The Law as a
System of Signs

TOPICS IN CONTEMPORARY SEMIOTICS

Series Editors: Thomas A. Sebeok and Jean Umiker-Sebeok
Indiana University

The Law as a
System of Signs

Roberta Kevelson
Pennsylvania State University
Reading, Pennsylvania

Plenum Press • *New York and London*

Library of Congress Cataloging in Publication Data

Kevelson, Roberta.
    The law as a system of signs / Roberta Kevelson.
        p.   cm. — (Topics in contemporary semiotics)
    Bibliography: p.
    Includes index.
    ISBN 0-306-42658-7
    1. Semantics (Law) 2. Law — Philosophy. 3. Semiotics. I. Title. II. Series.
K213.K48   1988
340'.11 — dc19   87-32716
                                                                                    CIP

© 1988 Plenum Press, New York
A Division of Plenum Publishing Corporation
233 Spring Street, New York, N.Y. 10013

Printed in the United States of America

To Lorin and Kenny and Karen and Erin, my children

I start from and in and with and as Motion. For me, in the "spiritual" as well as the physical world, there is of course no Rest as the ultimate goal or as the antithesis of Motion. The changeless is less than the dead, it is the non-existent. . . . I often say that I am determined to be free and free to be determined. Why? Because of the unnamed Third yet lying in the womb of Motion, to which both the determinate and the indeterminate have reference. . . . To me the ideas of the new, the young, the fresh, the possible, are deeper than any time-import, and are indeterminate only in a special sense.
. . . The best I can do is to say, "I wish instead of the Future, we could begin to talk of the Unreached as the Yet distant!"

Charles Sanders Peirce (November 20, 1904)

Preface

Even if Peirce were well understood and there existed general agreement among Peirce scholars on what he meant by his semiotics, or philosophy of signs, the undertaking of this book—which intends to establish a theoretical foundation for a new approach to understanding the interrelations of law, economics, and politics against referent systems of value—would be a risky venture. But since such general agreement on Peirce's work is lacking, one's sense of adventure in ideas requires further qualification. Indeed, the proverbial nerve for failure must in any case be attendant.

If one succeeds, one has introduced for further inquiry the strong possibility that should our social systems of law, economics, and politics—our means of interpersonal transaction as a whole—be understood against the theoretical background of a dynamic, "motion-picture" universe that is continually becoming, that is infinitely developing and changing in response to genuinely novel elements that emerge as existents, *then the basic concepts of rights, resources, and reality take on new dimensions of meaning in correspondence with n-dimensional, infinite value judgments or truth-like beliefs which one holds.*

If such a view, as Peirce maintained, were possible and tenable not only for philosophy but as the basis for action and interaction in the world of human experience and practical affairs, one would readily say that risk taking is a small price for the realization of such possibility.

It was with these views in mind that I began studying legal semiotics nearly a decade ago. Other scholars, of similar intent and purpose, have also approached the investigation of the practical sciences from the perspective of modern semiotics. But semiotics is not a term that has acquired stable and consensual definition. Other approaches to a legal semiotics are not largely Peircean, but are, nevertheless, rich and informative and thus contribute to this project in a complementary and supportive manner. At the time of this writing, there exist research centers of law and semiotics throughout the world, and it is hoped that this study will assure Peirce's place in the current global effort to develop a comprehensive notion of what it means to talk about legal semiotics.

The goal of this study is modest: I am walking the field and attempting to establish some intellectual landmarks. The ground covered is vast, including not only the interrelations among the practical sciences as its topics, but also selected aspects of modern linguistics, jurisprudence, aesthetics, moral philosophy, metaphysics, with side excursions into logics, philosophy of science, and the history of thought.

Out of this study it should be possible to construct a model that would exemplify semiotic methodology in Peirce's sense and thus be capable of providing a framework for linking diverse systems of inquiry into new unified relations. At the least, I hope to present material from many of Peirce's still unpublished manuscripts that is generally not known, and thus introduce to the reader more of Peirce than has heretofore received attention. In this kind of exploration, one cannot take issue with other arguments in the air on the various problems which have been identified, because such arguments do not exist. One confronts the silence, addresses it, and waits for a sign.

Acknowledgments

Research for this study was made possible by several grants from the Pennsylvania State University. In particular, I wish to express my appreciation to the Commonwealth Educational System of Penn State, the Office of Liberal Arts and Graduate Studies, the Institute for the Arts and Humanistic Studies, and the Berks Campus and Berks Campus Alumni for their support of this project.

I also wish to thank the Berks Campus Library for its special efforts in locating and making available some of the necessary material. I thank also the Huntington Library, the Firestone Library at Princeton, the Law School Library at the University of Virginia, the Special Collections and Law Library of the Library of Congress, and especially esteemed colleagues who opened their personal libraries for research on selected topics.

Earlier versions of a few chapters appeared as articles; I thank *Semiotica, American Journal of Semiotics, Indiana Law Review,* and the publishers of *Semiotics 1981* (Plenum Press), *Man, Law and Forms of Life* (D. Reidel) and of *Semiotics, Law and Social Science* (Gangemi Editore and the *Liverpool Law Review*) for publishing material in its earlier forms.

The manuscript was prepared for publication by Cindy Palecek, to whom I also express appreciation.

Contents

PART I

Introduction to Legal Semiotics

The field which Justice Holmes has tilled is a limited one . . .
his legal and social philosophy is great, not limited. It is an
expression of the processes and issues of law seen in an infinite
perspective, that of a universe in which all action is so experimental that it must needs be directed by a thought which is free,
growing, even learning. . . .

John Dewey (1931:36)

CHAPTER 1

Legal Semiotics

THE PEIRCEAN FRAME

It is over thirty years since Huntington Cairns wrote that for the first time since the ancient Greek philosophers "law as a field of speculative inquiry is a subject in which philosophers nowadays evince little interest" (1949:1). On the other hand, he pointed out, lawyers have become increasingly interested in the philosophy of law. As jurisprudence became a science of relations in its own right, the historical link between philosophy and law was severed.

Cairns notes that different methods of inquiry distinguish one discipline from another. Even when the jurist and the philosopher ask the same question—What is law?—not only will each answer differently, but each will apply his own appropriate method of analysis to the question, to the implications of the question, to the answer, and to the context in which the question is framed.

Philosophy in this century has tended to model its methodology on the exact sciences; thus, it tends to be analytic rather than synthetic. But philosophy and jurisprudence alike have perfected no techniques either for the discovery of knowledge or for its successful application once that goal has been reached.

During these past thirty years a new discipline and methodology has emerged: Semiotics, a method of inquiry into the process of inquiry, is based on the sign theory of the American philosopher, Charles Sanders Peirce. This method assumes that inquiry, always dialogic, is a process of communication or message exchange by means of signs and sign systems. Law is one such sign system, as are other social institutions, e.g., language, economics, politics, the family, and so on. In recent years the area of legal semiotics has begun to develop its own kinds of questions.

The following briefly reviews some basic tenets of general semiotics:

The purpose of "semiotic methodology," or "speculative rhetoric"—terms Peirce used synonymously—is to account for the process of how one thought or judgment sign, grows out of another, of how decisions and beliefs develop, and of how new knowledge evolves. (In this volume, when a term or concept is shown in quotes the first time, I mean by that that thereafter it should be understood in its Peircean sense or frame of reference and not necessarily its contemporary dictionary definition.)

The emergence of the discipline, semiotics, has provoked widespread interest among scholars of traditional disciplines, especially those concerned with accounting for communicative interactions in principled ways.

Two of the major assumptions shared by semioticians are:

1. All communication is a process of exchange of meaningful signs, and signs and sign systems such as natural language mediate between communicating persons and those objects in the phenomenal, physical world of experience to which they refer.
2. All human societies have developed complex systems of both verbal and nonverbal sign systems which are not static but which evolve continuously to correspond with and to represent changing social norms and the evolving, growing social consciousness of any given community.

To these major underlying assumptions I would add a third, namely, that not only can the legal argument be understood as prototypical of ordinary argument and discourse as Toulmin suggests (1958) but the entire notion of a legal system, consisting of interrelating communicative processes between legal discourse and legal practice, functions almost universally as a model of dialogic thought development. In relation with the economic or price system, law is a prototype of intersubjective social exchange of value as a whole.

Law and justice—legality and legitimacy—have throughout the development of legal history at times been regarded as opposing terms and at other times been regarded as terms with equivalent meaning. Also, the changing perspectives on the relationship between legality and legitimacy are brought about through specific rhetorical strategies. As the late Baron Chaim Perelman (1968) pointed out, by an argument of convergence two formerly opposing terms may be brought into a relation of meaning equivalence. By contrast, if we define only one of the terms in an equivalence relationship we extend the meaning of that term and thereby bring it into a new relationship of opposition with the other term. This rhetorical tactic is called an argument by dissociation.

What is significant here, because for centuries law and rhetoric were intimately allied, is the classification of rhetoric in semiotics as the highest determining division of Peirce's "expanded logic." But it is nothing new to regard logical terms and modes or patterns of reasoning as signs and sign systems. Aristotle speaks of signs in this sense. But Aristotle's logic is primarily concerned with syllogistic reasoning, that is, with formal analysis of the relationship between truth statements in valid arguments. The legal argument is not a formal argument. Its premises are neither true nor false, but hypothetical. Therefore it was believed for a long time that analysis of legal discourse must necessarily be much looser and less conclusive than discourse proceeding from true propositions. Yet it was Peirce's genius to recognize that at bottom all propositions are hypothetical and all arguments are enthymemic.

Enthymeme is a term known from classical rhetoric which describes an argument that presupposes, that is, does not make explicit, either the major or minor premise or the conclusion. Peirce convincingly shows that all argument is based on unexpressed presuppositions. These presuppositions are part of the public knowledge and as community property form the foundation for conventional meaning, that is to say, for representations or signs that stand in a general way in place of actual phenomena.

Peirce's influence on modern Continental legal science was direct through François Gény and indirect through Oliver Wendell Holmes and other Anglo-American jurists. More will be said of his influence and its effects in subsequent chapters. In this brief introduction to legal semiotics—to some of its goals and the problems engaging its practitioners at present—emphasis is on the unique contributions that semiotic methodology has to offer in inquiries concerned with accounting for changing legal systems in relation to changing social systems and evolving human values.

Although Holmes's famous paper "The Path of the Law" largely accords with some of the basic assumptions of semiotics, his opening line, "When we study law we are not studying a mystery but a well-known profession," invites challenge. One problem of interest to legal semiotics is the thesis, in modern jurisprudence, that legal procedure is properly divided into two distinct parts: legal activity and legal discourse. Legal semiotics holds that in each case there is a legal event, in which legal discourse is one kind of legal act, and that legal procedures, as communicative events in which both legal actors and nonauthorized persons participate, are exchanges of official messages by means of verbal and nonverbal signs and are also legal acts of a nonverbal kind. Francis Lieber, in his study of legal and political hermeneutics (1839/1963), was perhaps the first nineteenth-century jurist to advance this view. Lieber will be discussed later.

Legal semiotics does not insist, as does Learned Hand, for example, that the law must always be written (1954:104). But it holds that it must be expressible in the words of natural language. All natural languages are sign systems. The network of legal subsystems which compete for dominance in any given society is derived from such natural language and the interrelationships themselves are signs of dialogic conversation, of an iconic nature with respect to signs and their functions.

Fact, or experience, according to Peirce, is the ground of our perceptions. It is to the world of fact and experience that we must submit our logical conclusions for verification. Peirce's insight into the relation between logic and experience led to the development of a logic of signs—a semiotic process for reasoning—which included his concept of pragmatics and his notion of logical consequences. This latter theory of logical consequences had enormous influence on continental legal theory at the turn of the century. It underlay the then emergent thesis of such juridical spokesmen as Gény in France, Hagerström and Olivecrona in Sweden, and Holmes, Jerome Frank, and others in this country, that there are no absolute, eternal codes of law, but rather that legal decision and legal reasoning as a whole must reflect its social context and therefore must take into account as part of the basic process of legal reasoning the facts of change and the changing facts.

Holmes's and therefore Peirce's theory came to be called "legal realism." This stressed that the business of law was not to preserve and perpetuate ideals of justice as though they were permanent and unchanging values in a society; instead, law was to concern itself with facts and the interpretation of encoded laws in relation to the fact of the case at hand. This point of view was made explicit by Holmes especially in his famous lectures "Possession" and "The Path of the Law" (1921/1952).

We know that formal logic based on syllogistic reasoning cannot show us how an idea evolves and grows. A conclusion of formal reasoning gives us no more information than is contained in its premises.

How, then, Peirce asks, do we account for the fact that thoughts do grow and develop, that an idea accumulates its meaning through the process of discourse? There are patterns of systematic, directive thinking that permit new information to be introduced, interpreted with reference to the discourse theme, or topic, and that also permit communicating persons to take other directions in their discourse—directions not determined initially by the leading assumptions of the discourse. Therefore there must be not only a logic of justification but a logic of discovery. This logic of discovery, according to Peirce, must correspond with a method of inquiry. Thus, what are the forms that interrogation by communicators takes in their participation in open-ended and dynamically evolving exchange?

It is no mere accident that Peirce developed his "expanded logic" through frequent illustrative reference to known and conventional procedures in law. He followed a long tradition in this respect. For example, the forms for interrogation as a legal procedure constituted a major part of the training of legal professionals at the earliest law schools in Milan and Bologna in the twelfth century. Rules for questions and answers—for methods of inquiry—were carefully documented and followed for many centuries since and to the present day. The process of discovery is intimately linked with rules for definition. Both discovery and definition are those aspects of legal inquiry that fall under the heading of legal hermeneutics. The topic of sign interpretation in law, or legal hermeneutics, is discussed more fully in Part IV of this book.

Peirce does not restrict his use of rhetoric to verbal discourse only. Modes of conduct and forms of procedure also persuade; for example, it is assumed that the influence of one pattern of behavior upon another exerts what can be called a rhetorical force and that processes express and convey this rhetorical force just as rhetoric in speech does.

But there is a major distinction to be made between what speech act theorists call the "perlocutionary" force of an utterance and the kind of rhetorical persuasion referred to here.

Peirce's "methodology" is another word for "speculative rhetoric." Speculative rhetoric is the highest division of his "logic," the first part of his "normative science," followed by "ethics" and in turn by "esthetics," which he came to understand as the "science of value."

To digress, the first division of semiotic logic is "speculative grammar," which accounts for the syntactic relations of a sentence. The second division is "critic," or "formal logic," which is composed of "abductive, deductive," and "inductive reasoning;" the order in which they are here named corresponds to the stages of reasoning in the analysis of arguments.

Legal semiotics accepts the legal argument as the prototype of all ordinary argument. The legal argument as sign was the structure of discourse in actual experimental life to which Peirce referred as the symbolic sign structure upon which other various modes of argument are modelled.

Thus, if speculative grammar accounts for the syntactic level of arguments, critic accounts for the semantic level of arguments, and speculative rhetoric accounts for the pragmatic level of arguments. Rhetoric, as understood by semiotics in general and by legal semiotics in particular, is not to be identified solely with its persuasive force but also with the interactive force of dialogic exchange, which emphasizes the underlying erotetic and paratactic structure of discourse.

The notion of speech acts, on which abundant literature is available from many disciplines, has recently been directly identified with law and legal acts. But at present a deontic approach to speech acts in general derives from legal theory, particularly from that philosophy of law associated with the English jurist John Austin which holds that law is the command of the sovereign.

An alternative approach to the concept of speech acts would avoid identifying it with Austin's controversial theory and at the same time would place it in the proper context of the legal system from which the term derives. It would also show that legal discourse is based on an erotetic, that is, question-and-answer logic and not on a deontic logic of commands only.

Legal semiotics considers speech acts in prototypical form to be a kind of legal activity, that is, of verbal legal acts of which there are three basic kinds:

rules, commands, and decisions. A comprehensive analysis of these speech acts would require the application of a number of different logics: erotetic, deontic, and nonmodal. It is particularly with respect to the legal decision and to discovery procedures that the interrogative construction and interpretive process are most pronounced and the pragmatic aspect of semiotic methodology is most apparent and useful.

Still another area of concern to legal semiotics is the legal decision, from the point of view of the questions raised by Frank: (1) Do judges make or discover law? (2) Are judicial decisions law or merely applications of law? (3) Do laws exist antecedent to judicial decisions? (1963:159–160). The position of the realists, including Frank, is discussed in Part IV of this volume.

As mentioned above, the relation between legal decisions and legal consequences, as set forth by Gény in his classic exposition *Méthode d'interprétation et sources en droit privé positif* (1899/1963), is of special interest in legal semiotics. Here the social context is seen as an interactive function of a legal event, together with the shifting roles of addresser and addressee (official and nonofficial actors), the channel (the conventional signs of the natural language, the courts and legislative bodies, etc.), and the code (the code of laws as well as the technical terms and structure of law language). These five functions, together with the message (all verbal and nonverbal legal acts) constitute according to Jakobson (1960) all semiotic, including legal, events.

It is in the *Méthode d'interprétation* that Gény first credits Peirce's logical consequences with providing a principled way of taking into judicial account the wishes, customs, values, and technology of society in transition. Thus Peirce's semiotic philosophy was decisively instrumental in the development of much of both continental and Anglo-American law. W. Friedmann, speaking of Gény's work, says, "From very different premises, English and American jurists came to conclusions not very different from those of the continental jurists and legislators. . ." (1959:24, 25).

Peirce's influence on Holmes is not widely known. During the early 1870s Holmes and Peirce were members of a discussion group, the Metaphysical Club, which met frequently in Cambridge, Massachusetts (Fisch, 1964:3–23; 1942, *JP* 39 12 85–97). In *The Common Law* (1881), we recall, Holmes said that although the formal growth of legal systems and legal codes may appear to conform at times to the logic of the syllogism, in substance law follows from popular feelings and behavior relating to revenge and retribution, loss and compensation. Law ". . .will become entirely consistent only when it ceases to grow" (pp. 31, 32). Law is an "idea" or sign in this respect, in a Peircean sense.

The problem of interpretation in law remains paramount in juridical thought. According to Peirce, every interpretation of a sign results in a new, more complex sign, which carries its reference along cumulatively, thereby adding something at each stage of interpretation to the reference which did not previously or initially exist. The notion of the accumulation of information in discourse is the central focus of Peirce's methodology. However, this perspective on the dynamic growth of discourse is not peculiar only to Peircean-based semiotics. It is also characteristic of most current functional approaches to discourse analysis and is especially identified with the Prague linguistic school.

At present, linguists, philosophers of language, and semioticians distinguish three levels of language: the syntactic, the semantic, and the pragmatic. The syntactic has been, until very recently, the domain of linguistics. The semantic, with its emphasis on the meaning of logical terms in propositions, has been the traditional domain of philosophers. At present, through a growing understanding of what Peirce intended by his methodology or speculative rhetoric, there is the realization that not one but the several distinct types of discourse may be systematically accounted for by Peirce's highest division of his logic, governing the dynamics of thought.

A mention should be made of Peirce's preliminary approach to discourse analysis, which he called "phenomenology." This phenomenology described by Peirce antedated the continental phenomenological tradition associated with Husserl and differs essentially from Husserlian thought. The latter intends to reduce the phenomena perceived by the perceiving self to an absolute notion of a self which observes. Peirce's phenomenological approach, on the contrary, begins with the carving out of phenomenal experience a general "quality" to be investigated methodologically. Thus "quality" is not yet a sign. The next stage, which is the establishment of a quality as a "fact"—something that is this and not that—is not a sign yet either.

But the next stage can be described as the socialization of the fact. By a kind of social contract the investigator reaches an agreement of how this fact is to mean within the context of the particular inquiry. Thus the fact acquires the status of a "sign or representation." The next stage of the process of semiotic analysis leads to the progressive interpretation of the "sign as given," first with respect to logic, then with reference to ethics, and third with respect to the considerations of the esthetic. Logic, ethics, and esthetics constitute the three divisions of Peirce's normative sciences. The final stage of philosophical inquiry in Peirce's scheme involves the metaphysical.

Here we need not discuss the metaphysics except to note that Peirce stressed that metaphysical considerations may not enter into or color the logical, pragmatic analysis of discourse. Yet the methodology of which pragmatics is an essential part may investigate types of metaphysical discourse.

One main interest is in the relation between Peirce's semiotics and law, where legal discourse is a symbolic type of discourse, and other natural-language discourses are tokens of this type.

Peirce introduced into his methodology known legal procedures. Methodology is his method of methods which investigates modes of inquiry that

characterize the various academic disciplines, the scientific approach to investigation, and, in fact, the methods of all our institutionalized systems of reasoning
including systems of legal reasoning (Kevelson 1985a,b,c).

Methodology, or speculative rhetoric, as noted, was defined by Peirce as
that highest part of logic which intends to account for the actual process of the
development of a thought or idea, to some conclusion or judgment which is
regarded as if it were a law, and which functions as a law until it is called into
question and then becomes the theme or topic of a new process of inquiry.

Law-like truth in semiotic analysis is never absolute but always provisional.

In its lawlike function a judgment sign is predominantly symbolic. As the
topic of a new inquiry, this same judgment sign functions iconically. In the
process of redefining the terms that constitute a law, this same verbal "shape"
of a judgment sign becomes predominantly indexical in its function.

Just as there is not one ideal legal system, but rather a legal system as
actually a network of competing and conflicting legal subsystems (L. Friedman
1975), so there is not one type of legal discourse but conflicting modes of legal
reasoning which interact in any given period of time and are coeval in any given
society. For example, a mode of deductive legal reasoning intends a different
purpose than does a mode of inductive legal reasoning; both inductive and
deductive types of legal reasoning may be sharply distinguished from hypothetical
legal reasoning, which is primarily concerned with discovery procedures and
with establishing working assumptions that act as leading principles in making
judicial decisions.

If it is accepted that a legal system is never completely a closed system,
and that a code of law is never finished once and for all, then the task of integrating
new law with established law falls to the interpreting judiciary. The crux of the
problem lies here: there is not yet a consistent account which adequately and
systematically describes the process of hypothetical reasoning as it specifically
applies to law and as it generally applies to human discourse.

Further, there is no agreement to date on what the term *methodology* means.
As Horovitz (1972) points out, the term is ambiguous. Within some systems of
analysis of legal reasoning, methodology is *prescriptive*; that is, it provides a
model for official legal actors to use. Other analysts of legal reasoning regard
methodology as *descriptive*, in which case it accounts for the way reason actually
proceeds. Peirce's methodology is descriptive. As an alternative to the closed
system of syllogistic thought processes, Peirce offered a dialogistic mode of
reasoning which he demonstrated to be no less valid than the syllogism. But
Peirce's dialogism is a form of argument, or discourse, which leads to a conclusion with two or more alternative possibilities (Kevelson 1982a). It is an open-
ended mode of reasoning capable of leading to further inquiry and indicating
that although one and only one decision may be made in each case other options
do exist and through this manner of possible reasonings may be explored. Herein

is the key to analyses of the structure of reversed decisions and of contradiction between rules of law.

In concluding this chapter, let me stress the fact that in the present abundance of semiotic literature we find that certain general concepts continually recur. These concepts include hermeneutics; forms of interrogation *vis-à-vis* dialogue: conversational interaction; the logic of questions and answers; code; discovery procedures; and, not least, speech acts. All of these terms are rarely acknowledged today to have originated within the context of legal discourse and legal practice.

It should also be noted again that Peirce prefaced his paper "My Pragmatism" (1909) with a description of the Metaphysical Club. In this essay he mentions Holmes but also speaks with great admiration of the lawyer Nicholas St. John Green and Green's contributions to criminal law and "to the improvement of the Common Law as defined in Massachusetts."

There were, according to Fisch, at least six lawyers in the club, including Holmes, who was lecturing on jurisprudence in the spring of 1872. Fisch says we must assume that much of the discussion of that year focused on Holmes's prediction theory of law (Fisch 1964:16–17, 20). Throughout his writings Peirce uses examples from legal activity and legal discourse to illustrate important points in his semiotic philosophy.

There are at least six major areas of concern at present in legal semiotics which will be discussed in subsequent chapters of this volume:

1. Legal systems considered as complex structures of signs and sign relationships. Included in this topic is the relationship between legal systems and their referent, social institutions. Comparatist legal semiotics is included under this heading.

2. The widely held assumption that legal codes are "mirrors" of society (Dietze, in Friedrich 1964:63–88). Here the chain of relationships between social customs and values and the judicial decision with its consequences for social life can be viewed as arguments, or signs of argument structure. Such arguments progress and evolve. Initially hypothesized social values are subjects or themes upon which legal codes are predicated. Legal codes become, as judgment signs, subject themes for rules of law. Rules are thematic for the speech-act command, and sometimes for the decision, but the fact that activist judges may decide in particular ways for "justice" and "equity," in response to actual life, is thus contrary to decisions by precedent: in such cases society itself acts as a direct subject or theme.

The subject or theme of an argument has a predominantly iconic sign function. The rheme, or that which is predicated of the subject, is predominantly indexical. A code of law as such, and as a habit of decision, functions also as a symbolic sign. "Icon," "index," and "symbol" are the three primary sign functions in Peirce's scheme. Their predominant functions change with respect to changing contexts. All objects are multifunctional signs; their dominant functions are determined by context and by agentive purpose or aim.

3. Structures of legal reasoning, both according to syllogism and to what Peirce calls "dialogism," which yields two or more alternative conclusions and is an open-ended but complete structure of argument.

4. Relations between logic, ethics, and value, the three parts of the normative sciences in general semiotic theory. Value as used in this study is synonymous with what Peirce means by esthetics.

5. Roles of fiction in legal procedure, both according to Bentham and as defined in current jurisprudential writings. Relations between legal fictions and "legalisms" (Shklar 1964) should be examined. Vaihinger's and Peirce's opposing views on fictions in reasoning could be compared with special uses of legal fictions.

6. The conflict between Holmes's concept of law and the Austinian concept of law as command of the sovereign.

From the perspective of modern semiotics, especially that branch now know as legal semiotics, it is believed that not only can Peirce's semiotic methodology account for the structure of legal reasoning, or discourse, which takes place as an exchange between official legal actors, but that it must also begin to describe the kind of legal discourse that involves communication between official legal actors and the general public. This, too, is dialogic, in which meaning is transacted through the mediation of signs. In this regard the marketplace, or the economic relations to law, is a coordinate of the basic semiotic event.

Following Peirce, it is the task of legal semiotics to explore various kinds of "rhetorical strategies" which are used in the exchange and interpretation of signs. One needs to know how value equivalences are decided upon and agreed to, as in contracts. If we consider the class of legal actors as one social subsystem and the class of the general public as another social subsystem, one wants to know how systems interact and how intersystemic communication may be described. What are the bridge laws that connect systems of legality with systems of legitimacy?

Finally, from Peirce we learn that with each reinterpretation of a sign we create new meaning. Thus part of the process of describing how a legal discourse develops includes the continuing action of making new judgments and therefore of making the laws of thought.

CHAPTER 2

Staking the Claim/Walking the Field

When jurisprudence became a science of relations in law in its own right in the nineteenth century, the historical link between philosophy and law was severed.[1] It is now nearly thirty-five years since Cairns appraised this rift between philosophy and law. In the interim new links have been forged. The most conspicuous philosophical-legal tie is, perhaps, in the area of rights. A less visible relation between law and philosophy can be seen through Peirce's pragmatic thoughts. The name for this fresh approach to the study of law and other social systems is semiotics. A special area of this new field of inquiry is legal semiotics with its ramified inquiry into economics and politics.

When Justice Holmes came to the Supreme Court in 1902 he had rejected the use of formal, deductive reasoning as primary in judicial decision making, but he had not rejected logic as an indispensable method in the whole of legal reasoning. The logic that underlies Holmes's decisions is not, as Dewey notes, one of "rigid demonstration," but rather it is a logic of "search and discovery."[2] It is a logic of inquiry or, in Peirce's words, an "expanded logic," which includes but goes far beyond syllogistic reasoning in its attempt to account for the actual process whereby all thinking persons may interpret their ideas in order to act upon them and thus to verify them with reference to the actual world. In this sense, an idea such as the Constitution of the United States is an experiment, or sign, which permits one to perform certain mental operations or thought processes. This is Holmes's contention and applies to parts as well as to the whole of any given *open* legal system.

According to Peirce's view, nothing is ever absolutely given as an eternal and fixed truth. Rather, one constructs a hypothesis in order to test whether it is workable as an idea. Thus, when Holmes speaks of the Constitution as an "experiment," it is reasonable to assume that Holmes's experiment in the context of constitutional law is of the same nature as an idea or possibility in Peirce's system of thought.[3]

Holmes maintained that the only way a society ever approximated and even sometimes realized its ideal values was through what he called the "free trade in ideas," analogous with what Hayek describes as the free marketplace.[4] Peirce's pragmatism is grounded on the conviction that value in thought and in reality accumulates through a process of transacting and exchanging ideas by persons who contract to accomplish a mutually agreed-upon purpose.

According to Peirce, the growth and development of ideas is equivalent to the growth and development of real value. Recall that *real value*, like real estate, alludes to the elemental, basic relationship between portions of the earth's surface, defined and titled, and a person's property in a comprehensive sense. Property in land was synechdochal of the entirety of a person's value in the world; property represented a *sign* of that value. This process takes place as a social enterprise between persons in community.[5]

Holmes's conviction is that this "free trade in ideas" is the basic assumption on which our Constitution rests. The Constitution, he says, is "an experiment, as all life is an experiment."[6] Dewey interprets this idea of the Constitution as an experiment as a manifestation of Holmes's liberalism. According to Dewey, "Liberalism. . .(is) a method of experimentation based on insight into social desires and actual conditions. . . . It signifies the adoption of the scientific habit of mind in application to social affairs."[7]

Historically, as mentioned above, there is evidence that Holmes's first introduction to these pragmatic notations came not from Dewey or even from James, but from Peirce himself, through their association in the Metaphysical Club in Cambridge in the early 1870s. Holmes's correspondence with Laski refers to and discusses in an interesting and guarded way Peirce's writings: this discussion continued over many years.[8]

Yet these significant associations between Holmes and the founder of American pragmatism are not sufficient in themselves to claim that Peirce's ideas directly inform Holmes's contribution to constitutional law. It will be necessary to examine in close detail the resemblance between Peirce's thought on particular topics, for example, cause, discovery, interpretation, and Holmes's decisions in particular cases. This volume introduces the principal topics, which will be examined in depth in a later study.

Examining the possible relationship between Peirce's ideas and Holmes's contributions to constitutional law requires an analysis of more than one third of constitutional law to test the hypothesis that American pragmatism has become an integral part of modern law in this country and, by extension, is interwoven in the very fabric of modern social life. Before the society as a whole may be examined for evidence of an active pragmatism, however, certain special areas of law must be compared with the concepts in philosophy with which they are customarily identified. Among these are the concepts of legal code, rule of law, and the widespread notion in jurisprudence that a legal system is a mirror of society. The idea that a legal system reflects a social order is problematic and would thus require that the philosophical concepts of resemblance and representation be distinguished. In Peirce's terminology, the words *representation* and *sign* are synonymous and are so used throughout this study.

Although the term *sign* has been variously defined throughout the whole of legal history, Peirce uses it in a special way. His special understanding of a sign, as discussed throughout his philosophical writings, must also be interpreted in its relation to the specific sense of the term *legal sign* as it is variously understood in jurisprudential writings, in legal drafting, and especially in system-specific rules for interpreting laws and statutes. Thus, in presenting the general background for this project, it is helpful to include mention of some of the forerunners of American pragmatism, Lieber, for example, whose classic work, *Legal and Political Hermeneutics* (1839/1963), signified a sharp break with older traditions of legal interpretation, for instance, Savigny's and Vico's. But one might expect to find not only a radical change of procedure in legal interpretation since Lieber, who remained a loyal Kantian as Peirce did not, but an increasing emphasis on the openness of social systems as opposed to the assumed closed social systems of more traditional thought.

Paralleling these developments in American law are new developments in the physical sciences. Around the time that Holmes was creating his portion of constitutional law and Peirce was making significant breaks with earlier Kantian-influenced ideas, the very basis of inquiry in the physical sciences was being seriously questioned. For example, when Duhem refers to a fact as a complex of judgments and not an actual phenomenon or thing in itself, the fundamental concepts of observation, verification, falsification, causal explanation, and so on can no longer be assumed. Rather, the interpretation of basic concepts or ideas becomes the object of inquiry.[9] Against this ferment of debate and discussion in philosophy and in the physical and social sciences Holmes's position that law is a science and, as such, "deals with nothing but questions of fact" calls for reappraisal.[10] Holmes sees himself as a scientist in law; his major experiment is the Constitution. More than a third of the Supreme Court's total litigation was contributed by Holmes, as I have noted.

Similarly, Peirce's "method of methods," that is, that which he called the pragmatic method, or semiotics, was intended to adapt scientific method to philosophical purposes.[11]

This approach regards law as a sign system, interrelated with other social sign systems such as language, economics, government, family, and the many cultural institutions historically recognized and designated as such.

Although not all current semiotic investigation is grounded in Peirce's theory and method of signs, his work is acknowledged to be the richest source of information and the foundation of semiotic study and research as his total works, including unsigned and unpublished manuscripts, become more readily accessible to scholars. Peirce's conviction that through the method of sign interpretation ideas may continue to grow without end and that the vitality of human thought ceases only when inquiry itself ceases is an idea that permeates Holmes's writings.[12] "Law," according to Holmes, ". . .will become entirely consistent only when it ceases to grow."[13]

In the preface to his paper "My Pragmatism" (1909), Peirce described the membership and the activities of the Metaphysical Club. As noted earlier, Peirce mentions Holmes and also St. John Green. There were at least six lawyers in the club who lectured on various aspects of jurisprudence during the spring of 1872. Fisch notes that we may assume that much of the discussion of that year focused on Holmes's prediction theory of law.[14] We may also safely surmise that Green's thesis on proximate cause in law was the reference for much of the discussion among that group on causation in law and philosophy. Throughout his writings, it is stressed, Peirce used examples from law to illustrate his philosophical concepts.

Current interest among students and investigators of legal semiotics covers a broad range of topics, including the relation between the philosophical interest in speech acts and the juridical notion of legal acts, (Kevelson 1982a, 1984, 1985a,b,c); law in relation to other social systems and social sciences (Greimas and Landowski 1976); and semiotic investigation of rights and norms (Jackson 1985).[15] These are but a few of the areas under current investigation.

When Friedman referred to Gény's *Méthode d'Interprétation* (1899/1963), he suggested that English and American jurists' views of law resembled those of the Continental jurists, notwithstanding each other's differing starting points.[16] Cairns and others also gave some evidence that Geny was familiar with Peirce's logic of consequences and adapted it directly to their own legal theories.[17]

It can be assumed that Peirce's philosophy of signs had a determining influence on the changing structures and activities of social institutions and that his pragmatic philosophy has significantly contributed to the development of American constitutional law through Holmes and the catalytic force of American legal realism. Continued investigation in law as a system of signs should yield important results.

A possible consequence may be that pragmatic methods can be seen as useful for investigation of problems in the relation between legal systems and other social institutions that may utilize the prediction theory of Holmes in new ways. For example, by introducing the notion of genuine novelty into investigations causality becomes merely an ordinary-language term for explanation, as

Peirce claims. Social institutions will then be seen more accurately as dynamic systems rather than as successive states of affairs.[18] Investigating *procedures* will change.

Any timely report on legal semiotics is inadequate in this field, which is vital and expanding in many directions (e.g., Kevelson 1985b). Such a report errs in its clock-stopping limitations but like a photo may present a composite representational survey. These reports are such iconic layouts of legal semiotics as it appeared at the time of their writing (Kevelson 1980, 1981)

An account of legal semiotics at present must be in a significant sense also a history of its development. It is accurate to say that since Aristotle's well-known observation that logic came into being as a method of legal reasoning, law, from its inception, was regarded broadly as a social system, that is, a network of sign relations. But it is not only a system which consists, as Berman (1977) notes, of the "mass of legislative, administrative, and political rules, procedures and techniques in force in a given society. . . ." It is an index, as well as icon and symbol, of all the academic disciplines and social institutions that inform and are informed, that chart and are charted by law. Berman (1977) reminds us that it is particularly in the twentieth century, with traditional bonds between religion and law virtually severed in the West, that law as a consequence has increasingly come to be seen as a "matter of practical efficiency."[19]

A mere subdivision of the concept of law into three subdivisions or domains—or "devices," in Berman's sense: (1) political and analytical juris-prudence or positivism; (2) "historical and social-economic jurisprudence" or "historical school"; and (3) relations between law and society, or the "social theory of law"—is not adequate. What is wanted is an integrated jurisprudence, he argues, that includes these three approaches but goes beyond them.

Berman's approach includes faith in this higher view of law, that is, a faith based on the value or conviction that law requires not only reason, but emotion and intuition as well, or in his words, a "total social commitment."[20] In this he cites Holmes's advice to his law students: "Your business as lawyers is to see the relation between your particular fact and the whole frame of the universe."[21]

Law, Berman argues (1983), is to be seen as more than a body of rules and as a body of values if indeed the operative forces that historically have contributed to the development of law as a whole are not to be lost. Thus the recovery and discovery of values that law embodies for civilization, Western civilization in particular (see especially Berman's *Law and Revolution*, 1983), are the motives for introducing new approaches and more integrative methods for understanding the law.

It is a misconception, Berman points out, to distinguish Eastern notions of law from the traditions of law in the West. It is generally but wrongly assumed that in the West law has been shorn of nonlegal references to mythology, religion, customary ritual and formulaic observance, the family, marketplace, and the councils of government. It is not the case, according to Berman, that there is a fundamental difference between East and West in the view that law must and does imply all the attitudes and institutions of the society it is intended to serve. In the West, however, there has been the deliberate tendency to make sharp distinctions between legal orders, which manifest law in relation to other social orders, and legal systems which originate self-consciously as data to be studied for the metalegal purpose of self-reflection, self-correction, and growth. In brief, the notion of law in the West, especially since the twelfth century, is based on the purposes implicit in the idea of a legal science.[22]

Whereas in legal orders, as distinguished from legal science by Berman and others, the value force comes from behind or from the past, the impulsion to realize the goals and values of a society comes by projecting the values into the unknown and unknowable future. The notion of legal science in this sense corresponds precisely with the goals and methods of pragmatism and semiotics as pioneered by Peirce and continued by investigators of a legal semiotics.

The law as a whole as a text may be compared with a message or with any cohesive, discursive sign system the meaning of which can be correctly interpreted by regarding it in relation with other coordinate functions of the semiotic event under inquiry. This event consists of: the addresser, or the official legal actors; the addressee, or the general public however structured; the context of situation and environment including its history and future; the channel, which in the case of the law is not restricted to the courts, to the streets, or to the official places for doing law but includes also all areas which are involved in the law, that is, the market, the government, and today even those spaces in society once outside the claim of the law: the family and interpersonal relations. The code is the language of the law, as inscribed in law books, and in modern society no longer the unwritten code of legitimacy, of felt moral and customary values. Contact is the coming together in appropriate setting of addresser and addressee, with minimal noise, that is, minimal ambiguity, ellipses, or contradictions, in order to assent to the force of law.

It was a growing frustration among jurists from the eighteenth century into the nineteenth century that traditional presuppositions in law no longer held. For example, simple compliance no longer implied assent or contract. The growing complexity of society and emphases upon systems that can be objects of scientific inquiry made simple contract between official legal actors and general public extremely problematic. Rules for interpretation, and not merely a process of interpretation, began to be constructed in the latter half of the nineteenth century, thus preparing for a contemporary approach to the law through the method of legal semiotics as we now recognize and describe it today.

Berman's writings and those of others on the protostages of legal semiotics will be discussed throughout subsequent chapters. Properly speaking, one may speak of legal semiotics as such when investigators intentionally acknowledge semiotics as a theory and method and when they deliberately conduct their research according to the assumptions of semiotics.

In the case of a semiotics of law, the caption or title to a growing body of theory and resultant method called legal semiotics does not actually begin to appear before Lieber's *Hermeneutics*. But following this work one finds a wealth of literature, primarily from the area of jurisprudence, in the United States, Latin America, Scandinavia, and Europe on the semiotic aspects of law. It must be admitted, however, that the philosophic and theoretical foundations were rarely made explicit until the pluralistic movement of legal realism, following Holmes, began to emerge.

With the exception of such distinguished scholars as Robert Summers (1982), there has been too little written on legal realism and its philosophical foundations in the last quarter of a century. But Summers identifies the movement in law with Dewey's interpretation and understanding of Peirce's semiotics rather than directly with Peirce himself.[23]

Any discussion of legal semiotics must deal primarily with its very recent history. This history coincides with the emergence of semiotics as a distinct field of inquiry. The first recounting of American legal semiotics appears in Kevelson (1985b). This paper recapitulates the inseparable connection between a legal semiotics and semiotics as a whole universe of discourse. For example, whereas traditional disciplines rely largely on the "self-evident" truth, semiotics begins with a tacit agreement between speaker and listener that certain truth statements in propositions are signs or representations of consensually held values which function *as if* they were true; actually they are contracts about *ideas* of the True which, it is agreed, work as if true for purposes at hand.[24]

Thus, as Reichenbach (1947, 1976) and others suggest, the prototype in the search for truth is the legal contract. Similarly, Eco (1976) points out that it is the creative construction of the lie rather than the identification of Truth which characterizes semiosis. The lie is nothing other than a mediating invention, or representation of what the truth is provisionally taken to be by consensus or contract.

If traditional rhetoric was designated as the "mother of lies," legal rhetoric as the quintessence of semiotic rhetoric or methodology must identify the strategies of rhetorical argument with legal rhetoric and legal argument. The enormous contribution to this aspect of legal semiotics is found in the work of Perelman, noted throughout this book.

Perelman's *The New Rhetoric* (1969) antedated the emergence of legal semiotics as a modern field of inquiry by only a few years. His work is referred to especially in earlier introductory works of legal semiotics (e.g., Kevelson-

1977, 1980, 1985). Kevelson (1985c) accounts for development of this significant branch of semiotics up until 1980. Its forthcoming appearance will be immediately perceived as obsolete. Yet, despite its being outdated at the time of this writing, it describes the goals of a legal semiotics, points to some of the outstanding problems as perceived by 1980, and offers references to works that are both explicitly and implicitly of a semiotic nature.

The range of topics in law and semiotics theoretically may grow to include any topic whatever that falls within the general notion of law and related social systems. The point to be stressed is that the unique contribution of legal semiotics is not its range of topics but its theory and method of inquiry. Such problems that may exist in the law and may be responsive to a semiotically oriented investigation will define the role of legal semiotics for the next decades.

It is anticipated that in the next few years the main issues in methodology will have been identified and, if not resolved, will become an area for systematic inquiry and step-by-step agreement on what, why, and how the broad general area of legal semiotics should be approached and worked through.

It is expected that intersystemic problems will emerge, for example, on economics and law, on political science and law, on civil law and common law, on comparative law diachronically and also synchronically. It is expected that continued emphasis on law language and the legal argument will bring together the fields of law and communications in general, including technological communications and cybernetics, into the domain of legal semiotics. The entire field of medical science is today inseparable from the constraints of the law, and one would expect to find growing concern about this relationship, especially within the interdisciplinarian field of semiotics.

Consider the example of a complex legal issue in recent history: There was an overlapping of international law and maritime law in the 1986 incident of the United States capture of a hijacked airplane in which the terrorists, who had pirated an Italian luxury cruise ship docked in an Egyptian port, escaped, and during which event an American citizen was murdered as so-called counterretribution for retributive actions of the state of Israel which, at the same time, involved Tunisia and various other nations. Each separate faction involved in this event represents a *separate law system*. The outcome of this event will require an approach which is not now available but which, in the future, a legal semiotics may be expected to provide. A Solomon in twentieth-century garb is not what is needed. Rather, a method and theory upon which such complicated legal decision making is based requires an understanding of how each separate method of inquiry is structured with reference to its respective legal order and/ or legal system. How can all of these several references be understood by a method of methods or what Peirce characterized as the method of semiotics? In Chapter 22, on the problem of conflict of laws, some of these and other selected issues will be discussed further.

NOTES

1. The Cartesian elimination of rhetoric from logic which dissociated the respective aims of modern logic from law was opposed, implicitly, by Peirce. Peirce's emphasis, for example, on a logic of discovery in contrast to a logic of justification was anticipated by Gore (1878, 1882) and followed by Dewey's *Logic*, which linked logic with law as early as 1924: "Logical Method of Law," *Cornell Law Quarterly*, 17.

2. For discussion of contract as a higher stage in the development of law, see Morris Cohen (1933), 69, 70.

3. See H. A. Rommen's discussion of the relation between philosophy and sociolegal history (1936; in translation 1947).

4. See Kevelson on Peirce's method of methods (1987, originally written 1984).

5. Economics as well as the emerging physical sciences offered a new method of analyzing jurisprudential and political theory. For example, see Posner (1972), especially Part 1 on property, value, and economics.

6. Morris Cohen's frequent linking of Peirce and law occurs throughout his voluminous writings; it was also at Cohen's suggestion to Oliver Wendell Holmes that Peirce's writings on pragmatism became known to Holmes, as he noted frequently over a period of more than a score of years with his close friend Harold Laski in their correspondence.

7. Laski traces important influences on Holmes's thought, from the Stoics to modern pragmatism, especially in his celebration of Holmes's 89th birthday. See "Mr. Justice Holmes," in Franfurter's edition (1931), 138–167. The influence of Stoic thought on Peirce is referred to in this volume, especially in Chapter 6.

8. See Frank (1950).

9. See Cohen (1933), 323, with special reference to Laski (1931).

10. See J. P. Plamenatz's discussion (1968), 1–25.

11. For an opposing point of view see Jolowicz (1963).

12. For discussion of Peirce's use of Hamilton's "imaginary" as a kind of reserved space for emergent new meaning in a continuous discourse, see Kevelson on Peirce's dialogism and the continuous predicate (1982).

13. See Peirce (1958), 2.422.

14. See Kevelson's work on Peirce's notion of time as method (1987), chap. 9.

15. See especially Chapter 8 in this volume for discussion of speech acts in law.

16. For discussion of the historical development of freedom of speech and creative speech acts in law see M. Cohen (1933), 73 ff.

17. See R. S. Lancaster (1958), 13–19.

18. See Pound (1956), 242–243.

19. See Kevelson (1977); also Perelman (1969).

20. See Holmes's distinctions between property and possession in common law (1881).

21. See Chapter 16 of this volume for discussion of strict interpretation in law.

22. See D'Entreves (1963), 687–702.

23. See L. Friedman (1975) for discussion of legal fictions as stabilizing function in open legal systems.

24. Legal realism, in general, opposed the authoritative precedent in law. For a discussion see Rumble (1968).

CHAPTER 3

Perspectives on the Legal System

For many it was the discovery of semiotics as a method of analyzing sign systems and communicative interactions that coincided with the realization that one had been doing semiotics for a long time, often under the umbrella of other more traditional disciplines. Although some scholars do not describe their work as being within the frame of semiotic method and theory, they seem to be nevertheless much involved with the semiotic process.

One such study is Friedman's *The Legal System* (1975). His work has important things to say about legal semiotics. He speaks of legal acts as messages exchanged between legal and other coexisting social systems. He reminds us that legal codes are languages and as such are constructed of signs and sign relationships. He shows, also, that each kind of legal system persuades through its structure and style and with its own special rhetorical force. He thus suggests an important correlation between the practical rhetoric of legal speech acts and the theoretical or speculative rhetoric of Peirce.

Although semiotics does not lay exclusive claim to the term *system*, this is a key word in the lexicon of modern semiotics and has been given close attention by Peirce and others. From Peirce, for example, is the concept of a system as a unified, cohesive sign—a continuum—which is itself constructed of sign relationships (CP 3.637,6.111).

Friedman's study has been selected for comment because he holds some basic assumptions that may stimulate further interest in the structure and function of legal semiotics.

The next section of this chapter will give a brief overview of the context of Friedman's thought from which has been abstracted those major ideas with which this chapter deals. In the last part of the chapter focus will be on the correlations between Friedman's analysis of legal systems and Peirce's semiotic philosophy. The main ideas from Friedman that will be discussed are:

1. There is no dominant legal system in any given society; there are only networks of legal subsystems. Friedman says that "law is only one of many social systems . . . [and that] other social systems in society give it meaning and effect" (vii). Any concept such as "the legal system" derives from the ideal of law as imposed upon society from an external source; it is not the case, he maintains, that legal systems evolve through conflicting internal forces within given societies as a result of a dynamic exchange of messages between legal and other social systems.

2. Legal acts are of three kinds: (a) decisions; (b) commands, requests, and orders; and c) rules. Legal acts are both verbal and nonverbal. Any person, structure, or institution, that is, any sign in any social organization that carries legal authority is a legal act or legal actor. Legal acts are communicated in two kinds of messages: (1) substantive, to the general public or special-interest public groups; and (2) jurisdictive, within the official organization of legal authority. A speech act is a type of verbal legal act. Because speech acts have been a special topic of interest to semioticians, more detailed criticisms against prevailing theories will be offered below.

3. Assumptions of authority, which are usually deleted, or, as rules, ellipsed in legal acts, refer primarily to traditional, symbolic signs that are presumptive of trust and legitimacy. These presumptions most often refer to closed societies with closed legal systems and are no longer adequate, Friedman suggests, in modern, evolving open societies, or in relatively closed societies in transition. Thus a legal act such as a speech act in Friedman's sense (and in Austin's, Searle's, Grice's, and that of others in the Austinian tradition) does not describe the dialogic structure between legal systems and other social systems that does in fact exist and makes it possible for new information to grow and for values to change.

4. Coexisting legal subsystems in modern societies compete for power and legitimacy. Underlying each type of legal system is an appropriate structure of reasoning and logic. With particular reference to Peirce's work, this assumption will be explored more closely.

Essentially, Friedman argues against a view of legal systems that would identify any comprehensive legal system with a body of law, that is, with ideal written or unwritten codes of norms or rules that appear to be reflected in prevailing social customs in any given society, and that would suggest that society's dominant values concerning "right and wrong behavior, duties and rights" are timeless. Such a view, Friedman says, fails to account for interactions between laws, codes, motivations of conduct, and the demands of groups and individuals within pluralistic social contexts.

This view of an ideal, autonomous body of law stresses the authoritative role of the judge but does not consider the reaction of the judge to demands from society and how the judge's response takes the form of changes in the attitudes and instrumentality of authority.

Like Hayek, who speaks of two great traditions of the function of law in society (1973), Friedman also refers to a continuing opposition, throughout the history of legal systems and legal cultures, between "legal pluralism" and the tendency toward unification of a legal system, based on juristic or legal "rationality." Friedman finds that a "reduction of pluralism . . . is a natural historical process" (1975:219).

Hayek, on the other hand, sees a contemporary reduction of pluralism since around 1960 as the outcome of a power conflict between those who want to control the legal system in order to bring about utopian social ideals and those who still wish to consider legal actors, such as judges, as "institutions of a spontaneous order." (Hayek 1973:94–95) Hayek equates this "spontaneous order" with a free society in which "law and liberty are inseparable." This tradition, Hayek says, had its strongest origins with the Stoics. It became a motivating force to the Humanists of the Middle Ages. It was fundamental in the legal philosophies of Locke, Hume, and Kant and in the writings of Peirce, whose 1893 work, "Evolutionary Love," is cited (Hayek 1973:51–53). In contrast is the modern view of legal science or rationalistic legal system, which Hayek calls a "made legal order"—an organization that evolved as a natural consequence of the discovery of the powers of the human intellect. Hayek's contributions to legal semiotics are discussed in closer detail in subsequent chapters of this book.

It should be noted that Friedman's "innovative legal system", of which more will be said later, directly corresponds to Hayek's "made legal order." But in Friedman's view it is this rationalistic legal system—an innovative system—that is representative of a more open society and in a more open legal system is less dependent on the authority of legal precedent. The confusion between Hayek's and Friedman's interpretation of a "made" legal system seems less to be a problem in semantics than the result of the way in which particular legal systems choose to be rhetorically represented. Clearly the notion of the inseparability of law and liberty means different things to different men and depends to a large extent on the interpretation of terms such as *law* and *liberty* in different frames of reference. This problem is one that semiotics has not resolved yet. Peirce's speculative rhetoric, or methodology, offers some workable solutions to this and similar problems of terms as signs, (Kevelson 1985a,b,c).

Friedman speaks of still a third tradition of legal systems which developed in the twentieth century and is called "legal realism." Under this system legal speech acts that Friedman calls "decisions" were made by comparing two texts of legal codes, for example, an article of the Constitution with a statute that was challenged, and finding points at which both texts coincide. Thus one text reinforces another and the myth of court objectivity is sustained. According to this style, the Old Testament, the Koran, customary procedure under English Common Law, and so on, serve equally as corroborating tests for a statute in question. Under this system messages are conveyed which say, in effect, that the country is a country of laws, not of men. Friedman points to the role of the activist judge in more recent times to indicate the rhetorical force that each kind of a system uses to persuade us of its justness.

Friedman classifies four major types of legal systems according to their dominant modes of reasoning (1975:238–244). Systems are first subdivided from the whole of the legal system to subsystems characterized as open versus closed. Under "Closed" we find legal systems that refer to sacred codes and those that refer to specific codes of legal science, such as Justinian's Code, which served for the first law schools in the 1200s. Under "Open" there is the system of customary, opposed to the system of instrumental. Innovation is accepted in both instrumental and legal science systems but denied in sacred and customary systems. Of course there are no pure systems, but all interact to a greater or lesser degree in any given social culture.

How this process of interaction occurs, and what the method is by which the rhetoric of systems, operations, classifications, language, and so on, acts to produce change is not really discussed by Friedman, except that he cites examples to show that change does in fact occur in conflicts between opposing social wills. A later chapter examines how the process of intersystemic communication falls within the domain of semiotics. In the following section of this chapter I will suggest that existing semiotic theories, particularly those developed by Peirce, can begin to explain in some principled ways how legal systems in the context of specific social cultures interact and evolve.

Friedman speaks only of inductive and deductive kinds of reasoning to characterize various legal systems. Legal systems based on inductive reasoning are opposed to those based on deduction. Friedman says that both kinds of opposing systems make use of reason in an instrumental way, or as a method intended to bring about opposing kinds of action. For example, inductive systems aim for what Friedman calls *welfare legality*; deductive systems aim for *revolutionary legality* (1975:243). Both *welfare legality* and *revolutionary legality* are "ideal" modes of legal systems directed, instrumentally, to mandate and effect prescribed changes in social conduct.

Thus, in a relatively open legal system, in which Friedman finds both customary and instrumental legal systems, systems of legal science and sacred codes are excluded. In the latter, their referent codes "are the sole source of law; judges must link every decision to some concrete text of a code" (1975:241).

In these closed systems the only innovation possible must be within a fixed canon of premises. If we are to focus on legal systems that have an open canon of premises and that accept innovation, Friedman suggests that only instrumental systems offer this possibility. The subsystem of the instrumental kind, which he calls "revolutionary legality," abolishes older codes of law entirely, or attempts to do so, and replaces them with codes that are directed to further "revolutionary principles and the expediency of the situation" (1975:243). It is clear that either these new codes become stable, and thus the system encloses itself, or they become in turn replaced by counterrevolutionary systems.

But the system that Friedman calls welfare legality admits as starting premises for legal reasoning many kinds of assumptions from many sources outside the domain of legal authority (e.g., see Chapter 13 of this volume). Strictly speaking, such a system is really outside any conventionalized system of legal reasoning (1975:245), which rests, Friedman says, on a closed set of legal premises that can be known and argued by people with legal training. This kind of legal reasoning is, even in an open, instrumental legal system, based on the logical structure of the syllogism. On the other hand, in any ideal open system that does not have a finite, closed set of legal premises the conclusions of a legal argument are not necessarily contained in the premise but may open unpredictable possibilities.

Such a form of reasoning would not be based on the syllogism but rather on the kind of open-ended logical structure that Peirce describes and calls a "dialogism" (CP 3.172, 3.197, 3.623; Kevelson 1982a,b,c,d; 1985a,c). In syllogistic thinking in relatively open legal systems the premise is given and so is not unlike the precedent in closed legal systems. The conclusion, or legal decision, cannot move beyond what is given. By contrast, the dialogism—a term that represents, in legal argument, a rhetorical strategy or method—permits the legal speech actor to evolve from a single premise two alternative conclusions (Perelman 1969). The purpose of the dialogism in legal argument is to present possibilities other than that given in the legal proposition, or syllogistic premise, and so to increase the scope of what may be considered and further examined. The purpose of the dialogism in Peircean terms is to represent the actual way in which ideas, as signs, evolve and new information grows. Both in Peirce's speculative rhetoric and in the rhetoric of applied, or instrumental, legal reasoning, the dialogism opens a field of inquiry in order to introduce further innovative interpretation of the present data. Peirce's theory on the opposition between syllogistic and dialogistic structures of reasoning is discussed elsewhere (Kevelson 1982a,b,c,d; 1985a,c). Here primary concern is with the implications of dialogistic reasoning in open legal systems.

Friedman identifies syllogistic logic with those legal systems in which legal acts and actors have what he calls derivative power and *derivative authority*. He describes these systems as "formal," in opposition to nonformal, innovative systems in which acts and actors are not necessarily members of the official legal community.

In other words, in a maximally innovative legal system semiosis is a process of a shift of authoritative power between legal actor–speaker and public actor–speaker, where each in turn assumes the role of legal or public patient–listener. With this shift, a change in legal style takes place. The message exchange is no longer that of legal sentence or sequences of sentences but is an interactional, agonistic dialogic transaction.

However, Friedman cautions that no society, however open, can tolerate a wholly open legal system but requires for stability some elements of a closed legal system in which the rules and the decisions issue in the form of statements from a legitimate authority. Thus, even an ideal open, innovative legal system would have an underlying, conflicting logical structure. This necessary opposition between structures of discourse is clearly described, with respect to aesthetic texts, by Mukarovsky (1976), and is discussed in Kevelson (1987). Here we find a continuous opposition between monologic and dialogic structures. This opposition constitutes a kind of "semantic reversal" which permits new information—new rhemes or "legisigns" in Peirce's terms—to evolve.

As mentioned above, conflict between social forces and social systems of reasoning produces rules of law and processes of law. With reference to Peirce's semiotics, such conflict occurs as a sign of "secondness," on the level of actual existence. On the level of thirdness are the law-like signs, or rules, that govern the particular process of reasoning in focus. Signs of firstness may be likened to emergent anarchistic sorts of phenomena, or to patterned conduct of such social outsiders as cultists, religious revivalists, political dissenters, public action groups, and others. They appear as surprises, to disrupt a relatively stable legal system and to bring about a rethinking of what constitutes public trust in an established legal system. The function of the anomalous in effecting systemic creativity is discussed in Kevelson (1987).

Legal acts are persons and things—conventionalized sign structures—which are legitimized, authorized, and empowered with the ability to communicate all aspects of the legal system to a public and to carry with their message the "threat of official punishment or the promise of official reward" (L. Friedman 1975:28).

There are verbal legal acts and nonverbal legal acts. Nonverbal legal acts are such signs as police uniforms, traffic signs, codes of public conduct which are usually sanctioned by custom, ritualistic behavior in courts of law and other legal places, and certain signs of deference to dignitaries which are not strictly legal but which seem to observe unwritten codes of lawlike social behavior. Although not all acts are enforced, like going through redlights at intersections at 2 A.M., they may be so.

Speech acts, or verbal legal acts, which Friedman characterizes as commands or requests, and orders, have been examined against the background of legal reasoning, but against the kind of legal reasoning that has been identified with closed systems, or legal systems in which authoritative decisions are based on precedent. Speech act theories, from Austin through Searle, appear to consider only the authoritative statement, or sentence, without also accounting for the rhetorical force or style of such sentential speech acts. A theory of speech acts which would allow for the interaction between official actors and general public actors might also seek linguistic models in legal reasoning but would focus on open legal systems, particularly those that, following Friedman, are described as maximally innovative.

When we come to what Friedman calls the decision part of legal speech acts we find an area of speech acts which has received too little attention. A decision, like an order or command, is particular, compared with the rule part of a speech act which is general or axiomatic. But a further distinction between decisions and commands or orders should be made: Whereas a command expresses the will of authority which must be carried out without question or debate, a decision is a response to a claim, or question as complaint. Further, a command or order may be ignored or disobeyed, but with consequences that refer back to a rule. Thus, technically, and within a legal system, commands and orders are not questioned. But decisions may be appealed; that is, they may be questioned. So in the first stage of a total process of legal speech act the decision presumes a question and in turn may be questioned. Decisions may avoid appearing questionable by resort to legal fiction. "A fiction is phrased so as to look as if the court merely followed old and legitimate ways" (1975:252). Legal fictions form a bridge between ideology and fact, when an institution asserts either that less change has taken place or more than is actually true (1975:252). To interpret Friedman, a decision made based on the assertion of a legal fiction is an example of the rhetorical argument by convergence (Perelman 1969).

In subsequent chapters the underlying logic of question and answer is discussed in terms of speech acts that decide or define. Here it is possible to suggest the correlation between the three stages of a legal speech act—decision, command or order, and rule—with Peirce's three stages of phenomenological inquiry (Kevelson 1982b; 1983a).

Briefly, Peirce's phenomenology has also three stages: quality, fact, and representation. In terms of the first stage of a legal speech act, there is an initial quality of conflict that is abstracted and perceived. In the second stage the facts of the conflict are established. In the third stage the phenomena are evaluated and judged with reference to a shared body of signs and are said to be representations or signs of a kind of legally defined conflict. The representation in phenomenological inquiry is like a decision in court. The conflict as quality and the conflict as fact are not yet within the framework of a legal system. It is only with the decision that the representation, in terms of a legal system, has meaning.

As in legal procedure, the next stage of semiotic analysis would be to analyze the hypothetical decision logically. In a closed legal system the hypothesis would be analyzed either deductively or inductively. But in a maximally open, innovative system it could be examined provisionally, that is, in a manner of logic that approximates Peirce's abductive reasoning and is followed by deduction and then by induction. The conclusions of the logical analysis may also be made on "legalistic" grounds, that is, according to some form of legal fiction. Thus "legalism," or legal fictions, are governed by what Peirce calls speculative rhetoric. Friedman notes that "the legal culture—particularly theories of legitimacy—influences the *language* and *style* of the law as well as the forms of legal reasoning" (1975:259–60). Whereas older systems of law relied more on formulaic phrasing of legal problems and their solutions, even today modern legal systems tend to use law language to "protect professional cohesion and prestige" (1975:263). Not all legal acts can be challenged, but when they are they must indicate how "they link to higher authority" (1975:237).

One can perhaps carry this comparison between Friedman's legal systems and Peirce's semiotics through Peirce's ethics and esthetics in his normative sciences, and probably even through the divisions of chance, continuity, and evolution in his metaphysics (for example, see Part II of this volume, especially chapters 11 and 14).

A few words in conclusion: In the case of relatively closed legal systems, legal reasoning assumes a mode of formal logic: "The blocks of legal reasoning are propositions which serve as premises" (1975:237). When a decision is said to be based on or validated by so-called legal premises, of which in any closed system there are a fixed number, distinctions are sharply made between propositions that are legal and those that are not. The notion of a legalism refers to nonexisting legal premises which are used, in open legal systems, as though they were legally encoded. A maximally open legal system goes further and does not distinguish at all between legal and nonlegal propositions. In this sense a maximally open legal system resembles semiotics. All premises, or topics of inquiry, are suitable grist for the semiotic mill. Here there are ruptures or openings where new information may be introduced that permits new knowledge to evolve (see Part V of this volume). The idea of creating new value through intersystemic juncture is discussed more fully in Kevelson (1987).

Finally, according to Friedman, the ideal legal system contributes to the creation of new, major social values in much the same way that Mukarovsky (1970) says that the primary function of aesthetics is to create new social values which contribute to social change. Friedman speaks of both direct and indirect forces or demands that "produce legal change which lead in turn to major social change. . . . The main vehicle for this process is legislation" (1975:276). This is a direct force. A more indirect force are those groups or individuals who stand to profit from legislative changes. Still more indirect but no less effectual are reformers: "A reformer is a person who spends his energy on an issue where he has nothing *personally* at stake—no interest, direct or indirect" (1975:151). In this sense, one can speak of the aesthetics of legal systems. Esthetics as the science of value is further examined in later chapters.

A Comparatist View

Modern semiotics rests on the basic assumption that all human societies have developed complex systems of both verbal and nonverbal sign systems and that these sign systems are continually evolving as members of any given society continually reassess their future goals and values and attempt to reinterpret existing codes of rules and values to meet current changing needs and wants.

Some of the more familiar nonverbal sign systems are the ritualized forms of acknowledgment and politeness between members of a culture which contrast with the manner by which persons outside one's society are recognized and acknowledged. Actually, within any single cultural group the nonverbal signs for greeting and farewell, for approval and disapproval, for respect and disrespect, are part of a highly complex system, constructed of conventionally classified subsystems. These subsystems are also signs understood and adhered to by the community.

Infractions of these rules for social behavior are not always codified within a society's predominant legal system. As discussed above, there is not actually a single legal system except as an idealized concept of law in any society. Rather, as pointed out in the previous chapter, there are legal subsystems, in continual conflict and competition with one another, vying in various ways for position and for dominant power.

Peirce defines the legal expression *proximate cause and effect* as an "obscure term like most of the terms of Aristotelianism." He says that students of law and logic should be shocked by the practice of justifying the payment of damages in law by reference to a "term in Aristotelian logic or metaphysics." That such practice does occur underscores and "illustrates the value of PRAGMATISM." Peirce reminds us that in English law the term *witness* does not mean a person who testifies to his own experience, "but to facts which he knows by the immediate testimony of others" (Baldwin's *Dictionary* Vol. 2, 281–282: in CP 6.2391).

Practical law, Peirce suggests, results from persons whose knowledge of the facts of experience are formed in dialogue with others whose experience confirms one's own. The dialogue is immediate; the knowledge is mediated through signs. From the viewpoint of Peirce's pragmatism, which he saw as an integral part of his semiotic methodology or speculative rhetoric (mss: 774, 775), this chapter assumes that there are distinct types of legal cultures and that each may be regarded as a method of inquiry for the purpose of realizing social values. The relation between laws and societies—systems of legalities and legitimacies—will be regarded as culture-specific modes of dialectic.

It is proposed here that Peirce's methodology—his method of methods—may account for the way in which "patterns of conceptual change reflect the presuppositional structures of conceptual systems" (Toulmin 1958:70–71). Within the framework of a semiotics of law various ways in which the idea of the legal system has been interpreted will be examined.

Among nonverbal social sign systems are the structures of social institutions. For example, in closed societies the subsystems of such societies—the legal system, the economic system, the mating system, and so on—are characterized by the kinds of relationship they hold with one another. Primitive societies or cultures based on an underlying belief in predetermination, on fate, on a universe completely created by divine forces, not only reflect these beliefs in customs of interpersonal relationships but extend these relationships as well to the hierarchical concepts upon which social institutions are founded, and even to the architectural structures of the edifices that house institutional activities.

It is the conviction of many people who study the semiotics of culture that all cultural activity rests on culture-specific linguistic structure. That is, the natural language that characterizes each community, or family of communities, is a primary symbolic sign or point of reference upon which all other social systems are modelled and which provides the set of structural norms from which evolve notions of right and wrong, correct and incorrect, and even legal and nonlegal. This widely shared conviction is a collective judgment held by a particular community of inquirers, that is, semioticians. The conviction may or not hold up. If further research on the facts disproves it, a new working hypothesis will have to be established.

In other words, the method of semiotic inquiry following Peirce's methodology corresponds with the practice of law in open, rather than in closed societies. Not only is a belief acted on as though it were true—much as a person in a democratic society is believed to be innocent until proven otherwise—but its predominant sign status is symbolic of the assumption that there is such a thing in reality as scientific truth, just as there is such a thing in reality as legal innocence.

An open society, in which an open legal system usually predominates, rests not on the assumption that the world is fully created once and for all, but rather on the belief in the possibility of real change in the world, that is, on the conviction that the universe *becomes* and not that it *is*, that something really new may be created, and that this real novelty is not manifest in the actual order of things but is present in the evolving concepts of signs which stand for a reinterpretation of values and meanings of relationships between things.

Thus in an open society a code of laws is never fixed and eternal, although the official legal authorities may judge and decide particular cases as though it were. In a closed society the official legal authorities are duty-bound to find a rule within the codified laws that fits the crime, carries with it an appropriate punishment and/or penalty, and may justify judgment.

It should be noted that the more centralized the legal system is, the less open it becomes. The written law then becomes associated with a kind of permanence and is thus a sign to the people, as well as to the legal actors whose responsibility it is to enforce the law, of a fixed, unchanging symbolic nature. This is not to imply that an oral tradition of law in certain societies does not also appear to its society as a fixed, symbolic code. But a culture that depends for its stability and order upon an oral tradition of law must necessarily remain a simpler social structure if for no other reason than the fact that human memory, despite highly sophisticated mnemonic devices, is fallible.

Even with highly complex codes of law the problem of interpretation is paramount in juridicial thought. Frank, who was closely identified with legal realism, raised the crucial question in the 1930s: Is law discovered or is it created? By *created* he meant: Do judges in their decisions actually find an apt correlation between the law as it is written and the case before them, or do they freely interpret the existing code of law and base their decision on their interpretation?

According to Peirce, every interpretation of a sign results in a new sign, a more complex sign, which carries its reference with it cumulatively and adds something to the reference that did not previously exist.

In England, since the middle of the nineteenth century, through the influence of Austin, law has become a stabilized though controversial concept defined as the "command of the sovereign." Law, seen here as a system of commands, refers to a code of rules or statutes which may be amended or interpreted to fit the case in question but may not be fundamentally changed. This conception became embedded in American jurisprudence as well.

The responsibility of the highest legal actor, the judge, is to decide in conformance with the will of the original legislators who framed the laws; and clearly, in this understanding of law and legal systems, it is not within the province of the judge so to interpret law as to create new signs of law. This notion of Austin's derives from the belief that civil law is an extension of divine law. Thus behind both the concept of law as command—a much debated concept in jurisprudence today—and the concept of law based on semiosis, or communicative exchange between members of culture as in the social contract, stands a root concept of natural law.

The Stoics, who were among the first to translate natural law into civil law, were also among the first thinkers to develop the concept of signs and sign systems. They were advocates of the social contract. Well-known for his seminal writings on signs in the *Essay Concerning Human Understanding* and the treatises on law and government, John Locke was also a proponent of the idea of social contract. It is a concept that has evolved as Western civilization has evolved. Basic to the concept of social contract, in its rudimentary as well as in its current form, is the belief that it is the function of the will and the voice of the people to oppose and check the will and the power of the highest legal authority, whether it be the king, the priest, or the judge.

The two fundamental components of the concept of social contract are the ideal of personal freedom and the belief in justice in the courts of law. The Stoics gave this two fold concept, and it is from them that our modern Bill of Rights derives. It is also from them that the tradition of anarchism derives, which is based on beliefs in self-government, in self-correction, in mutual aid, and in the reciprocity of communication and interpersonal action. Thus the prototypical idea underlying modern semiotics implies intersubjective communication through the exchange of signs, the meaning of which is agreed upon by both speaker and listener, who are said to share and participate in a universe of discourse.

Systems of legal action and systems of legal discourse are complex signs of shared communal signs. Legal codes have long been characterized as mirrors of ideal social order. Breaches in the code represent rents in the fabric of social order. In relatively closed societies the purpose of the legal system is to restore damage done to society by infractions of social norms and rules. In open societies the legal system, which is usually an open system, mediates between established social norms and emergent social values.

Just as no society can be regarded as absolutely open, through legalisms or legal fictions the established code of laws is referred to as though it were fixed and eternal in order to maintain social and legal stability. There is no absolutely closed society or absolutely closed legal system. "Open" and "closed" are attributes that refer to the dominant features of specific cultures and social organizations and that make it possible to distinguish one type of cultural system from another. Because no code is ever fixed forever and complete, every definition, like a rule of law, may be doubted, questioned, and reinterpreted. Although some modern jurisprudes have suggested that legal procedure as a whole has two distinct parts, legal activity and legal discourse, legal semiotics makes no such distinction. *Discourse as a mode of communication is action, and every action presupposes a consequence.*

It was Peirce's idea of logical consequences in his semiotics that functioned as a catalyst in modern legal science and reintroduced into legal thinking the significance of legal consequences. Gény, in 1899, stressed that every legal system must involve consideration of the social customs and the wishes of the people. Customs and community must be seen to interact in a mutually reciprocal manner with existing and established codes of law. This was a revolutionary concept influencing jurists on the continent. Very similar conclusions were evolved in the United States by Holmes.

Four major assumptions of this chapter earlier stated are as follows:

1. There is no dominant legal system in any given society; there are only networks of legal subsystems.
2. Legal acts are both nonverbal and verbal, for example, speech acts.
3. Assumptions of authority, usually implied and deleted in explicit legal acts, characterize traditional presumptions of trust and legitimacy. Such presumptions are no longer adequate in modern transitional societies but characterize closed rather than open types of culture.
4. Coexisting legal subsystems are each reinforced by underlying systems of reasoning, each of which has an appropriate logical structure. The mode of logic predominant in any society is the referent model for other social structures and cultural institutions.

More than a half century ago the then famous legal historian John H. Wigmore compiled a monumental three-volume study that he called *A Panorama of the World's Legal System* (1928). Although legal historians since the writing of Wigmore's comparatist approach to legal systems may raise questions about the accuracy of particular dates he cited, there can be no doubt that his "semiotic" approach to the interrelations between legal signs in culture-specific law systems is a truly innovative introduction to this aspect of law and semiotics. It is Wigmore's contribution in this new direction that is stressed here. His point of view, which was nonorthodox at the beginning of this century, was that the primary code of laws of every culture is not fixed and eternal but instead reflects the values that predominate in the culture and that the most powerful members of a society want to see enforced. This view accords with Friedman's study (1975), which holds that the legal system is a predominantly symbolic sign. Subsumed in this sign system are many interlocking relationships of competing subsystems (as discussed above in Chapter 2).

Wigmore illustrated his enormous study with photographs and drawings of architecture, of sculpture and other art works, and of styles of script and printing to indicate how different styles of art and nonverbal structure reinforce and correlate with a particular style of law. Thus we want to understand by the term *rhetoric* not only the oratory of lawyers as verbal persuasion to some selected point of view but also as the persuasive force of all structures and procedures that are constituted of signs. This is Peirce's radical understanding of rhetoric.

In this sense of rhetoric, there is a perceivable relationship between legal actors and the general public, between codes of law and other structures of a society, for example, its kinship structure, its spatial structure in the layout of townships and villages, its calendar of significant ritual times in relation to ordinary workdays.

Communication is a semiotic event, which subsists of the functions of (1) speaker, (2) listener, (3) code of conventionalized language signs such as law language, (4) channel or appropriate medium for conveying language signs such as a court of law, (5) contact in the sense that a message does not overreach or fall short of its targeted listener but touches the other, and (6) context or the environment in flux that provides the background for the interaction. A context may be historical, conventional, geographical, temporal, referential, or the like and is usually a complex organization of all these factors and others as well.

In Wigmore's typology of legal systems there are sixteen distinct types, past and present: Egyptian, Mesopotamian, Hebrew, Chinese, Hindu, Greek, Roman, Japanese, Islamic, Keltic, Slavic, Germanic, maritime, ecclesiastical, Romanesque, and Anglican.

Since Wigmore's writing, anthropologists' studies have provided data for assuming other distinct types of legal systems of which Wigmore was unaware, such as those among American Indians. There is recent work done by scholars involved in legal studies and legal anthropologists to suggest kinds of relationships between law and society that we must consider. The following briefly surveys some of the varieties of legal experience from a semiotic perspective. The signs that each culture chooses to represent its significant space for justice to be done are multifunctional signs.

For example, the open clearing outside the limits of an old English town with its bar separating the pleaders—now barristers, or lawyers—from the bench of the judge is an iconic sign reflecting the significance of justice as a ritual apart and away from the daily business of practical life. Kevelson (1977) compares aspects of English law to theatrical productions, as suggested by Huizinga's classic *Homo Ludens* (1955). The lawyer may not pass the bar, that is, cross over from pedestrian to significant legal space unless he masters the correct formulae for presenting his plea to the highest legal actor. At the same time the plaintiff and the defendant must repeat the ritualistic formulae accurately before they are permitted to cross over from ordinary life into the space concerned with dispensing justice.

The place of justice in old England was like a theater, separated from real life only by words. These words in law language had to be correctly, that is, formulaically, phrased and uttered. Law space was structured, as icon, dramatistically, recalling the ancient *agon* between man and the forces of nature. The court rituals reenacted the primitive struggle between man the violator of the earth, and man the cultivator of the earth. As struggle, or *agon*, the court trial is an indexical sign, or in Peirce's terms a sign of "secondness," indicating the opposing forces and facts that actually occur in existential life. At the same time the reenactment of this drama which led to reconciliation between man the violator and man the cultivator, through the mediation of justice, is a symbolic sign, restoring the damaged society to its former wholeness. Holmes, in *The Common Law*, notes that law enters into human society as a mediator, or a substitute for vengeance.

Wigmore says:

> Let us recall to the eye the *edifices* in which various peoples of various cultures dispensed law and justice (whether temples, palaces, tents, courthouses, or city-gates); their principal *men of law* (whether kings, priest, legislators, judges, jurists, or advocates); and their chief types of *legal records* (whether codes, statutes, deeds, contracts, treatises, or judicial decisions). (Wigmore, 1928:6)

Law has been associated in many cultures with the word for "straight." For example, in ancient Egypt the goddess of justice was *Maat*, which meant in ancient Egyptian both "true" and "straight." Similarly, the Greek word *Kanon* was the sign for "straight rule" and thus came to be the word, or sign, for "law." We find the same association in Latin, wherein *rectum*, which meant "straight," also came to signify "right"; and in modern Italian the word *diritto* has the triple meaning of "straight," "right," and "law."

Thus the word, or sign, for "law" was iconic, in that it represented a visual image of a nonwarped or straight, that is, "upright" object.

It was indexical in the sense that the physical uprightness and the moral and ethical concepts of uprightness fused. Thus an act that was right was opposed to one that was crooked or bent or warped rather than one that was wrong.

The word *law* has had a duel meaning since Aristotle; it was the symbol for encoded legal action and at the same time the symbol for justice. These two meanings have often, through the argument of convergence, been conjoined. It is stressed here that although the verbal sign "law" connotes both legal rule and justice, it is by the strategies of argument, that is, by rhetoric, that equivalent terms have become opposed—through what Perelman notes is the argument by dissociation—and that opposing terms have become equivalent, through another rhetorical tactic known as the argument by convergence. It is these strategies by which arguments in law evolve, and it is this legal argument that is the model, or referent sign, by which argument or discourse in ordinary life evolves.

There has always been much interest in the role of women in all legal systems. Wigmore points out that in the ancient Egyptian system of law it is the woman "who has the option of divorce, and retains the greater property-interest" (Wigmore 1928:26–28). It is surprising that the Egyptians were the only people who retained for centuries in an institutional manner the equal rights of women.

In most other modern societies the role of woman as legal entity is reduced in direct proportion to the complexification of the culture. This phenomenon in large measure parallels cultural life: crime, family, property, commerce (Wigmore 1928:88). However, Egypt is the only culture known that fostered a native, enduring legal code, through a strong centrally organized system, which did not provide for the specific training of legal professionals.

By contrast the Code of Hammurabi, despite deference and reference to the deity, was clearly a civil code, in sharp contrast to the Mosaic or Talmudic Code, which was modelled after it.

It was not until around 500 A.D.—some 2,500 years after the Mosaic Code became the law of the Hebrews—that a legal system as such as established. The Mishna, or book of learning, was brought together with the Gemora, or Talmudic commentaries by the Priests, into an encyclopedia of law which defined in a legal framework the major topics of Judaic culture into a unified text. These topics included history, mathematics, medicine, theology, metaphysics, and specific topics of civil law. The term *law* refers here to the recorded legal arguments and the legal decisions on "rules and cases adjudged by the doctors of law" (Wigmore 1928:119).

What is found here is not a record of statutes as rules, but rather a documentation of discourse in the form of dialogue and questions and answers, conforming to the underlying logical structure of the Hebrew language. One finds the logic of questions and answers—the emphasis on dialogic exchange—even more pronounced in the Islamic system of law and exemplified through legal riddling, as discussed in Chapter 7.

As mentioned, the role of the woman and her power in decisive positions of cultural life is always reflected by a society's legal system. For example, in Egypt the marriage contract specified the sole right of the woman to sue for divorce. According to the Hammurabi code, the husband who opted for divorce had to restore to his wife her dowry. According to the Assyrian Code, the husband had to restore to the wife only part of her dowry, and only as much as he chose. The Hebrew law says nothing about the restoration of dowry by the husband.

A point in passing: An important recent text that examines the laws concerning women in modern societies as a key to changing cultural morals and values, *Sex Laws in Law and Society* by Kanowitz (1973), can be tied to the evolving significance of the written word together with the restriction of literacy among women. The study of women's legal systems and their roles in the legal systems of various cultures must be a separate task, exceeding our limits here.

Although there was no profession, as we know it, of advocates or lawyers in the Egyptian system of law, the lawsuits that we know show that the "practice of written pleadings had been devised" (Wigmore 1928:30).

There is no continuation of a native Egyptian legal system into modern times. The native Egyptian legal system, which at the end of its period of ascendancy held proceedings before the god Osiris—"the supreme last judge of all men"—evolved into a highly complex system which resisted the influence of many foreign conquests. It endured from about 3200 B.C. until about eight hundred years before Christ, when it underwent enormous modification that reflected the changing society and internal cultural revolutions in Egypt at that time. These changes were the result of war, of trade, and of renewed perspectives on the deity, which shifted over time from the supreme lawgiver, Menes, to Osiris.

In contrast, the Mesopotamian legal system, nearly as old, dating from about 2500 B.C., changed hardly at all. As Wigmore notes:

> In any of the surviving European systems, the lapse of a thousand years has given rise to successive new phases of thought, and thus has witnessed radical change both in the procedural methods and in the style of the records. . . (but) after reading a mature development by B.C. 2500 . . . the system exhibits little noticeable change. (Wigmore 1928:72–76)

The earliest people of that area were the Sumerians, a non-Semitic people. Fragments of their codes—the earliest code text to be discovered in modern times still intact—anticipate the "pillar code" of King Hammurabi (c. 2100 B.C.), which is the oldest national legal code known to us in its full text. It is older than the Hebrew Code and also older than the Manu Code of India.

This code shows how the legal system directly relates to controversial and/or unsettled areas of cultural life, particularly those that are in flux and in transition insofar as the values of the community have been called into question to meet the newly perceived facts of life. Laws pertaining to sex roles are subdivided into the following areas: marriage, employment, public accommodatons, pornography, media, military, sex preferences and appearance, birth control, rape, double standards of sexual morality, sex-based age requirements for marriage, for voting, for jurisdiction in juvenile courts. The "traditional" legal status of the woman is examined here, that is, as a nonlegal person, as chattel, as dependent, as constitutionally and physically unstable, and as recipient of social benefits.

Nancy Reeves says: "Even if nature is the common law, culture is its codification: form follows function . . . woman's patterns are cut to fit the cloth of the community in which she finds herself" (Reeves 1973:23). While Reeves notes from a cross-cultural perspective that there is a greater freedom of women's roles in totalitarian societies, L. Friedman (1973) suggests that we must look not only at the legitimized changing sex roles but also at how they came to be legitimized. For example, in a totalitarian society women may be permitted to assume and practice traditional male occupations, but if this legal right has not come about because the people wish it to, the appearance of greater legal status for women may be not freedom in the sense we understand it at all but an imposition of greater obligation to serve the nonpersonal, political goals of the state which acts as highest legal actor.

Friedman points out:

> In a democracy, the interplay between social opinion and the law-molding activities of the State is a more obvious and articulate one [than that in totalitarian government]. . . . Because of this constant interaction between the articulation of public opinion and the legislative process, the tension between the legal and the social norm can seldom be too great. But, a strong social groundswell sooner or later compels legal action. Between these two extremes, there is a great variety of the patterns of challenge and response (1973)

The interaction between public opinion and established legislation in any given society is predominantly an indexical sign. We speak of this communication in ordinary language as an index of social change. In Peirce's category of signs this index is a sign of secondness which directly refers to existence, experience, and the opposition between factive components of the actual world. Any change in the legal status of women is like a finger pointing to fundamental alterations in the cultural values of a society.

There are countless examples through history of dual legal systems. For example, Wigmore points out that the Jewish term or verbal sign for "deed" and *shetar*, or *starr* are from the Hebrew word *starra*. This word written in both Latin and Hebrew occurs in the Private Codes. It means "bond" as well as "deed" in Jewish and is etymologically derived from the Hebrew word meaning *memorial*. The origin of bond or contract in English law conflicts with the Hebrew concept of bond: There was a special court established in thirteenth-century England to deal specifically with suits between Jews and Christians. Presumably emergent from this cultural semiotic interaction in this special court is the concept of the English bond, which became the contract of the early thirteenth-century stage of English law. Thus the meaning of the bond in the Jewish legal system signified a *release* from indebtedness, whereas in the English system of law, *contract*, or *bond*, signifies an *agreement to action made between equals* or between persons of equal legal status (Wigmore 1928:124–126). The contract of English common law will be examined in later chapters.

In the Chinese legal system, as in the Semitic, in opposition to the systems of law in societies with a predominantly Indoeuropean language subsystem, the logic of science and the logic of practical affairs and morality were not opposed. The underlying logic of legal discourse in the Chinese system appears to be a logic of questions and answers. The Chinese legal system did not include professional training for lawyers and they had no enduring legal code: as in Egypt. There were, in China as in Egypt, notaries and brokers, but no technically trained "legal actors." Unlike the use of the *quaestiones* in Roman law, questions in Chinese law aimed at corroboration of understanding of the listener and not at clarification of the problem or point of law.

The basic maxim of Confucian law, which developed after about 500 B.C., was that government is of men, not of laws. This is precisely the "reverse of the basic occidental maxim" according to Wigmore (1928). Until around 400 B.C.., this maxim predominated, and justice was derived from the wisdom of the supreme ruler rather than from the interpretation of a legal text or code of laws. However, between 400 B.C. and 200 B.C. a group of reformers, called the Legists, completely rejected the Confucian maxim and pressed for a government of laws.

The history of Chinese law can be understood as a "struggle for rights" according to the German jurist Rudolf von Ihering (1924). The role of the Chinese "governor" whose office, or *yamen*, was the heart of local governments, is not to be found in other legal systems. His function was to create appropriate distinctions between legal relations and other cultural relations and at the same time to show when appropriate that no distinctions between legal relations and other cultural relations existed and that no distinction should exist. No single written code of laws existed before 1200 B.C., although an oral code can be traced back to before 2500 B.C. With the establishment of the Chinese Republic in 1912 a provisional legal constitution was drawn up. This was discarded and replaced in 1923. The native Chinese legal system at this time was replaced by a constitution of six codes, modelled on European legal systems and the product of European-trained legislators. This system, of course, has undergone revolutionary change during the past sixty years, and these changes are paralleled by the radical changes in Chinese culture during this period.

Berman (1977/1983) has insisted that we cannot truly speak of the existence of a system of law until the twelfth century, when universities were established at Bologna and Milan and special schools were established for the sole purpose of training lawyers. At this time the Codes of Justinian were recovered and questions of law—encoded rules of law—were problems regarding the meaning of laws which required interpretation.

The Greeks constructed no codes. They reported no reasoned decisions. They wrote no doctrinal treatises. "Their one juridical contribution, the popular jury-court, took a form most susceptible to caprice and [was] essentially incompatible with any science of law," Berman writes (1977:358–59).

But Roman code of law was from the start "procedural" (Wigmore 1928:374–75). That is, it was an algorithm for official legal action rather than a commandment for good conduct. The Roman legal system reached maturity under Augustus, between the second and third centuries A.D. "Professional jurists in copious treatises expounded legal principles in systematic form. Schools of law study arose and multiplied" (Wigmore 1928:419).

At this time one can speak of a "Roman juristic science," and it was around this time that scientific "purity" became a sign of the search for objective truth and impersonality. It was precisely because the Roman legal system had so successfully become interpreted as a sign of clear-headed monitoring of civil life in accordance with a finite set of regulations that it was so widely adapted by other cultures. A strong central legal seat together with a standard legal code reduced the force of local codes of law, of customary law, of tribal power, and, presumably, of ambiguity. Principles become superordinate to persons. It should be pointed out that the raising of principles over persons has had a dynamic impact on the development of all those cultures that modelled their legal systems on the *system* of Roman law and not necessarily on the expressed code of laws as such.

For example, there is no distinctly native Slavic system of law. In the vacuum created by a succession of conquerors, particularly after the disintegration of Germanic law around the thirteenth century, modifications of the Roman legal system were brought into the region from Italy. The first appearance of Roman law in Czechoslovakia was in response to problems concerning rights in the mining district of Kutnahora; a complex mining code, based on Roman law, was drafted there around 1400. It was first scribed in Latin and opens with the first chapter of Justinian's Digest (Wigmore 1928:741).

Roman law formed the basis for Polish and Czech legal systems, but the Balkan countries developed a very different kind of legal system, one that eclectically fused together Romanesque and Greek ecclesiastical and civil law. This code, in Serbia, was drafted by King Stefan Dushan, in Cyrillic. But by the mid-nineteenth century the adopted legal code was replaced by another civil code that was largely based on a Germanic-Roman model brought in from Austria.

Even the Russian code of Yaroslav, which dates from between 1100 to 1300 A.D., was not native but was incorporated into a legal system that was actually a hybrid of "Germanic, Slavic, and Greco-Roman elements" (Wigmore 1928:768). The Code of Yaroslav was called "Russian Truth" (Pravda Russkaya) and was inspired by the Greek religious courts. The second period of the Russian legal system begins around 1400 with Ivan the Great. This system, like the English baronial system prior to the Normans, was not derived from the model of Roman legal science but was "based on local customs" (Wigmore 1928:770). Not until the later influence of Peter the Great did the idea of law pass from the belief that justice was the supreme ruler's prerogative to the concept of law as a legal process, with official legal acts and legal actors.

This chapter concludes with a brief summary of the Islamic legal system. In this system it is presumed that everything a member of the Islamic culture should know, should believe, and should do was written in the summaries attributed to Mohammed and written down after his death as gleanings from what he said and wrote. These didactic summaries include all aspects of "theology, morals, law, politics, and industry" (Wigmore 1928). These dicta could be easily practiced, unlike the sacrificial ideals of Judaism or Christianity.

The Islamic legal system reached its greatest heights precisely during those four centuries between 800 and 1200 A.D. that are referred to (Wigmore 1928:538) as the Dark Ages in Europe: "In the sciences and arts, the Saracens were the preeminent people. . ." bringing intellectual and cultural activity and progress throughout all Europe. But by the 1200s the renascence of cultural life in Europe had begun and the influence of Islam was running down. It should be stressed that from its inception the Islamic legal system was a complex, comprehensive sign of interrelationships between all areas of cultural life: religion, morality, politics, law, art, kinship—and all this derives from revealed command.

As in the Rome of the emperors, the Islamic legal system two hundred years after the death of Mohammed was divided into judicial and juristic functions which were separated from the executive function. At this time a system was so well organized that the writings of these jurists form the third major source of Islamic law. The first is the Koran itself. The second is the commentary on Mohammed's sayings and writings. The work of these professionals became the third.

The separate sects of Islam were originally distinguished as five separate schools of law, each with its own characteristic theory which was the development of the legal concepts of a particular revered jurist. The four major sects of Islamic law are: the Malekites along the Mediterranean and in middle Africa; the Hanefites in Turkey, Syria, and parts of India; the Shafites in lower Egypt, central Asia, and what is now Vietnam; and the Sunnites, who are considered the most orthodox practitioners of Islamic law. The Shiites are the Iranians and traditionally and ironically, in view of recent history, were the least orthodox, the "heretics" of Islamic law. The Hambalites in Saudi Arabia is still another sect. "Each sect has its own extensive body of legal literature, ranging back through ten centuries" (Wigmore 1928:552). All of the enormous body of Islamic learning, it should be stressed, is entirely apart from government codes and statutes and is wholly the work of jurists (Wigmore 1928: 554). Wigmore's geographical distribution is in need of updating but still serves its purpose here.

Wigmore tells us that the oldest law university in the world was in Cairo, the Mosque El Azhar founded in 970 A.D. As a legal institution it has endured primarily because of the following functions: "Judiciary organization, careful documentation; role of counsellors, use of authority and precedent in argument and in decisions, theoretically religious background of its legal principles" (1928:552–554).

This is the formula or recipe for a legal system that reaches into and affects virtually every corner of every life in every aspect of a global cultural system. It is not, however, a system of law that exemplifies semiosis as open dialogue. It is a closed system. As such it is a complex sign of shifting sign interrelationships and as such should be studied in depth as a vehicle for communication. Its function, as sign, is not to evolve new information, but rather to retain its predominant status as symbolic sign, a symbol that incorporates many millions of persons, thousands of subcultures, hundreds of languages, scores of sovereign nations, and at least five competing, conflicting legal subsystems.

Finally, legal systems are systems of behavior. One of the principles of semiotics is that all behavior can be regarded as the exchange of signs and that the exchange of signs is never nonconsequential. In the past the so-called social character of law has been investigated by the movement of sociological juris-prudence which is usually associated in this country with Roscoe Pound. This view "seeks to bring legal policy in line with the interests of society as a whole" (Black and Mileski 1973:1).

A second major line of inquiry derives from legal realism, originating in this country with Holmes and finding chief spokesmen in Frank (1934) and Llewelyn (1962). Legal realism seeks to expose the myth of law's ideality and uncover its contingent history. This inaugurated a systematic behavioral approach to law contrary to traditional legal thought.

The work of legal anthropologists in this area begins with Malinowski, who compared the legal system of the Trobrianders with modern legal systems in the United States. The joint study by Llewelyn and Hoebel (1941) on the system of law of the Cheyenne Indian is most notable.

From another perspective, Becker's work on antisocial or "deviant" behav-ior (1963) has spurred research into legal systems that permit the label or sign of deviance to be applied to some persons. He has also looked at those legal systems in which the same targeted, or alleged, deviant behavior is considered normative. This recent work on law as a normative system has been historically valuable in the rebirth of legal sociology.

> [But] because it has continually referred legal practices to legal ideals, the sociology of law has been, at its core, evaluative. It has failed to treat law as an entirely empirical phenomenon, since the legal ideals it discusses are not observable in the world of human action. . . . Like any values, legal ideals have no objective meaning shared by everyone. . . . The interpretation of legal signs takes us outside of sociology . . . and into the realm of legal criticism and advocacy (Black and Mileski 1973:4)

A major aim should be the linking of "patterns from legal systems of different times and cultures" (Black and Mileski, 1973:5).

It is not possible to even describe the position a legal system has in the general structure of a society without taking into consideration the value of that system to the people of the particular culture.

First, the punitive impact of laws on people is not the only source of punishment for individuals. For example, the culture with its specific values always has other sources of rewards and punishment: family, co-workers, friends, and these private sources may be qualitatively measured and compared with the impact of the legal system on the conduct of life.

Second, each person is not force-fed values and ideas but produces them in interaction with others. A person is a creator of signs and therefore of culture. As L. Friedman suggests, legal "commands" do not strike a person directly from the outside but are filtered through his subjective scale of straights and crookeds.

Finally, no person is a passive object of the law. He can bribe, cajole, outwit, outtalk, or in other ways use the forces of rhetoric at his command to bend the rule. The use of rhetoric, as Friedman points out, is neither compliance nor noncompliance, but the act of a person engaging in a communicative event, using signs in persuasive ways, toward some desired consequence (1975:105).

It is the task of legal semiotics to investigate the various functions of signs for their rhetorical forces, some of which are viable in one culture and totally ineffective in another. What is also needed are the *equivalents* of such rhetorical signs, in much the same manner that one seeks equivalents when translating literature from one language to another. As George Steiner reminds us (1976), every act of translation is an interpretation.

Every reinterpretation of a sign according to Peirce is really the creation of new meaning. Thus, the process of finding equivalences between legal signs from a cross-cultural perspective is the search for new meaning in the world.

CHAPTER 5

Global Developments

This chapter prepares for subsequent sections of the volume which will examine the evolving meaning of the concept of contract in law, the changing function of contract throughout the history of legal systems in Western civilizations, and, finally, the alleged "death of contract" in twentieth-century law in the United States' tradition of common law.[1] Contract, in both theory and praxis, is regarded from the point of view of legal semiotics as a referent sign, or interpretant in Peirce's terminology. In common law the concept of contract is closely related to the ideas of legal cause and consideration.[2] This chapter also leads up to investigation of causation in law.

We shall presuppose parallels between, on the one hand, the dialogic, contractual basis of semiotic processes as now currently accepted in general by the community of semiotic researchers[3] and, on the other hand, the notion of contract central to legal systems throughout the Western world and indeed the basis of civil law on a more global scale. It is now a virtual commonplace among semioticians that semiosis as a structure of exchange, transaction, and contractual agreement between interacting parties implies that value, or signs of value in money, words, gesture, or any system of commodity whatever, acquires a working or functional valuation through mutual consent. Such a given sign is to be regarded as representing some assignable meaning and transactable value.[4] The assumption implied herein is that the legal contract may justifiably be regarded as the prototypical structure of exchange in general and, further, may be understood as the quintessential symbolic structure of all other semiotic processes and events.

I shall discuss concepts basic to an understanding of legal cause. Cause in law corresponds in significant ways to the concept of authority and its function in any discourse or system of discourse. If the notion of legal cause has become in the twentieth century multiply ambiguous, it is no less ambiguous than the concept of authority in the modern world.[5] Together with the predominant admission among scholars in all fields of inquiry today that absolutes may be useful but only provisionally true has come the realization that the conceivable universe may no longer be represented as a closed system, nor even as an open system, but rather as a "motion-picture system" in which both the system and its referent frames of authority are moving and changing in relation to one another simultaneously with their respective motion and change in relation to other so-called possible worlds.[6]

As the notions of truth and absoluteness have evolved to a working hypothesis in modern thought, at the same time the once venerable "authority of the precedent" in law has in a similar fashion become open to question and to doubt and through the semiotic process of developing ideas or interpretant signs has become susceptible of revision and revocation.

Peirce's semiotics and his pragmatic method are the major influence on legal realism in the United States, as I have noted.[7] Among the two main characteristics of legal realism are "the conception of law in flux, of moving law, and of judicial creation of law," and "the conception of society in flux, and in flux typically faster than the law, so that the probability is always given that any portion of law needs reexamination to determine how far it fits the society it purports to serve" (Llewellyn 1931/1962:54–70).

The permeation of Peirce's semiotic theory and method into what has been called the most revolutionary development of law in the United States is the main topic of chapters which follow.[8] The underlying structure of contract and the shifting meaning of the use of authority and cause in law are also principal topics. But non-Peircean approaches to legal semiotics should also be discussed and compared with a Peircean perspective on some main points.

The comparison will be made in part by induction. Legal realism, as a movement or a school, has eluded any single definitive concept and description but has been recognized by Llewellyn and others as a trend, a tendency to converge on certain principal issues which, it is said, characterize legal realism and distinguish it from other approaches. Llewellyn refers to this general movement as a "ferment" of interest, in which there is agreement on the wish to see law as concerned not with words only, but with people, with changing environments, with emerging social values. We "want to check ideas, and rules, and formulas by facts. . . . They view rules, they view laws, as means to ends. . ." or as means as ends in the service of the larger, dynamic semiosis of human society (Llewellyn 1931/1962:42–44).

This venture into legal semiotics may be regarded as such a movement.[9] The most challenging aspect of this new project is not to draw hard definitions of legal semiotics, but rather *to distinguish the method and perspective of a legal semiotics* from other older and more traditional approaches to the law. At such an early and formative stage of this growing field, an inclusiveness, rather than exclusiveness, should be stressed. Eclecticism may also, with qualifications, be encouraged insofar as the inquirer's free choice of materials and content of investigation does not negate or compromise in any way the goal of systematic representation of all aspects of legal theory and practice from the special point of view of general semiotics.

Initially, it is important to point to areas of commonality between Peircean and non-Peircean legal semiotics. Secondly, one wants to perceive relationships between, on the one hand, the legal system which respectively is each one of ours by a kind of inheritance or windfall, that is, of chance and circumstance, and that which respectively becomes each of ours, through interest, concern, and hard learning.

From a Peircean point of view, it is proposed that one begin with one's own experience, with those unavoidable "prejudices" as Peirce calls them which provide a ground and point of departure for further exploration and move ever closer to a more central, more universal position from which future studies of both a comparative and a specific nature may grow.

It is becoming apparent that the term *legal semiotics* is generic, covering an enormous variety of legal structures and systems. Both synchronic and diachronic analyses of legal systems are much needed, such that a comparative approach to legal semiotics may include the multiple subsystems of law that coexist at any given time within any given culture and that taken together comprise that network of law that, abstractly, we call the legal system of a given society (L. Friedman 1975). Another area that can be identified but that still lacks even basic information and analysis might be the structure of contradiction between equity and justice since ancient law, from the contrastive perspectives of an Aristotle and a Plato to the present day. And work is needed on the so-called materialistic basis for contract which derives from the Stoics and which, to this day, remains controversial, involving in current literature the admixture of morals, ethical positions, and creeds, in the judical attitudes toward the facts of contract cases in courts.[10]

From the viewpoint of semiotics, the dichotomy between legitimacy and legality, that is, between legal orders and legal systems, also warrants close investigation. All of legal semiosis may be correctly understood as a legal discourse, as Greimas and Landowski postulated in their seminal work (Greimas 1976:79–128).[11]

The important question also arises as to which is the predominant logical structure of legal discourse: deontic, as claimed by von Wright (1967) and others, or erotetic as is otherwise argued (Kevelson 1981a, 1982b, 1985a,b,c,).

Inquiry should be made into the relation between the way in which a textual code may be said to correspond with a legal code. This is a particularly difficult task, for we must look closely into the function of legal codes in not one but a number of legal systems. For example, if one assumes that a legal code is, as has been traditionally claimed, a "mirror of society,"[12] are we then to understand the legal code as an iconic mode of sign representation which resembles or replicates its referent? A mirror image is such a replication. But, as Peirce convincingly argues, any sign that has a predominantly iconic function need not resemble its object. Indeed it should not. It represents its object as a *verisimilitude*, that is, as an interpretation of its referent object.[13] This interpretation, or immediate interpretant sign, *makes present* the object of inquiry by showing it in terms of its spatial relationships, for example, as map, model, diagram, image, or even as a formulaic, axiomatic, equational structure that is not intended to state a truth but *is* intended to show equivalences between relates which, for the purpose at hand, may act as symbols of what has been and can be used at truths or zero-sign points of reference (Kevelson 1987)

From this perspective the imposition of one legal code upon another, for instance, through conquest or in societies that sustain dual legal systems, opens up fresh fields for researchers in legal semiotics. For example, in Kevelson (1977) a legal system in the process of transition, that is, English common law from the time of the Roman conquest, was examined from the perspective of semiotics. Here in a complex manner, the system of a society in flux with respect to its nonlegal institutions—economic, political, familial, artistic, and so on— may be brought into a more comprehensive system with a legal system undergoing radical change and transformation.

One could continue developing a possible classificatory schema for legal system, one that would have "fuzzy boundaries" and would, as any constructed system of types, tokens and topics, be open to change and revision. This task is the task of evaluating current literature specifically and intentionally written from the point of view of legal semiotics, together with the vast, untapped source of legal material that was not written from a semiotics perspective but nevertheless is invaluable for continuing research in legal semiotics.

This latter task requires, at least initially, less commentary than identification. In other words, a quality that we might call for our purposes here a "primitive notion" in legal semiotics must be abstracted from its usual ground and lifted from that ground so that one may evolve it, in Peirce's sense, from quality to fact to semiotic representation, thereby making it available for systematic semiotic analysis. This process of *prescinding*, of abstracting qualities from their customary ground, evolving a quality to a fact or judgment that is based on the contractual agreement of at least two members of a community of inquirers and is that which is agreed to be this and not that, is the equivalent of what in science is called an *observable*.

The fact is followed by the representation, which is given a name and thus becomes eligible to be included among the signs of verbal and logical discourse. This whole process, Peirce says, is what he means by phenomenology, a term not to be confused with continental phenomenology. This phenomenology, or "phaneroscopy" (as Peirce later refers to this process), is preliminary to all semiotic inquiry.[14]

It is critical, also, that those concerned with legal semiotics should distinguish a legal hermeneutics, or sign interpretation, from the ongoing mainstream discussion of phenomenology and hermeneutics that has stirred up much interest both on the Continent and in the United States. Of course there are overlappings; but the differences must be identified and discussed.

Paramount among tasks in the near future is the need to distinguish a semiotic concern with law from the various legal concerns that are not semiotically oriented. For instance, how do we contrast and compare any set of given topics in legal philosophy, in jurisprudence, in actual legal practice? Here, again, there are some basic differences between the approach to the study of law in general in the United States and in Europe.

In the United States, as a rule, legal philosophy is taught and studied within the liberal arts framework of the university, and jurisprudence, badly neglected, is part of the law school curriculum. In Europe, little distinction is made between philosophy of law and jurisprudence, and the persons principally involved in these studies are usually trained in the practice of law and are members of law school faculties. Without a careful distinction between these frames of reference, legal semiotics runs the risk of initially confusing and confounding its own special point of view. This confusion becomes even more complicated when we intend that our research in various areas of legal semiotics should cut across all national boundaries and achieve a global significance.

Among some of the questions that will inevitably arise, for example, are those that touch on the relationship between structural and semiotic approaches to law. For some purposes a close distinction is relatively unimportant; for others it is crucial. Certainly one must speak of constructions in a predominantly semiotic approach. Certainly, also, one is concerned with sign relations and sign systems in predominantly structural approaches. If one assumes the responsibility of clarifying for newcomers to this field the appropriate domain of legal semiotics, the historical and philosophical distinctions must be painstakingly made and brought into the paradigmatic base of inquiry.

In very recent years, both in the United States and on the Continent, various articles have appeared in the professional law journals that introduced structuralism and semiotics in the study of law as nearly indistinguishable terms. By contrast, there are a number of papers published in American journals in the past decade or so that specifically show the influence of Peirce's semiotics and pragmatism on the law in the United States; for example, papers focusing on Holmes's contribution to legal pragmatism, legal realism, and legal instrumentalism trace his ideas to direct contact with Peirce and with Dewey. Perhaps the earliest paper of this kind was Fisch's paper (1942) on the predictive theory in law. The most recent, to my knowledge, are Kevelson (1984, 1985b, 1986).[15]

Thus two major trends must be identified and compared: the one is Saussurean in origin and characterizes much of the early semiotic work in the United States which is of a closed-system or closed-structure nature: the other is that emanating from Peirce's philosophy of signs which has found its way across the Atlantic in a number of important ways, with important consequences in each case.

Of these transatlantic Peircean crossings two will be mentioned: the first is related to the emergency of a legal realism in Sweden in the 1930s (Olivecrona 1938).[16] There is much speculation but no hard evidence that Peirce's writings were known to the proponents of a Scandinavian legal realism which, in its fundamental ways, stressed the dialogic responsiveness of a changing legal system to a society in flux. The second major impact of Peircean semiotics on European law occurred much earlier, shortly before Holmes took his place on the United States Supreme Court and a few years prior to Peirce's major revisions of his semiotic logic. This Peircean influence on Gény's *Méthode d'interprétation* became apparent in 1899[17]:

> In contesting the then prevailing notion that laws are fixed and eternal . . . Gény's view, now strongly supported on both the Continent and in English and American legal systems, is that the judge not only must consider himself as an "ideal legislator" and act as a legislator might if confronted by actual, changing circumstances, but it is the social and cultural values which are hypothesized, and which function as the leading premise in free judicial decision. In other words, it is not the statute which is the antecedent . . . but it is the *consequence of a legal decision*—the custom and value of a society—which is takèn hypothetically as the primary assumption in the process of judicial interpretation, definition and decision making. (Kevelson 1980:243)

Gény's major contributions to French law have been especially consulted by realists in the Holmesean and Peircean pragmatic traditions of thought. For example, Roscoe Pound (1920/1943) points to Gény as one of the most valuable Continental legal thinkers.[18] Llewellyn, in commenting on Pound's discussion of Gény's *Science et Technique*, notes that not only in this cited work but especially in the *Méthode* Gény performs the "most magnificent single job that has ever been done of *mediating*, by way of a single, simple formulated way of work . . . between any ideal, and any authoritative text. . ." (Llewellyn 1963:499–500). Llewellyn suggests with the term *mediating* that Gény himself is a sign, a sign in the evolving understanding of the relationship between law and society. Llewellyn goes on to say that Gény's contribution is not only a work of intellectual genius, but it is "also lawyering, it puts jurisprudence to work, for anybody." It is to Pound's great credit, Llewellyn notes, that he has "sniffed out" this greatness in Gény which, except by Cardozo, has been for too long neglected, or even missed.[19] Elsewhere the affinity between Gény and the American legal realists is discussed in more detail (Kevelson 1985a,b,c). Here it suffices to emphasize one of the major areas in which Continental and American approaches to legal semiotics may fruitfully begin to share a common point of view.

Gény points up the corresponding approaches between discovery procedures and interpretation in law in particular and the interpretation of signs and
the logic of discovery in semiotics in general. Further, his work permits us to
see sharply how some of the now accepted and customary approaches to semiotic
analyses can be linked. For example, he suggests the following adaptation of
Jakobson's semiotic "functions" which were referred to earlier:

The *social context* is an interactive function of a legal event, together with
the shifting roles of addresser and addressee (official and nonofficial legal actors);
the *channel* corresponds with the conventional signs of the natural language, the
courts and legislative bodies, and so on; the *code* refers to legal codes as well
as to the technical terms and syntactic structure of law language, as Greimas
and Landowski point out in their analysis of the three levels of law language—
the syntactic, the semantic, and the pragmatic—in the Charles Morris sense
(Greimas and Landowski 1983).[20]

Future work in semiotics and law should attempt to correspond with the
predominant theories and methods of semiotics in general. Perhaps by regarding
law as a prototypical system, as suggested above, such efforts may make significant contributions to some of the unresolved, even unidentified problems in
the current general semiotics literature.

It is suggested that the following topics be given careful consideration:

- Authority in relation to precedential law and statute
- The desirability of incomplete codes of law, in opposition to the Benthamite position
- The question of whether legal discourse in it widest sense is based on a
  deontic logic or on a logic of questions and answers, or whether there
  are appropriate circumstances in which one rather than the other predominates and is a sign symbolizing a particular aspect of the legal
  process
- Similarities and differences in concepts of legal realism that point up
  Peirce's direct influence or minimize that influence, for example, as in
  the current view holding that Dewey's pragmatism is more in evidence.
- The emphasis on the dynamic process of law
- Inquiry into the role of fiction in legal procedure and the deliberate use
  of "constructions" or legalisms in order to sustain the belief in the contextual society that the law is a stable system[21]

From the diverse points of view of many kinds of legal systems, Islamic,
Judaic, Roman, civil, common, and so on, how does legal semiotics describe
and account for the following: fact finding; testimony; evidential procedure;
judicial lawmaking; interpretation according to system-specific rules for interpretation and free interpretative processes; discovery and the selection of admissible
fact; the transaction of value between the official legal actors and the general

public? These are but a few among possible topics for further global perspectives on legal semiotics.

NOTES

1. See Leon Green (1927), 132–134; see also Holmes 1881/1963), 200–203.
2. See Bruce Ackerman (1984), 6–22, 72–104. See also Twining (1973).
3. See Kevelson (1982a).
4. Kevelson (1987); see also Simmel (1907/1978). and Hayek (1960/1978), 174 ff.
5. See Laski (1969). Laski carries forward the influence of Dewey's pragmatic approach to legal controversy on philosophical hermeneutics in Europe, and especially the views of Gadamer (1983). Of special interest is Kantorowicz (1958). The classic on legal hermeneutics is Lieber (1839/1963).
6. See chapter 7 in this volume.
7. See also Kevelson 1985, 1985b,c,d,e.
8. See Summers (1982).
9. See Herbert (1981). See also Kevelson (1985b and 1985c).
10. See Berman on *Sachenspeigel* (1983), 503, 505, 526, 633; also his references to Stoic law and interpretation. 143, 146, 16, 275, 279, 287, 51.
11. See also Greimas and Landowski (1983).
12. See Dietze on special discussion of law and legal codes as mirrors of society (1964), 63–88.
13. See discussion on Peirce's distinction between resemblance and respresentation as "versimilitude" in Kevelson (1987).
14. See Kevelson (1983a).
15. See Fisch (1942).
16. See also Twining (1973), 380, 530.
17. See also Kevelson (1982d), 241–254 and Cairns (1941/1977), 339–351.
18. See Dewey (1916); also W. Friedmann (1959).
19. See Llewellyn (1962), especially on Holmes and pragmatism, *en passim*, 31–146.
20. See also Aarnio (1977); Hintikka (1976); and also Lindahl (1977).
21. See L. Friedman (1975).

PART II

The Open Hand

Only the existence of an argumentation that is neither compelling nor arbitrary can give meaning to human freedom, a state in which a reasonable choice can be exercised. . . . The theory of argumentation will help to develop what a logic of value judgments has tried in vain to provide, namely the justification of the possibility of a human community in the sphere of action when this justification cannot be based on a reality of objective truth.

Chaim Perelman (1969:514)

CHAPTER 6

The Art of Conversation

A point of view that still provokes considerable controversy is Toulmin's opinion that logic's most important reason for being, in terms of its significance as a human function in human affairs, is as a practical method of working out some of the knots of social relationships. Logical theory, in Toulmin's hierarchy of significant values, is clearly subordinate to logical practice (Toulmin, 1958:6). In his view:

> Logic is generalized jurisprudence. Arguments can be compared with law-suits, and the claims we make and argue for in extra-legal contexts with claims made in the courts, while the cases we present in making good each kind of claim can be compared with each other. (Toulmin, 1958:7)

Toulmin presents the case for a "working logic" which will enable us better to understand how we rationalize our verbal interactions with others. It is more essential to use arguments, Toulmin says, than to describe arguments as though they were objects in formal rather than functional ways. Toulmin finds that the legal argument is the prototype of rational discourse. It is the means by which habit, or customary behavior, becomes interpreted as law. Later in the chapter some of Horovitz's counterarguments in *Law and Logic* (1972) are discussed.

The term *discourse*, for all practical purposes, will be considered nearly synonymous in this chapter with *message, dialogue*, and *argument*. In a broad sense *discourse* may be either oral or written, but it must be characterized by certain features of cohesion and unity which enable us to distinguish between well-formed and ill-formed discourse. Criteria for well-formed discourse are far from comprehensively established, but, on the whole, it is commonly understood that a unified discourse is held together by a ruling theme, by a nonambiguous system of cross-reference, and by certain implications, or presuppositions, which permit deleted verbal phenomena to be recovered in so-called deep structure analysis.

Toulmin talks about the "layout of arguments" and contrasts "working" logic with "idealized" logic. Toulmin finds an almost one-to-one correspondence between the stages in which a judicial argument is laid out and the stages in which one rationally supports a nonlegal point of view, or nontechnical assertion, in ordinary discourse.

First of all, there is the stage common to both kinds of arguments in which evidence is given in support of a claim.

Secondly, the argument has to refute a real or imagined countersuggestion or objection to the argument thus far. The usual second stage *implies* the conditional—for example, "If what you say is so, then. . ."—but more commonly the argument expresses its qualifying claim with a relative rather than a disjunctive: "That being the case more or less, this is the more likely possibility. . . ." Peirce's contention that all propositions are basically hypothetical will be discussed in passing.

The final stage expresses the conclusion as a necessary conclusion, even when the conclusion is heuristic and results in two or more additional premises, as in Peirce's dialogism.

All rational arguments, Toulmin suggests, are justificatory. The traditional legal argument was held to be a justificatory argument. Whether one is interested primarily in the judicial or in the rational process of discourse in general, one observes certain basic patterns; that is, in order ultimately to justify a conclusion (to arrive at a judgment) one begins by presenting a problem: ". . .this can be done at best by asking a clear question, but very often by indicating only the nature of one's confused search for a question" (Toulmin 1958:17). When one cannot, from the start, formulate a coherent question, one must search for it. In his logic of inquiry Peirce refers to this having to search for a coherent question as the method of "abductive reasoning" in discovery procedures.

It is important to note that Toulmin's description of the stages of argument—extrajudicial as well as judicial—are contextual, between an addresser and a receiver who share in addition to a common language code certain conceptual and other cultural assumptions including rules for turn taking and conversational interaction.

Toulmin's thesis accords with Jakobson's communicative functions and factors. Argument, or discourse, is a social, pragmatic process. Toulmin, whose thought runs counter to the logical positivists' concepts of formal arguments, seeks to reintroduce a new appreciation of dialectics. His working argument is a dialogue that strategically evolves in the manner of Perelman's new rhetoric. Toulmin's three stages of discourse, considered to underlie all different types of discourse or argument, can be summarized: ". . .first, of setting out the candidate-solutions requiring consideration; then, of finding one particular solution unequivocally indicated by the evidence, ruling out some of the initial possibilities in the light of the evidence, and the rest—may be encountered equally whether our argument is concerned with a question of physics, or mathematics, ethics or law, or an everyday matter of fact" (Toulmin 1958:22).

Toulmin's perspective is insightful in the manner in which it enables one to see unmistakable parallels between the structures of legal discourse and ordinary purposeful, persuasive and/or justificatory dialogue. It is, however, a dangerous point of view because it tends to equate the formal logic of the positivists with descriptivism and nonformal working logic with prescriptivism. The distinctions are explained in Horovitz (1972) and are taken up elsewhere. The distinction has become traditional since formal logic historically began to be identified with logic proper and dialectic with rhetoric.

The predominantly prescriptive function of nonformal argument has been reinforced by interpreting legal behavior within the conceptual framework of legal action and/or reaction, where a legal act implies obligatory, responsible behavior. A logic of choice, in this framework, implies a logic of permission and obligation: a deontic logic.

In the sense that speech acts, from Austin (1965) through Grice (1968), Searle (1969), and their associate "speech act" philosophers connote *legal acts*, that is, social acts based on contractual obligations, the notion of pragmatics of dialogue has undergone strange transformations. According to these philosophers and their fellow linguist-pragmatists, analysis of discourse becomes a matter of distinguishing between truth and not-truth in discourse rather than a proceeding to realize new functional goals of communication that relate to common shared interests of society.

Horovitz, for one, notes that the term *logic* is so thoroughly ambiguous that some attempts to define its various meanings have resulted in contrasting legal and mathematical formal logics with legal and dialectical nonformal logics and with legal and dialectical nonformal logics. He says, "The basic ambiguity of 'argument' is to be found, naturally, in all fields of reasoning." Therefore it makes no sense to claim that "the semiotics of legal argument is essentially pragmatics, whereas the semiotics of mathematical argument is essentially syntax and semantics" (1972:129).

The confusion between formal and nonformal analysis of argument carries over in this century from philosophy to linguistics, from linguistics to semiotics. The prevailing view appears to equate transformational linguistic theory with formal logic and functional-structural linguistic theory with nonformal, even "antiformal" logic.

So, on the one hand, there is a notion of discourse presupposition, wherein discourse is conceived as a sequence of sentences, and 'P' and 'Q' are meta-variables ranging over sentences. . . (such that

1. P semantically presupposes Q if P's being either true or false necessitates that Q be true.

On the other hand, a *pragmatic* definition of presupposition, introduced and described by Stalnaker (1974:200–203), says that

2. "P pragmatically presupposes Q if whenever the utterance of P is conversationally acceptable, the speaker of P assumes Q and believes his audience to assume Q as well."

In his paper "On Pragmatic Presuppositions" Schwarz (1977:247, 257) points out that (1) and (2) are systematically distinct from one another and with few exceptions should not be considered with reference to the same theoretical framework.

In this chapter there is less concern with (1) than with (2). Our purposes are distinctly different from those of Schwarz, who is clearly within the camp of linguistic semantics and its concern with formally analyzable speech acts of the above-mentioned language philosophers.

It may even be more profitable here to review what the Stoics defined as structures of meaning, that is, the *lekta*. A *lekton* is "that which subsists in conformity with a rational presentation." *Lekta* are signs of meaningful structure. The Stoics maintained that a rational presentation is such that the topic or theme that is presented is presented as a focal part of a verbal transaction, that is, a discourse (Mates 1953:15). It suffices here to point out that a propositional kind of complete meaningful structure, or *lekton*, was also itself a sign that presumably referred to an antecedent sign. *Lekta* referred to structures that were not linguistic but were, iconically, diagrams of interactions. Such an antecedent structure is presumed to be a question–imperative type of *lekta*, grounded in materiality, that is, referring to a physical, material object, such as the actual dialogue *structure* it represents. Thus even reported dialogue refers, as a sign, to an actual, material, conversationl situation. This view reemerges in modern semiotic theory.

According to this interpretation, every statement or sentence of the indicative type will be considered a reply or a response, in relation to an antecedent utterance that functions for said reply or response as a question. Even if the question is given in the indicative mode it is nevertheless a question on the semiotic level. It functions as an index that points to and asks for a comment or answer.

To review: the Stoics' concepts of sign systems are built on the basis of minimal meaningful structures, *lekta*. There are, in this concept, complete and deficient *lekta* which are the other nonpropositional, complete meaningful structures. *Lekta* are not grammatical units but are meaningful units according to the Stoics' distinctive logic. A sentence was considered an incomplete and deficient meaningful structure. Clearly, in Stoic semiotic thought a sentence is not synonymous with a proposition, as it appears to be in some modern linguistic writings in which the implied synonymity often remains unchallenged.

Mates observes that deficient *lekta* are "those the enunciation of which is incomplete. . . ." Mates also discusses the two basic kinds of deficient *lekta*, for example, the Stoics knew two kinds of sign classes of deficient *lekta*, one of which corresponds with the part of speech called a *noun* and the other with the part called *verb*.

The parts of speech, according to the Stoics, were signs and therefore were physical objects in the sense that all signs have materiality. One must not confuse the term *physical object* with *sensible object* in terms of human abilities to perceive such objects sensibly. Rather, the Stoics conceived of the materiality and physicality of signs much as the physicist today conceives of the materiality of quarks and the material effects of charm. Peirce himself seems to have come to this appreciation of the Stoics' notion of physicality quite late in his own work, around 1902, in the context of his reinvestigations of cause and time (Kevelson 1983c, 1987).

A sign, according to the Stoics, was material precisely because it did its functional thing: it played an effectual role in relation with other signs.

What appears to be a remarkable similarity between Peirce's dynamic and final interpretant signs and the Stoics' semiotic—and dramatistic—subject–predicate sign function will be discussed elsewhere. Here we merely note that the function of the Stoic noun and verb is to indicate what kind of questions they answer and are completed by. According to Stoic logic, things–signs appear in language because they have been called for, or are missed, that is, are significantly absent as a zero sign.

Mates called attention to the Stoics' logical categories, of which there were four, in addition to one "highest notion." The "highest notion," Mates says, was an indefinable, "indefinite something" which, one may infer, played an important role in the Stoics' systematically vague categorical boundaries and thus contributed, in ways that are not discussed here, to the Stoic concept of shifting sign functions and dynamic sign processes.

These four categories were called subject or substratum, quality, state, and relation.

Again, the similarity between the Stoics' categories and Peirce's triadic sign divisions is particularly strong if one sees subject or substratum as the point of phenomenological perception which, as Peirce insisted, was propodeutic to an understanding of a logic of inquiry based on a theory of sign functions. For discussion, see Mates (1953:1–26) and also Pinborg (1975:79–120) and Sandbach (1975:18, 75, 92, 97). The Stoic structures of meaning will be discussed in passing in subsequent chapters.

The Stoics knew that the world was not complete. The task of human beings was not merely to arrange the parts already created, although that is undoubtedly a formidable task, but to participate in its creation. Because the world is not finite, however, creation can never be finally accomplished.

The Stoics conceived of a kind of Universal Egg somehow held together by a porous membrane which enabled new elements to enter into the world structure and interrelate with the existing parts. That the Egg was set in the context of its own void leads us to assume that the void was not merely nothing, but a significantly disorganized nothing—rather like the chaos that preceded the canonical genesis of the Old Testament.

Not only did the Stoics conceive of an open-ended or porous, world system, but this system was a motion-picture system as well. To carry the sign of the World Egg a bit further, it must have rocked in its waterbed kind of contextual void, which then tended to shake up and dislocate the internal order of its subsign systems. Correspondingly, internal agitation of the subsystems, as they attempted to reestablish themselves in relatively stable relationships with one another, undoubtedly contributed to faster, or slower, but ever to-and-fro motions of the Egg in its substantial, nourishing void. This is not altogether fanciful, in the light of what modern science understands about the relation between motion and emergent creative energies.

The Stoics believed that all of nature was a process of craft making, that is, doing art. Such a concept of nature as craftsman is based on a sense of dynamic interplay of forces that, together, are materialized in signs.

As Hahm (1977) shows, the Stoics considered nature the larger system of which chance and art were functional subsystems. In the sense that they considered the world always becoming more, that is, more in complexity and meaning rather than larger in space, the creative person was he who understood how to interpret the really new information that came quite by chance out of the void and into the universe: "In a sense chance and art are concerned with the same objects. . . .'Art loves chance and chance loves art'. . . .Art. . .is a kind of disposition which creates with correct reasoning."

In this study the art of conversation as a concept functions as a dialogic theme to relate American and Eastern European semiotics in ways not previously explored, but it also views certain aspects of Stoicism from a fresh angle with respect to law and values. The main emphasis lies in the importance the Stoics placed on the human usefulness of art and chance, that is, on the pragmatic aspect of the relationship.

Peirce also speaks of change in harmony with the goals of the creative person: "Peirce argues (i) that chance is an observationally verifiable element in the world, and (ii) that the recognition of chance does not abrogate the governance of events by law" (Gould 1970:221).

The unifying bond is that in an "art of conversation" interactions can go on and on from one point of agreement to others. The art of conversation, much like "conversational art" or talk for the sake of talk, functions as a symbolic sign. *We need not ever talk ourselves out anymore than the world can ever come to an end.* This attitude underscores the major beliefs and the basic epistemological ground of semiotics from the ancients into modernity and to its reemergence in the twentieth century.

The structure of art in semiotic theory and the structure of all predominantly aesthetic structures is imbalanced. Mukarovsky's (1970) schemata of cumulative information indicates that the relation between new and old information is asymmetrical. Also, in the Shapiro and Shapiro study (1976) of the relation between asymmetry and poetics we learn that not only are poetic structures asymmetrical but the structure of all creative inquiry is open-ended and off-balance:

> It is important to note that the question of ultimate cause or the "principle of universal causation" is practically banished from the realm of inquiry of the philosophers of science. Although a *Why Question* can be significantly asked at each stage of explanation of an explanatory hypothesis, there is no ultimate end. . . . (1976:4)

There can be no one final answer, but there can be alternative answers. Such is the form of the dialogism that Peirce recovered from the Stoics. The Stoics' unique "disjunctive proposition" thus forms the basis for transposing a predominantly aesthetic sign of dialogic interaction into a sign of logical relations, in a logic of pragmatics and significant human interaction.

It is important to note that the term *pragmatic presupposition in discourse* is different for the linguist and for the semiotician and that the structure of the data under consideration is presented for analysis in a different manner. It is not simply that semiotics investigates natural language systems differently and at a higher level as a communicative process than does linguistics, but the *methodological procedures* of each are structurally different.

Therefore, the terms that seem to be signs referring to the same linguistic phenomena for both semiotics and linguistics do not, in fact, point to the same referents but to quite different referent themes. In different contexts the terms presuppose different authorities. Words such as *pragmatic* and *semantic* and *discourse* have one (or more) kinds of functions within the framework of linguistics that are significantly different from their use in semiotic analysis of discourse structures. A thorough discussion of this problem cannot be undertaken here.

One of the problems that can be mentioned here is that while linguistic analysis can be described with reference to some models of analysis already established, such as standard Bloomfieldian structuralism, or standard Chomskean transformationalism, modern semiotics has not yet settled down to what might be one or more relatively stable modes of investigation. Its openness and pluralistic view of the need to synthesize in an interdisciplinary way "atomistic" kinds of arts and sciences has made it vulnerable to many kinds of criticism and, worse, it has permitted itself to be divested of concepts that appropriately belong in its domain. Such terms are *pragmatics, discourse, conversation, presupposition*, and so on, and generally those concepts that specifically have to do with conventional use of language in cultural interrelationships.

It is this problem that Maruyama stresses in his interesting paper on par-
adigmatology (the structure of scientific paradigms):

> The difficulty in cross-disciplinary, cross-professionaal and cross-cultural commu-
> nication lies not so much in the fact that the communicating parties use different
> vocabularies or languages to talk about the same thing, but rather in the fact that they
> use *different structures of reasoning.* (1974:136)

Coming from a different direction, Uhr's (1973:268–274) work in pattern
recognition explores the relation between natural and artificial conversational
models. Because natural systems are "ill-formed," anomaly and chance are naturally involved in patterns of exchange and value formation. In order to construct
useful machine models we must understand the process of shifting controls in
conversation. This shifting enables unpredictable new information to become
thematic and therefore to take a controlling position.

Uhr understands natural conversation to be of three kinds: (1) verbal interaction between two people; (2) verbal interaction between a person and his
environment, for example, a poem, a report, a question–answer game; (3) verbal
interaction between a person and himself. In all these kinds of conversations a
major problem arises that relates to the transfer of control. There are many kinds
of control in conversation. For example, distraction is subtle control. Delayed
response, or hesitation, is another subtle control. This problem of shifting control
implies that sometimes authority permits the conversation to evolve in certain
ways and sometimes the authority is controlled by other functions of the
conversation.

In relation to legal systems and to the legal fictions that constitute referent
signs of law in society is Cherry's notion of conversation as a "coded-cycle,
goal-seeking activity proceeding by a continual modification of the two comun-
icants' states of belief." Cherry says that we need not interpret a listener's "every
response to a sign (as) a 'verdict' arrived at rationally by conscious logical
methods after weighing the evidence he has heard. . . . Instead, we describe the
process *as though* it were of this nature" (1957:251).

One of the principle leading assumptions in semiotic thought, deriving
from Volosinov, Mukarovsky, and Bakhtin as well as from Peirce, is that dialogue is a method of establishing intersystemic communication, such as between
disciplines and between different cultural subsystems, that is, the legal system,
the economic system, and others (Kevelson 1986). For example, Mukarovsky
(1976) considers the persons participating in dialogic interaction as two (or more)
systems in communication, as does Peirce.

Following a brief review of Volosinov's concepts of dialogic function, in
contrast with current notions about speech acts, the historical and archetypal
functions of dialogue, and particularly the legalistic argument as the art of
conversation, will be referred to in passing.

At that point, Toulmin's point, namely, that all arguments have the same
basic structure as the legal argument and that they should be radically qualified

and described as a normative hypotactic style of legalistic argument, is critical. If a kind of argument resembles another, can we then speak of the isomorphic, iconic relation between kinds of argument? Does all argument, indeed, justify something? Or, on the other hand, did the art of conversation as the paradigmatic form of legal argument derive from an earlier, archaic mode of interaction that was not justificatory in purpose?

If this last question has some real basis in fact as, for example, Jane Harrison's study (1903/1959) of the chthonic foundations of Greek culture appears to suggest, the most deeply embedded structure of discourse and argument would resemble not so much the hypotactic but the paratactic style. Thus a prescriptive, *secular* legal style is such that it contrasts with a prescriptive, *sacred* legal style, where the latter carries forward the notion of sovereignty in common law.

For example, the style of practical argument that emerged in the twelfth century used the language of the Romans and the logical proposition of the Greeks in a multiply-embedded, subordinate-structured, hypotactic style of legal discourse. This was in sharp contrast to the laws of the Old Testament, given in a paratactic style that was, as Perelman points out, "more favored by the Hebrew culture" (1969:157–158).

Perelman also cites Auerbach, who in his *Mimesis* (1946) emphasizes the effective "strategic" construction of the hypotactic style of argument: Hypotaxis establishes "precise relations between the elements of discourse" whereas the opposite style, the paratactic style of argument, is "characterized by the absence of precise constructions" (1969:157).

The effect of the hypotactic upon the receiver is that of an unbroken continuum, it would seem, whereas the effect of the paratactic is to resemble a range of expression peaks separated by intervals, by significant absence. For example, the hypotactic sign of an argument resembles, by a stretch of the imagination, the nondiscreteness of perceived reality; through its resemblance to such continua as time, thought, feeling, space, value, and color, it would be a more likely vehicle for expressing propositions of a true–false nature than the paratactic sign, which has a striking likeness in its structure to unverifiable truth or falseness in attitudes expressed through conversational interaction. Thus the paratactic structure seems suited for expressions of belief and subjective emotion— aesthetic expressions, as in dramatic dialogue—and the hypotactic structure more suited to judging the yes or no of a case.

This line of reasoning is highly speculative and will be explored further elsewhere. Perelman calls attention to the "mysterious, magical character" of the paratactic construction, in contrast to the prescriptive structure of hypotaxis:

> The hypotactic construction is the argumentative construction *par excellence*. Auerbach considers it to be characteristic of Greco-Roman literature in contradistinction to the paratactic construction favored in Hebrew culture. Hypotaxis creates frameworks, constitutes the adoption of a position. It controls the reader, forces him to see particular relationships, restricts the interpretations he may consider, and takes

its inspiration from well-constructed legal reasoning. Parataxis leaves greater freedom, and does not appear to wish to impose a particular viewpoint. (Perelman 1969:158)

Perelman's understanding of the "new rhetoric" will be referred to again, from the point of view of the rhetorical force of imperatives and questions in legal discourse and other legal proceedings.

Certain discourse structures, or stylistic configurations, have come to stand for certain modes of reasoning in the world and certain conventional and culturally significant modes of justifying perspectives on given themes. Hypotaxis has come to symbolize manipulative verbal behavior; at the same time it is considered the characteristic structure of literary narrative. Can one infer, then, that the narrative discourse is a kind of justificatory argument? Barthes in *S/Z* certainly argues that the influence the "classic text" has on its reader is manipulative, coercive, and legalistic. Volosinov (1973: 120–123) came to similar conclusions and refers to narrative as a kind of waning authority in western Civilization.

By contrast, the paratactic structure has come to be associated with atten-uated play, with ineffectual "academic" questions and answers, with senility and certain kinds of aphasia. The paratactic style of dialogue will be discussed elsewhere in connection with the conative function in communication. Finally, hypotaxis represents the structure of ultimate authority; parataxis represents inter-subjectivity and growth.

Certain syntactic structures act as structures of commonly held pragmatic signs of meaning. This is evident in the active–passive distinction in headlines (Kevelson 1977); Kuno in a similar fashion describes this phenomena in terms of empathy in discourse.

In hypotaxis the "head" is clearly identifiable; the subordinate relation of clause to head is similarly clearly identifiable. However, there is no such fixed authoritative head in paratactic discourse. In fact, as Mukarovsky (1976) describes in depth, dialogic authority shifts from speaker to speaker, and the meaning of the discourse grows with each semantic shift, or "semantic reversal." There is a continuous theme, quite different in concept from a head noun phrase (NP).

A speech community shares, with all its other conventions, this conven-tional distinction between two fundamental different kinds of discourse style. It is a universal feature of languages that all cultures have a way of distinguishing between sacred and profane, between language-specific equivalents of hypotaxis and parataxis. It is not only that there are shared presuppositions but that the speaker always has a choice from among possible shared presuppositions. Fill-more suggests this also in "Subjects, Speakers, and Roles" (1972:21).

Fillmore says it is not enough to talk about presuppositions as shared assumptions between addressers and receivers. It is also crucial that we identify, from the point of view of pragmatics, which of the two participants in a speech is even doing the presupposing to begin with and which of the two, in conse-quence of the speech act of the other, must interpret the other's choice of

presupposition. Dialogic interaction requires also, in addition to reciprocal interpretation by each of the participants of the other's response, the ability of each
to interpret and evaluate the underlying why's, the ellipses "between the lines."
    One of the most powerful and thoroughly encompassing statements on the
metaphysical functions of dialogue is from Bakhtin, in his remarkable study of
Dostoevsky's poetics:

> For all dialogical relationships constitute a much more far-reaching phenomenon than
> merely the relationships between speeches in a literary composition; they are an almost
> universal phenomenon which permeates all of human speech and all relationships and
> manifestations of human life and, in general, everything that has meaning and sig-
> nificance. (1973:34)

Bakhtin sees a microdialog, which is the inner dialogue judging the external, or interpersonal dialogue which takes place with a "wholly other" in the
consequential world. This interiorized dialogic monologue is the drama between
one's *ad hoc* state of identity and the conflict of other possible identities or
selves. It is the state of one's self to which one refers as to an authority; but as
authority, it is no more stable than myth.
    The central emergent point here is that an underlying, paratactic dialogic
structure corresponds with

1. The Stoic ideal of the natural rights of man. Following the Stoics, the
   Epicureans especially emphasize the intersubjective and paratactic
   structure essential to justice by calling attention to agreement between
   men as the basis of social rights and values.
2. The symbolic and predominantly aesthetic sign of dialogic interaction
   that is assumed to characterize self-governing societies and is a foremost
   value within the anarchistic tradition of mutual aid.

The ultimate art of conversation becomes the interiorized judgment to
oneself. Volosinov finds that dialogue is implicit in all authorial texts, that is,
in all reported speech (1973:155–123).
    Until the enormous renascence of semiotic activity in the 1970s it had
become accepted practice and even commonplace to use the terms *discourse,
interpersonal communication, conversation, discussion, verbal interaction, dialogue,* and even *speech act,* as if they were nearly synonymous and metonym-
ically interchangeable. In some contexts they are; in others, they have metaphoric
function.
    Argument appeared to refer in some manner to a more formalistic frame
of thinking and so was diametrically opposed to the terms in the above list that,
together or as a class, signified "loose talk."
    An *argument* even in a nontechnical sense, in ordinary use, connoted the
development of a serious idea. Even at the time of Toulmin's *The Uses of*

Argument, argument could somehow, however dangerously, be equated with *discourse* but was conceptual worlds away from *dialogue*, and certainly it "outclassed" *conversation* as an art or otherwise.

Generally, among semioticians, *dialogue* is considered the basic kind of verbal semiotic process. In following Mukarovsky's distinctions, *conversation* is here regarded as a basic kind of dialogue.

Mukarovsky (1976:394) speaks of the three most important kinds of dialogue, namely, the *personal*, the *situational*, and the *conversational*. Conversational dialogue includes a "talk for the sake of talk" in which the aesthetic function predominates; this kind of conversation therefore not only is improvisional but also appears to resemble dialogic art in drama.

Mukarovsky does assume that conversational dialogue is largely "disengaged from a direct relation to immediate reality, though not completely detached from it" (1976:397). But he does not want to include practical argument, that is, legal discourse, among the kinds of conversation in which he presumes the aesthetic function to be dominant.

And yet, the art of conversation on which we focus here is a kind of euphemism for the dialectic process that has traditionally been associated with legal reasoning: The art of conversation as such came into being in the first and second centuries, B.C.; its roots are presumed to reach back to chthonic, mimetic performances of the sacred rites of judgment in pre-Olympian Greece. Rites of judgment is a term that refers to the dialogic exchange between performers, mostly women, in rites often enacted during the days "left over" between the end and the new beginning of a solar year. The official emissary from the mainstream government was sent to look upon these rites; this emissary was the *theoros*. By looking on, he violated a sacred taboo. To exonerate himself he was forced to take part in the rites of judgment, and thus he became part of the cultural subsystem of taboo (Harrison 1959:624 ff.).

Further analysis of the art of conversation will lead, presumably, to a more or less principled account of what Eco refers to as the "dialectic between codes and messages" (1976). This dialectic, he says, is the process ". . . whereby the codes control the emission of messages, but new messages can restructure the codes. . . ." The art of conversation, in this sense, provides semiotic justification for the "basic creativity of language . . . (with) . . . its double aspect of 'rule-governed creativity' and 'rule-changing creativity'" (1976:161).

To recapitulate: Peirce regards dialogue as a primitive, signifying a fundamental struggle between existents. To Peirce the very process of inner dialogue—of thought—is dialogic (CP 6.338).

Current studies, however, on cognition and language learning are often in disagreement with Peirce's description of the semiotic process of thought in inner dialogue. But Volosinov (as does semiotic theory on the whole) reinforces the symbolic or metaphoric notion of interiorized dialogue as a psychological reality.

Volosinov says "Everything vital in the evaluative reception of another's utterance . . . is expressed in the material of inner speech" (1973:118). Volosinov shows the breakdown of authoritarian dogmatism "characterized by the linear, impersonal, monumental style of reported speech transmission in the Middle Ages . . ." to its present-day *"relativistic individualism"* (1973:123).

Concern here is with continuing influence on certain aspects of Stoic thought in relation to dialogic structures that are not within the framework of modern semiotics. Of special note is that the art of conversation translates the Stoic principles of the natural rights of man and of freedom in community into the social interaction of dialogue as event.

Throughout the Middle Ages and into the Renaissance concepts such as authority, faith, reason, and revelation were split into common meanings on one hand and into marked, system-specific meanings on the other. For example, MacDonald (1933:4–5) discusses the fact that emphasis continued to shift from common to private meanings until the late Middle Ages.

By the time of Duns Scotus (d. 1308) MacDonald says, dialectic reasoning had come to be equated with the art of conversation and was generally regarded as "mother of the art." By contrast, the patristic authority of the scriptures had come to be accepted on faith, as an act of revelation: as the speech act of a divine lawgiver.

To digress briefly, Romeo in "Heraclitus and the Foundations of Semiotics" notes that the tradition of revelation as "giving a sign" predates the Stoics and originates with the pre-Socratic philosophers, namely Heraclitus, from whose fragments he cites evidence for his insightful information on sign giving as a hallmark of divine revelation (1976:73–90).

The concept of the divine lawgiver, or speech actor, historically develops to a reversed, or inverse, concept of the lawgiver as the listener. It is indeed the attention of the listener that authorizes or permits the speaker to speak. This distinction is especially important when we examine in subsequent chapters the bases of contract in early law.

In one sense dialogic relations are presupposed by the listener's attitude toward the speaker, as a compliant receptivity of the listener to Bakhtin's "ideal of the other person"; that is, Ivanov discusses Bakhtin's notion of the speaker as text, the very structure of which is "evident manifestation of the archaic level of consciousness (1974:850–854).

Again, of Duns Scotus MacDonald says that he used the term *authority* in its loftiest, rather than in its alternative, everyday sense. "He appears to derive authority from its original significance as authorship. . . . Reason is contrasted with *written* authority, with the writings of scripture or of the Fathers, not with the authority of revelation" (1933:45, 47).

In other words, reason, in its highest sense, became identified with written authority, that is, legal speech acts—*legal acts* as recorded in the then referent legal text of Justinian's books of law. The preceding section of this chapter should clarify the concluding section, which deals with the relation between the art of conversation and law:

With the systematization of the legal institution in the twelfth century a dialogue began between *sacred* and *profane*. A new model was introduced that resembled mimetic rites of justice in ancient ceremony which themselves retained something of the magic, the mysterious, the taboo. The legal system of the twelfth century reinstated the art of conversation in an open, practical, legitimized context of secular, matter-of-fact law schools. This new model of the art of conversation (*techne dialecktike*) began as a question-and-answer procedure. But as the questions, or problem themes, became familiar enough to the conversational community they could be deleted and safely presupposed.

Eventually, from a speculative reconstruction of the legal discourse model, one surmises that the questions were implied by the solutions to the posed legal problems; and the solutions ultimately assumed the structure of multiple subordinate, hypotactically styled texts. In the same general historical period that the legal discourse style was becoming crystallized, the religious responsive prayer was becoming codified in Judeo-Christian religious services. Parataxis once more became linked with mystery and hypotaxis with rational argument.

From the perspective of historical change, one can point to an enormous change that the art of conversation, as a method, brought about. The art of conversation as method underlies the emergence of the first legal system in the Western world. Under the umbrella sign of dialogue, the Stoic creeds of fellowship, of freedom and responsibility in self-government, of art as a methodological process in which chance plays a leading role, entered into the practical sphere of human affairs. The realization of a legal system placed dialectics on its material grounds. Thereafter, ideology referred to an ultimately perceivable substance.

Judicial rhetoric and political rhetoric have the peculiar ability to signify, by their boundary-line divisions between the definitions of terms, the property rights of the things to which juridical discourse peculiarly refers (Volosinov 1973:122). Not only semantically, but also stylistically, a discourse begins to resemble in an isomorphic way the significant value of "things," considered as interpretant signs in Peirce's sense. Investigators do not yet understand the process of cognition and memory that permits one to make these kinds of isomorphic translations and semiotic association. But it is clearly not to be found in the analysis of static, semantic categories.

For example, the Stoics speak of a doctrine of "total blending" (*krasis di holon*):

> According to this two substances might occupy the same space, although each is continuous and contains no void. These substances retained their identities and their qualities, so that "blending" was distinguished from "fusion" in which the original qualities are lost. (Sandbach 1975:75)

At bottom this doctrine is the belief in the absolute difference between an I and a Thou, even while they interrelate in the unifying event of authentic dialogue. It presupposes the belief in the existentialist's Wholly Other. It is Peirce's basic relational unit.

In the Stoics' sense of total blending the process of change is dynamic, like all natural processes of crafting new material value. In this sense dialogue not only is verbal composition but is also a transformation of the whole through the shifting relation of its parts. When we describe separate dialogic functions, we talk about them as if they were separable in fact. In fact they are not. This point will be discussed further.

As for the emergent legal system in the twelfth century, Berman notes (1983) that although there always existed legal orders in human societies, and legitimate authorities that applied the Law, there was no legal *system* prior to the twelfth century. No earlier judicial structure had a set of rules, definitions, and procedures, together with a referent canonical text, that was entirely distinct from other coexistent social systems. Without the legal fiction of an apparently stable text there was no frame of reference for systemic identity. Without identity as such, it is suggested, an organization has no systemic status and therefore no semiotic validity; that is, it can not be a functional social sign capable of trans-acting business—in the exchange of value—with other social systems.

When in the twelfth century the legal system emerged full grown, it was recognized as an entity *as if* it were a distinct, identifiable "thing." With the discovery and adoption of the Justinian books of Roman law the legal system became an official and authoritarian institution, that is, a potential conversational theme (Berman 1977:895 ff.).

Berman notes further that the method of teaching law, like the Justinian texts of law, was not invented in the twelfth century but was rediscovered. Thus the art of conversation was brought forward with new value from the second and third centuries as a method of inquiry that had already become associated with the settlement of legal matters.

As mentioned above, the art of conversation was first mentioned in con-nection with legal disputes in the first- and second-century legal institutions of Rome (Berman 1977:910–912). By the second century legal questions, of the type of the Stoics' *lekton*, were first posed as "definitions" of previous legal cases. The legal definition, or legal judgment, was then as now nearly synon-ymous with the legal sentence passed by an officially designated judge. The relation between monologic and dialogic systems, engaged, as it were, in "legal conversation," is noted by Volosinov: "Judicial language intrinsically assumes a clear-cut discrepancy between the verbal subjectivism of the parties to a case and the objectivity of the court—between a ruling from the bench and the entire apparatus of judicial-interpretive and investigative commentary" (Volosinov 1973:123).

Peirce also insists that all semiotic processes involving meaning exchange has to do with the process of *giving* considered as a triadic relation: "Giving is a transfer of the right of property. Now right is a matter of law, and law is a matter of thought and meaning" (CP. 1.475). This idea radically alters an assumed axiomatic legal structure.

In this context Berman says that the sentence referred to the legal definition; at a later period the legal definition was used to signify an assumption that could act as a signified given. Still later, the given lost its association with the conditional aspects of the "if . . . then" conditional logical forms and became identified with *given* in the sense of "material implication," a causal rather than predominantly conditional structure and one that conformed more closely with authoritarian ideology than with dialogic, libertarian views. Eventually the legal definition came to signify only a legitimate statement to which questions would defer, as though previous decisions or statements were true answers. These general ideas are taken up in greater detail in later chapters of this volume.

The notion of reference in the twelfth-century art of conversation appeared to anticipate an impulse toward authoritarianism, Berman's work suggests, because by the end of that century the systematically arranged rules (*regulae*) in the Justinian text had already become opposed to definitions. Berman tells us that formal questions regarding possible legal interpretation began to be governed by the method of recalling constraints from the past. Authority was felt to come forward, one might add, as a *legal act*.

Note that a legal reaction may be either obedience or disobedience of the law as pronounced by the referent legal action.

The underlying logic, as the Stoics knew, and as Peirce explored in the the disjunctive syllogism that he calls a dialogism (CP 3.172, 613, 623), implies the belief in the freedom to choose to keep or to break the law. This stress on the highest value, freedom, is discussed in Parts I and IV of this volume. With reference directly to the Stoics' disjunctive logic Peirce says:

> . . . an individual is something which reacts . . . this is the stoic definition of a reality
> . . . that which alone immediately presents itself as an individual is a reaction against
> the will. But everything whose identity consists in a continuity of reactions will be
> a single logical individual. (CP 3.613)

Berman notes that the Stoics introduced into dialectic reasoning important distinctions from Platonic and Aristotelian concepts of dialectics. For example, the Stoics denied that meaning inhered in forms but insisted that meaningful signs have multiple function and that values emerge as a part of the process of *doing meaning. The Stoic art of conversation was a doing of meaning in relation with other doers, that is, "meaners," rather than a making of meaning out of some stated "things."*

Very briefly, some of the emergent features of the legal system of the twelfth through the fourteenth centuries will be mentioned: First of all, it reinterpreted Justinian's sixth-century text which was, in effect, a retranslation. The text consisted of the Codex, the Novels, the Institutes, and the Digest (Berman 1977:904). The general method of studying the law was by "glossing" the text and by raising a conventional set of questions that referred to the textual categories in known and conventional ways. In a conventional, semiotic process questions raised "problems" for disputation. In other words, it was then generally known what was not known, what the legal code encompassed. The art of conversation was firmly based on common assumptions and emerged as part of a closed system. But the art of conversation established the legal system upon a partnership structure: a *societas* as it was called in Roman Law (ibid.:900). Around the twelfth century the students organized the law corporations (*univ-ersitas*) and the professors formed the college of teachers (*collegium doctorum*).

For example, Gadamer says that there can be no conversation between people unless they are bound by shared presupposition, that is, common assumptions. These assumptions have little to do with the truth or falsity of their beliefs (1976:330 ff.).

Bentham and others postulate that the entire judicial process rests on a foundation of legal fictions.

Friedrich more recently observes that behind every legal rule—every law—lies a dialectic argument (1958/1973:5 ff.). Every rule can be freely doubted or believed—in Peirce's sense "questioned" or "asserted"—or changed.

The idea that we are free to choose either to doubt or to believe is part of modern semiotics' inheritance from the Stoics. In large measure this same legacy of freedom of choice reveals the art of conversation behind the Kantian under-standing of lawful action as ". . . the hypothesis of freedom . . . necessary for an acting person," according to Friedrich.

Thus the basic hermeneutic art is conversation, considered as the art of realizing interpersonal goals as if they were authorized or commanded. "Dialectic as the art of conducting a conversation is also the art of seeing things in the unity of an aspect . . . the art of the formation of concepts is the working out of the common meaning" (Gadamer 1976:331).

It is worth noting that the Stoics conceived of art as a natural process. Art and nature were not dissociated terms but were equivalent signs of the same crafting process. For example, Zeno and Chrysippus spoke of crafting as a "collection of apprehended preceptions exercised together to form some goal useful of life" (Hahm 1977:203, 204 ff.).

Berman explains (1983) the reinterpretation of the Stoic art of conversation within the context of the newly formed communities of law as a synthesis of the older dialectic arts of discovery and the arts of forming judgments. Law communities were recognized in their capacity to act as prototypes for self-governing societies, thus resembling what has come to be defined as the anar-chistic tradition.

Kropotkin, for example, once maintained that the ongoing dialogue between anarchists and statists has existed from the beginning of human culture. This dialogic opposition between libertarian and authoritarian social systems appears to parallel Bakhtin's notion of opposition between static and dynamic forces in society and also to resemble Mukarovsky's theory of the monologic/dialogic opposition in the interaction he called "semantic reversals."

Within recent years a number of disciplines have approached conversation as a subject of investigation. For example, Goffman has referred to conversation as a framed social activity. He calls attention to the way in which people's responses in conversation tend to "carve out" of the foregoing dialogue remarks that can serve as internal referential guides to define mutual meaning in further conversation. This "referential tract" of which Goffman speaks (1976:309) acts as a regulatory device and at the same time as malleable thematic material.

To summarize some main points of this chapter: In interpersonal dialogue the interaction between speakers is actually an exchange between social systems. As a complex unified organization, each speaker is a virtual system. In conversation the values of verbal message-signs appear to shift between systems and also to shift dimensionally as the cumulative meaning of repeated referent signs becomes more voluminous, that is, denser.

Briefly, it is helpful to review Mukarovsky's three basic kinds of dialogue: the personal, the situational, and the conversational.

No dialogue is purely of one type only, just as no sign in semiotic theory, has only one function. Dialogue is always a mixture of all three types. Sometimes one aspect predominates and the others function as background. One might say that the more complex the dialogue, the more interrelated are the three kinds of dialogue. The ways in which they interrelate have to do with the dynamics of the process, or with the metamorphosis of values and information in the total mixture.

But one can say, with Mukarovsky, that when the dialogic aspect in focus is of the personal kind the dialogue can be characterized as a token "dispute." And when the focus is on the situational aspect the dialogue is predominately indexical with reference to the extralinguistic environment shared by the dialogic participants. Thus the third, the conversational aspect of dialogue, is predominantly aesthetic in the sense that it is not instrumental toward immediate practical ends but is more or less self-referential, a kind of verbal interplay. In this interplay references that function as authoritative themes are created and processed by the players.

Themes may be only *ad hoc* points of reference or terms temporarily defined. In this kind of conversation speakers freely create rules for talk as they go along and switch, with mutual assent, to other kinds of rules in midstream. They play against a presupposed shared norm of conversation, with its conventional rules for turn taking, for introducing new topics, for playing dumb, for mending conversational ruptures, and so on (Sacks, Schegloff, and Jefferson, 1974, 1977; Goffman 1976; Moerman 1973; Labov and Fanshel 1977).

Shared experience, such as other social subsystems, can be introduced into conversation as themes. But to the extent that themes are grounded in organized systems they control the creative possibilities of the conversation. Politics, economics, law, for example, may function in aesthetically marked conversation as referent themes, but they control by introducing or imposing their own system-specific rules and definitions. In this sense such a systemic theme on conversation is like superimposing one language game on another. Further, the more stable the referent system appears to be to the conversationalists, the more the theme will interact as a monologic system with a dialogic exchange of messages. To a large extent all institutionalized systems are contextual statements. To mention them is, in a real sense, equivalent to using the mention as an index of the system's assertorial function. *Every institution appears as a statement.*

The relation of dialogic to monologic systems is far from understood. Mukarovsky speaks of monologue as a kind of inner dialogue. He distinguishes this use of monologue from theatrical monologue: "In theatrical usage this term means, in fact, a dialogue with an absent or imaginary partner, but for linguistics monologue means an utterance with a single active participant regardless of the presence or absence of other passive participants" (1977:425). Presumably the distinction would apply to semiotics as well.

Veltrusky, for example, finds one of the basic distinctions between dialogue and monologue to be found in the absence of the spatial continuum in monologue; that is, dialogue happens through time and space but monologue requires only a temporal medium. We have to realize that terms such as *spatial continuum* and *temporal continuum* refer to a dramatic visualization of spatio-temporality. We cannot speak of functions in a dynamic process and also of the static intersection of two planes unless we deliberately intend to mix systems of reference in order to speak from the Burkean "perspective on incongruity" (Veltrusky, in Matejka and Titunik 1976:128–144).

Another member of the Prague school, Serge Karcevskij, sees a resemblance between monologue and declarative kinds of utterances. He appears to equate a sentence with a theoretical declaration, in which the declaration is a coherent unit of discourse more complex than the grammatical unit of the sentence is generally considered to be. Karcevskij's "sentence" resembles Volosinov's lineal, authorial text (1973:15 ff.). To Karcevskij, monologic style in intrapersonal conversation is "internal speech in the form of a dialogue" (cited by Mukarovsky 1976:441–442).

One can speculate on how strongly Karcevskij's views on the asymmetric, dynamic structure of conversation was influenced by the Stoics' concept of the total mixture and particularly by their sign for structurally complete units of meaning, the *lekta*. To repeat, the two Stoic complete signs were the proposition and the question and/or imperative. In legal argument one first finds the question as complete meaningful unit in the legal definition. Karcevskij is very careful to distinguish between grammatical sentences and sentences that are nearly synonymous with monologically derived opinions or judgment: ". . . we converse with ourselves, we ask our 'interlocutor' questions, and we answer him. . . . The structure of the sentence is the synthesis of a question and an answer. The division of the sentences . . . has nothing to do with the distinction between a subject and a predicate, nor with any other grammatical opposition in general." What Karcevskij calls a monologue is really what Bakhtin describes as an internal dialogue. To Bakhtin understanding appears to be a kind of mirror reflection of conversation. He says that "to understand someone else's utterance means to orient oneself with respect to it. . . . It is as though we layer on each word of the understood utterance a series of our own responding words . . . Every understanding is dialogic" (cited by Ivanov, in Baran 1976:321).

Here, too, we see the Stoic influence in the notion of the emergent sense transforming the total mixture of the dialogue situation, making it denser without requiring that it take up more space. In calling attention to the dialogic structure of all semiotic systems Bakhtin says that words change their value each time they are repeated in conversation. Mukarovsky and Jakobson speak of the continual opposition between static and dynamic meanings in communication (cf. Jakobson 1960 and Sebeok 1974).

Finally, anaphoric reference is always reference to a kind of contextual authority, and authority which is intra- as well as extra-linguistic. Repeated mention points *cataphorically* to an emergent but not yet codified sign of some former relatively static meaning. The new meaning is a comment on the old; it judges it and thus revalues the sign as an interpretant sign, in Peirce's sense. The revalued meaning, Bakhtin suggests, is then acted on by the speakers who use it, who make it a part of themselves, and so in a very direct and personal way become the shapers of their social context.

In other words, through the art of our conversation we change the world. The art of conversation in exemplifying the value, or aesthetics of legal discourse, presumes that law is an instrument for the realization of new value in society.

The following chapter will relate a moving, dynamic approach to decision making in law with the predominantly iconic structure of question and answer, which also indicates as sign the dialogic structure of legal exchange and also the symbolic use of the interrogative, modal structure of the possible in legal judgments in general.

Riddles, Legal Decisions, and Peirce's "Existential Graphs"

As the title suggests, Peirce's existential graphs, legal decisions, and riddles are members of a relationship that has not been examined from the perspective of semiotics. It is a relationship that, at first glance, seems to resemble Lewis Carroll's conjunct, "cabbages and kings." And, like the walrus, this chapter discusses paradox, nonsense, and incongruity in a significant way as they relate to legal semiotics.

By juxtaposing two or more conventionally established and well-known frames of reference, the riddle presents the possibility of new relationships: the solution, which is a sign of evaluative, interpretive judgment, is initially perceived with surprise, the same quality of surprise that attends the perception of the grotesque in aesthetics. The function of the grotesque, as we know, is to convey new value. Although the riddles' propositions are given as if they were truth statements, the underlying logic of the riddle has the same structure as Peirce's modalities of possibility.

The problem of the legal decision is central in discussions of philosophy of law and of jurisprudence today. Consider, for example, the previously noted issues that Frank has raised: (1) Do judges make or discover law? (2) Are judicial decisions law or merely applications of law? (3) Do laws exist antecedent to judicial decisions? (Frank 1963:159–160). From the viewpoint of a semiotics of law, none of the implied alternatives is the best possible solution.

Rather, by emphasizing the multifunctionality of legal signs—the shifting roles of icon, index, and symbol in context—legal semiotics finds: First, that judges' interpretations of encoded legal signs, through a discovery process, create new signs of judgment that when encoded act as new law. Second, that judicial decisions are neither absolute judgments nor applications of eternal laws but rather are provisional, open-ended judgment signs that are (a) symbolic with reference to the context of the particular case, (b) iconic as assumptions, or topical references for some future case in some other context, (c) indexical when the decision is made to appear similar to or analogical with the established encoded rule and thus is said to be predicated upon it. Third, that in terms of nonrelative logic an analogical decision would be a specification, or token, of the general law, or type. In Peirce's relative or "metamorphizing" logic, however, the decision as interpretant sign would be in effect a new idea and new sign of emergent value judgment.

Thus the broad context is Peirce's methodology, synonymous with what he calls "speculative rhetoric." The purpose of methodology, or speculative rhetoric, we recall, is to account for the process of sign interpretation that results in signs that represent new value judgments. The grotesque element is *marked* in riddles but concealed and *marked by its absence* in legal decisions through the rhetorical strategy of what is generally known as legal fiction, or legalism. In Peirce's methodology such strategy is theoretically presented; in the graphs, namely, the modal graphs, the theories of paradoxical reasoning and innovative decision making are visually demonstrated. The limitations of this chapter prevent reproducing graphic examples here, but reference to appropriate sections in Peirce's own descriptions of the existential graphs will be offered.

Between the element of surprise, that is, the perception of incongruous, unsuspected relationships as in the riddle, and the element of doubt, that is, juridical doubt with respect to the applicability of encoded laws and new habits of thought, or law-like judgments, lies methodological inquiry: the process of discovery which is the process of dynamically interpreting known signs into new meaningful signs.

The focus in this chapter is on the manner in which the existential graphs illustrate aspects of Peirce's methodology, especially aspects of possibility, that is, the existence of an illusion as a reality (Peirce 1869: ms 206), and how signs of possibility contribute to the growth of information, the evolving of an initial thought sign, and the underlying interrogative modality that characterizes methodology. Here the riddle and the legal decision are regarded as two other kinds, or tokens (in Peirce's sense), of the type of interrogative structure that underlies his semiotic methodology. With respect to different kinds of literature the riddle is prototypical; with respect to ethical, cooperative, enforceable social interaction the legal decision is a prototype of provisional, questionable, appealable legal acts. Peirce's methodology has received less attention than the other two parts of his "exact logic," although critic and speculative grammar—the other two parts—are subordinate to it. As early as 1892 Peirce discusses these three divisions of his exact logic, within the context of his explanations of the diagrammatical aspects of logic (CP 3.429).[1]

Peirce says that in its widest sense exact logic consists of (1) speculative grammar, following Duns Scotus; (2) critic, which purports to "consider to what conditions an assertion must conform in order that it may correspond to our 'reality'" or, in other words, what we assert, as relatively stable beliefs, concerning the relation of facts in the actual world; and (3) "methodology," which is that part of the general doctrine of logic that "must embrace the study of those general conditions under which a problem presents itself for solution and those under which one question leads onto another. . . . we might term this last study speculative rhetoric" (CP 3.430).

In 1869 Peirce wrote that the real riddle in philosophy was not, as Kant believed, how *a priori* synthetical judgments are possible, but, rather, how "synthetical reasoning is possible at all." The answer to this problem, he says, "is the lock upon the door of philosophy" (1869:ms 206). It is absolutely a matter of life and death, Peirce says, that the initial assumptions one brings to the process of reasoning are syntheses of values shared between an individual and a community. All logical methodology has its origins in the identification of self-interest with the interests of one's community. So we find in our analyses of riddles that their answers are definitions presupposed and shared by a community of some commonly known object or fact; similarly, the legal decision is valid insofar as it refers to an institutionalized, accepted code of either statutory or unwritten law.

Peirce suggests that many universes of thought—ideational continua—coexist in one's mind. While deliberate attention may be focused on one unity of thought, other thought relationships are gestating, as it were, below the surface of conscious attention. By chance, it may happen that a submerged thought is perceived by the observer who is in the process of attending to the development of another idea; he perceives the previously unnoticed thought as if it were fresh, as a quality, stripped in this immediate context of former connotation. This perception of a quality, which phenomenologically develops to a fact and then to a representation or sign, can be seen in relationship with that which one has been at present investigating. Thus two or more continua the relationship between (or among) had not been seen before are now understood in their interaction, as an index. One cay say, therefore, that although Peirce did not conceive of the existential graphs as such in the 1860s, in retrospect his writings of 1868 prefigure his later thought. In other words, the ideas he presented and examined in the 1868–1869 work were later seen in relationship to the work he was concerned with that dealt with topography, spatial relations, and new information (or rhema), and illusion, that is, signs for that *not* present, in diagrammatic thinking.

For it is as early as 1868 that we find Peirce distinguishing between the essence of a thought, as its "first intention," and the accident of a thought, as "second intentions." Years later, when Peirce compares the existential graphs to a moving picture of thought, he says that he does not mean by thought "merely the operations of human thinking to which psychological and other accidents attach. I mean a moving picture of the essence of thought" (ms 298, draft 2.11). In 1868 he is already stressing the fact that a conceptual essence is primarily an indicative sign and that it is the subject index of a thought the predicate of which is primarily diagrammatic, or iconic.

For example, in the question *Who is that man?* the interrogative index sign, the pronominal *Who*, refers anaphorically to the actual but deleted subject of the proposition: an antecedent *Someone.* The answer will necessarily identify or predicate that *Someone* is a member of the class of persons. This function of identification has to do with establishing equivalences and provisional class memberships. Elsewhere is discussed the concept of legal definition, in relation to shifting class membership and class categories that refer to contextual universes of discourse. Briefly, the problem of definition and classification is more crucial on the level of pragmatics than on the level of semantics; but the relation between classes and individuals has largely been considered from the semanticists' point of view. Yet, in legal semiotics, we clearly see that such traditional class distinctions between animate and nonanimate or human and nonhuman are rarely respected within the systems that regulate or legitimize the actual relations between people in society. For example, except in societies that observe the primitive *lex talionis,* currency, livestock, and labor may be considered equivalences for some "inalienable personal possession" such as the loss of an eye, a limb, or a life. Thus the definition of a right arm might be A right arm is ten Hereford steers, or the loss of an eye might be defined as *An eye is $500,000.* These are legal equivalences and represent *as signs* the nonformal, or relative, logical equivalences that actually underlie community values. The relationship of money to an eye is clearly not metaphorical, nor is it analogical; but it may be hypothesized that the good derived from $500,000 will be equivalent to the good or value derived from the use of an eye. We will return later to the distinction between analogy and hypothesis in Peirce's sense.

Thus, in our example, the someone referred to by the question *Who is that man?* is usually expected to be a member of the class of persons. If the answer to the question predicates characteristics generally associated with creatures or things not believed to be human persons, the answer is felt to be absurd, comic, and incongruous, as if two distinct worlds had become commingled. Indeed, two universes of discourse have overlapped. However surprising or paradoxical the answer appears, it is nevertheless a judgment that evolves from an earlier interpretant judgment sign and is thus a continuing forward of the subject of discourse, the genesis of which is ideal, hypothetical, and, in an antiplatonic sense, incomplete.

Although it is true that Peirce did not develop his graphs fully beyond the Alpha and Beta parts (that is, only partially through the Gamma system), he did indicate the need for a system of Delta graphs, which he supposed could map relations between commands, questions, and other modals in discourse.

The Delta graphs are mentioned not at all by Zeman (1974) and only in passing by Roberts (1973), who refers to a letter from Peirce to F. A. Woods (begun in 1913; ms 477) that mentions the Delta graphs. Roberts interprets these Delta graphs as a proposal for examining modal logic. However, although one might agree that the Gamma graphs were intended to express the modals of obligation and permission—of deontic logic—the Delta graphs were envisioned as expressing a more inclusive and fundamental system of modality, namely, modalities of possibility, through constructions of questions and answers: what has since come to be associated with the broadest sense of erotetic logic, the logic of inquiry.

We may be reminded here of Morris's observation that the word *methodology*, in the context of pragmatism and semiotics, refers to the area of philosophy having to do with epistemology, or the theory of knowledge. Thus a semiotic methodology implies that knowing is a process of inquiry, "by inquiry into inquiry" (Morris 1970:48, 50).

In Peirce we find not one but three purposes for inquiry into inquiry: (1) to ascertain what men inquire about and to establish a formula that may express these basic areas of inquiry; (2) to fill the need or needs that are satisfied by such essential questions; and (3) to find the general principle that underlies the form of action that is "designed to fill that need" ("Logic of Relatives," 1892, 3.515). In other words, inquiry into inquiry seeks (a) fundamental questions or subject–topics, (b) needs that motivate the raising of such questions, and (c) the action or process that relates the question–answer procedure to the initial motivating want or need.

Just as the answers to folkloric and literary riddles refer to objects or allusions well known to the solver of the riddle, and as the legal decision presupposes a referent code of law, the existential graphs are based on the assumption that the graphist and the interpreter share a mutually familiar universe of discourse.

In passing, it should be noted that Peirce refers to the Delta graphs in 1911,[2] two years earlier than the 1913 date given by Roberts. The 1911 date is significant because, as we will see, it is around this time that Peirce began to conceive of expressing modality through the medium of the stereogram. This chapter presumes that we share a general familiarity with Peirce's development of the graphs, from the Alpha to a possible Delta. His own writings are the best source of this development, and Zeman's and Roberts's studies of the graphs are invaluable secondary sources. Here we will be examining primarily the problem of overlapping reference. We will recall, as mentioned above, that to Peirce an idea is a continuum. As discussed elsewhere, the methodological development of a thought sign from the initial assumption of a subject to fuller, more complex expression of that subject is what Peirce calls a "continuous predicate"; the example he gives is of the extensive, consequential relationships that necessarily follow the passing of a legal sentence, that is, a juridical decision, implying all the ancillary legal acts the decision sets in motion, such as the serving of the prison term and all the parts thereof until its completion. With respect to the existential graphs we note that there are two kinds of continuous existential graphs: the graph of identity and the graph of coexistence. In the notion of true continuity we expect that a question as well as an assertion logically constitutes the continuous line of developing thought, Peirce says (ms 293.36). For example,

1. **Q:** Who is that man?
2. **Q:** Do you call that a man?

Question 2 asks for two definitions, or redefinitions, of (1) *Someone*—(2) *Man*.

In the context of this imaginary conversation the usual definitions of *someone* and *man* are inadequate. By questioning the common code of referential meaning, of someone and man, a third term may be introduced in the conclusion of this dialogue. Peirce has compared this logical structure, in which an alternative term may be introduced in the conclusion, with the syllogistic argument, and has called this a dialogism.

The following suggests relationships between "imaginaries" and other modalities in Peirce's existential graphs.[3] The correspondence between the structure of riddles and modalities in the existential graphs such as the Delta graphs might be imagined to express. In this context it indicates the comic aspects of relative logic and hypothetical reasoning. In passing it will be suggested that the nonstable and comic aspects of legal decisions follow the riddling pattern and that of the modal graphs. Here it will be noted that legal riddles are a significant part of the whole tradition of riddling in almost all cultures where riddles exist, that is to say almost everywhere from the beginning of recorded human culture. Finally, the conclusion leaves open the question of the relation between Peirce's concept of the role of esthetics in semiotics and the relationship between esthetics as the science of value and the emergent, often incongruous, value judgments that are discovered through the process of inquiry capable of expression by means of the existential graphs as an *instrument* of semiotic methodology.

The purpose of methodology is to show how one thought grows out of another, how one "sign gives birth to another." Methodology's special interest is in the "devices which have to be employed to bring new relations to light . . ." (CP 4.370). Every definition presupposes a question (Caws 1959). Every definition tends to establish a belief, or *provisional law*, in Peirce's sense, which, like a legal decision,[4] behaves like a final, or absolute judgment that may be, in turn, appealed, that is, questioned. A riddle is such a definition, but marked in relation to the unmarked, a usual kind of definition which inductively, or in the rhetoric of "working logic" synechdochally equates the attributed parts with the whole. The riddle definition presents a strange, unsuspected relationship as an equivalent of the whole, or subject–answer. In discovering this unlikely relationship one feels surprise—a comic reaction—and begins to doubt what was formerly believed to be true.

Peirce says that it is not the perception of disorder that provokes surprise, but the discovery of an unsuspected order which jars belief and which leads to further questions. Peirce's own method of working was to set out questions in writing and to avoid including those questions that depend on other questions not already thoroughly considered and then to set out arguments pro and con on either side of the question. This process corresponds to the "growth" of the question in focus (ms 311.11, 16); but the process is set in motion by the emotion of surprise, a sign equivalent to a judgment, as Savan (1976) explains.[5]

Referring to the poet Schiller, Peirce says, "The sense of Beauty never furthered the performance of a single act of duty," implying that he did not equate the *summa bonum* with beauty, although tradition holds that beauty as the highest good is predominantly esthetic because it opens onto new value, that is, new freedoms that are valued. We know that the grotesque, as a category of the esthetic, has universally signified the emergence of new value. The function of the grotesque is discussed more fully elsewhere. Attention is given here to the comic-grotesque aspects of hypothetical reasoning which we find in the juxtaposition of multiple frames on reference, including references to imaginaries, which the modal graphs express. As mentioned earlier, Peirce's conventions, or "rules for the game of Existential Graph," presuppose "mutual understandings between two persons: a *Graphist*, who expresses propositions according to the system of expression called that of *Existential Graphs*, and an *Interpreter*, who interprets those propositions and accepts them without dispute" (1958:4.395). At the outset a code is selected and agreed upon. All coherent or directed discourse must proceed from such a code, or matrix, as Koestler stressed.

Koestler (1970) says that "drifting from code to code characterizes the dream; (and) in the routines of disciplined thinking only one matrix is active at a time" (1964:39,40). However, when two or more codes are juxtaposed or overlapped in a noncustomary way we find in the interplay a predominance of the comic aspect of the esthetic, particularly in the variety of the comic usually associated with the absurd. But when out of this clash of codes, this seeming paradox or nonsense, new value emerges and/or is discovered, the new clue appears as grotesque—a sign, or judgment of grotesque. In myth, grotesques appear as the offspring of the fusion between human and nonhuman, such as the sphynx whose riddle requires a new definition of man, that is, an emergent new value in relation to a former judgment of man. Other grotesques are the result of metamorphoses, or the clash of ideality with actuality. The grotesque is a sign of transition from one level of understanding to a new level. In Koestler's words, "Comic discovery is paradox stated—scientific discovery is paradox resolved" (1964:95).

Some notions of Peirce's understanding of play, or musement, as preliminary to his logical "inquiry of inquiry" are suggested, but not developed in the following.

In 1905 Peirce wrote in a letter to the philosopher F. C. S. Schiller that his logic of relatives

> sets everything in logic in a new light and greatly enlarges or metamorphizes every conception. Corresponding to generality in *non-relative* logic is continuity in *relative* logic, and the development of the principle of continuity in the light of that logical view and the adoption of it as the central principle of metaphysics is an indication of what I mean by synechism. (1905: ms 371)

Here Peirce speaks of a "transfigured esthetics" and refers to his 1903 lectures in which he explains how "logic ought to be founded on Ethics and Ethics on a transfigured Esthetics which would be the science of values, although now wrongly treated as a part of Ethics." In the following year, 1906, Peirce wrote that, although the name of existential graphs was first given to his new system of expressing propositions in 1896, he had actually conceived of the graphs as a means of expressing his metamorphizing logic some fourteen years earlier, around 1882 (ms 498.2). Discussion of the relation between ethics and esthetics is continued in the next chapter.

The graphs are anticipated as early as 1868, especially in his paper "Some Consequences of Four Incapacities." Here his anti-Cartesianism is most explicit when he insists that philosophical inquiry never begins with complete doubt but begins ". . . with all the prejudices which we actually have when we enter the study of philosophy. . . . Let us not pretend to doubt in philosophy what we do not doubt in our hearts." It should be mentioned here that to Peirce what we believe in our hearts is what we feel to be true, and this feeling is a kind of law, or judgment, or "legisign"; but we may come to doubt what we formerly believed to be true, which we learned from our experience was true, when we are confronted with something that causes us to correct our beliefs. Every idea, or sign, selected to be the subject of inquiry must be the result of a previous semiotic mediation; and at the same time, in its specific function, as a feeling perceived with fresh attention, it is not, in this role, "susceptible of mediation"; it is perceived *as if* it were immediate.

In this same 1868 paper, Peirce goes on to say that we never have any absolutely "first cognition of any object" but we must always begin with a "process of cognition" that parallels and seems to "most closely follow" the processes of interrelation and growth between facts and signs of facts in the external world.

Although, on the one hand, Peirce says there is an equivalence, or analogy, between the process of discovery and increase of knowledge of a selected subject, and the process of evolution in the external world that is expressed by syllogistic reasoning, there is another process, probable reasoning, which depends for its validity on the "nonexistence of some other knowledge" (1868b:141). As opposed to deductive reasoning, both inductive and hypothetical methods of reasoning must assume the nonexistence of some other knowledge, but, as Peirce stresses, we choose one or the other mode of inquiry depending on our purpose. Thus "the function of an induction is to substitute for a series of many subjects, a single one which embraces them and an indefinite number of others . . . it is a species of reduction of the manifold to unity" (1868b:144), in the Aristotelian sense. But hypothesis, in contrast with induction, substitutes "for a great series of predicates forming no unity in themselves, a single one . . . which involves them all, together (perhaps) with an indefinite number of others. It is, therefore, also a reduction of a manifold to unity" (1868b:144). In fact, all deductive, syllogistic forms of reasoning may be expressed as hypothesis, for example, *If A, then B; but A, (therefore) B.* Peirce says it is important not to confuse an "argument from analogy with hypothesis."

Because every minor premise of hypothetical reasoning appears as an "antecedent" of a hypothetical proposition, hypothetical inference is seen as "reasoning from consequent to antecedent"; whereas the argument by analogy, in either deductive or inductive processes, bases validity on identity or quasi-identity.

In an argument from analogy we can say, for example, that there is some general thing that we know as a sign, that is, a name for a class of things or a system of predicated attributes, or tokens, of the general type, which equal the sum of the type in a nonrelative logic. Thus, inductively, what is not known or included among the attributes of a general may be inferred; the non-known, in this sense, may be assumed. For example, X is eyes, nose, and Y; Y is inferred as mouth; therefore X is a face.

But in hypotheses we find the prototypical structure of the riddle; for example, X is three legs at dusk, two legs at noon, four legs at dawn; therefore, X is man. Here are at least two overlapping frames of reference: dusk, noon, and dawn are signs within a conventional code referring to times of day marked by a solar calendar; legs are signs with a code of objects requiring support; the numbers *three, two,* and *four* refer to a code of measurable things. At the same time each of the three descriptions stands for something which it is not, that is, is a sign, predominantly symbolic, for something it literally represents. All three of the descriptions share reference to a unified concept, like time, caused by time, contiguous with time, namely, age. The three basic principles of association are operant here: resemblance, contiguity, and causality. The riddle process is twofold: It illustrates the establishment of a stable relationship out of an unfamiliar series or set of predictions; at the same time it codifies an apparently incongruous relationship between a subject and it relates so that a new, if provisional, definition emerges.

Peirce denies that continua are real, but he does not ascribe to the Kantian notion that such continua as time and space are only subjective. To the question, What is reality? Peirce admits there may not be a *really Real* at all. Rather, what we call reality "is but a retroduction, a working hypothesis which we try. . . . [It is] . . . our one desperate forlorn hope of knowing anything." He goes on to say, "But if there is any reality, so far as there is any reality, what that reality consists in is this: that there is in the being of things something which corresponds to the process of reasoning, that the world *lives*, and *moves*, and *has its being* in a logic of events" (ms 439.28, 29). Thus all deductive reasoning and inductive reasoning must be viewed within the more comprehensive mode of hypothetical reasoning, or what was earlier referred to as his "metamorphizing logic."

To begin with, one assumes that the continuum is always "all that is possible in whatever dimension it be continuous. . . . The continuum is that which the logic of relatives shows the *true* universal to be" (ms 439.27, 28).[6] But the point is that one always knows, as a realist must, that some true universals are fictions, for instance, the binding force of law.

What immediately follows is a lengthy digression on the concept of "event" as Peirce used the term and anticipated its further development in pragmatic thought.

Peirce says that every intuition or cognition grows out of a previous cognition and that the "striking of a new experience is never an instantaneous affair, but is an event occupying time, and coming to pass by a continuous process" (1868b:147). It is one of the problems of ordinary language that Peirce, in using the word *time* in the above quotation, seems to be referring to the usual sense of spatial or extensible temporality, which suggests the idea of time as a function of historical, pragmatic consequence. When he uses the term *event*, it is surely anticipative of Whitehead's notion of time–space function of significant, momentous organizations, which we have come to call the process of semiosis. It is clear that Peirce knows time not only as an aspect of a calendar or clock temporal system, but also as a durational, intensive aspect of recollection and association, somewhat in Bergson's sense. It is the intersection of both temporal systems that the existential graphs attempt to express in every stage of the growth of an idea. Peirce says that,

> in addition to the principle element of thought at any moment there are a hundred things in our mind to which but a small fraction of attention or consciousness is conceded. It does not, therefore, follow, because a new constituent of thought gets the uppermost that the train of thought which it displaces is broken off altogether.

> On the contrary, . . . its prominence in consciousness . . . must probably be the
> consummation of a growing process. (1984:209–210)

In germinal form here we find Dewey's notion that when an experience is consummately known it is experienced esthetically.

The thought one is deliberately examining is always concurrent with other, submerged thoughts; these undercurrents, as it were, can always be brought into relation with the mainstream at any time. We note that Reichenbach, influenced in many ways by Peirce, developed his notion of "random pockets of energy" which oppose the tendency of the mainstream to run down; these random pockets feed into the main and so resist its entropic tendency (Reichebach 1956). We also find this same idea expressed in the semiotic theories of Mukarovsky, Bakhtin, and others, as discussed in the preceding chapter, especially in the notion of "making strange" (*ostrenenie*); in this sense the esthetic work is said to be a deformation of the norm, or everyday modes of communication. In a similar sense, the anomic, or outsider—the grotesque as Kayser defines it, for example—infuses, either from a subterranean level, or from a position external to the main, the established system of society. The subculture and the counter-culture are, in this respect, "random pockets of energy" or undercurrents of thought in Peirce's sense.

The process between the main and the submerged thought is dialogic. Further,

> the logical comprehension of a thought is usually said to consist of the thoughts
> contained in it. . . . thoughts are events, acts of the mind. Two thoughts are two
> events separated in time, and one cannot literally be contained in the other. . . . Two
> thoughts cannot be similar unless they are brought together in the mind. . . . It is
> plain that the knowlege that one thought is similar to or in any way truly representative
> of another cannot be derived from immediate perception, but must be a hypothesis.
> (1984:225–226)

It is only a matter of speaking to say that one idea is contained in another. When we represent an embedding of ideas what we are expressing is a judgment of relationship by various signs for implication, in which a subject signifies one concept and a predicate represents the other (1868b:148): ". . . the association of ideas consists in this, that a judgment occasions another judgment, of which it is the sign" (1868b:154).

Morris Cohen says that it is in this 1868 paper that Peirce emphatically denies that the process of thought is a succession of images. Peirce says that what we call a succession of images is actually a succession of judgments.

Thus an image, or picture in the mind, is not a copy of an actual, real thing, but an iconic sign, or representation of a judgment which, in a previous stage in the development of the process of association of an idea, was a predominantly symbolic sign. Of course, as subject of a thought, the picture of such a subject in the mind is predominantly indexical. Peirce denies that there is actually an "ideal first image" as a "thing-in-itself." This ideal first image does not "exist as such. . . . Real . . . is a conception which we must first have had when we discovered that there was an unreal, an illusion; that is, when we first corrected ourselves" (1868b:155).[7]

In "Questions Concerning Certain Faculties Claimed for Man" (1868a:105) Peirce says that prior to Berkeley's book on vision it had been assumed that one could immediately perceive the three dimensions of space; since then we have known that three-dimensionality is known by inference. Both Zeman and Roberts point out that the existential graphs are a two-dimensional instrument for representing a three-dimensional process. However, when we come to the modal graphs, we are talking about four or more dimensions. Just as film presents a four-dimensional representation of an action by its ability, through montage, to emphasize the temporal function of events, Peirce continues to compare his graphs with motion pictures. In 1906 (ms 298.4), 1907 (ms 905.12.7.07), and 1908 (ms 296.7, 300), Peirce uses this comparison. It is in manuscript 296 that he says that the graphs' function should not be restricted to the representation of necessary reasoning because they are equally adaptable to the representation of "explanatory conjectures . . . as well as the whole process of induction." In this same year Peirce says that the comparison of the existential graphs to moving pictures should not be taken as a literal resemblance but as a simile. Although we see only one side of a picture, we know it also represents a nonvisible, obverse, and therefore a three-dimensional object. At the same time, more than one graph may occupy the same space; thus in the overlapping of two frames of reference—graphs—on a context, or universe of discourse, we express in this interrelation an opposition, or antagonism, which is consequential and therefore four-dimensional. We can experiment with this perception of four-dimensionality with our illustration of the hyperstereogram. In 1911 Peirce wrote that he was convinced that there is a better method than diagram to express the process of reasoning, and that might well be stereoscopic moving pictures.

We know Hamilton's influence on Peirce's graphs and on his concepts of multidimensionality; we also know that Peirce's father, Benjamin, improved on Hamilton's graphs by introducing imaginaries into the quaternion. We must also assume that Peirce was well acquainted with Hamilton's invention of the holograph which, briefly, has to do with the relation between two continuities of a particle, each with its own frame of reference and function, and with the manner in which they—the continuities—interact.[7]

But it was in 1903 that Peirce decided to replace the single sheet of assertion with the "book of separate sheets in order to deal with logical possibilities" (Roberts 1973:88). By 1906 he explicitly says that the inner area of a cut was to represent possibiilty, and that the cut should be envisioned as opening up many layers of the surface sheet, so that each of these strata would be differently tinted to represent different kinds of possibility (CP 4.578).[8]

The relation of the modal graphs to possibility in the future has been least understood. Yet Peirce is consistent in assuming that value derives not from what is immediately, that is, presently thought, but in the relation of present thought to subsequent thought—to thought in the process of becoming. It will be recalled that even in the Alpha and Beta graphs, which require only one sheet of assertion, the sheet itself, without being "scribed," or impressed, is still a graph. A blank sheet in the Alpha and Beta systems is like a zero sign, or a possibility inherent in present time. The first assertion thus expresses a possibility. The sheet itself represents an initial presentation of data. In this case the data are the inquiry of inquiry. These data must be imagined. Peirce says that "imaginary observation is the most essential part of reasoning" (CP 4.355).[9]

We are dealing with aspects of modality even in the Alpha and Beta graphs. That is, we are not talking about proving the truth of falseness of assertions, but, rather, about the *fidelity* of the assertions with respect to the agreements between graphist and interpreter that they are referring to the same universe of discourse. In terms of fiction, a thing—a subject or actor—can said to be "in character" and yet in no way be true. This is precisely the point played on, for example, in the absurd drama of Pirandello and others, except that in the drama we have more than one level of untruth. With respect to the existential graphs, the graphist may assert the following proposition, "The Real Thing comes in pints, quarts, and gallons" and we know that the agreed-upon universe of discourse is the universe of soda-pop. Or if the assertion is, "The greatest carver does the least cutting," we know we are in the universe of the Tao; we know, also, that in this universe paradox and contradiction are indices of truth.

The point here is that in order for there to be agreement between the graphist and the interpreter they are permitted to agree to a universe of discourse that may, itself, be a fusion or intersection of two or more other familiar universes of discourse. Just as it is possible to argue that black is white, as Peirce does in "Validity of the laws of logic" (1868c.201, 202), it is possible to say, according to Permission 7 of his Code of Permissions, that "Whenever we are permitted to scribe any graph we like upon the sheet of assertion, we are authorized to declare that the conditions of the special problem are absurd" (CP 4.415).

We note that a graph may be scribed on its converse or inner side as well as on its outer surface. Graph replicas of graphs may overlay the basic sheet of assertion, so that the replica, which is a *blank*, can be understood to correspond with that which may possibly be predicated of the subject but either is not known or has not yet come into existence. The graph is a type and the graph replica, in relation to the initial graph, is a token, or "individual instance of the graph"

(CP 4.414). Now it is permitted to erase the graph replica, but in doing so the graph, or type to which it has provisionally been found to relate, is also erased; that is, the relationship requires correction. Similarly, a legal decision, as a token of a statute as type, may be appealed; the appeal throws up to question the soundness of the interpretation of the type.

Peirce concedes that the Alpha and Beta graphs are inadequate not only because arguments must be represented as a succession of sheets, representing the multiple embedding of clauses in hypotactic types of discourse, but also because they do not represent signs such as music, or commands and requests. Later, when he says that questions as well as assertions may be represented in sequence, he begins to speak of a corresponding signification between two kinds of existential graphs: one is the graph of identity and the other, which is to be represented by a blank, is the graph of coexistence (ms 293.36). Therefore, where in the Alpha and Beta systems, the graph replica, also a blank, represented a system, or class of predicted objects, or characteristics of a subject, the blank graph of coexistence may be understood as an entire system, constituted of both type and tokens, which is brought into relation with another system. The graph of coexistence is the "rhema," or new information, which becomes upon being scribed a present graph of identity, thus bringing about a new level of inquiry. Every graph is a composite, complex system of signs which, like all feelings, are meaningless in isolation but acquire value insofar as they become connected with other signs as graphs. Feelings are never single; when other elements, such as the motion and time we know through experience to accompany feeling, are absent, they are said to be *logically* absent. Similarly, we can logically imagine an uncolored space, through a process Peirce calls *discrimination*; that is, we discriminate color from space (ms 296.27, 29).

When Peirce begins to speak of the modal graphs, he says they would have to express relations that neither the Alpha nor the Beta graphs are capable of doing. First, they must be able to express two kinds of hypotactic abstraction: one kind of abstraction would express absence in the sense that some feature is deliberately left out of the picture; this absence, which he calls "prescissive abstraction"—which, we recall, is the first stage of his phenomenological process—prescinds a *quality* that becomes, through development, a representation, or sign. We are to imagine this prescised quality, or subject for investigation, shorn of its usual connotations; it is as if we perceived it immediately.

The other kind of abstraction is a kind of paraphrase, akin to the concept of word order in functional language perspective. Its purpose is to establish a hierarchy—a new order—of the terms of an assertion so that the greatest emphasis will fall in the most prominent position, on emergent information. Thus Peirce proposes that the usual order of subject and predicate be inverted and that the operation should change the predicate into a subject. Now we find exactly this process in the riddle: the riddle–question, which is often referred to by riddle scholars as the subject of the riddle, with the answer being assumed to be the predicate, is actually, as we analyze its structure, just the other way around. *The answer to a riddle is the subject of the riddle,* and presents the newest comment on the iconic, predicated signs of the riddle description.

But this type of predicate relationship is particularly difficult to express as a picture. Peirce says that the "representation of Modality (possibility, necessity, etc.) lacks almost entirely that pictorial, or Iconic character." In fact, to represent modality iconically is a false representation, and "properly speaking" modality "is not conceivable at all" (ms 298.18).

However, we recognize the "difference . . . between possibility and actuality much in the same way as we recognize the difference between a dream and a waking experience." Peirce then suggests that the Gamma and presumably Delta graphs express not one, but two opposed universes of discourse: the actual and the dream kind of world, "ever so detailed, reasonable, and thoroughly consistent with itself and with all the rest of the dreamer's experience."

The meaning and value expressed by modality is not self-referential only but is its relation to an iconic representation of actuality as well. If we are to represent this relationship in a nonpictorial way and yet retain the graphic instrument or method, we may color the logic that will be shown to relate to actual experience. In this way Peirce introduces the system of tinctures (ms 96.2).

The use of color in the graphs is a study in itself. But let us look briefly at the code of tints that Peirce invents. The code of tinctures is subdivided into three types: metal, color, and fur—the traditional mineral, vegetable and animal "kingdoms" that correspond with his three categories; firstness, secondness, and thirdness. It is suggested that the three divisions correspond with three universes: metal represents the actual or existent; color represents the questionable, the possible, and "things possible in themselves"; and the fur represents the universe of command and compelled (ms 295). Each of these three universes is subdivided into subuniverses.[10] Each of these subuniverses represents a different kind of possibility. Thus, when a line of identity extends from one tincture, or subuniverse, to another tincture, or universe, we have a double bisociation in thought brought about by simultaneously referring to two or more frames of reference, or sign systems. This may seem to be a problem. However, the problem disappears when we realize that the double bisociation, in carrying with it an expression of the comic, represents a fusion of two separate judgments of identity, such as the fusion of animal and vegetable in the grotesque *Tales of Hoffmann* and in other discourse wherein metamorphosis signifies by incongruity a new synthesis or value judgment.

Just as two perspectives focused simultaneously on a single object result in what has been called a *perspective by incongruity,* two sources of light focused on a single spot may result in a third sensation, in both color and intensity perceived. Peirce writes of this phenomenon in his review of Rood's book on modern chromatics (1879/1975 [Nation]:59–61): "By a mixture of lights is not meant a mixture of pigments but the effect of projecting two colors—for instance by two magic lanterns—upon the same spot."

As we have seen, by inverting the relation between spot and light, that is, by having a single perspective focused on two spots, we perceive the illusion of four-dimensionality. It would seem, although Peirce never developed the concept, that the proposed Delta graphs would have been able to express such incongruity. To follow, by presenting an incongruent overlapping or juxtaposition of two universes of discourse to a single interpreter, the graphs could express the logic of the absurd, that is, the relation between the possible and its verso: the impossible as conceived.

The problem for semioticians is not how to eliminate the element of confusion from the process of reasoning about possibilities, about the association of signs of possibilities, but rather, as in semiotic approaches to the circus and the carnival and the joke, to understand how to make confusion clear, *as confusion*.

A semiotic study of the riddle will not be attempted here, either from the perspective of the riddle as a kind of literary text and therefore a sign, or from a perspective on the structural elements of the riddle as presented, for example, by Scott (1965). Rather, a few generally agreed-upon definitions of the riddle will be offered, some illustrations, and some relationships other than those already mentioned will be suggested between the legal decision and the existential graphs.

One begins by observing that the riddle places something that is not expressed—an imaginary, virtual something—within the possible grasp of expression. The riddle deletes its subject, which is always revealed as a familiar object well known to both riddler and interpreter. Riddles are always expressed in the interrogative construction, in dialogue, and thus express some aspect of modality. Also, whereas the answer, or subject, of a particular riddle may function in such a context as a general or type, no sign may be absolutely indefinite, singular, or general. As Peirce points out in a letter to William James with reference to modality,

> The distinction between the Indefinite, the Singular, and the General is obviously only another application of the distinction between the Potential, the Actual, and the Necessary. By *Potential*, I mean the Possible in the sense in which the Possible is not a mere negation of Necessity, nor a mere ignorance, but is a germinal mode of being. . . . A potential occurrence is a Past one, an actual occurrence is a Present one, a necessary occurrence is a future one. (1905:9)

The fact that the actual subject of a riddle appears as the last word indicates a necessary conclusion of an exploration of possibility, toward something in the future. The riddle, by transposing the usual subject–predicate positions, brings the subject from the past into the future.

Distinctions are made between the riddle of oral folklore and the literary riddle by scholars who specialize in the study of the riddle. As a text sign it is found almost everywhere in ancient written texts except, curiously, in English, where it does not emerge as a literary form until around the end of the fifteenth century, coinciding with the final stabilization of what we know as modern English—an analytic rather than a synthetic language type. The oral tradition has been traced to the beginning of what is known of human cultures. Although riddling, like many other sacred forms of augury, has become attenuated in modern times, just as sacred play of which the riddle is a part has become a pasttime, many literary riddles trace their origin to popular oral riddling traditions; these popular riddles have been transposed for use in ritual riddling, such as in the Rigveda, which dates back to at least 10000 B.C. In both Old and New Testaments examples of the riddle in many forms are found. The riddle of the Sphynx, perhaps one of the oldest of the known riddles, directly concerned Peirce. It is strongly suggested that it was Schiller's influence in this case, rather than Emerson's (as is sometimes believed) that led Peirce to associate the riddle with esthetics and ultimately with the existential graphs. This distinction will not be discussed here.

In the resurgence of Arabic riddling, especially between the tenth and the sixteenth centuries, coincident with the establishment of the first law schools in Europe, we find a number of famous riddlers who wrote only legal riddles. One such riddle master was the logician Al-Hariri (c. 1050–1120; Taylor 1948:18–24). Al-Hariri's collections of riddles were called Assemblies and contained, together with problems of grammar and syntax, legal puzzles and puns on legal complications (Taylor 1948:26). The main actor in these assemblies was the improvisor.

As a general observation, it has been found that in every culture that has had an enduring legal system we find a corresponding tradition of riddling. This has to do, perhaps, with the fact that legal codes, especially in closed legal systems, appear to be absolute, as givens by supreme authority, but are continually open to reinterpretations. We see this, for example, in the Talmudic, Chinese, and Arabic legal codes. The codes themselves are constructed of riddles; therefore, although the law is apparently fixed and established, interpretation is left to the succession of legal actors—judges—who "decide" with reference to a code but may actually distort the code so that the "decision" appears as a judgment, that is, as final.

There are many definitions of the riddle, none of which is considered to be adequate. The following are among those most widely accepted (Scott 1965:14):

> A riddle is that in which little things play with each other, inasmuch as they put trifling questions to each other, which no one understands. (Cledonius Pompeius Julianua, c. 400 A.D.: *Aenigma est, quo ludunt parvuli inter se, quando sibi proponunt quaestinculas, quas nullum intellegit.*)

Guiseppe Pitre's long definition will be given only in part (also from Scott):

> The riddle is an arrangement of words by which is understood or suggested something
> that is not expressed; or else it is an ingenious and witty description of this unexpressed
> thing by means of qualities and general traits that can be attributed quite as well to
> other things having no likeness or analogy to the subject.

Let us consider the following simple question–answer routine: The spelling bee. Here the student is asked to spell, for example, WORD. Initially, WORD is pronounced, its constituent letter parts are named, and then WORD is pronounced again, in conclusion. The student's participation resembles a process of deductive, or syllogistic reasoning, except that in this case the question that led into the reasoning is explicit. Now this is straightforward: WORD is *doubleyou, oh, are, dee,* WORD. But let us now transform this dialogue into riddling activity. Thus the riddler might ask: What is *not me two times, an open mouth, an old man leaning on a cane,* and *follows everything eyes do*? The answer to the riddle, of course, is the verbal sign WORD.

Now the principles involved are precisely those that Peirce ascribes to the process of the association of ideas or judgments, namely: resemblance, contiguity, and causality. For example, the letter D is contiguous with the letter C, and by entertaining a notion of resemblance in the sound shapes of C (the letter) and the verb "see" we have the last part of the riddle that solves the questions as a whole. The letter R, by some stretch of the imagination, graphically resembles an old man leaning on a cane; the letter O, following the principle of causality, is that which happens when sound comes from an open mouth; the letter W also follows the principle of contiguity, in the sense that we know the opposition between an I and a *Thou* is universal—a *me* and a *you*, in other words. Therefore, "not me two times" is necessarily *you two times,* or *doubleyou,* by hypostatic abstraction, or paraphrase.

This riddle was invented here partly to illustrate Pitre's definition and partly to point up the process of principles of association in modal expressions of the existential graphs. By abstracting each of the component parts of the riddle predicate from the class with which it is usually associated, and then by regrouping each of these abstracts as members of a new class—a possible system—the familiar subject becomes linked with an unfamiliar predication in a potential line of identity which is continuous with the line of coexistence of several frames of reference. This process is an example of hypothetical reasoning and does not at all resemble inductive reasoning. For we cannot say there is an *old man leaning on a cane, an open mouth,* and *something which follows everything eyes do,* and infer from his sampling either the missing part—the *not me two times*—or the type sign, WORD. Each part requires the interpreter, or riddle solver, to begin afresh after each part is deciphered. As Archie Taylor, the classic authority on the riddle in folklore and literature, says,

> The literary riddle ordinarily contains a long series of assertions and contradictions and is often put in the form of a speech made by the object that is being described. In order to accumulate details enough to permit the listener to guess the answer, the riddler often sacrifices the unity of his conception. The first assertion and its denial are almost certain to conflict with the next pair. Yet the author goes on and on, while his conception becomes more and more incoherent. (1948:3)[11]

Around 1500 we find a resurgence of the riddle in Renaissance and Reformation Germany (Taylor 1948:72). Usually these riddles were long comparisons between two objects that were supposed to represent the opposition between old and new law (Taylor 1948:96).

Scott (1965) tells us that in some Persian and Arabic societies the riddle contest was set apart from everyday life, just as we recall that *the thing*, or courts of pre-Norman English common law, were set apart from the community and represented a playhouse, or theater.

We note in conclusion that the nucleus of the joke is the riddle "which the listener must solve. . . . By doing so," Koestler says, "he is lifted out of his passive role and compelled to cooperate, to repeat, to some extent the process of inventing the joke, to recreate it in his imagination" (1970:85, 86)[12]

As noted, Peirce was profoundly influenced by the poet Schiller's concept of aesthetic play from as early as 1857, when he wrote that Schiller's *Formtrieb* was equivalent to the "I impulse and faculty"; the *Stofftrieb* was equivalent with the "It impulse and faculty"; and the *Spieltrieb* with the "Thou impulse and faculty" (ms 1633:9, ISP). Years later, in that significant year 1911, Peirce was to say that it had been fifty-five years since he had "read the only book on esthetics in general, the only one professing to cover the whole subject . . . the work of the poet Schiller . . . (whose) theory was that beauty is the expression of the Spieltrieb." Peirce goes on to say, "I am willing enough to admit the truth of all the great poet said of that kind of beauty that is a matter of play, whether idle play or busy play" (ms 675, draft:14–16; c. 1911).[13]

In speaking of beauty and its relation to hypothesis, Peirce remarks, "Both sensations and conceptions are hypothetic predicates. They are, however, hypotheses of widely different kinds. A sensation is a sort of mantel name. To assign a name to a thing is to make a hypothesis" (ms 357.2).[14]

Finally, we recall Haeckel, who, like Peirce, expressed great enthusiasm for the future of evolution. Peirce, we know, believed continuity and evolution to be the two most important concepts of this century. In his book Haeckel concluded that six of the great riddles had already been solved; that is, the problems of the "structure of matter" and the "origin of life" had passed from doubt to belief. What remained, the seventh riddle, dealt with the question of "man's experience of freedom and choice" (Koestler 1964:250). According to Haeckel, this was not a real question, or riddle, put "pure dogma" based only on the illusions of freedom and choice, and therefore it could not be seriously considered. Peirce associated freedom and choice with Schiller's aesthetics, that is, with value. This esthetics, deliberately constructed on illusion, or play, for the purpose of creating and disclosing new values that can be acted upon and acted out in real life, is what is expressed in the existential graphs, as they imagistically represent a semiotic methodology as Peirce conceived it. The discourse of legal systems, both verbal and procedural in structure, needs to be examined with the use of these existential graphs.

NOTES

1. These references are to the *Collected Papers* (1958); the figures indicate volume and paragraph respectively.

2. In manuscript 500, p. 2, Peirce says, "The better exposition of 1903 divided the system into three parts, distinguished as the Alpha, the Beta, and the Gamma, parts: a division I shall adhere to, although I shall now have to add a *Delta* part in order to deal with modals." Peirce goes on to say that the Alpha, Beta, and Gamma parts of the existential graphs are not supplied "with any means of expressing mere feelings, such as abound in the arts of music and painting. Nor has any need been found for furnishing it with means of expressing commands—not even such as take the softened forms of requests and inquiries" (ms 500.10, 11).

3. Speculatively, Benjamin Peirce's improvement on the Hamiltonian Quaternion, by introducing the imaginary, seems to be closely related to Peirce's realization that imaginaries are essential for the expression of modality in the existential graphs. See CP 3.56n, 130, 326, 557, 647 (in which Clifford's "nonions" are referred to), 6.420 (on signs to indicate on diagram some future, anticipated value, which is a possible).

4. According to Friedman (1975: 24,25), "A decision is usually elicited as a response to a definite claim." Also, Friedman says that the main function of a legal decision is to communicate a message (1975: 75,76).

5. Savan says that "living emotion is an affective condition in which some brute force beyond our control has disturbed or destroyed our prior emotional equilibrium, so that we cannot return to it at will (1976: 21). Affect develops when emotion encounters opposition and conflict. Frequently it is the shock of surprise that triggers the violent response" (1976: 21).

6. Cohen (1916) says that Peirce, in going against the grain of thought which held that "all social changes (are) due to an imminent dialectic force," clearly realized that changes in society are directly dependent on changes in individual habitual thinking. "His keen psychological insight is shown perhaps at its best in his attack on the now classical tradition that makes the process of thought consist of a succession of images . . ." (1916: 626–637). Peirce (1868b) says that because an idea has not yet been consummatedly realized or is not at present the object of inquiry, that does not mean that one's previous consideration of it has broken off, but rather that it is a continuous thought which exists, unseen or attended to, in some subterranean stratum of consciousness, to rise now and again and rejoin the mainstream.

7. We may compare Peirce's "real" and former "hypothesized" selves with a "normal" class which does not contain itself as a member of the class or set of phenomena investigated. The nonnormal class includes the investigator as a member of the class being investigated. Thus in terms of the nonnormal class the investigator is nonexistent, that is, an illusion, but is still the antecedent of the actual self—outside the investigating process—that becomes illusory at every stage of thought development. Peirce says, with respect to this phenomenon, that "whenever we think, we have present to the consciousness some feeling, image, conception, or other representation, which serves as a sign. But it follows from our own existence (which is proved by the occurrence of ignorance

and error) that everything which is present to us is a phenomenal manifestation of ourselves. This does not prevent its being a phenomenon of something without us, just as a rainbow is at once a manifestation both of the sun and of the rain. When we think, then, we ourselves, as we are at that moment, appear as a sign" (Nagel and Newman 1964:24, 25). To suggest that we are beside ourselves is to imply that we are off-center, that is, eccentric; from the viewpoint of a relative logic, we would say that we shift in relation to shifting center, or focus.

8. Related to what Peirce sees as a graph of coexistence is what had been described prior to and during 1904 as a "Diagram in Pairs"; this indicates "that a point in the diagram corresponds to a point in another diagram. . . . If the diagrams are drawn on the same piece of paper we may indicate corresponding points by drawing a line from one to the other, taking care that this line of correspondence is so drawn that it cannot be mistaken for a real line in either diagram." The stereoscope permits us to view the two two-dimensional diagrams as three-dimensional bodies.

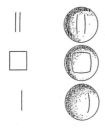

Figure 1. Euclidean and non-Euclidean spatial relationships. From Nagel and Newman (1964, pp. 18, 19). Copyright 1964 by New York University Press. Reprinted with permission.

Further, additional events may succeed one another, so that each new level represents a kind of a replica of its predecessor and at the same time a comment or new definition of it (Figure 1). The non-Euclidean geometry of Bernhard Riemann can be represented by a Euclidean model. The Riemannian plane becomes the surface of a Euclidean sphere, points on the plane become points on this surface, straight lines in the plane become great circles. Thus a portion of the Riemannian plane bounded by segments of straight lines is depicted as a portion of the sphere bounded by parts of great circles (*center*). Two line segments in the Riemannian plane are two segments of great circles on the Euclidean sphere (*bottom*), and these, if extended, indeed intersect, thus contradicting the parallel postulate.

9. At the same time, Peirce was experimenting with the way in which the graphs could express the relation between an anomaly and a norm, or shared belief. Thus anomaly could be expressed by a kind of paradox; for example, a "line of identity across a cut" would express that something both is and is not. But the possibility should express something else, namely, that a line of identity should hold except for the possibility that one or more characteristics were absent, in actuality or in conjecture.

10. We might say that the sheet of assertion on which paradox is expressed is akin to comic discovery, and the conclusion of the argument, in Koestler's sense, is similar to what he calls scientific discovery.

Disagreement with Zeman's interpretation of continuity in the graphs is argued more fully elsewhere (see Zeman 1968: 147). He says, "The unactualized is in a definite sense discontinuous with the existent, the actual insofar as it is not a part of the universe of existent individuals" (p. 147). But one need not agree that nonexistence is synonymous with discontinuity or discreteness in the graphs because Peirce consistently explains that imaginable thoughts, that is, those that are in process but have not yet come into existence, are continuous with and coexistent with that which perceivably exists (see Peirce 1868b: 149). Further, he says that we may imagine points on a graph representing existence to indicate what will come into being in the future.

11. The subuniverses are further distinguished as to the kinds of possibilities: for instance, there are four subuniverses of color: azure, gules, vert, and purpure; color distinctions of possibility are indicated by fine line-shadings in four directions: azure is horizontal; gules is vertical; vert is

obliquely from left to right clockwise; purpura, obliquely from right to left counterclockwise. The furs are distinguished by alternate rows of marks, or motifs, some joined as in the cross-hatching of sable; others, open circles, as in vair (a squirrel-skin prized in the fourteenth century), and crosses in point-counterpoint. Metals are either bland, as in Argent, or crosses (Or) or rows of horizontal and vertical dashes (Iron, Plomb). As mentioned, each subuniverse is a different kind of possibility; for example, vert expresses the interrogative mood: azure, a logical possibility; gules, or red, "a more objective mode of possibility"; and vair, that which is commanded, and so forth. It seems certain that each of these representations of possibility is symbolic with reference to some universe of discourse, perhaps that of alchemy or cabalistic enigmas, or heraldry, or other codes in which the paradox is a sign of potentiality; but this area requires a separate study, which is most interesting from the point of view of modern semiotics. Roberts (1973) says there is a problem when a line of identity extends from one tincture to another kind of surface texture or tint; but I would like to suggest that this is not really a problem but, rather, an intended double bisociation, which carries with it the expression of the comic and of the grotesque in particular, such as when a line of identity extends in the grotesque tales of Hoffmann from the vegetable to the animal or human universes of discourse. The notion of metamorphosis as a process in relative logic is thus expressable in this way in the graphs. Border areas, tinted on the sheet of assertion, are called marches; areas abutting the borders are called provinces; provinces adjacent to provinces but not abutting a march are said to be superimposed on the provinces which are adjacent to the border; that is, if a province is contiguous with a linking province it is, in some way, contiguous with the kind of possibility expressed by the tint of the border. We are clearly in the domain of games, play, and strategy. It is particularly interesting to realize to what extent Peirce's photometric researches influenced his semiotic methodology, and how, especially, they seem to anticipate his introducing tinctures to the modal graphs. For example, Lenzen (1969) calls our attention indirectly to the relation between Peirce's earlier interest in the sensation of light and his later uses of color as a function of light in the graphs. In his paper "Charles Peirce as Atronomer" Lenzen refers to Peirce's 1878 work on photometric research—the same year in which his doctrine of chances appeared. Lenzen explains that Peirce uses the term "noumenal" light to designate light as something in the external world; light that is considered as an appearance and as a function of sensation he calls "phenomenal" light (1964:45).

12. Riddle scholars distinguish between true riddles and other riddle types of enigmas and puzzle questions. The distinction lies in the subject matter rather than in the structure of the riddle, which seems to be of a general type shared by all riddles. In the study of folklore it is customary to assign riddles to such categories as things living, persons, animals, plants, one person, and so on. The comic effect of the riddle is achieved when two categories overlap and a totally new relationship is perceived. Williamson says, "A riddle is a comparison or equating of the answer to some other object, be it an animal, a person, a plant, or a thing. The point lies in the fact that the answer and the object suggested are totally foreign and unrelated to each other" (Williamson 1977). Taylor (1948:2) says that whereas literary riddles have answers that are usually abstract ideas, folk riddles select themes commonly found in everyday life. The folk riddle often contrasts "a vague description with one that is understood literally." Baum (1963) gives the following example of a translation of one of the Anglo-Saxon riddles of the Exeter Book which illustrates Taylor's point:

I was alive but said nothing;	even so I die.
Back I came before I was.	Everyone plunders me,
keeps me confined,	and shears my head,
bites my bare body,	breaks my sprouts.
No man I bite	unless he bites me;
many there are	who do bite me.

Baum says the answer to this riddle is onion but adds that it is onion with salacious overtones

(p. 32). Here two frames of reference—two kinds of modalities—are seen freely to "borrow themes from one another" so that in the culture's tradition of riddling there is an embedding of riddles.

13. See also Taylor (1948), in particular pp. 28–32, 34, 35, 41, 53, 54, 76, 96.

14. Peirce says of the relation between beauty and hypothesis: "Both sensations and conceptions are hypothetic predicates. They are, however, hypotheses of widely different kinds. A sensation is a sort of mantel name. To assign a name to a thing is to make a hypothesis. It is plainly a predicate which is not in the data. But it is given on account of a logical necessity, namely the necessity of reducing the manifold of the predicates given to unity" (1967:357.2). Peirce suggests that there would be a theorem, a demonstration, and a corollary in Esthetics (1967:649.22–27). Max Fisch's file note of this later classification of the sciences emphatically suggests that this is a surprising development and one that invites inquiry (Fisch 1969).

Speech Acts

DECISIONS

The concept of speech acts has in recent years been of major concern to linguists engaged in analysis of context-sensitive discourse. Philosophical interest in speech acts derives from a longstanding tradition in which ethics and law were originally interrelated. In this century, in assuming that human conduct is predisposed by language, the philosopher John L. Austin (1968) introduced the term *speech acts*; his work has been germinal in this area of philsophical concern, as noted earlier. Modern semiotics, developed largely from Peirce's pragmatic methods of inquiry, analyzes structures of communication that are understood to be complex systems of sign relationships. Such a system is natural language. Another such system is the legal system. Legal semiotics is one of the most recent branches of general semiotics to evolve.

In this chapter the notion of legal speech acts is further applied. It is assumed that legal speech acts are not statements but rather question–answer constructions. Focus is particularly on the underlying interrogative structure of the legal decision. There is no attempt here to present either a linguistic or logical analysis of decisions. Because this concept is new, the chapter proceeds in the form of general discussion.

As discussed in Part I of this volume, Lawrence Friedman shows that legal acts are both verbal and nonverbal. A nonverbal legal act, or sign, may be a badge, a uniform, a system of traffic signals, or even a legal environment such as a court which traditionally conveys its message through certain structural features that set it apart from everyday spaces and events (Kevelson 1977).

All legal acts are messages. A legal system is a process of communicating such messages through legal speech acts. This chapter does not discuss the technical, idocyncratic sublanguage system known as "law language," although the application of semiotic methodology to the semantic and syntactic levels of legal argument, and law language in general, would be a fruitful undertaking. Actually, one's understanding of the uses and meanings of argument requires that we apply semiotic methodology, a term Peirce uses synonymously with speculative rhetoric, to practical argument as noted above (CP 3.160, 2.105, 4.615, 4.116, ms 645.19, 754.8, 311.11-16, 312, 622.2, 425, 425.18, 95.7). Toulmin, as noted, considers the legal argument prototypical of all ordinary argument (1958); and the late distinguished semiotician Perelman described the basic intercommunicative functions of modes of "the new rhetoric" in argument (1969). But there has been little *systematic* study of the pragmatic level of law language, or legal speech acts in which speaker, listener, code, channel, message, and context are coordinates in a legal event. From the viewpoint of semiotics, the three levels of a communicative event are syntactic, semantic, and pragmatic (Morris 1946).

Here the main concern is with the pragmatic level of the legal speech act called *decisions*. In passing, linguistic and philosophic interest in the semantics of speech acts as "meaning" will be discussed in the sense that has to do with propositional attitudes and the relationship between law and ethics.

Jurisprudential and philosophical concern with the act centers on how volition, action, and value derived from felt wishes and desires are interconnected, especially in the context of the legal act. Briefly, the jurist John Austin's (1879) definition of the term *act* will be given. Reference is also made here to Mead's *The Philosophy of the Act* (1938). Rayfield's thesis, which holds that choices, decisions, and acts are equivalent and interchangeable and which opposes the now prevailing "additive analysis" of acts in legal theory, as developed by Austin, has important bearings here; it supports the notion that a legal decision is not a consequent stage of the juridical (and ordinary) decision-making process but, rather, that the decision is a coherent question–answer unit of language, in which the question part may be below the surface, that is, ellipsed but implied (Rayfield 1972). In recent history Sanders has called attention to the fact that "there are . . . linguistic constructions which are clearly larger than the sentence and which include sentences. One such construction is the question-and-answer exchange, or what might be called the interrogative dialogue" (Sanders 1969:38–39).

Sanders is not original in his observation. As discussed earlier, the Stoics distinguished various kinds of *lekta*, or complete units of verbal meaning; for example, a proposition is one kind of complete meaning structure; the question is another. The answer by itself was regarded as an incomplete unit of meaning. No attempt will be made here except in rudimentary fashion to describe some advances in the last twenty years on the logic of questions and answers.

In talking about the kind of legal speech act called rules, it will be assumed that rules are communicated in two distinct kinds of messages: (1) substantive, in which the message is directed to the general public or special-interest public group, and (2) jurisdictive, in which the message is exchanged between authoritative, offical legal actors. Except in a minimal way there will be little discussion of the kind of legal speech act called commands, or requests, where brief investigators help to point up the interrogative in decisions.

For example, there is a widespread tendency to analyze legal discourse from the point of view of deontic logic, the logic of permission and obligation. There is no doubt that the nineteenth century concept of the law as command of the sovereign, although highly controversial today, nevertheless seems to justify regarding legal language as a construction of imperatives and commands. The work of Rescher (1966) for example, and others suggests that legal discourse is predicated on the theme that the law is a tool, instrumental in bringing about social conformity to its leading principles, encoded law. The fact that a command signifies an order and is deontic in this respect does not warrant regarding all legal speech acts as having an underlying deontic logic. On the contrary, one can consider the rule and the command as signs of certain verbal structures which, through their rhetorical force and their structural similarity to actual quasi-propositional rules and quasi-directive legal commands, convey a stylistic meaning. It was recalled in this context that Peirce considers all proposition-like statements, including nonpropositions such as imperatives, to be, at bottom, hypotheses.

For example the word *let* which prefaced writs in early English law and has come to mean both *permit* and *restrict* originally indicated a question of possibility, that a "may be" rather than a "would be" was implied by the plantiff. Similarly, the word *if* such as in the *if . . . then* conditional, derives in English from the word *gift*, or *given*. While the *given* is understood in positive law as that which is axiomatically encoded in law, the earlier meaning of *given . . . (that)* was always dependent on an antecedent question: "it is possibly the case" or "there is a question of" followed by the disjunctive *but* and the exploration of one or another possible alternatives.

Unlike the rule kind of legal speech act that Friedman (1975) says is a *general*, that is, which represents as a sign, a *given*, and conveys an axiomatic or truth-like rhetorical force, the command and the decision are particular. In terms of traditional grammar, the command represented by the decision is predicated on the subject of inquiry, the rule. In a logical sense the rule functions as a type and the command and the decisions are tokens of that type. But according to Peirce's relative logic the old subject–predicate and type–token relationships do not hold. As we will see, a decision can become a new precedent and thus a new subject or type in subsequent cases. The shifting role of provisional judgments will be discussed further.

It is customary to say that the command and the decision are not axiomatic and that, in general, imperatives and questions cannot be analyzed as truth statements in formal logic. However, as Susan Haack (1978:84) suggests, the truth conditions of imperatives and interrogatives may be satisfied by considering the consequential truth of question or directive. Thus the result, in a pragmatic sense, of a command or a question yields an accomplished fact that can be verified as true. Now it is not possible here to examine Haack's suggestion fully except to note that by regarding the result of a question or a command as a truth sign, or proposition, we would only be perpetuating the prevailing tendency toward additive analysis of legal and other acts. In this theory the consequence is a second stage derived from the first; the decision would be a discrete unit subsequent to its antecedent. Actually, however, by regarding the deliberation and decision as complementary units of a single process or act, just as the question–answer is a complete, unified meaning structure of language, we will have introduced a radical and more satisfactory way of accounting for acts.

There is another important distinction in the surface structure of decisions and commands. A command presumably expresses the will of authority which must be carried out without discussion or debate, *whereas* the decision is markedly a response to a claim, or question as complaint against the accused. Further, in relatively open legal systems a legal decision by an activist judge is also a response to public sentiment and to the extensive common value of his referent society. Still further, in the inner dialogue that involves the judge's questioning and interpreting the case with reference to established rule, and in selecting one alternative from among possible decisions, the process of judicial inquiry is clearly a dialogue of questions and answers. Finally, unlike the rule or command, at least in Anglo-American courts, the legal decision may be appealed. That is, it may be questioned by either party involved in the litigation.

A decision may avoid appearing as a question when there is resort to the device of the legal fiction. Again, in Shklar's sense (1964), the use of the legalism may conceal an innovative decision within the appearance of maintaining the stability of the legal order.

As Friedman says, "A fiction is phrased so as to look as if the court merely follows old and legitimate ways. Legal fictions form a bridge between ideology and fact, when an institution asserts either that less change has taken place or more than is actually true" (1975:262). As for legalisms, especially in relatively closed legal systems in which legal reasoning assumes the mode of formal logic, "the blocks of legal reasoning are propositions which serve as premises" (237).

When a decision is said to be based on, or validated by, fixed legal premises, of which in any closed system there are a finite number, distinctions are sharply made between propositions that are legal and those that are not. Although the notion of legalism refers primarily to nonexisting legal premises as though they existed, a maximally open legal system goes one step further and does not distinguish at all between legal and nonlegal propositions. Here in this ideal open system the judge makes and does not merely discover law.

It was pointed out earlier that a legal code has been regarded as the mirror of society (Dietze 1964:63–88). It is the iconic sign, or subject of the continuous discourse in a legal system. That which is predicated of it—the legal acts – are indexical signs. But we want to recall that in the dynamic process of developing an idea, or any continuous idea such as the concept of law, sign functions shift with reference to shifting contexts. Thus, from this perspective, *the laws from which the rules are inferred are also questions.*

Berman (1977) shows that the medieval lawmen understood problems in the Codex, or codes of law, to be questions of law, or *quaestiones.* He discusses at some length the process of questioning the law (906–909) and says:

> Dialectical reasoning is distinguished above all by the fact that it does not start with 'propositions,' that is, with declarative statements that must be either true or false, but rather with 'problems,' or questions about which people may differ, although ultimately the disputed question will be resolved conclusively by a proposition, or first principle, in favor of one side or the other if valid methods of dialectical reasoning are used. (1975:911)

He also adds that it was the Roman jurists who changed the process of the Greek dialectic "from an art of discovery (*ars inveniendi*) to an art of judging (*ars iudicandi*)" (916).

But it is to Peirce that one owes the understanding that all feeling— impression as well as conviction and belief—are actually signs of value judgements, or interpretant signs, throughout any given process of inquiry. A legal decision at each stage of the continuum of law appears as a symbolic kind of sign, or legisign in Peirce's sense. Actually, in each case of inquiry, the final judgment is always provisional and passes in function from predominantly symbolic sign to predominantly iconic sign or subject–theme of a subsequent argument or inquiry.

In this context one can suggest some clarification of the concept of *stare decisis.* Particularly in Anglo-American legal systems, the legal speech act, decision, rests on at least two distinctive "ideal" procedures.

The first is procedure by precedent, which requires that in each particular case the judge must appeal to existing, relevant rule, that is, to that which is inferred from the code.

The second of these two ideal procedures may be described, following Wasserstrom (1961:7), as procedure by equity in which the judge decides the particular case by "appealing to that which is just or equitable for the particular case." Still a third procedure, suggested by Wasserstrom, is one we identify with relatively open legal systems; this third procedure does appeal to established rules for precedent, but in each case it is not bound by precedent. Neither is equity in itself a sufficient condition for decision. But the judge acts as an ideal legislator (in Gény's sense, 1899) and refers to his own personal values which presumably reflect or mirror general social claims and values, and thus acts as a legislator might if the present facts of the social context had been known at the time of legislating. The judge in this case conserves the code, but in actuality the innovative decision introduces new law based on the judiciary response to the implied or articulated questions of society.

The concerns of philosophy, linguistics, and law have traditionally been intertwined. The methods in each case distinguish the disciplines; a method of inquiry has to do only incidentally with the sharing of certain data, for instance, legal speech acts, but essentially with the kinds of questions that are raised in response to these data.

Philosophers and linguists all recommend that their respective analyses of speech acts be applied to legal procedure. The irony is that just as ethics cannot be separated from legitimized conduct, the idea of acts—of legal speech acts— continues to reveal its initial implication of law. It is recalled, for example, that the bifurcated concept of law in Aristotle holding that, on the one hand, the purpose of law is to effect compliance with such legal instruments that represent the will of society, holds on the other hand that law aims to bring about justice. As positive law evolved, particularly in the late eighteenth and nineteenth centuries, law and ethics or morality again became conceptually opposed. Again we find that the legal act presupposes ethical moral conduct. This conduct, according to John Austin, must be externally observable, yet it derives from wishes and desires and the need to realize one's wants in social intercourse, that is, from questions. Austin's emphasis, as in other theses on positive law, assumes that the will of the people will coincide with the ideal code of law, as commanded. But in common law, the legal system is clearly a system or instrument, directly responsive to the wishes of the people. The basic underlying principle of the controversial concept of the social contract is again revived in modern legal realism. The problem of mapping morality into law is examined later.

The concluding part of this chapter touches on a few significant topics in the following order: First, it discusses some of the philosophical notions of speech acts that influenced the now abundant literature on linguistic analyses of speech acts: Sadock (1974), Longacre (1976), Kevelson (1977, 1978b), Kuno (1972), Bennett (1977). Second, it gives an overview of Maitland's famous study (1909/1971) of the forms of action in English law, especially as it pertains to interest in legal speech acts and to the interrogative construction of decisions. Third, in a few words it attempts to summarize some basic tenets of Rayfield's *Action: An Analysis of the Concept* (1972).

It has become customary to credit the philosopher J. L. Austin with introducing the term *speech acts* into our legal lexicons. As Lyons notes (1977:727), Austin challenged "the restrictive view of meaning held by the logical positivists, according to whom the only fully meaningful utterances were empirically verifiable statements. . . ." The linguistic concern with speech acts countered the early Chomskean view which excluded *meaning* from language analysis, and adopted his revised position in which he maintains that a theory of "generative grammar must provide a general, language-independent means for representing the signals and semantic interpretations that are interrelated by the grammars of particular languages" (Chomsky, in Searle 1971:71–82).

J. L. Austin's concern relates to a philosophical persepctive holding that human conduct is determined by the underlying verbal structure of natural language and that a study of speech acts is really a study in human interrelationships and human goals as signified by ethical concepts and values. In the 1960s Austin defined action as the goal of deliberate purpose. Austin says here that the Aristotelian problem of the Good, with which ethical behavior has been confused, has led to problematic distinctions in language between statements that have a so-called truth value, that is, *substantives*, and utterances that may or may not be true but that effect interpersonal communication; these latter he called *performatives*.

The study of speech acts is the study of performatives (J. L. Austin 1968:1–31; 1975). Austin asks what makes a statement true. Further, he says that there are some statements that are not statements at all, in the sense of being analytical, that is, derived from true premises from which true consequences may be inferred. Speech acts are communicative acts because we require that there be a shared system of conventionalized verbal signs which a speaker can produce at will and which an audience can "observe" or understand (1968:121).

A statement is not a statement "when it is a formula in a calculus: when it is a performatory utterance: when it is a value-judgment: when it is a definition: when it is part of the work of a fiction . . ." (Austin 1968:131). Austin did not add that a statement is not a statement when it is an answer to an implied or explicit question, such as a definition (Caws 1959). In this context it is worth mentioning that Peirce distinguishes between an immediate action that refers to ethical standards and signs and a projected or imagined action that refers to ideal goals and aesthetic values (CP 7.201; 1.591–2).

It is evident in many works on speech acts in both linguistics and philosophy that the legal model is often implied in analyses of speech acts. This is especially apparent in Grice (1968) and to a lesser extent in Searle (1969). One might say that an obverse analogy holds, namely, that just as the legal argument is the prototype of arguments in general, the legal speech act is the prototypical speech act.

So deeply is it ingrained in Western thought that only responsible people act and therefore that only "actors" are legal entities whereas irresponsible people merely *behave*, that it is easy to see how the principle actors of a society came to be identified with authoritative, official legal actors: these legal actors comprise the agents of a legal system, the highest-ranking of whom is the judge. Technically, an *act* is part of an official legal system whereas *conduct* in the ordinary sense of the term, is not official but is related to everyday and nonlegal behavior.

Similarly, the notion of *justice*, however defined, is rooted in a community's sense of what is legitimate in interpersonal transactions which may be but are not necessarily regulated by explicit law.

According to this understanding, only legal persons, that is, those recognized as responsible under law, commit legal acts. Maitland's book, coming at the turn of the century (1909) is remarkable in its attempt to systematize the forms of action in English common law so that we understand each action form as a particular kind of sign structure with characteristic functions and styles, each with respect to the context of the larger, ideal process called the legal system.

Although each action has its own process of originating, of concluding, of expressing formulaic utterances, for example, in pleas, trials, and judgments or decisions, all actions in English law share in common basic features: "It is not enough that in some way or another [a man] should compel his adversary to appear in court and should then state in the words that naturally occur to him the facts on which he relies and the remedy to which he thinks himself entitled" (Maitland 1909/1971:1–9).

Maitland speaks of eight levels of questioning, each described as a form of action: from the time a plaintiff considers presenting his case to official legal actors to the termination of the legal sentence imposed by the deciding judge. An act in this sense is a consequence, or decision, at every stage of the legal procedure and correspondes to what Peirce's methodology attempts to explain.

Following the Judicature Act of 1873, the rules that were supposed to underlie the forms of action were ultimately disparaged, Maitland says. It is around this time that the period of modern law begins, in which law and justice become opposed and not "administered concurrently" (1909/1971:7).

Maitland goes on to say that, following this act, English law

> no longer . . . knows a certain number of actions and no more, or that every action has a writ appropriate to itself; the writ is always the same, the number of possible endorsements is as infinite as the number of unlawful acts and defaults which can give one man an action against another. . . . There may be as many forms of action as there are causes of action (ibid., 5).

A few remarks to conclude: Following H. L. A. Hart's distinction (in "The Ascription of Responsibility and Rights" 1963) between doing and acting, Rayfield argues against John Austin's concept of voluntary action as a willed obedience to command and against his "additive analysis" of acts, referred to earlier. Rayfield suggests that a theory of acts must include a more satisfactory approach to omissions, or forbearances, in law and must include, as John Austin did not, acts that are not external but refer to internal dialogues and deliberations. As noted, Rayfield says that a choice and a decision are one and the same. Also, a choice, a decision, and an action considered as an answer to an implied question in decision making are but different aspects of the same act. Rayfield correctly notes that there is a problem in talking about acts: for example, to say that X *did* Y is merely descriptive discourse is prescriptive; that is, presuming the head legal actor finds the accused guilty of such and such and utters the selected decision, the decision carries with it the whole ensuing consequence of legal action against the guilty person.

Peirce describes this process as a "continuous predicate." This aspect of hypotactic discourse structure was discussed earlier. The prescriptive aspect of a legal decision in referring to an act does, as Hart points out, "ascribe responsibility."

In concluding this chapter I suggest that further study of legal speech acts, particularly of the decision in modern courts of law, must deeply question whether nonresponsible persons, in the traditional legal sense, can perform legal acts. If they cannot, as is still the fact in the case of young children, question their rights, or as in the case of incapacitated persons or convicted criminals, be considered responsible persons, how does the court talk about their *acts*? The kinds of decisions courts make will indicate, as answer, the nature and complexity of the question the legal actor investigates.

CHAPTER 9

Pure Play

RULES OF LAW AND RULES OF CONDUCT

This chapter is not a polemic. It provides links between legitimacy and legality. It opens inquiry on the following questions:

1. In what sense can Peirce's concept of aesthetic freedom—free play— be reconciled with the prevailing prescriptive notion of a normative aesthetics?
2. If a process of inquiry is itself a sign in Peirce's philosophy, how do we communicate our objects of inquiry through philosophical dialogue which, in this case, is inquiry into aspects of American legal philosophy? If the process is undetermining and open-ended, how do we identify and define the goal?
3. How may the process for choosing leading principles of inquiry be applied in the selection of those underlying principles or values that determine the structures of legal codes and of the ethical codes that regulate behavior of official legal actors, for instance, jurists, legislators, and lawyers?

Because Peirce used the term *Semiotics* or *Semeiotic* synonymously with the whole of his pragmatic philosophy, it is appropriate here to consider that legal semiotics be firmly grafted onto the broad girth of American philosophy and American legal philosophy. The kernel of Peirce's semiotics is found in the three papers of 1868 and 1869 in *The Journal of Speculative Philosophy*: "Questions Concerning Certain Faculties Claimed for Man," "Some Consequences of Four Incapacities Claimed for Man," and "Grounds of Validity of the Laws of Logic." These and other sources of specific focus on Peirce's semiotics are suggested in "The New Tools of Peirce Scholarship" (Fisch, Ketner, and Kloesel 1979).

Law and philosophy at this time are confronted with questions that suggest confidence in the advancement of American traditions of thought, but that, at the same time, do not clearly predict the directions vanguard studies might possibly take. Apropos of this uncertainty is an anecdote about the late Justice Holmes: When, in his retirement years, Justice Holmes was traveling through one of the southern states, he was approached by the train conductor, who asked to see his ticket. Holmes fished through the pockets of his vest, his trousers, his topcoat, but could not produce the ticket. Now the conductor recognized Holmes as a vaguely familiar, distinguished public figure and said, "Sir, there's no problem. All you have to do is mail in the ticket when you find it, or send in the money if you don't." But Holmes, pulling himself up to his full authoritative stature, said, "My dear conductor, you don't seem to realize precisely what the problem is. The problem is not the ticket. The problem is, just where is this train going?"

This chapter will not ask the obvious but rather will remind that, as John McDermott points out in *The Culture of Experience* (1976), the focus on pragmatics, or on experience in American thought, is not merely a preliminary approach to American philosophy but is quintessentially its core. As in philosophy, so in jurisprudence. . . .

According to Peirce, rational inquiry proceeds from simple to complex signs, that is to say, from simple perceptions of experiential life to more complex judgments, or sign relationships of life experience.[1] The actual world is the ground or origin for each process of rational inquiry—a mediating process of signs and sign relationships—into the actual world which is then reinterpreted and recreated more meaningfully. How does it happen? What is the process of such inquiry? How do we know with which hypothesis to begin? Peirce suggests that through play, or musement, a hypothesis is entertained, is evolved into a rule of behavior, and then becomes subject to logical analysis.

Pragmatists like Dewey and James, taking their cues from Peirce, agree that the actual, experiential world far exceeds and overflows our ability to know it.[2] We know it to the extent that we create more complex systems of signs to communicate about it. The signs we use to express our thoughts and judgments—our feelings which are value judgments of our immediate sense perceptions—are the ways by which we define reality.[3] But definition is a device which is very useful, in science and especially in law, for setting out problems, as Caws points out (1959). The definition considered as a provisional judgment is nothing less than a question: a question that is open-ended but is nevertheless presented in the familiar sign structure of the propositional truth statement. In this sense these questions before us are part of the constituted code of philosophical inquiry. The definition in law *is* the "rule of law."

Dewey reminds us (1939:1043) that in an empirical philosophy the notion of continuity governs the traditional opposition between concepts of nature and experience. Max Fisch points out that in classic American philosophy with its focus on experience, "Anticipation is . . . more primary than recollection; projection than summoning the past; the prospective than the retrospective. . . ." Therefore the possible, imagined values projected into the future, govern our activities, according to a pragmatist's view (1951:21–25, quoting from Dewey's *Creative Intelligence* [1917]).

It should be noted that the term *code* is often used in a figurative sense: language codes, codes of social conduct. The term *Code* in its nonfigurative sense refers to legal codes, for instance, the Justinian Codex. The Codex is specifically associated with those legal questions (*questiones*) or problems that circumscribed the domain of inquiry for students of the early law schools.[4] Since the development of modern semiotics, particularly in the last twenty years, *code* has come to stand for any normative, prescriptive set of rules that is said to regulate behavior. Thus it has come to stand for any normative, prescriptive set of rules that regulates sign systems. A language code, for example, refers to both natural language and artificial languages considered as sign systems. Economic codes refer to currency transactions and exchange. Codes of conduct refer to sign systems that in a more general way regulate sex, talk, and agreement. More specifically, we have legal codes that refer to rules for legal acting and include what has been come to be called speech acts.

Each of these systems is not identical with the way we order experience in an immediate way, that is, according to patterns of sensation. Neither do they necessarily refer to one another or represent one another. Yet they are in some basic sense isomorphic with one another in any given social system. Such institutionalized systems are mediate organizations of signs and sign systems that stand in place of immediate experience and permit us to make communication of experience possible.

The genius of Peirce lies largely in his having distinguished the Cartesians who discount from rational inquiry that which experience permits us to rest our beliefs on, from the pragmatists who say that experience is mediated through signs.

The subject of a discourse is predominantly an iconic sign. The comments or predications of a subject are predominately indexical sign functions. Our conclusions or final judgments are like laws—"legisigns"—of a predominately symbolic sign function, but such judgments are provisional and become the themes—logical types or grammatical subjects—for further inquiry. The provisional nature of a judgment implies that the world as we can conceive it is indeterminate.

As McDermott emphasizes (1976), it is Peirce to whom we look in order to understand "the dialectic between the press of experience and the wisdom of reflection."[5] The action from experience occasions doubt which leads to inquiry and thus to new belief and new value. The form that surprise takes, which Peirce identifies with the impact of experience on belief, is a form of the comic. Thus surprise, or the awakening of disbelief, is identified with an aspect of traditional aesthetic classification. Specifically, the aspect of the comic that introduces new form and value has been identified with the grotesque,[6] as discussed earlier.

Traditionally, the grotesque has signified the fusion of two or more frames of reference, or universes of discourse, in a novel and deliberately distorted form. It is precisely this distortion that is perceived against the background of familiar, normative forms that form the setting for the emergence of new values. Consider what Peirce regards as a universe of discourse: ". . . the total of all that we consider possible is called the *universe* of discourse, and may be very limited. One mode of limiting our discourse is by considering only what actually occurs, so that everything which does not occur is regarded as impossible" (CP 3.174). But he proposes that the term *universe* include and denote frames of reference that on different occasions denote different aspects of individuals in their sign relationships (CP 3.65, 174, 573).

Peirce suggests that new values emerge through the overlapping of universes of discourse in the kind of modal reasoning his Delta and Gamma graphs were intended to express and describe. It is his logic of relatives, he says, viewed against the background of nonrelative logic, that sets "everything in logic in a new light and greatly enlarges or metamorphizes every conception." This observation, made in 1905 in a letter to the philosopher F. C. S. Schiller (CSP/FCSS 5.12.05), takes place in the context of a discussion of a "transfigured esthetics." In this same letter Peirce refers to his 1903 Lowell lectures, wherein he says that "logic ought to be founded on Ethics and Ethics on a transfigured Esthetics which would be the science of value, although now wrongly treated as part of Ethics."

Peirce's relative or metamorphizing logic is not founded on the sense of beauty, the *summum bonum* of traditional esthetics, but rather on emergent value, which initially is seen as plausible, possibly credible, and which tends then to displace prevailing judgment which functions as a symbolic sign and as a rule for ethical behavior.[7] Peirce's subordination of ethics to esthetics leads to principles—motivating principles—upon which ethical behavior is defined. Ethics in turn is subjected to logical analysis on the three levels of syntax, semantics, and pragmatics that correspond with Peirce's subdivisions of speculative grammar, critic, and methodology (speculative, rhetoric, or methodeutic).

Analogously, in law as in ordinary behavior which falls outside the bounds of legal authority, ethical codes are based on commonly assumed prevailing values, that is, on presuppositions that themselves are not clear-cut but are vaguely sensed to correspond with predominant, changing social customs and mores.

For example, in *The New York Times* (August 19, 1979)[8] was an article on the changing ethics of lawyers. It was suggested here that a lawyer's code of ethics should parallel the legal code that serves to prescribe legitimate interpersonal behavior for society as a whole and that such a code or responsibility should function prescriptively for legal practitioners.

The first such code was introduced about a hundred years ago. Its ruling principle was little more than the subjective appeal to the conscience and compassion of each individual lawyer. In 1887, a more formal code of legal ethics was adopted by the Alabama State Bar Association, based on the stance taken by the already deceased Justice George Sharswood. His lectures, interpreted as a sign, were then reinterpreted into a revised code of professional legal ethics. But when the code was again revised in 1970, the leading principle was not much different from that of a century before, despite the fact that society had changed in radical ways and that the consciences of lawyers had, correspondingly, changed. Now, however, instead of individual conscience we have collective lawyers; we have the corporate legal department, the legal team. The new code has had to consider a number of new questions, among which are the following: (1) What is the distinction between an incompetent lawyer and one who performs poorly? and (2) Who, precisely, is the legal client represented by the lawyer; for example, is the lawyer of a corporation representing its shareholders or its trustees, and is the lawyer appointed to represent the poor, unable to pay for fees and services representing this person or, rather, an ideological state principle? A new code of legal ethics will have to distinguish between actual, subjective lawyer's bias and the judgment that results from intercourse between the law and the public.

It will be suggested in this chapter that the values that may underlie ethical codes for lawyers, as well as those codes that regulate the behavior of self-controlled individuals in society as a whole, may be derived and accounted for through one neglected aspect of Peirce's philosophy: his normative esthetics, which was profoundly influenced by Schiller's concepts of aesthetic play.

As mentioned in Chapter 7, in 1857 Peirce wrote that the poet Schiller's *Formtrieb*, which he understood to be equivalent with the "I impulse and faculty" may be interpreted as corresponding with the then prevailing lawyers' code which, as mentioned above, appealed to lawyers' conscience. Peirce finds that the *Stofftrieb* of which Schiller speaks is equivalent to the "It impulse and faculty"; this, we may infer, corresponds with a kind of legal positivism, with its emphasis on precedential rules and on deductive, syllogistic reasoning, and offers lawyers a kind of objective ethical code. But the *Spieltrieb*, which Peirce says is equivalent with the "Thou impulse and faculty," corresponds with a code of ethics which presumes that governing values and value judgments are the result of interactive, dialogic communication, that is, a process of semiosis, in which the *I* and the *Thou* are shifting functions (ms 1633.9 ISP; also Kevelson 1977).

Years later, in 1911, Peirce said that it had been more than a half-century since he had read what he considered the only significant book on esthetics, the "only one professing to cover the whole subject . . . the work of the poet Schiller . . . (whose) theory was that beauty is the expression of the Spieltrieb. . . ." But by 1911 Peirce understood that what is meant by beauty has only peripherally to do with artistic beauty; it has largely to do with beauty in the sense of emergent value—that traditional antithesis to beauty that has been called the grotesque and that Peirce wrote "is a matter of play, whether idle play or busy play" (ms 675, draft pp. 14–16, c. 1911).

Recognition of beauty, in Peirce's sense, is less closely related to his phenomenology as suggested by Kent (1976) and others than to his concept of abductive, or retroductive reasoning. Peirce considered that all reasoning is, at bottom, hypothetical. He related beauty to hypothetical reasoning in the following: "Both sensations and conceptions are hypothetic predicates." That is, they are indexical signs, commenting on antecedent subjects, or predominantly iconic signs. But the hypothesis of sensation and that of conceptualization are very different manifestations of indexicality. While a concept evolves to a kind of predominantly symbolic sign function, the sensation, processed to become a sign of feeling in its first instance, culminates in a lesser kind of symbolic sign function, that is, a name. "A sensation is a sort of mantel name. To assign a name to a thing is to make a hypothesis" (ms 357.2).[9]

In their remarkable and sensitive commentary on Schiller's *Aesthetic Letters,* Wilkinson and Willoughby stress that Schiller did not associate the play spirit with art only, but that he intended to relate the *Spieltrieb* with "its manifold functions in human culture as a whole." They point out that Schiller's point was entirely missed by Kant, by neo-Kantians, and by the pregmatists such as James and Dewey who followed Pierce. Baumgarten, who introduced the concept of a normative aesthetics in 1750, understood, as did Peirce, that normative science should be subdivided into logic, ethics, and esthetics. Baumgarten stressed that esthetics was not primarily concerned with taste or with sensations; but, rather, esthetics should account for a mode of knowledge (Wilkinson and Willoughby, p. xx).[10]

Herbert Spencer introduced a notion of play which he attributed to a "German author whose name he forgot" which associates the play spirit with aesthetics. We know that Spencer was a senior member of the Metaphysical Club with which Peirce was associated (1870–1872) and we may safely assume that the discussions here focused on the senior members' concern with law, with psychology as in Spencer's case, and with relative logic, as Peirce was beginning to explore it. Peirce did not formulate the divisions of his normative sciences until years later, in 1903: his rejection of Spencer's work was well known.

Discussion of play often turns to Huizinga because of his *Homo Ludens.* But Wilkinson and Willoughby correctly point out that Huizinga missed the point of Schiller's notion of play, which holds that the play spirit in esthetics is not merely an activity preliminary to the production of works of art, nor an activity— a consummate experience, in Dewey's sense, equivalent to the person's total apprehension of an event—but, rather, an experience of freedom. They find that particularly in Peirce's pragmatics Schiller's ideas are correctly interpreted, especially those concepts that treat the relation between differentiation and continuity and the relation between biological inheritance and capacities for creating values which are, in Peirce's sense, isomorphic with our physiopsychological dispositions. Wilkinson and Willoughby explicitly regret that Peirce did not fully develop the correlation between semiotics and Schiller's theories of play and esthetics. Of Peirce, Wilkinson and Willoughby write:

> . . . He possessed the two prime qualifications necessary for the task: unusual feeling for the work itself, combined with the logical and linguistic bias which makes him the acknowledged precurser of contemporary linguistic philosophies. . . . It seems more than probable that the importance Peirce continued to attach to the work (i.e., *The Aesthetic Letters*) was not unconnected with the conclusions he eventually reached [that although] aesthetics and logic seem, at first blush, to belong to different universes . . . that seeming is illusory, and that, on the contrary, logic needs the help of aesthetics. . . . When our logic shall have paid its *devoirs* to Esthetics and Ethics, it will be time for it to settle down to its regular business. (CP 5.402; 2.197–200)[11]

A primary requisite for a philosophical investigation of Schiller's play is the willingness not to be bound by any prior systems of thought but to be free of the tendency to make Schiller over "in the philosopher's own image" (Wilkinson and Willoughby, introduction). Peirce, especially in his concept of ideal value, returned to Schiller's concepts in his mature work:

> The beautiful is to be neither mere life, nor mere form, but living form . . . for it imposes upon man the double law of absolute formality and absolute reality. Consequently, Reason also makes its pronouncements: With beauty man shall only play, and it is with Beauty only that he shall play.[12]

A more penetrating comparison between Schiller's aesthetic and Peirce's semiotic philosophy is not possible at this time; but such a projected study should disclose that Peirce should be viewed not only as the precurser of pragmatics but also as the founder of a new mode of philosophical inquiry which identifies freedom as the highest value and which looks to law to release such value. Until Peirce's methodology is seen in relation with his esthetics, the normative function of ethical signs and of responsible behavior under law will not be realized in practical affairs.[13]

We have equated esthetics in Peirce's system with the science of value.[14] It is helpful to understand what is meant by *value* in contemporary research. The study of value and value theory is older than Plato, and Lotze may generally be regarded as the originator of modern value theory.[15] Ralph Perry defined *axiology* as the study of values; his definitions have guided inquiry since World

War II. Rescher, for example, says that pragmatists following Dewey argue against Aristotelian distinctions between "means values and end values" (1969), but he fails to consider that in Peirce the process of creating new value is itself the motivating value of philosophic inquiry.

Peirce asks,

> What does right reasoning consist in? It consists in such reasoning as shall be conducive to our ultimate aim. What, then, is our ultimate aim? . . . If we had . . . no other aim than the pleasure of the moment . . . we should have no ideal of reasoning, and consequently, no norm. It seems to me that the logician ought to recognize what our ultimate aim is. It would seem to be the business of the moralist to find this out, and that the logician has to accept the teaching of ethics in this regard. But the moralist, as far as I can make out, merely tells us that we have a power of self-control, that no narrow or selfish aim can ever prove satisfactory, that the only satisfactory aim is the broadest, and the most general aim; and for any more definite information, as we conceive the matter, has to refer to the esthetician, whose business it is to say what is the state of things, which is admirable in itself regardless of any ulterior reason. (CP 1.611)[16]

In this comment Peirce brings together the two traditionally disparate goals of a legal system: civil law according to statute and equity according to custom and the will of the people. These two goals were bifurcated in the Aristotelian system of ethics and have remained in dichotomized relation until the turn of this century.[17] Their relationship is controversial today, especially with respect to the mapping of morality onto law. (See Chapter 12.)

In this same year, 1903, Peirce also said that all ideals are of a general nature. All ideas are capable of being represented by a sign, however complex the referent ideational sign relationships may be. It is essential, he says, that the ideal as sign be coherent. Every idea, as sign, must represent a single ideal. It must have unity, "because it is an idea, and unity is essential to every idea and every ideal . . ." (CP 1.613).

That which is admirable in itself—an ideal, or sign of the general of an idea—must never be considered stationary. The dynamics of every ideal—of every motivating value—spring from a feeling, an originating sign of judgment, such that the process of reasoning is never a closed process but is always vital and pragmatically consequential. "Reason looks forward to an endless future and expects endlessly to improve its results" (CP 1.614). This, as we know, is the basis for Peirce's doctrine of "fallibilism," which presumes that the world is continually becoming, being made or crafted in the Stoic sense, into the practice and conduct of life.

Thus every act is consequential and every consequence is tentative. Every act invites a reaction—a secondness, or sign of indexicality—which we find to correspond to conflict and interaction in the actual, experiential world. Every reaction has a potential corrective function and is therefore, from the view of aesthetics, comic; every new value resulting from such comic procedures is perceived as grotesque.

Traditionally, as we have said, the structure of ethical behavior conforms to the hypotactic structure of authoritative address; by contrast, the dialogic structure (parataxis) has come to be associated with attenuated play, and with dramatic dialogue in liturgical refrain, and ordinary conversation. But Peirce, following Schiller, bases his methodology on dialogic interaction and grounds his esthetics—his science of values—on an *I–Thou* event. It is this concept that gives impetus to Peirce's metamorphizing logic.

Again, Peirce contrasts syllogistic reasoning with dialogistic reasoning, the latter term having originated with Vico. The dialogism in its original sense (as an interpretant sign) is a rhetorical strategy of argument which "makes present" to the imagination objects which are actually absent and merely possible. Peirce, in his mathematical studies, followed his father, Benjamin Peirce, in admitting imaginaries into mathematical considerations; we know, also, that imginaries had a strong function in his methodology with respect to his understanding of possibility in modal logic. Peirce's dialogism is discussed in Kevelson (1982, 1985).[18]

Peirce writes in "Ideals of Conduct" (1903): ". . . the development of Reason requires as a part of it the occurrence of the more individual events than ever can occur . . . the development of Reason consists, you will observe, in embodiment, that is, in manifestation . . ." (CP 1.615).[19]

The year before, 1902, had found Peirce anticipating the pragmatic notion of the aesthetic function. In his paper "Minute Logic" Peirce says that we must come to a radically different interpretation of the traditional relation between logic, ethics, and esthetics. If, in the traditional sense, they are representative of the "arts of reasoning," the "conduct of life" and the "fine arts," respectively, a semiotic perspective can not consider these divisions as part of a normative science. Although the object of normative science is to study what ought to be, the normative processes, signs in themselves, are not *oughts* but *ises* which represent *maybes*. The normative sciences, viewed in themselves as a means–end process of semiosis, are not to be identified with an *account* of ideals.[20] Peirce, in referring to Pascal's observation, "La vraie se moque de la morale" (reality mocks morality), points out that the word mock should be understood as another word for representation, that is, an interpretant sign upon which actual, experiential life is modelled. Here the word *mock* corresponds to the colloquial expression *mock-up*, which is a model, or sign upon which full-scale and practical systems are constructed.

Peirce finds, in his review of Aristotle's *Ethics* (*The Nation,* 1906),[21] that Aristotelian ethics overlooks the fact that people do not immediately will their behavior but, rather, that will is the result of the cultivation of habit. The habit of willing, so closely tied to what Peirce understands as the result of freeplay,

requires "repeated performances of any action in vivid and detailed imagination . . . almost as effectual in creating a habit of so acting, as if the outward
acts were really performed" (reprinted in Ketner and Cook 1979:278).

This acting out of the desired ideal in imagination, as a means of developing
the will to act virtuously, or ethically, is one of the consequences of what Peirce
calls play or musement. Another consequence is that through play one strengthens
one's hypothesis of the ultimate ideal, of the hypothesis of God. In play one
proceeds from inner to outer "nests" of hypothesis and sequentially considers
the ideal in each of the three hierarchically ordered universes. The first universe
"comprises all mere Ideas," the second universe encompasses "Brute Actuality
of things and facts," and the third universe is "everything whose being consists
in active power to establish connections between different objects in different
Universes." Speaking of these connection, Peirce says:

> Such is everything which is essentially a Sign—not the mere body of the Sign, which
> is essentially such, but, so to speak, the Sign's Soul, which has its being in its power
> of serving as intermediant between its Object and a Mind. Such, too, is a living
> consciousness, and such the life, the power, the growth, of a plant. Such is a living
> constitution—a daily newspaper, a great fortune, a social 'movement. . . . (from
> "The Neglected Argument," 1908; CP 6.467)[22]

Of the value of freedom, Peirce says, "The very first and most fundamental
element that we have to assume is a Freedom, or Chance, or Spontaneity, by
virtue of which the general, vague nothing-in-particularness that preceded the
chaos took a thousand definite qualities." Next, we must assume that there may
possibly have been an infinite number of accidental modifications of such qualities, and the possibility of what did not occur is part of our view of what is
(1898, CP 6.200).

In this same year, 1898, in "The Logic of Events," Peirce contrasted the
"boundless freedom" of nothingness—the all-in-nothing potentiality of zero
sign[23]—with the delimitations of pragmatic freedom. Pure boundless freedom,
pure potentiality, can only annul itself: "It remains a completely idle and do-
nothing potentiality; and a completely idle potentiality is annulled by its complete
idleness."[24]

As Schiller insisted, in the society "where conduct is governed by beauty,
in the aesthetic State," persons do not seek to restrict the freedom of another by
force or by the support of restrictive and legitimated codes of law; rather, in the
esthetic state persons confront persons in the mutuality of free play: "To bestow
freedom by means of freedom is the fundamental law of this Kingdom."[25] Yet,
if the legal institution of a society is to protect the deepest values of its people,
then free play, as a manifestation of the esthetic function, must be integral with
our system of law. Indeed, the free play of the market, as will be discussed,
has such a function.

Peirce's view of freedom as the leading principle or the esthetic ideal governing ethics may be represented in the following: "Pure play . . . is a lively exercise of one's powers. Pure play has no rules, except this very law of liberty. . . . the one ordinance of Play (is) the law of liberty" (1958:6.458, 460, 461, 463, 467).[26]

The *summum bonum* is thus the freedom to break the rules that have been codified. It is the freedom to doubt what one formerly believed. It is the freedom to modify one's habitual conduct and the freedom also to will such change. It is the freedom—the only absolute freedom—to reject any law or system of laws that has previously been referred to *as though* it were fixed and eternal. It is the freedom to regard all judgment as provisional and nevertheless to act freely according to one's existing judgment in a controlled, responsible, and ethical manner.

The main point herein is that when the highest good is conceived as freedom, rather than as a form of constraint, then a normative code of specifically legal enjoinders in the form of possibilities will replace a deontic code. Thus the code of *may be*'s would supplant the code of *ought to*'s which characterizes the analysis of law based on commands. A normative freedom would be the object of a quest from a Peircean perspective on ethical and legal orders.

NOTES

1. See Peirce's "On the Origin of Signs" (CP 3.159). Also, refer to his 1893 paper "Association," on the "occult" source of signs in the imagination and on the "free play" of imagination.

2. See Dewey (1934:272–297). See also McDermott (1976) who says that ". . . aesthetic sensibility does not denote exclusive or even necessary relationship to the world of art. In this, we follow the lead of John Dewey, for whom all experiencing is potentially aesthetic" (xii, xiii). See also Morton White (1955:174, 176) on the "mediating" ethics of Dewey; see also his interpretation of how pragmatism evolved, so that "Peirce's pragmatic theory of meaning was carried over to 'true' by James and by Dewey to 'good' . . ." (17).

3. Peirce, in "Forms of Consciousness" (CP 7.540), discusses how Kant has distorted Tetens's concept of feeling. Peirce says that what he will mean by feeling directly follows Tetens: "Take whatever is directly and immediately in consciousness at any instant, just as it is, without regard to what it signifies, to what its parts are, to what causes it, or any of its relations to anything else. . . ."

4. This point is made by Berman (1977).

5. See McDermott (1977:16, 17).

6. Kevelson writes on the relation between the grotesque as an esthetic category and the tradition of anarchism in western societies (forthcoming 1987). See also Prall (1936) for discussion of the domain of the esthetic (1936:4, 5, 8, 11, 12, 13, 25, 29, 172, 176, 196).

7. See Morris (1970, 1946).

8. See Tom Goldstein's "Attorneys Pondering the Ethics of their Trade," *The New York Times*, August 19, 1979, E7.

9. See Kent (1976).

10. See Wilkinson and Willoughby (1967); they discuss in their introduction the singular ability of Peirce correctly to understand what Schiller means by the Aesthetic (clxxxiiii–clxxxix); see also their translations, particularly, of Letters XV, XIV, XXVII, XXVI, XXIII.

11. In addition to Kent's work on Peirce's esthetics (above) see also Hocutt ((1962); Morris (1939:131–150); Bernstein (1971:191–219); Feibleman (1949:402–404); Kevelson (1981, 1977); also Morawski (1974).

12. See Wilkinson and Willoughby (1967:105), Letter XV.

13. See Kevelson (1987).

14. Richard Rorty, presidential address, American Philosophical Association, December 1979, printed in *Proceedings and Addresses* (August 1980:719).

15. See Fisch, Ketner, and Kloesell (1979).

16. See Rescher (1969: particularly 54–59.

17. For discussion of the process, in Peirce, from the pre-ethical, through the ethical, to esthetic judgments, see Walter Krolikowski, "The Peircean Vir," in Moore and Robin (1964:257–77).

18. See Kevelson (1982d).

19. See Kevelson (1982a).

20. See Peirce's review of S. E. Mazes' work on Ethics (*The Nation* 73 Oct. 1901, reprinted in Ketner and Cook (1979). See also Peirce's understanding of the "magic" of imagination in scientific inquiry (CP 1.47, 48).

21. See Bernstein (1971).

22. See Peirce's review "Aristotle's Ethics" (*The Nation* 83 1906 226–7, reprinted in Ketner and Cook (1979).

23. See Kevelson (1978a).

24. See Kevelson (1987). See also J. Sully, "Aesthetics" in *Encyclopedia Brittanica*, Vol. 1 (1904:212–224; also C. J. Ducasse (1964:71–83). A distorted interpretation of Schiller's play is given in Croce, *The Aesthetic* (1909). See also discussion of play in Dewey (1920) and also a reduced, restricted concept of play in Santayana's *Sense of Beauty*.

25. See Nagel (1979:329–335) for discussion of what he calls a "fortuitous hypothesis" with regard to the Peircean concept of chance, spontaneity, and freedom.

26. See particularly Schiller's Letter XXVII (Wilkinson and Willoughby (1967:215).

CHAPTER 10

Limits of Authority in Law

The previous chapter pointed to freedom as the ultimate value of an open, moving society and its institutions. This chapter examines such boundaries as pushed open by the value of freedom and as resisted by authority and the bounds and constraints of spatiotemporal systems.

The nineteenth century has been characterized by scholars in many fields by its quest for authority. In this century the seat of authority has shifted from metaphysics to physics, from essential supremacy to existential supremacy. It is the age of the fact. Peirce himself stressed the ruling principle of dynamics which distinguished the age by identifying factiveness with his category of secondness.[1]

The distinctive feature of the fact is its oppositional, adversarial, agonistic, conflictual character. In its predominant sign function the sign represents experience. Peirce's own epithet for the nineteenth century was "the galvanic era."[2] Yet, although he has been a child of his age or, in his words, "a person of the strongest possible physicistic prejudices," it was surprising even to him to "have been brought to the deep conviction that there is some essentially and irreducibly other element in the universe than pure dynamism . . ." (1907; CP 6.322).

Peirce's search for nearly half a century, he said, had been for a "genuine triadic relation . . . one that does not consist in a mere collocation of dyadic relations, or the negative of such . . ." (CP 6.322). It is only through an understanding of a genuine triadic relation that we can begin to explain how life began and then to resolve the problem of causation, of ultimate authority.

Throughout most of his life Peirce's work had been based on the conviction that the principles of science may and must be applied to the method of semiotic, that is, logical inquiry and that the process of thought regarded as a dynamic, open-ended and evolving phenomenon is a fact capable of scientific investigation. Peirce's conviction was shared and promulgated by his contemporaries and associates. Peirce himself had been profoundly influenced and guided in his groundbreaking work in semiotics by Chauncy Wright, whose impact on the development of Holmes's commitment to a science of law has been variously noted.[3] In a letter to F. E. Abbott, written in 1867, four years prior to the meetings of the Metaphysical Club in Cambridge in which Peirce, Holmes, Wright, and others participated, Wright said:

> Words have reputations as well as other authorities, and there is a tyranny in their reputation even more fatal to freedom of thought. True science deals with nothing but questions of fact. . . . If the facts are determined, and, as far as may be, free from moral biases, then practical science comes in to determine what, in view of the facts, our feelings and rules of conduct ought to be, but practical science has no inherent postulates any more than speculative science. Its ultimate grounds are the particular goods or ends of human life. (Cited in Howe 1957:257, 312)

If the quintessential value, or authority, of investigation and procedures for discovery are the goals of human life—the not-yet existent, but possible and willed aims—fact-finding and the interpretation of fact are viewed as means requisite to net end, which is the satisfying or appeasing of a ruling value. As Peirce was to contend in his later writings, means and ends are not distinguishable as value signs, but, on the contrary, constitute in their relationship the whole of human creative activity and therefore constitute the highest good. The method of interpretation, in law and in ordinary life, may be seen as a configuration, or representation, or sign replete with complex inter- and intra-relationships of creative activity at its best.[4]

If logic is the science that investigates method, then semiotic as the method of Peirce's expanded logic is the "method of methods."[5] And this *expanded logic* is not that which Holmes rejects in his famous dictum that the life of the law is not logic but experience. The logic to which Holmes refers confirms and accepts as true those leading principles which can neither be verified nor disproved with reference to the actual world.[6] Thus discovery in the law relates to procedures governed by law for the purpose of ascertaining admissible facts. In this chapter there will be little discussion of discovery procedures as such; it will focus instead on the interpretation of rules stipulating how discovery is to be conducted (cf. Ross 1912).

Legal interpretation or legal hermeneutics is a method of inquiry, a kind of juridical behavior, or, broadly speaking, is a part of that which is implicit in the term *legal act*. The act of interpretation in law is the consequence of a method of reasoning. As Peirce has said, reasoning is phenomena manifested by action in the world. The action which a mode of reasoning intends to bring about may be regarded as ethical action, or right conduct. Thus logic, as Peirce points out, is dependent on ethics, which, in turn, is governed by the authority of value. In this sense, esthetics, to which ethics and logic are subordinate, is the science of value.

Peirce argued that whatever one means by a fact is not that which is directly or immediately perceived or observed. Rather, what one calls facts are judgments, inferred through modes of reasoning from observation which itself consists of multiple presentations to the mind of the inquirer of that object in question, that is, under observation. One proceeds from the vague quality of a thing in question to a more definite understanding or consciousness of any given observable. The process of abstracting the thing in question from its customary ground—of distinguishing it from its context—results in identifying the object *as* a fact. As a fact, it is an individual with respect to its referent system, or background. As a fact, it is a general with respect to its distinctive quality, or observable complex. When this fact acquires nomenclature it is then capable of functioning as an exchangeable unit of meaning, for example, as a sign, or representation, or, in Peirce's more exotic terminology, as an immediate interpretant. At this stage the representation or sign is capable of undergoing further transformation and modification, for example, growth. As subject, or typical sign, it acts as symbol of interpretive authority to which the ensuing process of interpretation must refer and defer.

However, since there is an element of error in all that we call our observation, and since the proposition represented by our immediate interpretant may not be absolutely true, our major premise in any process of reasoning is at bottom hypothetical and subject to correction and revision.

In this manner Peirce qualifies the nineteenth-century search for authority by establishing the concept that insofar as reference is required for thinking directed toward some end we may not dispense with signs that represent the authoritative function. Insofar as this authority is never to be regarded as absolute or infallible, authority as such in each particular case is provisional. *The means for challenging the rule must be part of the encoded rules in a coherent system of thought.*

Peirce wrote in 1866, in the Logic Notebooks, on the relation between liberty and necessity. The will to act in a certain way requires that "liberty and necessity do not conflict." Peirce's argument is remarkable. By redefining the key terms *liberty* and *necessity,* synonymous here in a loose sense with the terms *freedom* and *authority*, he illustrates his concept of methodology, or speculative rhetoric, in action, as it were:

Whereas the terms *liberty* and *necessity* have customarily been held in a relationship of opposition through previous arguments in the history of these terms, Peirce contests this dissociative relationship and, through what Perelman describes as an argument by convergence, brings the terms, or signs, of authority and freedom into a new relationship, which is not that of equivalence but rather of co-functions of a more comprehensive system, or idea, in which each is an integral part, interactive and interdependent one with the other.

In Peirce's outline of his "synechistic" philosophy the term *synechism* refers to a continuity in the development of a sign or system of thought which is brought about by mental operations upon that thought. This is not an oxymoronical argument: Rather, the etymological definition of synechism, which Peirce says is meant to bring something about continuously "by surgery," does not signify the reduction or diminution of the object operated upon. Rather, to offer an analogy, the surgery implied by synechism more closely parallels the kind of judicious pruning we associate with horticulture and husbandry in which constraints and inhibitions on rank growth tend to produce bountiful harvests. Thus to operate on a thought is to cultivate, in a selected fashion, its continuous development and fruitfulness.

Synechism, at this stage of Peirce's later writings, does not oppose or conflict with his concept of tychism, or pure chance—the occasion for the spontaneous, the possible, and the free—but rather subsumes chance, such that freedom and inhibition become correlated and reciprocal. If surprise can be said to be our response to chance and spontaneity—that which we perceive to be unmotivated and uncaused—then effort is the resolution of the vague and indeterminate to that which, in some degree, may be definitely known. "Effort and surprise are the only experiences from which we can derive the concept of actions," Peirce says. He continues by noting, "All inhibition of action, or action upon action, involves reaction and duality. All direction toward an end or good supposes self-control, and thus the normative sciences are thoroughly infused with duality" (ms 182.83).

Any reasoning is good, that is, ethically sound, if it achieves its purpose. The purpose of reasoning is to indicate, to specify but not necessarily to prescribe, conduct which itself is "good" if by it intended goals are reached. All thinking, which Peirce regards as an "active operation," is a kind of behavior. Whereas feelings may make no claim to authority, reasoning must make such claims if its purpose is not restricted to knowing itself only. The reasoner as inquirer values the phenomenal world and such experience in the phenomenal world from which emerges the indeterminate, that is, mere occasions that surprise and thus stimulate effort (ms 182.91–14).

Although Peirce's explicit definitions of this duality are merely mentioned above and will not be taken up here in detail, they are discussed more fully in later chapters. This same duality was tended to confuse the method and purpose of legal interpretation since the beginning of written law. Indeed, the concept of interpretation in law has been bifurcated since its inception.

What will be attempted here is a commentary from a Peircean perspective on some of the major and most provocative concepts of legal hermeneutics as selected from the now vast and varied literature on the topic. Selections have been guided by concern with the relation between freedom and authority, particularly as this relation is involved in the activity of legal interpretation.

Much of the current commentary on interpretation in law assumes that there are two main trends, or schools, of interpretive theory and practice. For general purposes one might say that the first is represented by Hart, who insists on a faithful and "literal interpretation of statutes"; his position is referred to, for the most part, as "conceptual jurisprudence." The second main stand is in the tradition of Iherius, followed by Pound and then by Fuller, and is called "teleological interpretation."[7]

But as Tedeschi and others point out, neither of these positions exempts the interpreter from the explicit role of interpretation as stipulated by that legal system to which the interpreter is committed: "In both 'schools' the interpreter must be faithful to given rules for legal interpretation" (Tedeschi 1967:9).

The inhibitory force, in Peirce's sense, is the authority implicit in the goal, or value of the legal system itself. The rules of interpretating the law are rules that may be seen as tokens of the type of system.[8] The rules themselves represent the general idea of their referent legal system and carry it forward into action. In other words, the rules for interpreting law in any given system are interpretant signs capable of continuous interpretation.

The rules for interpreting law may be considered to be canonical of ethical conduct in legal acts that refer to that system. This passage extrapolates from Tedeschi and also from Peirce. But it is important at this point to conceive of the interpretive aspect of law as that division that mediates between value, or esthetics, and the whole of what Peirce calls logic. In this manner one may show institutionalized law as a kind of *verisimilitude* of all of what Peirce intends to be represented by his normative sciences: logic, ethics, esthetics.[9]

It was Montaigne who called attention to Justinian's realization that although authority determines the interpretation of laws, freedom is part of the process of creating the rules of law (Tedeschi 1967:11). But this is hardly the case when we regard Savigny's insight into interpretation. Savigny proposes, for instance, that we regard legal hermeneutics as an art and interpreters as artists trained in the craft of interpreting the law. The interpreter of modern law must be guided or inspired by those ideal models of legal interpretation. Such an ideal model, he proposes, is the system of Roman law. In other words, he suggests that we hypothesize this system of interpretation in Roman law, which we cannot precisely recover. But insofar as it is representable to us today we may examine such a model for its flaws as well as for its excellences. Particularly because at the time of his writing in the middle of the nineteenth century all attempts to formulate a sound theory of legal interpretation were inadequate and defective in many ways, Savigny advises the construction of a theory that might evolve, as an invention improves upon its predecessor in some significant way, but does not emerge fully grown out of nothing (Savigny 1867/1979:170–171).

Here the maximum freedom is in the act of selecting the appropriate model—that reality in the world from which it is possible to abstract a working hypothesis. But once one has committed oneself to this hypothesis it must be analyzed in a manner requiring utmost self-control, or inhibitions, as Peirce said. It is doubtful that one can reconstruct the possibilities and alternative choices that confronted the Roman legislators, or the legislators of any system of rules; thus Montaigne's affirmation of Justinian's notion of maximum freedom seems misconceived, if not altogether misleading. But one may assume that the action of the legislator in framing laws of interpretation is bound and determined by many causes, that is, many authorities, from the dual domains of both theory and practice.

Peirce reminds us that "potential means indeterminate yet capable of determination" (ms 948.8). Indeed, every choice, or decision to act in this and not that manner, to follow this and not that inclination, originates in freedom and possibility and becomes realized through determination, that is, by authority.

To a small extent Savigny anticipates Peirce's idea of duality in all normative systems by his concept of the *jural relation*. The idea of a jural relation requires that the interpreters of a model of thought, in this case the model presented by the ancient Roman legislators, freely and imaginatively enter into the role of their predecessors by "placing themselves upon the stand-point of the legislator and artificially repeating to themselves his activity, that is causing the law to originate again in their thought" (Savigny 1867/1979:171).

It is suggested that in such re-creation of legislative intention described by Savigny the free play of the interpreter—what Peirce calls musement or pure play—is no less operative in authentic interpretation, that is, when the rules for interpreting the law are part of the written law, than it is in usual interpretation, when interpretation follows the unwritten rules determined by custom.

Both authentic and usual interpretation together constitute what is generally understood by legal interpretation. It is only when rules for both authentic and usual interpretation are inadequate or misleading or insufficient in some respect that the interpreter is sanctioned in his attempts to assume the role of legislator and create rules for interpretation as if he were the framer rather than the judger of law. It is assumed that in doctrinal interpretation there is greater freedom, because the referent authority does not exist as statute, or at the least as custom which the people served by the law fully believe has quasi-statutory force. These distinctions are Gény's. For example, in Gény's words:

> Custom is a second source, but one which is referred to only in the absence of written law. While custom may be considered a substitute for statute this custom must be of long duration . . . [and] lawlike. . . . Statute and custom are the only formal sources

of positive law. . . . In the absence of a statute or custom appropriate to govern the
contested case, the judge, designated . . . as the central organ of all positive interpretation, applies his free discretion. . . . (1899/1963:566–67)

As mentioned above, both Gény on the Continent and Holmes in the United
States were strongly influenced by Peirce's pragmatic logic and its apparent
application to juridical matters. Gény, undoubtedly the more conservative of the
two, remained firm in his advocation of what was referred to above, namely,
the method of interpretation that characterizes conceptual jurisprudence, with its
fidelity to the authority of the written statute. Holmes, more revolutionary in his
contention that interpretation in law must be vital and like life itself, creative of
itself, is much closer, as might be expected, to Peirce's ideas of general interpretation of signs.

With reference to the development of legal realism Tedeschi introduces
his argument against what he sees as anarchistic interpretation in law, such that
the choice of whether to regard the rules for interpretation in any given legal
system *as* rules, or merely as text, is entirely within the freedom of the interpreter.

Tedeschi restates the main propositions of legal realism: first, "The interpretive element is indispensable whenever a rule is applied," and second, "Interpretation does not confine itself to mere transposition, but is, by nature, creative"
(Tedeschi 1967:2). If there is to be continuity in law the interpreter must be
constrained by the law. The law as such must be prior to legal action. There
can be no science of law, Tedeschi contends, unless the function of a rule in
law, a leading principle, be constant. But if *function* is understood to be use in
context, the semantic shape of the rule remains, but the statutory meaning changes
from case to case (Tedeschi 1967:5–19).

But Peirce, if asked, would say that law may not be correctly regarded as
a continuum *unless freedom be an active element of legal interpretation.* Growth
is inconceivable without change, and change requires a ground of indeterminacy
or free play. On denying "creative interpretation" because it creates "fictions,"
Tedeschi and other proponents of conceptual jurisprudence seem to reject precisely what they admit, namely:

Interpretation is not a mechanical or physiological process. It is the reconstruction of
another person's thinking—normative thinking, in the case of legal interpretation. . . .
To interpret is to transpose the thinking of another into one's own mental universe. . . .
(Tedeschi 1967:1)[10]

Peirce, on this point, would concur.

In concluding this condensed discussion on the relation of freedom and
authority in legal interpretation from a semiotics perspective, we stress that
Peirce's theory and method must be closely examined although he rarely speaks
explicitly on legal matters. Nevertheless he asks many of the same questions

that have concerned investigators of legal interpretation for a long time, for instance, "What does it mean to speak of the interpretation of a sign? Interpretation is merely another word for translation" (ms 282.100).

Finally, the important manuscript "The Basis of Pragmaticism" written around 1905, should be cited: The passage quoted has been deleted from the *Collected Papers* (5.497–501), but it is significant and should be noted especially in this context:

> What are signs for, anyhow? They are to communicate ideas, are they not? Even the imaginary signs called thoughts convey ideas from the mind of yesterday to the mind of tomorrow into which yesterday's grown. . . . But why should this idea-potentiality be so poured from one vessel into another unceasingly? Is it a mere exercise of the World-Spirit's Spiel-trieb—mere amusement? . . . It is a part, perhaps we may say the chief part, of the process of the Creation of the World. (ms 282.101)

The law, like time and space, were real continua to Peirce and must be so regarded in our attempt to understand interpretation within the framework of a semiotics of law. The meanings of rules, of arguments, of systems, of law lie in their interpretation, according to Peirce. The end of interpretation is the realization of a value. The value is not implicit in the rule but rather, develops, as an act is consequential of the conduct of thought, that is, of the process of interpreting signs which, as signs, are invested with authority by the tacit agreement of their users.[11]

NOTES

1. See Peirce's 1903 Lecture III, in which the categories are defined and in which the sign functions of icon, index, and symbol are discussed (mss 307, 308). In Lecture III Peirce contends that firstness and thirdness—feeling and law—represent reality, whereas secondness, which is characterized by conflict and existence, represents the structure of the oppositional structure of facts in the existential world. Dynamics, it is also suggested, is the predominant mode of secondness and therefore permits fact to be established on a basis of contradiction and paradox. Peirce, in response to Mach's notion of "virtual velocities" (ms 130), identifies "virtual" with the scholastic notion of *potentia* and points to the idea of continuous transformation of both possibility and force, that is, power, in mechanical, dynamical velocity.

In 1905 Peirce brings secondness into the domain of the real by speaking of the real possibilities of facts; as possibility, therefore, a fact "is not subject to the principle of contradiction"; that is, a possible may be both truth and falsity; yet there are, Peirce says, "real vagues." In this manuscript Peirce says that the scholastic principle which most concerns pragmaticism is not whether there are real generals, or real necessity, but rather whether we can say truly whether there is real vagueness or possibility in facts (ms 290.16).

See also Norman Kretzman's paper on contradiction in scholastic thought (1982:270–276).

2. See Peirce's ms 1123; also mss 1124–1129 on great men and ideas of the nineteenth century.

3. See Fisch's (1964). Fisch also discusses the fact that more than half the members of the Metaphysical Club were lawyers. While Peirce had called James the father of pragmatism, which he claims came to birth during the meetings of the club, it was St. John Green whom Peirce dubbed

he claims came to birth during the meetings of the club, it was St. John Green whom Peirce dubbed the grandfather of pragmatism because it was he who pointed out to Peirce Alexander Bain's idea of belief as the basis for action and noted that in this sense "pragmatism is scarce more than a corollary." This information is in the introduction to the third volume of *The Writings of Charles S. Peirce* (Fisch 1986), who kindly shared it with me in a prepublication draft in spring 1983.

4. On the relation between diagrammatic thinking, or graphs, and interpretation, see Peirce's discussion, *CP* 4.395. See also Chapter 7 of this volume.

5. Peirce conceived of semiotics as the "method of methods," i.e., a method of interpreting the relation between the discipline-specific methods of inquiry of the various sciences, both theoretical and applied. See mss 655–657 (1910), ms 311 (1903); CP 3.33.

6. See Reichenbach (1947) on the inability to verify such nomological statements as "All men are mortal"; also, Peirce on the inadequacy of Aristotelian deduction with respect to reasoning about "occult properties, those properties of any fact which are brought to light by experiment" ms 1310. In this manuscript Peirce establishes the basis for discovery procedures and the disclosure of evidence. He traces the use of the term *manifestus* to Petrus Peregrinus, where it is a sign of that which "is open to direct observation" and which, he concludes, may be subject to the operations of inquiry in the analysis of thought and thought processes. Peirce regard Petrus Peregrinus, the teacher of Roger Bacon, as the first to write in the "spirit of experimental inquiry" and thus in the manner of modern scientific interpretation.

7. Traditionally a legal act refers to law which is written or enacted. But, as Plucknett points out, "the more one examines the historical processes by which the judicature interprets the written and the unwritten laws, the laws that are enacted and the laws that are unenacted, the more clearly one sees that the office *ius dicere*, to interpret law, involves also the office *ius dare*, to make law" (1922:vii of the Preface by H. D. Hazeltine). Also, see Bubner (1976) and Tedeschi (1967:8–11) on the two major traditions in legal interpretation.

8. Peirce's type is the authoritative type of any given discourse, and tokens of that type may be regarded as interpretations of the rule. See mss 291–95 (1906) for discussion of type–token as sign functions in pragmaticism.

9. In the 1905 Notebook ms 1334, Peirce redefines the dependence of logic on ethics and that of ethics on esthetics. Esthetics is concerned with the discovery of highest value, the *summum bonum*. Peirce introduces and discusses three kinds of discovery procedures: "prattospude," "taxospude," and "herospude," that is, discovery for acting, for application of knowledge, and pure discovery for its own sake; all these bear on legal discovery.

10. The prevailing, if not the dominant issue in legal hermeneutics is how far freedom in interpretation may be stretched before interpretation, as the making of new law, becomes anarchistic. Peirce's concern with limits in topical geometry may be understood as an approach to this issue by using the methods of mathematics to investigate problems that are not mathematical but that require the methods of inquiry mathematics makes possible. Thus the question, What are the limits defined by a boundary? leads to a redefinition of boundaries as such, that is, as real vagueness or real possibilities (cf. FN 1 above). See 1967:950 on continuity and growth which require explanation beyond the principles of dynamics. See also 1967:948.2, on application of the concept of continuity, in geometrical topics, to other fields of inquiry.

11. Laski, unlike Peirce, is not concerned with meticulously distinguishing important differences in method between Aristotle's and Kant's sense of the free spirit. However, when he insists that the "real significance of freedom . . . enables the individuality of men to become manifest," he is affirming Peirce's contention that freedom is such an idea, as is individuality, which may be scientifically examined and semiotically interpreted. See especially Laski's discussion of the responsible community as authority (1919/1969:89–109). To extrapolate from Peirce on this matter, it is the community, self-controlled in its logical or semiotic acts, that is a community grounded on an ethics that in turn defers to appropriate processes of thought as its principle value, that is, to correct argument and interpretation, which in an ideal legal system acts as model or interpretant sign for its society.

PART III

Quid Pro Quo

Liberty is essential in order to leave room for the unforeseeable and unpredictable. . . . It is because every individual knows so little and, in particular, because we rarely know which of us knows best, that we trust the independent and competitive efforts of many to induce the emergence of what we shall want when we see it.

Friedrich A. Hayek (1960:p. 29)

CHAPTER *11*

Contracts and Equivalences

When Justice Holmes reminds us that the earliest forms of contract in common law are covenant and debt, we want to be aware that, of these, debt is the elemental form.[1] The covenant, related to the promise under seal after the Norman invasion, is a distinct kind of promise. It represents, as sign, evidence and fact, which are themselves the outcome of a preparatory legal procedure. Debt, that is, the history of the action of debt in law, is more ancient and nearly universal throughout legal systems. It is tied to the doctrine of consideration, and, as is well known, consideration was rarely if ever required for contracts under seal. Consideration, in layman's terms, is equivalent to the proof of the existence of a contract. Proof takes a number of forms, but each of these forms may be regarded as a variation in the act of attesting to an agreement of *quid pro quo.*[2]

The purpose in this chapter is not to undertake jurisprudential account of the history and ramifications of contract in law but rather to show how this basic concept is semiotic in structure. Especially it is related to Peirce's semiotic theories and method. This chapter investigates ways in which Peirce uses these legal concepts in his writings and how, in using them, he adapts and indeed transforms them into elemental semiotic concepts.[3] It is remarkable that the indices to the manuscripts and to the *Collected Papers* contain, with respect to the former, no reference to these concepts and, with respect to the latter, incomplete references.

In semiotic terms the index is nothing but a sign, or sign system, pointing to topics regarded as significant to the indexer. Thus an index, like a code in any other system, is never complete.[4] Rather, the text regarded as an "eminant text" is replete with more than has been so far discovered; that is, it remains a potential source of inquiry and interpretation. The investigator brings something new to the text and thereby establishes relationary concepts that did not previously exist; something is thus discovered of the object of investigation which *interprets*, in Peirce's sense, its referent interpretant.[5]

When Peirce writes in "Notes on Scientific Philosophy" (CP 1.130) that we cannot assume that geometric postulates are "precisely true," and that "the matter is reduced to one of evidence," where "evidence" is understood to be always a result of "indirect observation," he is using the concept of evidence in a legal sense, that is, as a consequence of a mode of legal reasoning intended to establish the fact of the existence of a contract.

What is to count as evidence in science, as evidence has been traditionally regarded in law, is that factiveness to which the community of discourse assents. How such contracts are understood in science is only minimally different from how contract is understood in law. Indeed, the fundamental presupposition of contract underscores all of that which, in every given universe of discourse, is to count as evidence and as fact, that is, as held judgment. Such judgment symbolizes the assumed axiomatic truth of each particular inquiry.

It is claimed here that the legal contract, like the legal argument, is prototypical of all other social modes of exchange. It represents exchange of goods, as will be discussed in a later chapter. As prototype, the legal contract furnishes us with a basic model for semiotic agreement on the meaning of the meaning of a sign in question, in any type of discourse.[6]

The contract delineates a relational act of one kind of certainty. With respect to the question of certainty and modes of achieving exact and certain knowledge, theology, like physical science, has been a source of direct evidence, but even in the theological doctrine of "Evidences," Peirce points out, divine revelation as *undoubtable* evidence does not exist. There is no way of knowing that the evidentiary truth or revelation is true. The acceptance of such evidence is the result of a previous concurrence to accept *as true* the results of assumed, divinely inspired vision. But such concurrence is possible only through a kind of collective faith and with reference to a supposition that includes divine inspiration or revelatory evidence as a ground for continuing belief. However, Peirce insists, divine evidence is far less certain than almost any other source of evidence—far less than that certainty achieved through reason. And, one might add, divine evidence is less freely agreed to by those whose membership in the collective faithful is more circumstantially determined than freely chosen (CP1.143). Yet one of the basic forms of action which, in common law, substantiates the contract as such is the oath, that is, the *fides facta* or testimony of a hearsay nature to so-called observed fact and to contracts bound by seal in writing and record, for instance, the legal covenant referred to above (Kevelson 1977).[7]

These two brief examples of legal concepts are inextricable from Peirce's thought. We assume here, as I noted at the outset, that Peirce's semiotic theory and method is a mode of clarifying legal systems. Conversely, understanding of the foundation and development of certain basic concepts in law such as contract elucidates Peirce's sometimes dense semiotic theory and method. Therefore I hope that by showing how each acts as interpretant in turn for the other an examination of law from a semiotic perspective will contribute to Peirce scholarship in a significant manner and also will provide a basis for general semiotic investigations of law.

At present many writings that discuss signs and sign function are classified as semiotics. But such a general use of the term obscures and trivializes the really distinctive contribution that semiotics makes to scholarship as a whole, across disciplines and with possible application to the practical arts and social institutions.

Among the most perplexing problems one faces in current semiotic investigations of Peirce's work is how one uses systems of classification already established for issues that are beginning to emerge when such classificatory systems, or indices, explicitly omit all mention of the ground of one's inquiry.

Emergent problems may render disfunctional existing general rules for resolving problems. It is like attempting to examine critically any given system of law by disputing the existing norms, or constituents of a given legal code, in order to resolve the problem of *incompleteness* in the system of law as a whole. We know that such method was the basis for a systematic and scientific approach to jurisprudence in the tenth and eleventh centuries with the discovery of the Justinian Codices: the *quaestiones* were the problems presumed to be contained by the Codex under review.[8]

Actually this method of disputing given questions in law was not so much intended to restrict legal dispute to a circumscribed set of legal problems as it was a manner of structuring inquiry in general regarding the law. But if the set of problems, norms, or legal questions is regarded as a complete code, then one has no alternative but to regard the society which it serves as a closed and completed system, in need only of clarification. Contrary to the positivists, through Bentham and well into the twentieth century, legal semiotics claims that no code is ever complete so long as one admits the possibility of genuine novelty and real change.[9] Thus Peirce's insistence on indeterminacy—an indeterminacy further developed by the legal realists and others—supposes an open and continually developing universe in which chance is the occasion for something new to enter into the established order of things, and for new possible relationships to appear as signs; *this changes reality as such, that is, as sign.*

The predominant sign function of evidence, according to Peirce, is iconic (CP 2.279), but the iconic function of a sign—*any* function of a sign, whether iconic, indexical, or symbolic—is subsequent to the previous phenomenological or "phaneroscopic" process which produces an instrument as sign with which to proceed further in investigation of any topic.[10] These three sign functions are aspects of all of what Peirce means by representation.[11] As I have said, the concept of representation, or sign, evolves out of the notion of the fact, which, in Peirce's view, is not yet a sign. The fact depends on an elemental stage of inquiry, namely the quality that prescinds or cuts out the abstracted observable from a familiar and conventional ground for more intensive investigation.

These subdivisions are not so explicitly designated in any history of contract. Indeed, Holmes called attention to this lack of clear-cut division between revealed appearance in hearsay, factiveness as implied in the oath, and representation presupposed by written documents and/or records as in sealed contracts.[12] But Peirce in his phenomenology describes reconstruction in stages, parallel to the history of contract and corresponding with the process of establishing evidence for further legal investigation within the framed boundaries of the court. Thus Peircean semiotic analysis is analogous with procedure in law.[13]

Peirce identified semiotic iconic evidence with a rhetorical evidentiary mode in law. What he means by rhetoric, as I have stressed before, is methodology, that is, an intersubjective, or dialogic and pragmatic development of an idea, with real consequences in the actual and practical world of human affairs. We have covered this point already (see also Kevelson 1987). The following is a brief recapitulation.

Pure rhetoric, in Peirce's lexicon, is synonymous with semiotic methodology. Evidentiary rhetoric, then, refers to the stage of semiotic analysis that precedes the investigation of signs as signs, the purpose of which is to determine what shall and what shall not function as a sign for the investigation at hand. Peirce distinguishes his use of evidentiary rhetoric in this new sense from other more traditional uses of the term, for instance, in his "Elements of Logic" written about 1902.

Peirce says that the term *rhetorical evidence* should be understood as a part of his speculative rhetoric, which he says is the "highest and most living branch of logic" (CP 2.233). Further on in this passage Peirce says that once deductions, or "quasi-predictions" have been made based on accepted theoretical frameworks, that is, contractual bases for theorizing, "it is requisite to turn to the rhetorical evidence and see whether or not they are verified by observation" (CP 2.233).

A continuity of inquiry requires that any judgment become the ground from which further investigation may begin. Such ground may be abstracted from still further judgments, such that the initial concept in question—the law in relation to the case at hand—may be further defined and refined. The rhetorical evidence provides a new quality, in turn to become a new fact, and in its turn, to become a new sign or representation, an interpretant of its object. The final interpretant concludes a complete process of inquiry. These brief explanatory remarks may be useful for further discussion of semiotics and contract in law.

As mentioned above, every assertion according to Peirce is a relationship between a speaker and a listener: the listener may be merely hypothetical, that is, assumed as that aspect of the notion of one's self with which one has, as it were, an inner dialogue. The point is that in order for something to be an assertion it is *implicitly* a communal contractual relation between at least two signs of persons. The function of assertion, in Peirce, is to furnish "evidence by the speaker to the listener that the speaker *believes* something, that is, finds a certain idea to be definitively compulsory on a definite occasion." The passage continues, and is quoted here in full.

> There ought, therefore, to be three parts in every assertion, a sign of the occasion of the compulsion, a sign of the enforced idea, and a sign evidential of the compulsion affecting the speaker in so far as he identified himself with the scientific intelligence. (CP 2.225)

All three aspects are contained in the iconic function of the sign, and all three aspects in law are also implied in the evidentiary procedure that is preliminary to the fact selection of the total fact-finding process.

This iconic function, characteristically tripartite, is the initial and distinguishing feature of discovery in law. Indeed, it is that part of legal reasoning which corresponds with abduction, of which more will be said.

The "occasion of the compulsion" is the case at hand. The "enforced idea" is the encoded rule, or system of rules with respect to each legal system which legitimizes discovery procedures. And the third sign, designated above, is the affirmation by judiciary power of established systemic-specific convention with respect to this partiular procedure, that is, fact-finding and discovery.

Peirce's assertive function, analogously and isomorphically, is an assertive event in legal procedure.

This assertive event determines the framework, that is, sets the stage for the subsequent court procedure. Relevant prop and actors are assigned their places. They are selected during this assertive event for the role they will play in the courtroom drama, which is yet to begin. This preliminary stage, then, is a complex sign or sign system regarded both as a whole and also as a part of a larger relationship. The entire sign of discovery event is a coordinate structure of icon, index, and symbol.

Thus far, described briefly, are the aspects of the iconic function: the case in hand, or that which is present; the rule of law, or qualifying authoritative force; the representation of the whole by its part, that is, the whole of the community of legal system as represented by this special case. All this is iconic, and all three aspects of its iconicity are parts of the placement of the presentness— the *hic et nunc* of compulsion, as Peirce puts it—within its context. From the start the initial iconic relation is contractual.

The indexical function next becomes predominant. That is, the experiential character is dominant so that the selection process itself is to be given focus. Or, in Peirce's words;, ". . . it is requisite that these should be a kind of sign which shall act dynamically upon the hearer's attention and direct it to a special object or occasion. Such a sign I call an *Index.*" This, in the framework of legal semiotics, suggest that the predictive aspect of law, of which more will be said, is being emphasized.[14] This indexical sign in its basic function tells the "listener how to act in order to gain the occasion of experience to which the assertion relates, and is a basic *relationship.* Acting and being acted upon are reciprocal parts of the fundamental relation of any action."[15]

Because all action is of the here and now, that is, represents presentness and experience, the characteristic sign function of acts, Peirce tells us, is also of the character of presentness. The index must point out this selected experience as fact: ". . . that to which the index directs attention may be called the subject of the assertion . . ." (CP 2.336). It must be stressed that the use of the terms *subject* and *object* should not be confused here with grammatical subjects and objects.

An index need not be a part of speech, Peirce says. Neither must an icon be a grammatical part of the language system of any particular kind or type, English, Greek, Latin, or whatever. Thus in the proposition "all men are mortal" each of the terms is indexical in the sense that each points to all of that which in experience is represented by these language signs. This is not the appropriate place to discuss in detail what Peirce refers to here as the "logic of continuous universes," which, he says, still "awaits investigation." The third function of any sign is the symbol, and it has its special place in the contractual aspect of legal semiotics.

Peirce first introduced his concept of the symbol in 1867 as a "general representation." Shortly afterward, he redefined his terms, propositions and arguments. In the sense that every predicate is a symbol, it is an ideal representation of the subject with which it is likened. *Ideal* in this sense is to be taken not as 'identical with' but 'equivalent to' or 'having the same value as'. A symbol is evaluative. It carries the value of meaning within a community that has agreed to this value or meaning. At the same time a predicate denotes that which is characterized by such value meaning. And also it presupposes a "mental construction, or diagram of something possessing those characters, and the possession of those characters is kept in the foreground of consciousness." (CP 2.341).

What Peirce suggests is that if one similarly breaks down the process of judicial fact-finding and decision making these three sign functions, each of which is assimilated and subsumed in the other two at all times, correspond to the three sign functions described by Peirce in that part of any argument which is assertorial. An assertion is a rudimentary argument. Similarly, the fact-finding procedure in the courts may be regarded as a rudimentary trial or hearing resulting in a decision or new judgment.

In each of these stages of legal procedure, just as in each of the stages of any semiotic process in a Peircean sense, the notion and action of contract is involved, implying one or more of the basic forms of contract, as described by Holmes and others.

Elsewhere in this discussion of pragmatism (or "pragmaticism") Peirce explicitly shows the correspondence between an assertion, or judgment, and its function in legal practice. He says that in order to analyze an assertion and describe it within a pragmatic framework it is useful to compare assertion in argument in general with assertion and judgment in legal procedure. As assertion carries with it the solemnity of oath taking: "If a man desires to assert anything very solemnly, he takes such steps as will enable him to go before a magistrate or notary and take a binding oath to it."

Taking an oath is not mainly an event of the nature of a setting forth, *Vorstellung*, or representing. It is not mere saying, but *doing*. The law calls it an *act*. As such an act, assertion depends on an underlying agreement or contract because every judgment is the result of dialogic interaction:

. . . Even in solitary meditation every judgment is an effort to press home, upon the self of the immediate future and of the general future, some truth, It is a genuine assertion, just as the vernacular phrase represents it; and solitary dialectic is still of the nature of dialogue. Consequently it must be equally true that here too there is contained an element of assuming responsibility, of "taking the consequences." (CP 5.546, 547)

Especially interresting is that while Peirce's semiotics furnishes a tool for understanding legal systems as sign systems, the actual practice of law in its most general and basic acts had furnished Peirce with a model for explaining the fundamental process of developing thought. The notion of dialogic interaction is inseparable from this process. The underlying and elemental structure of this dialogue takes the form of question and answer, that is, of an erotetic logic, as discussed earlier. Historically, from the viewpoint of comparative legal history, it is found that the riddle has been one of the characteristic structures of many legal systems, for instance, Islamic law as mentioned above.

It is useful to recall that Peirce noted the need for recovery of contractual structure in semiotic inquiries. The referent interpretant or the consequential interpretant may not always be manifest, explicit. Thus this entire argument-like process may be fruitfully and correctly compared with the structure of the enthymemic argument in which suppression of first, second, or final premise is possible because these propositions are safely implied due to the underlying conventional and contractual context of the argument.[17]

Peirce follows his famous admission that he regards himself as a "pioneer, or rather a backwoodsman, in the work of clearing and opening up what I call semiotic . . ." (CP 5.488) with the remark:

it is to be supposed that upon every presentation of a sign capable of producing a logical interpretant, such interpretant is actually produced. The occasion may either

be too early or too late. If it is too early, the semiosis will not be carried so far, the
other interpretants sufficing for the rude functions for which the sign is used. On the
other hand, the occasion will come too late if the interpreter be already familiar with
the logical interpretant, since then it will be recalled to his mind by a process which
affords no hint of how it was actually produced. (CP 5.489)

What is then wanted, Peirce suggests, is a detecting investigation which
will successfully lead back to a causal explanation of the situation or case in
point. The problem of causation in law is·discussed in a subsequent chapter.
Here it is noted that the contract in its various forms underlies all acts of exchange,
whether of information or of services, or of goods and chattel as in the notion
of property in law. Consideration, or motive, is evidence of a contract in common
law. Although the meaning of *motive* in everyday speech has come to be nearly
synonymous with the reason why, or explanation, one should bear in mind that
the special sense of legal motive as a "causal factor" is closely tied to the implicit
sense of *consideration*, which is evidence for and explanation behind a contract
in law. Thus, it should be noted that the evidence of motive is equivalent with
causal factor. Property, that is, the idea of free property rights, is the basis,
according to Hayek and others, for the related idea of free contractual rights.[18]
This point will be also discussed as a separate problem.

Earlier it was pointed out that *quid pro quo* characterizes all contracts. As
Holmes points out, the common element of all contracts might be said to be a
promise, although even a promise was not necessary to a liability in debt as
formerly understood.[19] The assumption of indebtedness or an agreement to return
in reciprocal manner something of equivalent value for that which is taken
precedes the promise to do so. Also, liability in debt precedes the action of
assumpsit. Further, everything is form, which the law requires in order to make
a promise binding over and above the mere expression of the promisor's will.[20]

Holmes does not restrict the meaning of formality to written documents.
Covenants are, in common law, no more formal as contracts than "ordinary
consensual contracts." Freedom is prior to determining causes. Consideration
follows after voluntary consent.[21] In the development of common law contract,
consideration is as formal a sign of contract as the seal.

Now, of what does consideration consist in law, and in what sense is
consideration a sign of agreement in law which corresponds with agreement to
the semiotic meaning of a sign in ordinary conversation as well as with the
meaning of a sign in logical terms?

Consideration is a rather late development or sign of contractual agreement
in law. Prior to consideration was debt. The proof of debt was still earlier than
the notion of promise, as noted. Debt in its earliest sense is an implied duty
brought forth in response to receipt of some service or property.[22] Actual receipt
of goods was in early common law an observable fact, easily attested and sworn
to.

But if one wants to strip this action of debt to its bare logical bones what we have is a request, implicit or explicit, or a want by one party of another. The satisfaction of want is the responsive action of the second party to the first. The manifest, observable fact in law of the receipt of satisfaction carried with it the contracted duty to repay, or to repossess, that is, to have again. Debt is a sign of transitivity and relationship.

The force of the law to bring about repayment of a debt is not properly to be regarded as deontic in structure, except as the deontic feature is subsumed within the larger structure of a logic of questions and answers. The question, or problematic "want" that sets the ensuing legal acts in motion, is analogous to a question given a satisfactory answer. The answer becomes obvious or apparent just as in the appearance of the statement or command the question is implied and recoverable, but not obvious on the surface.[23]

Adam Smith, the first of the great liberalists, understood that the basis of contract is "the reasonable expectation which the person who promises raises in the person to whom he finds himself."[24] Discussing Adam Smith, Atiyah places the burden of obligation not on the person who receives expected satisfaction but rather on the person who must *deliver* the satisfaction expected. Atiyah interprets Adam Smith as saying that this obligation of expection, as the source of expected satisfaction, becomes in turn the "source of promissory obligation" (Atiyah 1979:83).

According to this interpretation, the initial obligation is derived not from a promise but rather a duty. What, precisely, is the nature of such duty? Or, to take the earliest significance of consideration as equivalent with reason or motive for action, what is the motive or reason for accepting the obligation of providing those goods for which the receiver is, in turn, indebted? The answer, from a moral perspective similar here to Kant and to Locke, is that community as such, as a fellowship, implies this contractual agreement to reciprocity, or, as the anarchist Kropotkin termed it, to "mutual aid."

The basis, as it appears, of an initial acceptance of obligation, that is, that which binds one party to another in the sense that one is obliged for some reason or motive to permit another to expect receipt of goods in return for which there is a new and binding contractual agreement or promise to repay, is not the promise, but its progenitor: *the trust.*

In common law, long before the Statute of Uses of 1535, medieval law recognized various kinds of contracts on trust. Trust is otherwise known as use.[25]

The ancient law of uses carried with it two requisites: privity and confidence. Confidence should be understood, literally, as a sharing of trust, or good faith. The laws of trusts, then, are more ancient and more primitive, historically and in semiotic terms, than promises. Trusts are initially confidences and thus relations of special privilege and privity. The early notion of trust is inextricably connected with a "chose in action," which is to say, with exempting some one from the obligations accompanying a right, or in transfer of a right as a transfer of use.[26]

According to Atiyah, ". . . there is not only an element of potential unjust enrichment in the trust situation, there is also an element of detrimental reliance." Partly because the law of trusts is older than the law of promises, and partly because the law of trust, or use, provides opportunity for third-party enrichment when the third party does not directly contribute to the transaction of equivalent goods, trusts remained outside the mainstream of transformation and development of the laws of contracts and quasi-contracts. Even today "the promissory element" is a "relatively insignificant part of trust law" (Atiyah 1978:56). However, it is the very structure of trust law that corresponds with the triadic relationship in semiosis. It is this triadicity which still obtains in modern laws of trust.

For example, the distinction between fully constituted and incompletely executed trusts is similar to the distinctions between completed and partially completed contracts. In both, the promise is implied by the partial completion of contract and trust. The promise in modern law thus links trust with contract. It is the promise that plays an evidentiary role in the identification of contractual duty.

But the merely evidentiary role of the promise is less binding than the evidence of consideration. Thus consideration—that is, reason or motive—is by far the stronger element of contract. As Atiyah notes:

> Promissory liability has still not overtaken consideration-based liability. The executor is liable, not because he promised, but because he received assets earmarked for a legacy. The promise is evidence of that fact; but it is not the promise which creates the obligation. (1978:162)

The question of moral obligation arises in this context. As discussed in seventeenth and eighteenth century law, the promissory obligation was less enforceable than the consideration-marked obligation. Yet it has been assumed, as suggested above, that the initial obligation not yet evident in fact is a moral obligation to deliver goods wanted and thus to place another under obligation characterized by consideration, that is, to interpret or translate obligation of an *ethical* system into obligation of an *economic* system.

What is the role of the moral obligation in law? Clearly, long before Kant, this question of moral versus legal obligation arose, that is, moral *as* legal obligation. Atiyah says:

> The key point about the moral obligation in doctrine is that in the mid-eighteenth century the courts were increasingly faced with a problem they had rarely encountered before . . . namely, a series of cases where there appeared to be a marked divergence between the law and morality. (1978:163)

In other words, as the system became less closed, and the changing values of society had to be taken into account in interpretation of the law, legality, and legitimacy became signs or terms no longer in equivalence relations but in dissociative relation. With the increasing divergence between the law and the moral order, distinctions between equitable duties and legal duties arose. It must be stressed that a legal promise is distinct from a moral promise in this context. A legal promise is based on such evidence as consideration. A moral promise is based on assumptions which originate outside the legal framework.

However, although it was generally rejected through the nineteenth century that moral promises were co-extensive with legal consideration, the notion of promise as implicit in contract developed: the promise, legal and/or moral, gradually began to create the "legal duty" and, Atiyah shows, "was not merely adding to it, evidencing it, or modifying it." But this was not a reciprocal, or reversible process. The moral duty was not created by the legal promise. Indeed, the moral duty "existed independently of it" (Atiyah 1978:164).

This is the general context of the situation that Holmes confronted in the late nineteenth century. It was a period in jurisprudential development when Kant's influence was running strong, when the categorical imperative that informs the Kantian theories of law and justice and of ethics were markedly finding their way into laws governing social rights and thus into the laws governing contract as well.

The relation between social contract and legal contract and the alternative mapping of the one on the other, wherein each is a sign system and in turn each is an interpretant of the other, is discussed in following chapters. This introduction to contract in law from the perspective of Peircean semiotics will conclude by stressing that the consideration that ultimately constitutes the evidence of contract, in common law, corresponds to the motivation or force of reason in Peirce that allows semiosis between a speaker and a listener—a receiver and a sender of messages—to proceed.[27]

In the 1905 paper "Consequences of Critical Common-Sensism" Peirce discusses the notion of individualism. The legal concept of individual is inseparable from the idea of contract. But an individual person, like an individual sign, is incomplete to Peirce. He says, "A sign is objectively *vague*, insofar as, leaving its interpretations more or less indeterminate, it reserves for some other possible sign or experience the function of completing the determination'" (CP 5.505). An individual person, as sign, requires the other who interprets to make its own meaning determinate, that is, an actor with a purpose or goal. Individuals are *relates* in Peirce's semiotics.

A resolution to act is that initial consideration which moves one to act, to satisfy the wants of another, to impose on this other an indebtedness to respond and to repay. Note that this is not, as Kant would have it, a "categorical resolve,"

Peirce insists, but is rather a "resolve conditional upon having a certain purpose." Yet, paradoxically, because all acts are future events with respect to resolves, and acts are "the most perfectly individual objects there are" (CP 5.529), every contract in its basic form is spontaneous and concoercive, that is, is a free extension of an actor toward a recipient of a good or a satisfaction.

This Peircean interpretation of contract and its consideration in semiotic terms closely anticipates Hayek's notion of individualism as an economic sign within a free community of transactors of goods according to the laws of the free market. In a subsequent chapter the economic basis of law will be explored from this viewpoint. The notions of trust and use as ancient concepts in exchange and agreement will be again reviewed.

It is the practical experience of each person, just as it is the relation between the practical sciences and their respective social institutions, that furnishes material for all meaningful acts. These practical affairs are the possibilities for new freedoms. At the same time, Peirce insists, they are the boundaries that define and constrain permissible freedoms, both in theory and in praxis: "I hold . . . that man is so completely hemmed in by the bounds of this possible practical experience, his mind is so restricted to being the instrument of his needs, that he cannot, in the least, mean anything that transcends these limits" (CP 5.536).

As will be seen, it is precisely this position that Hayek takes when he develops his theory of economics. Hayek represents the ideal of freedom as a consequence of change in which reason and culture are participants in a contractual kind of relation such that the possibility for freedom increases in direct proportion with the continued interplay of reason and culture, that is, of consideration and purposeful acts.

NOTES

1. See Holmes on the evidence of consideration in contracts in law (1881/1963:230, 31).

2. The concept of *quid pro quo* presupposes a principle of mediation in contract law and thus implies a method for establishing equivalent values. As discussed throughout, the sign is quintessentially a mediating function in all manner of exchange of value, that is, of information and of tangible goods as well. This is Peirce's basic principle in arguing for the mediating process of semiotics; it is also the main tenet of such legal realists as Fuller (especially 1971:305).

3. Fisch suggests that because more than half the members of the Metaphysical Club were lawyers discussion centered on legal examples and cases to illustrate more abstract principles in philosophy (1942:85–97).

4. Despite Peirce's admiration for Bentham and for his ideal concept of utility, it was Bentham's system of reasoning with which Peirce took issue; it was Bentham's logic that permitted him to uphold his theory of a completeness requirement in legal codes.

5. See especially Peirce's letters to William James (1958:8313-315).

6. See Toulmin (1959).

7. The basis of oath taking in early common law was belief in divine authority; Peirce shows that this belief rests on faith rather than on any verifiable certainty and thus places the subsequent arguments from oath taking on shared belief rather than on absolute truth.

8. See Berman on the use of the *quaestiones* (1983:148–151).

9. See Dickinson (1940:149–161).

10. Peirce changes his "phenomenology" to "phaneroscopy" to stress, it is assumed, the *instrumental* use of the phenomenological process in evidentiary procedure. See Kevelson (1987: especially chap. 10).

11. See Peirce on representation as sign, especially in CP 2.228–30.

12. Compare Atiyah and Holmes on the history of contract, especially with respect to the much later date of the binding contract in Atiyah (1979:1–218).

13. Procedures in law, as facts of law, can be understood, respectively, as predominantly iconic and indexical sign functions, as Peirce discusses throughout his writings. When understood from the point of view of his methodology, or speculative rhetoric, these sign functions are to be understood in terms of their power to produce effectual and consequential action. An act in law would be regarded as analogous and equivalent with action in the everyday world. For discussion on the function of facts and evidence see Loevinger (1958:154–175).

14. See Twining (1973) for recent critiques on realism and predictive theory in law.

15. Von Mises' closed system of reasoning (e.g., 1966) was rejected by his student Hayek, whose own approach to legal and economic relationships follows the Peircean method which attributes a positive function to uncertainty and chance in open-ended systems. See especially 1960:155–157 on Holmes and the instrumental use of the law in creating freedoms through its predictive abilities.

16. See Holmes (1881/1963:191–264).

17. For a discussion on the enthymeme, as related to Peirce, see Madden (1952).

18. For discussion of relations between free property rights and free contractual rights see Hayek (1967).

19. See Holmes (1881/1963:227).

20. In *The Common Law* (1881/1963) Holmes shows that assumpsit is a later development in law than liability in debt.

21. See Holmes (1881/1963:215).

22. See Plamenatz on consent (1968:20 ff., 108, 109).

23. See Holmes (1881/1963:208).

24. See Kevelson on interrogatives (1981, 1982b) and in chapter 6 of this volume.

25. See Atiyah (1979:84, 85), where he cites from Adam Smith's *Lectures on Jurisprudence* (1760).

26. For discussion on opposing views on trust and knowledge between Kant and Peirce, see Kevelson (1987).

27. See Holmes (1881/1963:316, 317).

CHAPTER 12

The Mapping of Morals onto Law

PROBLEMS OF RIGHTS, ETHICS, AND VALUES

This chapter, in continuing the discussion of contract in law, deals specifically with the relation between social contract—a philosophical concept—and contract in law. The linking terms are trust, obligation, rights, consideration, ethics, values, and the broad notion of equity or justice which spreads over both systems of thought throughout the history of civilizations, particularly western civilizations.

The implicit problem is the matter of how the establishment of equivalences takes place such that the meaning of an idea, concept—sign—in one universe of discourse is regarded as an equivalent of a verbal sign of the same or similar "shape" in another system.[1] The trade-and-barter system of exchange depends also on agreed-upon equivalences, but any standard system of equivalence requires the mediation of signs and the general ideas that value signs may represent.

In the previous chapter attention was called to the growing tendency to impose *moral* obligations upon the existing concept of contractual economic and economically measurable obligation, which had evolved but had remained within the domain of legal systems through the sixteenth century. By the seventeenth century the realization that law and morality had greatly diverged and had opened up in a dynamic and growing universe far from the cloistered medieval image of the world led to the evolution of two increasingly nonparallel systems.

Attempts were made to close this gap and to show that law was not a separate system with its own autonomy rooted in civil affairs but rather was subordinate to a higher law, such as that which adhered to, in all its various interpretations, the notion of natural law.[2] Although this is not a directly focused discussion on the problems of natural law, some of these problems must be discussed in the context of this chapter, which is explicitly concerned with the intersystemic and semiotic communications and cross-influences between meta-physical ethics and values and the practice and theory of law.

Almost proportional with the decline in the freedom of property and free-dom of contract in law especially since the end of the eighteenth century and into the first decade of the twentieth has been the emerging concern with moral aspects of rights in general, including property rights, and loss of confidence in contractual acts between individuals. The notion of obligation had been variously redefined, and with the growth of the corporate entity. At the same time, growing restraints on a free market, criteria for an ethical basis for law as well as for economics and related political institutions have settled upon philosophical bases, the appropriateness of which is critically disputed.

For example, the Rawlsian neo-Kantian position of rights reinforces[3] cer-tain philosophical assumptions that are not only not tenable but that predictably reduce rather than encourage new possibilities for freedom. These premises, which minimize, for example, the positive aspects of chance and indeterminacy, tend to emphasize the so-called long-range social benefits of necessary coercion, that is, the justification of means toward ideal end, as in the case of growing governmental regulations both intranationally and as international restrictive and coercive measures on a global scale. Similar criticisms apply to the utilitarians, who, however their language has changed, are still using the logic of the original utilitarian spokesmen, Mill and Bentham.[4] More will be said on this point. As is recalled from the previous chapter, the initial obligation that motivated a giver to provide a recipient with goods, services, and/or satisfaction and thus brought about the recipient's indebtedness in contract law was not an obligation imposed upon the donor by law, or by any other institutionalized social regulation. Neither is such an obligation which may or may not inhere in certain theological dogmas mandatory upon individuals. What was required in some instances was mandatory support by individuals of the Church, and also of the State insofar as it had the power to levy taxes upon individuals; but nowhere is it written that it is mandatory for individuals to recognize and to perform acts of kindness and beneficence to fellow citizens. Thus the initial obligation that sets in motion the act of contracting with another is required neither by church nor by state law (or both) but is a manifestation of free giving, of choice.

Now one may argue that the placing of another in a position of indebtedness to oneself is not an act of good will but rather a manipulative tactic designed to place oneself in an advantageous position, a position to receive riches over and above the gift given, that is, with interest. The "indulgences" of post-Reformation middle-class society are not divinely mandated but are implied contracts with divinity. It can also be argued that an initial presumed deontic obligation which establishes a contractual relation is indeed required if one is to carry out the mandates of one's ethical code; but this mandate is of a different nature than the first.

However, historically speaking, the attitude of *noblesse oblige*, a moral attitude, becomes integrated into legal and political policy of economic justice, or distributive justice.[5] The chapter on economic justice in this volume discusses the merging of these two frameworks in some detail with respect to the logic of Mill and Bentham, which tended to reinforce the notion of utility that carried moral obligation into the domain of law.

Atiyah calls attention to the well-known fact that we have little understanding today of whether or not seventeenth- and eighteenth-century societies tacitly accepted the contractual relation as a link between governed and governing on the one hand, and contractual relations as bond between persons or parties who contract with one another in a deliberate and consensual way on the other hand. In some sense, it has been variously argued, the contractual relationship between state and citizen rests on the same freedom of choice and voluntary or intentional will to interact as that characterizing legal contracts between persons.

Arguments against a voluntary social contract, that is, the choice by a people to "create a society in which free choice was one of their principal goals," the voluntary creation of a "society in which the voluntary creation of relationships would be permitted and respected," and freely instituted society "for the protection of their property in order that they could be free to acquire, exploit, or dispose of property to their best advantage" are all arguments that historical evidence rejects.

We have no documents in evidence to show that the term *social contract* represents any contractual act at all. That evidence that we do have is the phenomenal factiveness as a consequence of an idea; it interprets the idea of social contract, but the idea refers forward to a possible and not back to verifiable experience. Are we to say, then, where authoritative, coercive, and even totalitarian oppressive social institutions exist that no social contract with respect to this particular society took place? On the other hand, can one say that where the people remain and sustain the power of opposing and correcting the institutions of government, economics, and law such social contract must have occurred because the consequences of such an assumed contract are manifest in the structure of a free society?[6] Is it possible or plausible or even probable that a people would choose to be subordinate to institutions they created because such societies willed themselves to be and wanted to be controlled by their own self-created instruments? Unfortunately this possibility is not at odds with history. People can be observed to choose their poisons and to subjugate themselves to their own inventions. Thus even in the case of coercive and nonfree social institutions they may still be interpreted and understood as evidence of some social contract that allowed them to come into being and persist.

It may be recalled from the previous chapter that the legal contract, in the early days of its history, was regarded as legally binding long before the covenant or sealed document became evidentiary of a contractual relationship. Indeed, it was shown that consideration of a kind, as motive, antedates promises and covenants, that is, sealed writs and records, as evidence that a contract was chosen and mutually consented to by participants. One may ask what kind of consideration is evidence of the social contract, especially of social contracts presumed to underlie oppressive relations between state and people? In other words, what motive or reason can be understood as the necessary consideration for such contractual relations, which seem to contradict self-interested common sense? Clearly, as Peirce shows, the ethics of such a chosen relation must be derived from and governed by a value system that promotes relationships of subordinate people to exploitative rulers. It should be noted that such value systems may be manifest conclusions of incorrect reaesoning. One may simplistically, perhaps, trace such value systems to earlier, coeval theological values which emphasize the punitive role of the deity and the sinful nature of mankind. Indeed, this is precisely what we find in the Hobbesian concept of social contract. But, again, the holes in these arguments are well known.

Grimke, among others, places side by side two main theories that deal with the *reasons*, that is, the *consideration* in legal terms, for the establishment of governmental institutions. The first theory regards social institutions as copies or representations of divine institutions, such that the motivating impulse is in large measure utopian. The other theory speculates on the possibility that all government is the consequence of compacts, or agreements. From the proponents of the latter theory come a number of variations. For example, the compact may be presumed to hold between a people and its rulers, as in Locke's version. Or, as in Hobbes and Rousseau, the compact is "among the people themselves," who create out of themselves governing institutions, (Grimke 1848/1948:76, 77).[7] Grimke associates the utopian theory with the "advocates of the 'jure divino right' [who] have, at the same time, been the most idolatrous worshipers of the absolute power of governments . . ." (Grimke 1948:77).

Grimke argues:

> Compact is the only legitimate basis upon which government can stand. . . . Thus, in those communities which existed at a period anterior to written history, although we cannot conceive anything like a formal agreement to have been entered into, we can very readily suppose, indeed, we are compelled to suppose, that the minds of all the adult males, however untutored, spontaneously and without any set purpose conspired to that end. . . . We talk of tacit or implied agreements even in jurisprudence, and give the same force and authority to them which we do to express ones. (Grimke 1948:78)

What Grimke appears to be suggesting is that at some ancient prehistoric date our earliest human societies consisted of persons—males, he specifies—

who compacted with one another in the interests of creating a free society for all, or at least who set forth the rudiments of what has developed into representative governments and free societies. If one is to take Grimke's suggestion seriously—and there is no reason not to, since no possibility exists of falsifying such a supposition—then modern free societies were constructed by compact or contract and interpretants, in a Peircean sense, from some general idea the origins of which are lost to us historically but the rationale of which may be reconstructed semiotically, that is, by their consequents. Thus what is called a society based on social contract is a kind of *verisimilitude* of a more primitive, less well developed idea of itself. Such an idea is a continuum in Peirce's sense, and the evidence for such a fact derives from the resultant phenomena of societies whose members bind themselves together by the assumption of underlying social contract.[8]

The point in question here is whether this is a moral assumption on the part of persons, that is, an ethical attitude with respect to their own representative society, or whether their own representative society is a logical, a semiotic development of a previous general idea, one based not on prior convictions and predispositions in the Kantian sense but one that has evolved experientially, through the experience of people in society.

The semiotic view is the latter view. The Kantian notion of social contract as the result of a prior mandate inherent in human nature is strongly opposed to and contradictory of the semiotic position taken here.

One is not in any case talking about a lineal development of a notion of social contract. Clearly, ramifications of such an idea have been aborted, as historical records show; and the records show just as clearly that societies which in themselves do not have an ancient tradition of social contract become societies that in fact do represent social contract. When traditional continuity of the idea of social contract with respect to any given society is not the case, we may then begin to speak of intersystemic junctures between traditions which result in subsequent mappings of one system upon the other. In semiotic rhetorical terms one may speak of redefining one term or system so that it becomes equivalent in meaning with the other previously dissociated term or society (see Perelman 1969). This redefining, rhetorical strategy is discussed elsewhere in this book and in greater detail in Kevelson (1977).[9]

Grimke stresses that "our notions of right and wrong, of just and unjust, are not determined by our positive arguments, but the reverse" (Grimke 1948:78). In other words, Grimke, as Peirce, maintains that our ethical convictions determined by our value choices govern our positive actions, where *positive action* is a term understood within the framework of Peirce's pragmaticism as the logical consequences of correct reasoning. Such reasoning, in Peirce, may be said to correspond, with respect here to the concept of social contract, to the concept of consideration as it applies within the more special context of legal contract.

As late as the eighteenth century, Atiyah points out, "The very concept of contract was . . . in a transitional state." Traditionally, a contract was primarily conceived as a relationship involving mutual rights and obligations. There was not necessarily an implication that the relationship was created by a conscious and deliberate act of will, still less that the rights and duties thereby generated were the creatures of that will.

The passage is important and will be quoted in full:

> Some degree of consent may have been thought of as normally necessary, but consent is a complex idea itself, and there may well have been cases where no consent at all . . . was a necessary part of the relationship. If this is right . . . it will be seen that there was nothing very unreal in seeing a close relationship between 'ordinary' contract and the 'social' contract. Both involved relationships in which mutual rights and duties were created. The concept of contract was, in short, replacing customs as a source of law—that is, as the regulator of social and political obligations—and as the source of individual rights and duties—that is, as the regulator of private obligations. (Atiyah 1979:36–37)

If Atiyah is correct, there should not have been, and should not exist today, the schism between legality and legitimacy that is one of the primary sources of unease in most modern societies, even in those that, like Anglo-American common-law countries, still assume that customs play an active role within the law as an informing agent.

The problem of legality deriving from morality is far from settled. Custom is not, nor has ever been, the equivalent of morality. On the contrary, the customary or usual behavior of the man on the street has rarely been identified with the ideal ethical goals of his society. Rather, the sources of moral conduct are nonusual, and uncommon. Thus custom may be subsumed within law, as legitimacy within legality, Atiyah suggests, with respect to the transference of social contract to legal contract.

But ethical justification for new interpretation of rights theories does not derive from, and has rarely depended on, customary conduct. On the contrary, one is here confronted with three terms: legality, legitimacy, and morality. How all three become fused into a concept of social contract must be explored from a fresh perspective, especially since property is what ties them all together and the notion of property is itself transformed in the modern world.[10]

We are dealing with a number of sign systems, each of which is continuously undergoing change. As they are each in the process of change, they are also interacting with one another and thus, in these interactive relationships, the process as well as the participants contribute to the ongoing transformation of an enormously complex network which, because it is phenomenal, escapes our total knowledge of it. What we may know of this vast and changing network or sign system is limited by those operations of thought we are capable of performing upon it. Analysis by its nature is a reconstruction. But such constructions must be n-dimensional if the dynamics of the process and the parts of the events in process are to be understood and accounted for. Thus what we may gain through a semiotic approach is more comprehensive and more readily revisable than that which may be known by other, more traditional modes of inquiry.

An exhaustive discussion on social contract and legal contract is out of place here. What may be more appropriate is to suggest and, where possible, to illustrate, how a semiotics approach to these and other related topics may be fruitful. At the least, one seeks close discussion of the interdependence of modes of reasoning on ethics, insofar as one's choice of a mode of reasoning is an ethical choice, dependent in turn on a set of values.

For example, the choice of a mode of reasoning permitted Bentham to equate morals and laws in a manner that would not be used by those electing an alternative mode of reasoning. Similarly, a deductive approach to the concept of obligation, as in Kant, yields quite different results than a combination of abductive, deductive, and inductive reasoning, as in Peirce. Inductive reasoning, such as that characterizing the method of the social sciences, is incomplete, not only because the data with which it deals are resistant to positive analysis but, more important, because levels of possibility are not usually included in prob-abilistic accounts of cases under inquiry.

The selection of a method of reasoning is a choice among possible methods of reasoning. The traditional mode of legal reasoning has been deductive, based on assumptions which are not true but are only consented to be held as true with reference to values which are belief systems adapted to purposes which at any given period of time markedly differ from their original aims, when they were first set in practice

This is particularly apparent when we perceive the reintroduction of moral obligation into the domain of legal rights. This is precisely the point argued by Holmes, who rejected the place of morality and moral attitudes as determinant factors in legal procedure. Holmes's position on this point is reiterated throughout his voluminous writing. Not all pertinent citations are offered here, but only representative examples.

Holmes's important distinction between legal and moral liabilities in tort is recalled:[11] What must be asked if one is to decide whether a defendent is innocent or guilty of such liability in tort. How does one properly separate an illegal act from a moral shortcoming, Holmes asks. The full passage is given from *The Common Law*:

> The law of torts abounds in moral phraseology. It has much to say of wrongs, of malice, fraud, intent, and negligence. Hence it may naturally be supposed that the risk of a man's conduct is thrown upon him as the result of some moral short-coming. But while this notion has been entertained, the extreme opposite will be found to have been a far more popular opinion—I mean the notion that a man is answerable for all the consequences of his acts, or, in other words, that he acts at his peril always, and wholly irrespective of the state of his consciousness upon the matter. (1881:65)

Without restating Holmes's examination of both of these approaches here, it will suffice to say that with respect to the former, the leading assumption, which is not always made explicit, is that persons are determined in their actions by forces out of their control and their innocence or guilt depends not so much on whether, in fact, the law was violated, but rather on whether persons are unequally predisposed to obey the law. If unequally, should the court be authorized to correct these inequities and judge more severely those whose freedom to act involves fewer moral restraints, or more severely those who are more morally bound and thereby in conscience observe the limits of the law? Does the law reward or punish the free? The morally conscientious? Holmes takes the stand that "in spite . . . of all the arguments which may be urged for the rule that a man acts at his peril, it has been rejected by very eminent courts, even under the old forms of action." There appears to be an underlying contradiction if not a paradox at the bottom of this problem.

In other words, considerations of moral attitudes enter into the judgment and confuse the law. If the law is consistently to support its own rule which in essence holds that "an act is always a voluntary muscular contraction, and nothing else . . ." then observance of the law of the land is *not* a moral obligation, but the result of a reasoned choice.

The circumstantial series of "causative" events that culminates in an act do not and should not determine that act. Similarly, a chain of mental and emotional states that precede the act should in no way be regarded as causative of that act. In every case, to Holmes, the rule holding that acts are free does not allow for moral, emotional, or other contingencies.[12] Always, in Holmes, an act, whether within or without the domain of the law, implies a choice. This attitude of Holmes is based on a rejection of a mode of reasoning holding that cause and effect are both necessary and sufficient in their relationship. It upholds other quite different modes of reasoning which are multidimensional in the sense that between an alleged causative force and a consequential act there is an interlude of noncommitted possibility. There is a link of openness, by means of which one may choose freely and not be a compelled instrument of prior or previous determinants. The inclusion of moral considerations in legal judgments is, if one may so interpret Holmes, a denunciation of freedom and as such a claim for the determination of persons against their will, or indifference to the idea of will as such ("Trespass and Negligence," 1881/1963:62–103).[13]

At the same time, Holmes concedes:

The moral starting-point of liability in general should never be forgotten, and the law cannot without disregarding it hold a man answerable for statements based on facts which would have convinced a wise and prudent man of their truth. . . . The common law, a any rate, preserves the reference to morality by making fraud the ground on which it goes. ("Fraud, Malice and Intent," ibid.:109 ff.)

But Holmes does make his own conviction clear and nonambiguous, especially in his famous lecture "The Theory of Torts." He says, "Moral predilections
must not be allowed to influence our minds in settling legal distinctions;" (ibid.:
118). This view is amplified in the conclusion of the lecture on torts, quoted in
full:

> The theory of torts may be summed up very simply. At the two extremes of the law
> are rules determined by policy without reference of any kind to morality. . . . But
> in the main the law started from those intentional wrongs which are the simplest and
> mosts pronounced cases, as well as the nearest to the feeling of revenge which leads
> to self-redress. It thus naturally adopted the vocabulary, and in some degree the tests,
> of morals. But as the law has grown, even when its standards have continued to model
> themselves upon those of morality, they have necessarily become external, because
> they have considered not the actual condition of the particular defendant, but whether
> his conduct would have been wrong in the fair average member of the community,
> whom he is expected to equal at his peril. ("The Theory of Torts" ibid.:128)

Here one sees the shift from the authority of the moral code as derived
from religious and sacred codes to that which a consensus of fellow members
of a given community would tolerate. The general reference point or sign for a
legal judgment is thus the implied consent of the society in general. The shift,
it would seem, is from the moral to the customary. But the customary is something
more than, or different from, what might emerge from a poll of a given community. It is a value ascribed to a community, as an approximation of a general
and ideal social aim or value. These values are, in part, inherited from theological
sources as mentioned. But in part they are also the contributions from art, from
science, from industry, and in sum, from that composite, the image of which
constitutes the prevailing representation of current value.

If the "fair average member of the community" can be said to sanction
disregard for personal and private property, and if such fair and average member
can sanction irresponsible behavior with respect to the persons of others, and if
such fair and average member should hold as a value the continual rebellion
against authority in all forms, than defiance of the law is in a logical sense
compliance with the spirit and ethics and values represented by such a legal
system.[14] The iconic, representative image might then be the traditional scales
of justice smashed or weighted.

Holmes's understanding of the evolution of the moral element in law to a
consensual value in community has not been generally interpreted as anarchic.
Yet Holmes was particularly and favorably impressed by Proudhon's famous
slogan, "Property is theft."[15] The followers of Holmes, those who will be discussed in later chapters as spokesmen for legal realism, were very closely in
sympathy with selected aspects of the anarchic tradition. It is characteristic of
this Realist movement to question and to reject the authoritative power of the

legal precedent, to argue against the traditional referential function of the rule of law, and to approve of legal instability in the service of the changing values of the actual community.

Although the Realists' development of legal semiotics is discussed more fully later, here it is noted that Holmes's distinction between morality and legality is but one way in which he develops Peirce's semiotics and pragmatic method. Of the predictive theory in law, which had enormous influence on the development of legal thinking in the United States and abroad, and which derives from Peircean pragmaticism, more will also be said later. In general, as claimed here, Holmes interprets and thus transforms ideas which have their origin in Peirce.

In the words of Patterson, "Holmes . . . presents in a dramatic way the view that the meaning of law depends upon its operational effects."[16] Patterson goes on to say that this view, "derived from Charles S. Peirce's pragmatism . . . and resembling that of logical positivism . . . [rejects] . . . the notion that law is the product of deduction from ethical principles or axioms . . ." Holmes, Patterson notes, ". . . anchored law to decisions and other official acts . . ." (1953:119, 120).

Although Patterson's view is sound in identifying Holmes's predictive theory of law with Peirce's pragmatism, as Fisch, Dewey, and others have similarly done,[17] Patterson is incorrect in describing Peirce as a positivist. Because so little of Peirce's manuscripts and other writings was known or widely referred to at the time of Patterson's writings, there was a tendency among some selective readers of Peirce to class him among the logical positivists. But it was precisely this approach to logic and to analysis of thought and thought process—to sign systems as a whole—that Peirce clearly rejected and revised.

Yet, it was the positivist notion of logic that Holmes had in mind when he made his famous observation that the life of the law is not logic but experience.

Some of the late adherents of realism, such as the legal sociologist, Underhill Moore, were explicitly concerned with the relation between judicial decisions, institutional procedures, moral attitudes, and the changing social values that resulted from their interchange. Moore's studies are investigations of sign relations in such a manner that we want to regard him as having anticipated, in 1929, at the Yale Institute of Human Relations, that which emerged nearly a half-century later as legal semiotics. Patterson's discussion of Moore is valuable (1953:547).

In the problem of mapping morals onto law, Patterson also points to some of the attendant problems when he distinguishes between ethics and morals and correctly notes that this distinction is rarely observed. Patterson says *ethics* refers to the system of theoretical norms that should guide human conduct, *morals* to the attitudes and practices that prevail in any given society or class of society (1953:30, 31 ff).

One may thus describe the behavior of a group of people, that is, any community, class, society, as *moral* in some degree. But one associates ethical precepts with normative divisions of philosophical systems.

Patterson (1953) observes that there are requirements of law which are apart from and outside even the most logically convincing and valid of ethical arguments. The integrity of any legal system at least makes the claim of protecting and reinforcing those moral assumptions that are, in any cohesive community, believed to unite the society in common purpose and peaceful coexistence. It has become increasingly apparent, however, that contemporary writers on law and society tend to include ethics as an integral part of law and jurisprudence. Yet within the legal profession this is not appropriate, although it is becoming more and more usual to do so.

It is a long and honorable tradition that seeks to unite ethics with law and has its origins in Western thought in Aristotle. Chinese law is also inseparable from ethical considerations, as are Hebraic law and Islamic law. But the system of law that are identified both with Anglo-American common law and with the civil law systems that developed from Roman law do not easily and without fundamental problems integrate justice with law. Justice is an ethical concept, but it also connotes the moral convictions of communities as carried forward in practical affairs. The notion that responsibility in law is traditionally inseparable from moral or righteous behavior is closely tied to philosophical ethics; freedom and responsible choice are the manifestations of unification of ethical principles and existential acts.[18]

The obvious problem here is that intention, in an ethical sense, or the carrying out of intention in the moral sense, is quite different from the notion of intention in the legal sense. Similarly, as shown, the motivation of the actor, which is implicit in his intention to act in a certain manner, is in an ethical sense his reason or consideration for such an act. There is great opposition from some and just as strong support from others today to the claim that consideration and motivation on ethical level are congeners to consideration and motivation in law. The persuasive strength of those who see these concepts as basically the same in both systems, but functioning differently with respect to one or the other system, has created a situation in which morals are mapped onto law because, it is assumed, the legal use and function of such concepts as consideration, contract, promise, rights, and so forth, is but the practical aspect of the theoretical notion, the obverse and reverse of the same coin. Indeed, praxis is not actual practice and has never been understood as such. Praxis refers to the conceptual base underlying the operations of the practical sciences and arts. It represents the theoretical reference and/or adapts it to less abstract purpose.

Thus the systems of thought that inform and account for the practical acts and institutions of economics, government, law, psychology, sociology, and the like, were the base of Peirce's pyramidal construction of the classification of the sciences: At the apex was mathematics, not because it was more noble, if noble is an ethical judgment, but because mathematical sciences are more abstract and less firmly based in the practical affairs of people in society. Mathematics is linked with the practical sciences through logic, physics, philosophy, and other sciences which are less abstract than mathematics but also less in touch with actual experience than law, economics, and government.[19] Yet philosophy needs both the greater and the lesser abstract sciences. It needs to represent the methods of mathematics, that is, to adapt to its purposes the self-corrective operations of mathematics. At the same time it needs the base of the practical sciences if it is to draw from experience and not be subject to or determined by notions of essence, substance, intuition, prior knowledge, and so on, all of which are, claims Peirce, antitheses to freedom.

Thus the method of semiotics, including the method of legal semiotics, must show that logic—all of that which Peirce means by logic, which is all of that which he means by semiotics—is the connecting link between the positive mathematical approach and the praxis that characterizes the method of the social sciences. It is for this reasosn that Peirce has logic, in his expanded sense, determined by ethics, which is determined in turn by esthetics or the science of value. The esthetic division of the normative sciences in Peirce's thought is explicitly unconcerned with matters of taste, of beauty, and of art as bearers of esthetic values. Rather, his idea of the esthetic is primarily concerned with the growth of possible freedom and the necessary limits of freedom. The basic denial of individuals by Peirce, except as individuals in relation with other individuals, sustains intelligibility, he argues, and assures that consensus of meaning, that is, transactability and exchange of value-bearing signs, remain possible and usable.[20]

Ethics, in Peirce, must emphasize the role of relationship. If it does not do so, the meaning of the value of freedom is lost and the responsibility of ethics to its esthetic governor is abrogated. To follow through, the choice of a method of reasoning is an ethical choice. The logic one uses to account for the meaning of one's propositions must support and not contradict this meaning.

The measure of morality, Peirce suggests, is the extent to which a community of inquirers conducts its inquiries appropriately, that is, according to the ethical precepts that permit the value of freedom to be evident as acts. The choice of a mode of reasoning is an ethical choice.

The basis of Peirce's criticism of Bentham nevertheless has less to do with ethics than with logic. Yet implied in Peirce's rejection of Bentham's "utility" is the rejection of the value that governs the Benthamite logical support of utility.[21] Utility presupposes, it is recalled, a finite world and finite goods, distributable among members of a given society. Of particular interest is Bentham's analysis of the concept of motive, which, as discussed earlier, has been from early days on associated with the notion of consideration as evidence of contract. In the broadest, most general sense, Bentham says, a motive is that force which is capable of creating an idea, of generating an act, and of preventing an action of any kind. What Bentham does is to take this most general sense of *motive* and establish a classification of kinds of motives, namely, those that are aptly descriptive of various subclassifications of actions. There is nothing which is an action unless it be set in motion by a motive, according to Bentham. Thus there are motives for the most usual concept of action, that is, physical movement. But there is also, by implication, a genus of this general motive which is traditionally termed a *legal action*. Here is found the fusion between physical acts of both moral and nonmoral nature and legal acts according to the forms of action in law. If one follows Bentham's reasoning, not only in this particular chapter, but throughout his voluminous works, one finds that the relation of properties to subjects, which characterizes traditional Aristotelian logic, similarly assigns an attributive function of legal acts to the general topic of motives.

Schematically, the subdivision is: Motive branches to acts; acts to kinds and qualities of acts. Kind includes physical, emotional, intellectual, and legal; quality includes moral and nonmoral. The relation between moral acts in the physical, emotional,and moral senses is thus undeniably tied to legal acts, both moral and nonmoral. A close examination of Bentham's argument is beyond the aims of this book, but it particularly illustrates the structure of his thought in general and also emphasizes how consideration in contract in law becomes analogous with consideration or motive in contract, between persons interacting morally, immorally, or indifferently in their everyday, nonlegal lives (Bentham, *The Principles of Morals and Legislation*, (1780).

Peirce's criticisms of Bentham are many and appear throughout his writings. Here I will mention only those that are particularly appropriate to this chapter. For example, although Peirce praises Bentham for following Locke's example in attempting to establish the practical experience of ordinary people as worthy of scientific investigation, and in laying the foundation for the work of the economists and jurists, (for example, Smith, Ricardo) who bring to bear on their research the methods of science, he also applauds Bentham's contribution of utility to the problems of ethics (CP 8.199). It is not that he agrees with Bentham's *analysis* of the reasons for utility, but, rather, that the reasons themselves are laudable. In other words, the *motive* or reasonable considerations for utility are praiseworthy, even though Peirce rejects out of hand Bentham's justification of utility, that is, the presumption of happiness to be the highest good (CP 8.141).[22] In short, he admires the sentiment but deplores the methods that Bentham employed to argue his points: "Bentham may be a shallow logician; but such truths as he saw, he saw most nobly" (CP 8.158).

Although Peirce takes special issue with Kant also on a number of critical points—for example, Kant's upholding of *a priori* knowledge compared with his own rejection of knowledge not gained through experience; the Kantian concept of time, the distinction between noumena and phenomena; the discreteness of parts of a system—he does not explicitly call Kant to task for his inclusion of ethics within law.

On the whole, Peirce finds little use for and has less respect for ethics and the widespread use served by ethical systems lacking firm and unshakable criteria. And Holmes, especially in his lecture on possession, shows that Kant's emphasis on freedom as the "end in itself" of human values simply does not work when brought into the framework of the law in a Kantian frame of ideas.

Although Kant's influence is pervasive throughout the law of Holmes's time and throughout our own, Holmes shows that Kant fails to address the serious implication of the rights of possession. Kant's view—the basis of his ethics in law—is centered on the individual and not on the individual in relation with other individuals. The relational unit underlying all social structure, which provides a motive for engaging another in contract, is absent from Kant's ethics and, in effect, upholds the freedom of the individual will only at the cost of the freedom of the will of another to assent to the freedom in possession, and in free rights in general of both regarded as a unit of relations (Holmes, "Possession," 1881/1963:163–194).[23]

Holmes's criticism and rejection of Kantian ethics and of the imposition of morality on the law is ultimately based on his rejection of the set of values as well as the method that develops such values into reason that characterizes the Kantian concept of legal ethics. Yet, as mentioned above, Kant's influence together with adaptations of Bentham's principle of utility has produced in modern legal systems a tolerance for justification for this mapping of moral behavior gleaned from systematic ethics onto law. It is a morality that, as Hayek and others deplore, threatens in the name of freedom all that is possibly free. Freedom and the possibility of freedom, according to Hayek, depends on a spontaneous society, on chance, on risk taking. Freedom as ideal and idea interprets the model of a free market.[24]

The following chapters explore semiotic implications with respect to current theories of rights in law and also examine Hayekian views on the free economic system as warrantor of freedom in society wherein such freedoms are upheld by noncoercive and nonrestrictive but morality-based legal systems.

NOTES

1. The notion of isomorphism, which today is especially important in pattern recognition theory, was related by Peirce to representational equivalences and not to similarities or resemblances. In Peirce the idea of isomorphism is related to diagrammatic signs, where a diagram is a type of icon in that it is a "set of rationally related objects" (ms 293).

In this manuscript Peirce discusses the relation between evidence and this type of diagrammatic iconic function of a sign. But isomorphism, which depends on such visual evidence, is not itself identical with evidentiary features but rather with his complex notion of identity, which can only be mentioned here. Manuscript 293, reprinted in Eisele (1976: vol. 4), is entitled "Prolegomenon to an Apology for Pragmatism."

2. See Dewey's article "Austin's Theory of Sovereignty" in *Political Science Quarterly* 9 (1894:31).

3. See the essays on the basis of political authority by R. Taylor, C. Carr, J. Paul, and others in the special issue of *The Monist* Vol. 66/4 (1983).

4. See Hayek on the unfortunate consequences of mapping morality onto law (1984:330).

5. See discussion on distributive justice, Chapter 13 of this volume.

6. See Parker (1979:269–295).

7. See Grimke (1848/1968:218, 219).

8. See Kevelson on the Peircean notion of verisimilitude (1987:chap. 11).

9. See Ong (1958).

10. A full discussion of relations between morality and legality is found in Pennock and Chapman (1982). Of special interest in this collection is F. L. Michelman's "Ethics, Economics and the Laws of Property" (3–40).

11. Peirce's notion of free choice is closely tied to his investigation of genuine paradoxes, as discussed in Kevelson (in preparation) and in Chapter 21 of this volume.

12. See Holmes's "Ideals and Doubts" of 1915 reprinted in 1952:303–317.

13. See Chapter 15 of this volume.

14. See Cohen's linking of Peirce's and Holmes's similar notions of freedom (1950:66, 76, 77, 84, 88).

15. See Pound's discussion of free self-assertion (1958:153–175).

16. See Philbrick (1938:691–732). Note also that Holmes's admiration for Proudhon's "Property is theft" was thoroughly qualified throughout his liberalist career. Yet today legal realism has come to be identified both with anarchism and with radical leftism and is the topic of considerable controversy at present in the Harvard Law School, which is said to be split between the radical realists and the proponents of traditional jurisprudence.

      See also Holmes's so-called liberal opinions in *Lochner* v. *New York* (1905); *Hammer* v. *Saggenhart* (1918); *Abrams* v. *United States* (1919); *Adkins* v. *Children's Hospital* (1923); *Nixon* v. *Herndon* (1927); *Olmstead* v. *United States* (1929).

17. See Holmes on legal interpretation (1899; reprinted in 1952:203–209).

18. See Dewey (1931:210–212).

19. See Kevelson on the mapping of one system of thought upon another, according to Peirce's methodology (1987: chap. 11).

20. See Chapter 4 of this volume.

21. See Peirce's manuscripts on hierarchical order and classification of the sciences: mss 437, 601, 602, 605, 615, 655, 675, 728, 1135, 1341.

22. Peirce includes Bentham among the nominalist wing of the Lockeans (CP 4.33).

23. The notion of the individual is an economic and political concept but refers in Peirce, as in Whitehead and others, to the system of relations (of signs) that symbolically represent a unified and meaningfully enduring whole.

24. The notion of tangible, material consideration, once an equivalent term with motive in contract, has now come to stand primarily for the psychological impulse.

CHAPTER 13

Economic Justice

THE "TAKINGS CLAUSE" AND LEGAL INTERPRETATION

The topic of social or economic justice is most often appreciated in modern literature from the partisan viewpoint of those who claim that many have less than their equal share of society's goods. The problem of whether and how to compensate those members of society who, in the name of economic justice, have been required to divest themselves of portions of their property is of far less immediate concern to moral philosophy. Yet it is among the more perplexing issues with which the law has to deal. How the law decides in these matters depends largely on the methods of interpretation it employs.

It is more than coincidence that jurists of the mid-nineteenth century began to turn their attention to the investigation of juridical methods of inquiry, discovery, and interpretation, for it was precisely around this time that the concept of social or economic justice began to emerge, especially through the writings of Mill (Hayek 1976:66–71, 176–77).

As mentioned, Lieber in 1839 introduced the now classic text on legal hermeneutics as the interpretation of signs in law and politics. In the process of writing his major work, *Political Ethics*, Lieber recognized the lack of clear statement available on the interpretive process in law and addressed himself to this task. Unlike Savigny's work on interpretation in law which presupposed reference to a closed society and hence to the notion of fixed authority, Lieber's work introduced the problem of interpretation in the context of an open society with shifting authoritative reference. In this work Lieber anticipated Peirce's pragmatic logic of inquiry which emphasizes the dynamic process whereby ideas as signs may be infinitely developed through a method of inquiry that creates, evolves, and discovers cumulative meaning of the topic in question. Peirce's semiotic method of inquiry is dialogically structured and assumes that the author-itative precedent of norms, rules, and judgments are law-like, but provisional only and subject to doubt and to question. It was Peirce's contention that the belief in free will and hence in free inquiry must presuppose the possibility of doubt. It is only in "certain critical moments" of doubt that one is most free: "Hence the practical part of Ethics is the study of these critical moments" (1982:6). This chapter continues the discussion to this point but will focus on a particular aspect of the issue of law and morality.

The freedom to interpret and reinterpret leading principles is antithetical to closed societies, but such indeterminate review constitutes the basis of a free marketplace, in the context of what Hayek refers to as the "spontaneous order" of the open society (Hayek 1976).

Since the latter half of the nineteenth century the arguments for economic justice have largely been made on behalf of the multitudes of people who, by contrast with the rich and the privileged and from both personal and institutional viewpoints, lack well-being. It is in the interests of and with sympathy for the unfortunate members of society that the case for economic justice, however defined, has been advanced. Indeed, the appeal to economic and social justice in the name of countless special interest groups has, on a global scale, transformed human societies. At the same time this transformation has brought about critical changes in the nature, function, and general understanding of the marketplace. A free market, as conceived by classical economic theory, is an endangered species. As Hayek and others argue, this great cost does not and will not ensure that just societies will prevail, but only that the dubious concept of economic justice, or social justice—which he regards as synonymous terms, and we will so regard them here—will have had its day and inevitably come to be replaced by some other central mandate for the reorganization of society toward the alleged good of its own being.

Merely to assume that a society is a composite or corporate being of which can be predicated certain capabilities or properties such as that of goodness or justness is to step into the framework of an Aristotle or even of a Berkeley and to assume that the idea of a society may intrinsically possess attributes inde-pendent of human interpretation and evaluation, that is, of judgment.

One of the principal tenets of semiotics is that we are incapable of knowing anything directly or immediately but only through the mediation of signs and sign systems. Therefore, society and economic justice, as ideas, are stages in the development of signs and sign systems which represent, at any given time for any given community of inquirers within the context of any given universe of discourse, that which is commonly held and affirmed to be real. But this judgment of the real, with respect to the idea or sign used to refer to it, is provisional only. It is open to doubt and to question in an open system which encourages free inquiry and exchange. This chapter holds that free exchange on the marketplace for the purpose of transacting values, or value equivalences through the media of money and related tangible wealth, parallels the free transactions of signs of value in the exchange of ideas and signs of meaning in processes of inquiry and discovery of reality.

Because this chapter is not an investigation of specific relations between Peircean semiotics and the concept of economic justice but is rather an inquiry into some neglected aspects of the general theory of economic justice from a semiotics perspective, Peirce's work will be mentioned only in passing. It will also be noted in passing that the exchange of ideas between Peirce and his British colleague, the well-known logician and economist Stanley Jevons, may be assumed to have contributed richly to the changing role of economics in a philosophical approach to issues and problems, both of method and content, of modern society.

Jevons's work in economics marks for his contemporaries as well as for ours a turning point in the goals and theories of economic institutions (Kirzner 1960:10–17). Yet Jevons did not radically revise the utilitarian criterion but rather introduced the significance of methods of discovery. According to Jevons, the key concept in discovery and interpretation was substitutability, or commutation, in the establishment of equivalences between money and other social values. Peirce's major criticism on this point is that substitutability does not permit us to account for values that increase and decrease as a result of inquiry. What is needed, Peirce insisted, was the concept of permutability. This distinction is crucial in differentiating between methods of investigation appropriate to open and closed societies and hence to dynamic as opposed to static modes of interpretation.

The first part of this chapter will briefly present the problem of economic justice brought about by an activist legal system on behalf of society's less fortunate members. Regardless of whether state intervention does actually succeed in improving the well-being of the poor and underprivileged through activist judicial decision, it does so only by creating at the same time new ethical problems. Thus the problem of private property in an activist state has required as a last resort the need to interpret constitutional law for purposes quite novel in the history of the country. For example, the problem of private property in an activist state requires reference to the Constitution. Now, according to the method of inquiry that characterizes *closed* systems, the Constitution is *invoked*, whereas according to the method of inquiry that characterizes *open* systems the Constitution is *interpreted*.

In the United States it is, specifically, the Fifth Amendment that is to be invoked or interpreted in the interests of protecting citizens not only from incriminating themselves but also from other related acts of self-destruction. According to the Fifth Amendment, no person shall relinquish part of his well-being without receiving in the transaction value judged to be equivalent to the loss, "nor shall private property be taken for public use, without just compensation" (Ackerman 1978:1–10).

The problem not only concerns the difficulty in establishing limits to the authority of an activist court but also opens up for speculation in another light facets of economic justice which proponents of organized social welfare have largely chosen to ignore.

The second part of this chapter will review, also briefly, the major criterial bases for justice: legitimacy, utility, and fairness (Pettit 1980). It will be shown that all of these criteria, which rest on traditional and established habits of thought, are presumed to be law-like in Peirce's sense and may so function until new evidence casts doubt on these belief systems and thereby calls these time-honored judgments, or criterial bases for justice, into question and opens them to possible revision and correction. It will be shown also that each of these concepts—legitimacy, utility, fairness—connotes with respect to contextual closed systems certain meanings that are inappropriate and wrong with respect to open systems. The terms may retain their verbal shape, so to speak, but the meanings of each term will inevitably change and increase in the very process of inquiry and discovery.

Further, if inquiry increases our knowledge of the real, that is, adds to the sum of a society's goods and commodities which the terms *real* and *real property* represent and refer to, then that *knowledge* of the real must also be counted among the totality of a society's wealth. Thus the problem of the distribution of knowledge, which is already big business in a strictly economic sense in our day, must also be raised in connection with the general topic of economic justice.

From this point of view it is found that the need to take account of the potential and the infinite preclude establishing a clear definition of any starting point of social wealth, that is, a finite quantity capable of being measured and justly distributed.

In the third part of this chapter some of the more significant issues involved in economic justice from the perspective of efficiency will be discussed. Efficiency requires a starting point, and such starting points with respect to an economic analysis of law are indeterminate in most respects, as Baker (1980) explains. Similarly, Rizzo argues that unless efficient legal rules are identified, theorists may propose norms which in actuality cannot be implemented by the courts and have, in Rizzo's words, "little operational content" (1979:641–658).

The concluding section of the chapter presents a rejection of economic justice as a means of maximization of wealth enacted and enforced by central institutional authority. Some of the major objections to social or economic justice developed by Hayek and others will be referred to. The problem of the making of property through exchange and a free marketplace will be compared with the taking of property from individuals in the interests of public welfare and the predictable claim for compensation in the form of equivalent value. The question left open is whether equivalent values may be more justly determined through changing needs and wants in interpersonal and local transaction, or whether such standards of equivalent value must be imposed from a single and central authoritative source. With respect to either possibility, who should act for a free and just society as its arbiters?

Henry Maine reminds us that, far from being a simple concept, property can no more be defined and valued by reference to its nature than by certain distinctions such as movable or immovable, real or personal, transferable or inalienable. Yet one of the principal tasks of any legal order is to enact and enforce rules governing the protection and exchange of property. The changing classifications of kinds of property in a given society are always referent to those underlying goals and nonmaterial values that constitute the substructure of that social organization. When we move from one period of history to another, or from one culture to another, or from one region to another in some countries, we move also from one order to a different order of legal ideas with respect to property and value (Maine 1886:342–43).

One of the major revolutions in legal thought resulted from the assimilation of immovable property within the category of movable property. One of the consequences of this revolution in legal order is that a property may be valued not only for its present market price but also in terms of what it may become, that is, in terms of its potential value in the marketplace.

Thus a tree, once regarded as falling within the class of immovable properties, becomes a movable property when its potential value is taken into consideration. For example, the tree may become fine furniture veneer, building material, works of art, gasahol in our times by conversion, and even clean air by derivation. If a city decides to remove a tree from a property owner's yard in order to widen the street for a public throughway, what compensatory value may be assigned to that tree? What compensation, if any, may be demanded? A hundred years ago the question would have been easily answered. At the very least, compensation itself was assured, and the main business of the legal institution was to serve the status quo (Ackerman 1978:28).

But despite the fact that since the initial drafting of the United States Constitution the problem of unequal distributions of property has been deplored, various means have been sought and tried in order to correct such disparities; but property has been so firmly tied to power that the various attempts to legislate against status quo and monopolistic holding of property have met with firm but failing resistance. Power itself has until very recently been generally regarded as a kind of possession.

Adolphe Berle argued more than a quarter of a century ago that the kind of power one must be most concerned about was not related to property in the traditional and usual sense. He showed the evolution of power in four stages, namely, (1) the power of divine inheritance such as the power of priests and kings who were assumed to follow God in the chain of command; (2) the power of landed interest or that which accrues through title to land or real estate; (3) the power of property and affluence through property in general; (4) and, in our own time, the power of intelligence, that is, of brain trusts, decision-making expertise, and the authority vested in such brain trust to organize and control the entire social structure directly or through influence (Berle, 1959). According to Berle, this last is power without property. It is the power without property that authorizes modern institutions in this country to change the rules, that is, to reinterpret the "takings clause" of the Fifth Amendment in such a manner as to substitute a former concept of status quo for a new social state, one claimed to be of equivalent value in terms of a "just society."

Thus, as Ackerman shows, the clause stating "nor shall private property be taken without just compensation" may possibly be understood as "payment is constitutionally required *only when it will serve the purposes of justice*" (Ackerman 1978:28–9).

Assume that a property owner holds title to some natural resource, such as a piece of land which stands in the middle of a projected public park and on which is a natural pond. At one time, if the land were taken the property owner could successfully demand payment for the book or market value of the land. At a later time in our history, it became possible for the property owner to be required to open his park-like land with pond to public use. The value of the land could be taken and distributed so that the community owned the right of use. Today, however, the property owner may be compensated for relinquishing his sole right to use, but he may not be compensated for the loss of specific control over how the community may conduct activities on that land, and neither could he be compensated for the depreciation in value of what had formerly been a negotiable instrument. *The loss of power is not compensated under law.* Further, if the property owner wants his former state restored to where it was prior to intervention, the right to just compensation does not hold. The question is whether, under the Fifth Amendment, as interpreted today, the property owner can and should be compensated, in the interests of a just society, to the equivalent of full restoration of his former status and property. Ackerman's illustration has been modified for purposes of this chapter. The point is, although our property owner has suffered damages for which there may be determined an equivalent sum of money, it is not clear whether the interests of justice *permit* full compensation. *The justice of yesterday is different from the justice of today.*

Today it falls to the judge, or highest legal actor, to decide for justice or economic justice, in this sense. If the judge is an activist judge, this means that he is of the bent to respond to the felt wishes of the people in a way that, according to this understanding, best serves the highest social good. If he is a more traditional, or restrained, legal actor, he will attempt to understand and implement the intention of the legislators.

In order not to shake severely the semblance of a stable legal system, an activist judge may indeed refer to legislative intent and cite as grounds for his decision some authoritative precedent, but it may well be a nonexistent precedent and he may well be in such event the creator of a new law by means of legalism, or legal fiction. Thus the questions that Frank posed in the 1930s are still pertinent today: Does the judge, as highest legal actor, create or discover law?

To the extent that even the activist judge attempts to preserve the stability of a legal system the legislative intent will be, at least on the surface, honored. According to Hayek, it is the supreme responsibility of the highest legal actor to decide as a vehicle for legislators and not as an innovator of new law. By the same token it is the responsibility of legislators to refrain from making judgments that are not theirs to make. But the current practice of legislating regulations regarding the use and distribution of some properties, in the interests of a just society, is tantamount to judging and deciding the law.

Policymakers at all levels assume the role of the judge and in effect bring about radical transformations in the meaning part of the "takings clause" (Berle 1967:55–78).

Berle traces what he calls "the revolution in economic organization" and suggests that a council of economic advisors is urgently needed to protect business and the free market from government. His argument hinges on the point that the legal system in its present organization is inadequate to the economic challenges confronting them in a changing society; they need help.

Berle suggests that when the "takings clause" affects corporations the demand for compensation must come from individual persons—stockholders, workers, suppliers, and all the related members of society—because it is these persons whose rights may be unjustly ignored. This is a point of view rarely discussed in that literature most critical of capitalist institutions and free-enterprise market economy. This point will be returned to, in summary, with reference to Hayek's argument against institutionally organized deployment of economic justice.

As mentioned above, concepts are assumed to increase in their "real value" through the semiotic process of inquiry and interpretation. The changing status of the "takings clause" is but an example of the development of legal concepts with respect to social goals. In retrospect one finds that legal concepts change very slowly.

As Maine cautions, at all periods of social development, there has been a tendency to overesteem "the stability of legal concepts. . . . Their great stability is apt to suggest that they are absolutely permanent and indestructible" (Maine 1886:360). Maine sees this tendency to regard the association between relative stability of legal concepts and something resembling fixed and permanent truth as a flaw deriving from the juridical thought of John Austin and Bentham, who "sometimes write as if they thought that, although obscured by false theory, false logic, and false statement, there were, somewhere behind all the delusions which they expose, a framework of permanent legal conceptions which is [like] . . . looking through a dry light, and to which a rational Code may always be fitted" (Maine 1886:366).

The following adopts Maine's thought to the concepts of legitimacy, utility, and fairness, which are presumed to be the major criterial bases for the present prevailing idea of justice in the United States.

The literature of these topics is so vast that it will suffice to state only the main points and to add what is pertinent.

The idea of legitimacy based on proprietary rights derives from Locke. The idea of utility, as the maximization of social goods for the greatest number of people, derives from Bentham. The idea of fairness, deriving from Kant, finds its most explicit modern expression in Rawls.

This is not to suggest that legitimacy, utility, and fairness are distinctly different concepts. Rather, each relates to property in a different manner, and each respective tradition of thought presupposes a different methodological approach to the question of property distribution in an ideally just society.

Legitimacy emphasizes the "natural right" of inalienability of property to person, where property is that which extends from person to production and which may be translated into exchangeable equivalences, or signs of transactable values of a person, in Locke's sense.

Utility stresses the commonality of human purpose, which is to attain to the greatest possible happiness (the highest good or value) and the opinion that this good may be quantified and justly distributed through the medium of money. The end of utility is the maximization of public welfare. Happiness as topic extends to as many tokens as there are kinds of commodities and goods available which may be exchanged for money.

Fairness rests on contractual agreement and is enforceable by law. Violation of the fairness principle is nothing short of an infraction against society as a whole where the society is presumed to be the vehicle for liberties designated by law, in agreement with the felt needs of the people who constitute the society and who demand such liberties.

These three criteria together form the design or "charter" for a just society (Pettit 1980:75 ff). "The notion of legitimacy presupposes pre-existing standards of right and wrong," Pettit observes. Similarly, preexisting norms are also assumed for notions of welfare and the criterion of fairness. Fairness assumes mutuality, reciprocity, and cooperation between contracting parties. These expectations are ideal and unsupported by evidence.

Thus legitimacy, utility, and fairness, although distinct in their respective objectives, are alike in referring to qualities of human beings that are widely believed to be peculiarly human and of the very nature of being human.

Emphasis is on the static mode of human being, as opposed to the dynamic, open possibility of becoming more human. A concept of justice—of social or economic justice—that derives from states of being is antithetical to a concept of justice that would imply a process of becoming continuously and infinitely closer to some changing, continuously reinterpreted idea of justice. A definition of justice, in this sense, is an interpretant sign.

This is not to deny that regularity of conduct or established habits of thought are the bases of legimated norms. But criteria that derive from satisfied expectation of regular patterns of conduct and events exclude whole ranges of possibility and chance. Thus the free marketplace functions in a vital and viable manner precisely because it includes chance and possibility in transaction. The danger of eliminating chance and possibility in the organization and implementation of institutional social or economic justice is that the economic freeplay available to a justice-seeking society shrinks or becomes so constrained by imposed regulation that risk taking, upon which a free market depends, disappears.

The Constitution is constrained from enacting practice conducive to self-indictment and self-destruction; legislation that in a long-range view is reductive of human possibility should be suspect.

Pettit speaks of the relation between a legitimate, preinstitutional claim to rights and an institutional denial or obstruction to these rights as a "weak sense of non-institutional rights" (1980:76–79). He notes that it is precisely this kind of "right" that is referred to, for example, in the *Declaration of the Rights of Man and of Citizens of 1789*. It is this same weak sense of rights that underlies the *Virginian Declaration of Rights* of 1776. And it is also this same weak sense of rights that is so problematic in the *United Nations Declaration of Human Rights*.

By contrast, a strong sense of rights is concerned with manifest acts and practices. Practice is here understood as "regularity of behavior to which nearly everyone in a society conforms, and which is such that this expectation gives . . . some reason for wanting deviance discouraged, including his own deviance if that is a necessary cost of general discouragement" (Pettit 1980:76).

Thus, the argument suggests, a strong sense of rights based on all three criteria for justice—legitimacy, utility, fairness—is sufficient motivation for persuading one to act against his own self-interest. Even if one qualified this, such that a strong sense of rights might persuade one to act self-destructively in the short run if, in the long run, self-destructiveness would result in a just and free society, it might be condoned from the viewpoint of a moral philosophy; but it is highly improbable with respect to interpersonal transactions in a free marketplace, and in a society that is maximally free.

What one next must ask is, How and for what reasons has economic theory been so radically altered within the last hundred years that such a belief in self-destruction and the deliberate renunciation of power and property could have come to be assented to?

Despite the fact that Hayek correctly places the concept of economic justice within the framework of socialistic ideology, he concedes that the appeal to economic justice has, to a large extent, succeeded in transforming those societies that have reorganized toward this end (Hayek 1976:64,65 ff). He suggests that the phrase *economic justice*, or *social justice*, has been responsible on the pragmatic level of inquiry for bringing about such changes especially in third-world societies. However, the impetus to change continues its dynamic development in modern societies, and the denial of the free market in favor of social justice eliminates in time the resources for any justice in terms of wealth distribution and incentive to produce.

Hayek goes on to say, "Though the phrase has undoubtedly helped occasionally to make the law more equal for all, whether the demand for justice in distribution has in any sense made society more just or reduced discontent must remain doubtful" (1976:65).

Toward the end of the nineteenth century the appeal for economic justice was little more than a stirring of the consciences of the then ruling classes in countries throughout the world. They were moved but not mandated to take a caring and philanthropic position toward those of their fellow citizens who not only were impoverished but were without hope or assurance that basic survival needs might be met on other than a day-to-day basis.

The notion that only propertied persons in society were capable of contracting prevailed. Evidence of ownership of property was necessary in lieu of collateral. Thus lack of title to property prevented persons from engaging in contractual relations. The nonpropertied person had a relation to the propertied person not essentially different from that of servant to master, or wife to husband.

Spokesmen for the poor and unfortunate rose from the so-called privileged class. The status of the privileged class came to represent a standard against which deviations were measured and toward the attainment of which, for all persons in society, well-being was assessed. The notion of welfare and utility emerges in such a social climate of comparison in which the standards of the rich and privileged were adopted as the absolute standards of utility. The belief that happiness was accessible to all presupposed that by the improvement of physical life all other social disorders would also be righted. Poverty was viewed not only as the site of sin, but as sin itself, as bad in opposition to good. By extension, from the idea that welfare was economically procurable emerged the ethical norm from which the concept of economic justice evolves. Thus the initial appeal for economic justice shifted from appeals to conscience to prescriptive moral rules, and hence to laws to bring about conscionable acts (Laski 1919/ 1969:37–42; Cohen 1954:86–180).

The legislation of morality in other than the cause of economic justice is discussed in Thomas Grey's (1980) study of the development of a moral attitude in American legal practice and theory. Grey draws attention to the recent renewal of discussion during the last twenty-five years of Mill's notion of social justice.

He shows that the concern with just distribution of goods extends the notion of property to include the property of one's physical body. He raises as a particular question whether society or the individual decides what manner of sexual activity the body-as-community property may engage in. For example, the question of homosexuality and social rights brought about the Hart–Devlin debate subsequently led to legislative changes in laws regulating sexual behavior. On the one hand, the revised legislation corresponded to changing social values. On the other hand, a point not discussed by Grey, the Lockean notion of the body as property together with the property produced by one's body becomes reinterpreted and updated today in a manner not likely to have been in the minds of former legislators.

Major developments in economic theory led to reinterpretations of money. Money as representation of material wealth became money as a measuring-rod for values material and nonmaterial. Thus when Georg Simmel's *Philosophy of Money* first appeared in 1900 it was understood by Max Weber and others as a metaphysics of money.

Simmel's study has been since its publication variously and ingeniously misunderstood. He attempts to interpret economic events so that money is viewed as a complex sign—a symbolic sign, or sign of thirdness in Peirce's sense—by which the basic and most enduring of human values may be measured. Simmel describes money as "mediating between value and life in such a manner that money and exchange not only enable an objective comparison of subjective values but permit [one] to take up the problem of value itself" (1907:25; Kevelson 1983).

Very recent years have seen law and economics synthesized into a new discipline, characterized as that area that analyzes the law from the perspective of economics. This synthesis presumably "emerges to fill the intellectual vacuum left by Legal Realism," Horvitz notes (1980). It emerges as the youngest of the neutral, or practical, sciences. It attempts to base its inquiry on scientific method, to be "objective, neutral, and apolitical" and also mathematical (Horvitz 1980:905–912).

The prime goal of this new science is to gain legitimacy by assuming a cloak of science, that is, the accoutrements of "exactness." But despite its disavowal of partisan politics, its rhetoric has been largely persuasive of the need for central governmental control especially with respect to the broad, unclear, and largely controversial area of distributive justice, according to Horvitz (1980:905,906)

This organization of an economic-based legal system attempts to analyze, for example, the cost of crime and whether or not enforcement of the law would justify incurred expense.

Generally, the paradox this master plan presents is as follows: for example, those who are at present constrained from taking advantage could, in turn, be taken advantage of by those who at this time are assumed not to share equally in social value and goods which have an equivalent social-value money tag. The result of such legislated economic justice leads to rules which bind persons to act toward their own self-undoing. Further, the term *advantage* can be extended such that advantage taking in intelligence and knowledge would be forbidden by law. The knower would be required to relinquish private knowledge and permit it to be redistributed as public information. Aside from the problem this would create in terms of the "takings clause" of the Fifth Amendment, such rulings would play havoc with the First Amendment as well. Yet there are discernable steps in this direction, which will not be discussed here.

Constraints of this volume prevent more detailed examination of other problems presented in the approach to economic justice through efficiency, where efficiency as an economic concept becomes a legal concern and the basis for a radical reinterpretation of the aim of the law.

With respect to money as an equivalent of other nonmaterial social values, the commodity of knowledge must be seen in terms of its current unequal distribution in society. To rectify that inequality and to distribute power more justly among all the members of a society requires that one should regard knowledge as an exchangeable object, not unlike other factory-produced goods and items. Fritz Machlup, the well-known Hayekian economist, has shown in his *Knowledge: Its Creation, Distribution, and Economic Significance, Vol. 1* (1980) that the general term *knowledge* may be readily subdivided into classes of knowledge, for example, negative knowledge, qualities of knowledge, and that in this way one may establish a standard monetary basis for knowledge.

As a kind of manufactured goods, knowledge would have to pass inspection, presumably as it moves along the assembly line of knowledge inspectors. Shipping and receiving of knowledge is now and would further become an important cost factor. The problem of sitting with a large inventory of last year's knowledge would be bad for business according to any economic theory. There is evidence of this in most universities today and especially in the relation between knowledge producer and knowledge backer, or research granting institutions.

In the paper entitled "Notes on the Theory of the Economy of Research" Peirce formulates mathematical relations between cost and utility and then applies his method to the problems of relating the "scientific utility of a small fixed advance of knowledge" to a delayed or deferred return on investment, showing that the initial cost of an idea may not yield a profit for a long time (CP 7.159). Peirce's economic theories are discussed in a subsequent chapter. What should be noted at this time, however, is that Peirce successfully shows where Bentham's utility errs because the method of Bentham's inquiry is based on the notion of a closed and finite system with a fixed point of reference. In a similar fashion he refutes the economic theories of Ricardo and Malthus and is in fundamental opposition to Keynes.

James's notion of the "cash value" of an idea is directly influenced by Peirce's pragmatics and by his concept of interpretation and growth in semiotic transactions; it anticipates such a free market as argued for by Hayek and others.

We undertake to argue against economic justice with calculated risk. At best, one appears to be misanthropic and perverse. At the worst, one has failed to distinguish between assent to the ideal of a just society and denial of social organization to bring it about by coercive means.

Hayek says that despite the fact that the appeal to economic justice has been, over the past century, "the most widely used and effective argument in political discussion," its very success in bringing about better distribution of goods has also brought with it the danger of destroying the hen which lays the golden eggs. The imposition of a centralized authority on the marketplace can only vitiate free exchange and reduce the incentive for risk taking to the level of good will. The "spontaneous order" of the marketplace cannot withstand constraints on its activity and free activity to the extent they are proposed or even to the extent they are already effective.

Hayek questions whether economic justice as it relates to the marketplace has any meaning whatever except that which is invented and used as if it referred to some actual, phenomenal relation in the world of human affairs. Not least, he proposes that the very idea of economic justice is a lie which argues in the name of greater freedom while at the same time it reduces possible freedoms of exchange by restricting and regulating options and alternatives which, he claims, are essential if free men are to believe in their capabilities for making genuine choices, taking genuine risks, and testing the very nerve for failure, without which no real discovery and invention are conceivable.

He says:

> The type of social order in which individuals are directed to serve a single system of ends is the organization and not the spontaneous order of the market; that is, it is not a system in which the individual is free because bound only by general rules of just conduct, but a system in which all are subject to specific directions by authority. (Hayek 1976:35)

Finally, it is not so much that the various criteria of legitimacy, utility, or fairness are inadequate. But the idea of justice itself, as regulated by law and imposed on the free market, reduces the meaning of the terms to mere stipulations. Economic justice prescinds specific qualities of these broad and general terms and then proceeds to regard the abstracted quality as though it represented the whole ground.

As the concept of economic or social justice has evolved in the last century and has become an object for scientific inquiry, the various models suggested for theoretical exploration have tended to be substituted for the actuality they are assumed to represent. The actuality of a free society depends on the ability of people to negotiate in dialogic exchange and *to be capable of differentiating misfortune from injustice*. Further, a discriminative economic justice that leaves the property owner who is divested of his property in the name of public welfare without clear recourse for just compensation is neither just nor economically sound.

CHAPTER 14

Economic Links with Law

THE MARKET AS SIGN OF A FREE SOCIETY

Elsewhere (Kevelson 1987) I have proposed a semiotic approach to economics and have examined some of Peirce's most significant and, to date, neglected ideas on the relation between money and value, that is, on the correspondence between a free market and freedom as the *summum bonum.*

This chapter will expand some of the principles introduced in earlier chapters of this volume and will show the interdependence of economics and law, such that a legal semiotics may be seen to include economic problems and issues as significant semiotic structures. Such a chapter is exploratory in two ways: First, the interrelation of law and economics in traditional inquiry is still regarded as highly problematic. One ventures to tie these two social institutions into a unified relationship only if one is prepared to counter serious and qualified objections with counterarguments to justify this unification.[1] Secondly, the relation between law and economics has not previously been explicitly discussed to a great extent, partly because legal semiotics is itself so new a comer upon the scene of general semiotics and partly because semiotics as a whole is maverick in its assumption that it is not the content that distinguishes disciplines from each other but their respective methods, that is, the kinds of questions they ask and the reasons or motives underscoring the questions.

Nevertheless, one cannot do semiotic research without assuming risk because risk, or chance, is inseparable from semiotic theory and method in its totality.[2]

Scarcely more than a decade ago, Richard Posner's *Economic Analysis of Law* stressed the ground-breaking project of approaching law and legal theory from the perspective of economics. Posner notes that before the 1960s, except

for antitrust laws and related legislation, there was little or no attempt to discuss
the union of law and economics:

> . . . The hallmark of the new law and economics—the law and economics that is
> almost entirely new within the last decade and a half—is the application of the theories
> and empirical methods of economics to the legal system across the board—to common
> law fields such as tort, contract, and property, to the theory of practice of punishment,
> to civil, criminal, and administrative procedure, to the theory of legislation, and to
> law enforcement and judicial administration. (1973:15–16)

Posner suggests the obvious, that one cannot lift a part of a system to bring it
into relationship with another system without at the same time implicating all
parts of the subsystems comprising the total network.

Thus the earlier attempt to treat only antitrust laws as economically based
can be assumed to be the result of an atomistic premise holding that discrete
elements may be brought together to constitute a class or aggregate. We know
that Kant, throughout his writings, held to this view although in his posthumous
work there is strong evidence of his moving from the position of discreteness
to a theory of the continuum, such as is central to Peirce's thought.[3] This is not
an appropriate place for discussion of Kantian philosophy, except to emphasize
that so much of modern legal theory on rights and on legal ethics, as discussed
above, is Kantian in its origin and thus influences the development of modern
law in the United States and abroad.

Posner points out that the older linking of law and economics restricted
its scope to laws that were explicitly economic in nature, it but overlooked the
vast area of law dealing with the law of contracts. But, he says, the new union
of law and economics includes in its scope everything that is law and everything
that is economics. It must also come to include, one might add, all of that which,
within the discretely structured university of the twentieth century, is called
"political science," and also that which, within the halls of philosophy, is concerned with ethics, social and political philosophy, legal philosophy, and so on.[4]
In other words, the new law-and-economics marriage is no less cross-disciplinary
than is semiotics. The problems encountered by traditional scholars in law and
economics concern methods of bringing this new relationship within the prescribed methods of their respective fields. Semiotics deals with a similar problem
except that the semiotic methodology is not piecemeal, as are adaptations in
arbitrary manner from various traditional disciplines, but is systematically out-
lined by Peirce.[5]

Calabresi's and Coase's early 1960s work is cited as being one of the first
and most innovative attempts to map economics onto selected areas of legal
theory. This attempt and subsequent attempts successfully point to an economic
basis of a great deal of law which was not previously regarded from this point
of view. At the same time it established economics as a logical "individual" to
be sure, but an individual whose meaning is significant only in relation with

other individual sciences. Peirce's important principle has quietly and, for the most part without explicit discussion, been catalytic upon the development of legal and economic semiotics. This book, then, is the first attempt to make explicit and to provide further exposition of Peirce's semiotic concepts as they apply to and influence the development of the practical sciences of law, economics, and government.

Posner's main thesis is that an economic approach to law will possibly result in more "efficient allocation of resources" (1977:17). Efficiency is one of the basic concepts of economics, as is value. Both are technical terms as used within the framework of economic theory and will be briefly reviewed here for noneconomists:

Efficiency in modern utility concepts is a replacement of the Benthamite notion of the pleasure principle, that is, that which is satisfied when maximum available resources are so distributed as to afford the greatest number the greatest satisfaction with respect to available goods. Efficiency is more appealing to modern economists than pleasure primarily because one may more easily chart and measure units of efficiency whereas pleasure remains in the last analysis a fuzzily subjective and ultimately nonmeasurable goal.

Thus efficiency, more or less, is determined by consumers' willingness to pay. Efficiency is proportional with this willingness to exchange currency for goods. The greater the efficiency, the greater the demand and thus the more marketable the goods at the most profitable price. Efficiency is to vendors what value is to consumers. Money or its equivalent is the medium of exchange.

Analogously, with respect to the transaction of other values, that is, meaningful "commodities" such as information, efficiency relates to the clarity and nonambiguity of verbal expression, and value relates to the attention and intensive interpretation a listener is willing to expend for this information.

Jakobson's famous chart of coordinate functions between addresser, addressee, channel, code, message, and contact are all applicable here, and for noneconomic readers they provide a common frame of semiotic reference for discussion of economic terms. In this sense an economic transition is prototypically a semiotic event. This point will be amplified throughout the following discussion.

It was observed in previous chapters that all contracts are *quid pro quo*, based on some consideration or motive, that is, reason. The motive, or reason, within the domain of economics is money or its substitute, a note, a check, a promise, a service, or something tradable. Anything having a possible cash value, including ideas and the by-products of ideas, is worth money. The interesting problem one confronts here is that an equivalent of cash money is not only and not always a mere substitute, as Jevons and other nineteenth-century economists claimed. Rather, in some instances the equivalence is *qualitatively* different and, as Peirce argues against Jevons, the important factor in economic exchange, which relates to a difference between their logics, is *permutability* rather than commutability or mere substitutability.[6]

It is the emphasis on the transformations of signs as part of the process of transaction that is so important in Peirce and rarely emphasized in traditional economics (Kevelson 1985c).

With respect to the transformation of an idea, the idea of an invention or concept is efficient in direct proportion to the value of those who are willing to spend money, that is, significant energy, in acquiring it. The transformation of an invention, or a concept such as a slogan in advertising, a stand of black walnut saplings, an outline for a system of thought, or the like, into something *qualitatively* different is discussed by Machlup, for example, when he speaks of taking an "inventory" of ideas in order to include these goods within the whole of any hypothetical maximal resource or sum of goods of any given society at any given time.[7]

Machlup points out that utility is not feasible because there is no instrument for measuring ideas that have not yet emerged and taken their places among the published, that is, the evident *facts* of accumulated knowledge or goods of a society. There must be a place for possibility in a radical sense, Machlup suggests. Here he is anticipated by Peirce's theories of the potential and the possible[8] (Machlup 1980, also 1976:13–60).

Efficiency, in supplanting utility, has become a hallmark or criterion for economic value. However, in our modern and complex world one is not able to measure with any accuracy the extent to which a good is voluntarily acquired and is a measure of voluntary action. Still further complicating the issue of efficiency is the fact that some goods are involuntarily acquired and therefore one would have to include in one's analysis the amount of negative value of involuntarily acquired goods. The approach to these and other related problems is even further complicated by the fact that there is no way of achieving other than a static representation of an efficiency transaction at any given time.[9] What is possible are successive states, or discrete pictures of what in actuality is a dynamic process. This shortcoming in efficiency analysis of law and economics closely resembles the deficiency in structural analysis as a whole, as remarked earlier in Part I of this study.

Although *structuralism* and *semiotics* have unfortunately been used synonymously by some investigators, there are differences between the systems each denotes that are fundamental to each respective system; it is necessary continually to call attention to the fact that structuralism and semiotics, from Peirce's point of view, are not alike in aim or method.

By the same token, the union of law and economics which has grown over the last several decades has overlooked contributions that semiotics has to make. Peirce's contributioins to both economics and law are not well known even among seasoned Peirce scholars, largely because the manuscripts have not been readily accessible and also because there is no distinct section within all his writings that develops either law or economics or their union as suggested by Posner. It is one of the principal tasks of this book to make this Peircean contribution more widely known.

The influence of economics and economists upon Peirce's own thought is much more widely appreciated, as mentioned earlier. For example, Whewell and Jevons are among those trained in and renowned for their contributions to nineteenth-century classical economics who have been singled out by Peirce for special appreciation, although he takes issue with each of them on basic principles.

There are also passages in Peirce's writing that express his sympathy for the anarchists and his distaste for what passed in his day for a scientific approach to political economy. For example, within his famous essay "Evolutionary Love" Peirce takes issue with spokesmen such as Simon Newcomb, who was well known for his contributions to the science of political economy.[10] Yet he expresses enormous respect for the science of political economy as such. In fact he designates the nineteenth century as the "economic century." He says that political economy" has more direct relations with all the branches of its activity than has any other science:

> political economy has its formula of redemption, too. It is this: Intelligence in the service of greed ensures the justest prices, the fairest contracts, the most enlightened conduct of all the dealing between men, and leads to the Summum Bonum, food in plenty and perfect comfort. (CP 6.290)

Peirce unmistakably affirms the free market in a manner that anticipates the arguments of Hayek and his school in the first third of the twentieth century. Yet he also admires the sentiment behind utilitarian ideals. Self-interest in the market is never self-interest for any individual, but, rather, as Hayek was to explain later, property although individually owned binds the individual into a contractual relation with those for whom the product of property is intended. The obligation, here, is not an ethical obligation, but a responsive obligation such that a free market exercises in free manner. Peirce's logic of relations wins out for Hayekian principles. Reason, not sentiment unsupported by correct thinking, was to Peirce the only possible course to freedom, that is, to that freedom which may exist.

It is important to pay especial attention to Peirce's identification of the *summum bonum*, which is nothing else but the free interaction and free transaction between persons in society for the shared purpose of their mutual well-being. Freedom is the highest good, and this highest good—this value of values—is possible only in the free market, and only when this free market represents the choices and actions of a spontaneous society.[11]

Peirce asks whom are goods for, that is, who deserves the highest goods in a just and equitable sense:

Why, for the greedy master of intelligence. I do not mean to say that this is one of the legitimate conclusions of political economy, the scientific character of which I fully acknowledge. . . . What I say, then, is that the great attention paid to economical questions during our century has induced an exaggeration of the beneficial effects of greed and of the unfortunate results of sentiment, until there has resulted a philosophy which comes unwittingly to this, that greed is the great agent in the elevation of the human race and in the evolution of the universe. (CP 6.290)

What Peirce objects to is the generally accepted dictum among political economists of his day, Newcomb, for one, that the basic motivation to human action is love: love of self, love of a limited group with which one identifies, love of all mankind. Peirce says, Nonsense. Love is not the motive of human action and it is misleading to represent acts by such reason. But if it is not love, asks Peirce, then what is a "wiser motive?" (CP 6.291). He says that the sense of "public-spirit, or Benthamism" does not effectively teach this motive of love.

Indeed, Peirce goes on to rip to shreds the so-called virtues of Christian and Western tradition including thrift, frugality, and charity as expressions of pride.[12] Finally, Peirce says, it is never the striving of one individual to progress that permits progress for the whole of society to occur. Because one individual is meaningless, it is only insofar as each individual in an economic as well as in a metaphysical sense is in relation to and shares some common ground or stake in existence with others that makes progress possible.

To Peirce economic principle is not opposed to the principle of scientific metaphysics. Rather, the experiential and prototypical manifestation and model of metaphysics finds its strongest expression in economic transactions.

The rest of this chapter will introduce and comment briefly on some of the issues confronting a semiotic approach to the economic link with law. A close study of these and other issues requires a separate book.

It is important to show, for example, how the Keynesian principle of economics, refuted and rejected on the basis of its logic, was successfully contested by Hayek and others in our own time. It is indeed Hayek who is the principal present-day author of a semiotics of freedom in law, economics, and politics. He does acknowledge his indebtedness to Peirce in several ways. But he has taken Peircean thought much further than even Peirce perhaps had conceived it. For Hayek as for Peirce, the *Summum Bonum* is freedom.[13] And he declares not only that freedom is a meaningful sign of value but also that it is already possible to oppose the proponents of determinism at the first level, that is, the level of quality.

Posner emphasizes that the new approach to law and economics includes topics not previously regarded as appropriate. And Becker (1976) insists "on the relevance of economics to a surprising range of nonmarket behavior [including charity and love]. . . ." Although it is clear that Posner has not recently read Peirce on love and economics, both he and Becker have, inadvertently perhaps, reopened discussion on the "neglected arguments" of economics and law.[14] Posner reminds us that this new economic approach to law has already stirred up antagonism, "especially, but not only, among academic lawyers who dislike the thought that the logic of the law might be economics . . ." (Posner, 1977:19). The question raised by a semiotic approach to law and economics is not only *whether* the prevailing logic of the law is economics, but also, *which* economics.

This book has taken the position that although the legal argument is the prototype of all ordinary arguments, as maintained by Toulmin (1959), the economic exchange is the prototypical model of semiotic transaction as a whole.

The sense in which law is regarded as a prototype is not as a historical Weberian ideal form but rather as a model or representation of more general semiotic activity in society.

One of the first studies on the transactional basis of semiotics was Kapferer's edited volume, *Transaction in Meaning* (1976). But certainly Goffman's studies on transactions and exchanges of meaning and Laing's psychiatric studies of intersubjective transactions are also early semiotic studies with an implied economic model.

Posner also astutely reminds us that one of the main objections academic lawyers have to bringing together law and economics is that the prevailing philosophical basis of economic normative analysis is subject to challenge. This basis is a carrying forward of utilitarianism. Peirce's and others' criticism of utility is largely a criticism of the choice and method of reasoning. The assumptions, in other words, that underlie a method of reasoning utilitarian theories are, in Peirce's view, not only wrong-headed "values" but also examples of incorrect, that is, nonutilitarian, reasoning because they are based on inappropriate logics.

Posner does not take up this point, but he notes that ". . .the proper normative uses of economics—to clarify value conflicts and to show how to achieve given social ends by the most efficient means—are quite untouched by any debate over the philosophical merits of utilitarianism" (1977:20). The point is that from a semiotic point of view they are indeed touched upon and opposed.

As mentioned above, it is the static approach to economic analysis that predominates today. Yet, the dynamic approach is far older. As Posner reminds us, "the economic basis of property rights was first perceived in dynamic terms" (1977:27). One might add that it was perceived phenomenologically or, to use Peirce's term, *phaneroscopically*. This term derives from Bentham's "cenoscopy," which first attempted to bring economics within the range of scientific inquiry.

Posner's point is that although the dynamic approach is earlier it is generally rejected on the ground that it is "more complex and advanced than static analysis" (1977:27). Yet, property rights include the right to cultivation and use of property to produce value over and above the value of the property in any given state.

Land is a prime example of produceable property, and it is more than coincidence that property law was initially and for a long time primarily concerned with real estate, that is, with real property rights. It was not until the early actions in common law were becoming obsolete, as Maitland tells us, and the distinctions between movable and nonmovable property were becoming blurred (at the end of the nineteenth and into the twentieth century) that the privileged position of land laws in property laws was obliterated.[15] With this fusion also goes the last vestige of identification of land with a divine estate. As Posner remarks, the dynamic approach to property is ancient: "In contrast, the static analysis of property rights is little more than 50 years old" (1977:28).

This reduction of the meaning of property is analogous with Peirce's explanation of the decrease in meaning of a logical term (see especially mss 421, 422). For close discussion of the relation between increase and diminution of the meaning of a term, in the context of the concept of *verisimilitude* and discovery of new value, see Kevelson (1987).

According to Posner, "the economic theory of property rights implies . . . that rights will be redefined from time to time as the relative values of different resources change" (1977:38), and in this sense he is affirming the Peircean notion that the meaning of a sign increases with every interpretation of it. Increase as used here means more information and not necessarily additional or expanded attributes. A decrease in meaning is nevertheless an increase in significant information. This is not contradictory. To say that something that was once red is now faded is not to say that less information is available although "faded" but that less of the original quality, or the previously accepted representational meaning of "red," is given. Similarly, to say that someone who was once good is less good is not to say there is a reduction in information but merely that the attribute *good* is less applicable. Thus every change in meaning is an increase in information even though the change is a departure in some degree from a previous meaning.

In a similar vein, Posner notes:

> It is possible to object . . . that a process of continually redefining property to secure efficiency under changing conditions is bound to create instability and discourage investment. . . . Uncertainty itself is a source of disutility (especially for people averse to risk-taking). (1977:39)

Of the relational aspect of property rights, Posner correctly notes that with respect to some kinds of property, namely, the property of ideas, there are built-in incentives such that the "exclusive" right to property is useless without another as the *object* of production. (1977:54).

Three criteria are usually associated with an efficient system of property rights: exclusivity, universality, and transferability. Universality implies that "ideally all resources are owned by someone" with total power over the use or non-use of these resources. The universality or exclusivity criteria are both ideal only when one examines property rights from a dynamic perspective. Even Locke's well-known assertion that each person owns himself or herself as a universal and exclusive "property" is significant only if qualified by the understanding that the intention or motive for use remains with the possessor. But the other, as possible appropriator, is always implied in the very notion of *oneself*. Oneself is *for* someone, that is, for some other self.

For example, this point is related by Hayek to persons and their respective properties of knowledge. One *has* what one knows in the modern world. In the world prior to the advent of nation states, of capitalism, of international trade, of becoming, *one was what one knew*. Transitivity is the hallmark of modernity. The distinction between *Is* and *Have* is one of the few universals in language and yet this distinction blurs when one discusses property in terms other than those of inalienable possession and knowledge.[16]

Hayek says he believes his essay "The Use of Knowledge in Society" is not referring to scientific knowledge but rather to the "unorganized knowledge of the particular circumstances of time and place" which is our most important and richest resource. Peirce also maintained that our surprises, that is, our sources of new knowledge, come not from ordered systems but from the disorder characteristic of the world in the process of growing. Hayek's work establishes a "division of knowledge." He understands the "central problem of economics . . . [to be] the spontaneous interaction of a number of people, each possessing only certain bits of knowledge," as Leube explains in his introduction to *The Essays of Hayek* (1984:xxiii). According to Leube, such people, each with only a piece of special knowledge, creates "circumstances that could be brought about only by somebody who possessed the combined knowledge of all these individuals."

According to Hayek, "In our society, in which the knowledge of the relevant facts is dispersed among many people, the price system is the only mechanism that communicates information" (p. xxiii) The following, quoted from Nishiyama's introductory passage, is especially significant:

> The price mechanism is a system of signals that puts us in the situation of adapting to circumstances and experiences of which we know nothing. Our whole modern order and well-being rest on the possibility of adapting to processes that we do not know. (Nishiyama and Leube 1984:xxiii)

Nishiyama has succinctly summarized in this introduction many of the major ideas stressed by Hayek throughout his long and honored career. Hayek is not only an economist of great and deserved renown but he is a philosopher whose work is not customarily studied in departments of philosophy.

Hayek begins with the basic structure of experience in society. He begins, in other words, with that sign function which corresponds with the structure of the world of experience: the index or denoter of facts of opposition, of struggle, of antagonism. In brief, he begins where the ancients began but soon left off: with the *Hieros Gamos* or interplay between natural man and man the cultivator of the natural world. It is the basic relationship. It is the basis of contract. It is the foundation for a philosophy that rests on the knowledge of experience and on the material given by the world.[17]

Knowledge is open-ended in Hayek, as it is in Peirce. It is unpredictable and uncertain precisely because something new continually enters into this experience which neither any individual nor individuals collectively are capable of accounting for until either after the fact, or, predictively, through risk taking.

As Nishiyama points out, one of the basic and most important tenets of Hayek's thesis is that:

> He denies the possibility of anyone's becoming "complete" in his or her thought or of acquiring the whole range of knowledge. This is precisely the reason why he adamantly opposes any kind of planned economy and has consistently been distrustful of the various forms of governmental interventions. . . . And this is exactly why he asserts methodological individualism. . . . (Nishiyama and Leube 1984:iii)

Because this is not a study of Hayek in particular, one may only comment in passing that Hayek's "methodological individualism" rests on the notion of individuals *for* other individuals, in community by consent, by compact, by contract, and for mutual gain.

Hayek maintains that a philosophy need not and cannot be complete. To keep faith with its own promises,

> It is always incomplete and never closed. It keeps growing and evolving. Viewed as a logico-theoretical network, the Hayekian body of ideas keeps expanding both by knotting new nets and reknitting old ones and by connecting internal nets that had previously not been linked together. (1984:1)

One hears in this echoes of Peirce's explanation on the continuum of thought and the manner in which threads of ideas become plaited together to form new networks of thought. It is particularly in his discussions of musement, or pure play, that Peirce developed these explanations. An explanation, in Peirce, is a synonym for *cause*.

Hayek, like Peirce, is not a "system builder," and yet both are systematic thinkers. They are not system builders only if what we regard as a system is closable. Peirce's concepts of modality and possibility emphasize neither closed nor open systems, but rather "moving picture" systems of thought, representing the dynamic process of thought as it grows and builds out of itself. This is discussed further in Chapter 7.

Hayek says that classical economics developed as it did because Jevons in England, Menger in Vienna, and Walrons in Lausanne, had at about the same time all "made the subjective value of goods to individuals the starting point for their reconstruction. . . ." They did so because Mill, in his theory of value, had "explicitly returned to Ricardo." Yet all the classical economists, according to Hayek, "lacked a general theory of values which explained the determination of all prices by a uniform principle" (1984:196).

Peirce, as I have said, regarded Ricardo as one of the "Great Men of Science" (Eisele 1976:251–254). But he also, in his praise of both Adam Smith and Ricardo as forerunners in a new and scientific approach to commonsensism, remarks that his own pragmatism will go much further than they did "by emphasizing the point that there is no intellectual value in mere feeling *per se*, but that the whole function of thinking consists in the regulation of conduct" (CP 8:199, 1902).

Value takes on a new significance. Peirce provides one of the earliest bases for the science of value. The science of value is usually referred to in this century as axiology, but Peirce called it esthetics, the highest of his normative sciences. The value of freedom in Peirce is an esthetic value, as I have noted.[18]

For Peirce, the value of freedom had become linked with economics and with law. It is the links among cognition, market exchange, and legal codes that Peirce finds are already evident in Locke's *Essay Concerning Human Understanding* (1690; CP 8.199). One might add that it is also evident in the Locke of the Two *Treatises on Civil Government* (1690); it is there we find the first spare but serious treatment of property as a condition of freedom.

In 1968 Hayek presented one of his most controversial and important papers at the meeting of the Philadelphia Society in Chicago: "Competition as a Discovery Procedure" emphasizes competition as a method for the discovery of such facts as would not otherwise be brought to light. Whereas science aims at so-called general facts, Hayek points out, discovery through economic competition seeks to find "particular facts relevant to the achievement of specific, temporary purposes. . ." (1984:256).

The search for such particular facts is tantamount to the search for whatever novelty has entered into the structure of the known world, has made the world unknowable and unpredictable until and unless such novelty be discovered. The irony of such discovery procedures is that the new is always yet to be discovered. Even economic competition as method lacks real tests or proofs. "The validity of the theory," in other words, "can never be tested empirically" (Hayek 1981:155).

The following chapter will consider in close detail the notion of economic liberties and the United States Constitution together with discussion on the Constitution as an experiment.

In concluding this chapter, it is worth noting that Hayek regards the laws governing boundaries on property as one of the most significant legal-economic contributions to human liberty. One notes that boundaries are precisely those interpretable signs that may be stretched, changed, challenged, legislated, and competed for; and however fluctuating boundaries in the particular may be, their existence ensures the rights of property, the rights of exchange, and the freedom to engage in negotiations and to set values.

Peirce, in his studies of topical geometry, is similarly concerned with the boundary as a sign of possible freedom. Limits or boundaries may change shape, may be stretched, and may be altered so they are not recognizable limits of known spaces—known topics—but it is in the *testing* of boundaries, in the claims regarding the *limits* of properties, of terms and of land, that the limits of freedom, continually changing, are found. For this search and discovery the old geometries are obsolete and the old logics are inadequate.

NOTES

1. Alf Ross proposed that the law be regarded as a phenomenon, in much the same way that Peirce proposed that all ideas and thoughts, as signs with consequential effects on the phenomenal world, be regarded as phenomena. Ross attempts to synthesize a prevailing dualism in law by arguing that even positive, normative law is an ideal, that is, an idea of meaning not yet emergent but phenomenal nonetheless in its symbolic power and potential capacity for realization (1946:140–158).

2. See Cohen (1932:330).

3. Because Peirce was thoroughly familiar with Kant's published work, but clearly less aware of Kant's altered concepts of continuity, for example, in his posthumous writings, he saw one of the main differences between his thought and Kant's to inhere in their differing concepts of continuity and attributed the idea of discreteness to Kant, whereas his own later work, particularly, stresses primal relations of ideas that are always open-ended and continuous, and in act are infinite in their capacity to develop and evolve through semiosis.

4. Although Lieber's major contributions to the establishment of political science are rarely discussed in the current literature, he nevertheless holds a key position in laying the foundations for a semiotic understanding of the interrelations between economics, law, politics, and the modes of discourse specific to each. Lieber was influenced by both Savigny and Kant but evolved the concepts of both beyond the positions reached by his teachers.

The third edition of *Legal and Political Hermeneutics*, first published in 1839, was reissued in 1880 with full indexing and notations. This third edition follows Lieber's major contribution to the drafting of codes of war and laying the foundation for codes of international law and therefore for the current and urgent questions involved in the topic of conflict of laws. The topic of conflict of laws in relation to logical contradiction and paradox, following Peirce, is central to a forthcoming study by Kevelson.

5. What Peirce means by *method* is examined comprehensively in Kevelson (1987). The concept of method, in its current and general usage, remains ambiguous and difficult to define, as all multiordinal terms are.

6. Jevons (1873) refers to Peirce on pages 23 and 391 but misinterprets Peirce's notion of the transformation of signs throughout any given inferential sequence. For instance, when Jevons speaks of a substitution, especially on page 22, Peirce, who is referred to here, would speak of a process of permutation.

7. See Machlup on potential property as an equivalent of emergent knowledge (1980:vol. 1).

8. See Peirce's manuscripts on potentiality, especially mss 927 and 320.

9. See Posner's distinction beween dynamic and static systems of economic theory in relation to differing views on property rights and contract (1972:25–64, 65–100, 16,17).

10. See Peirce, CP 6.291–294.

11. Hayek develops his notion of a spontaneous society especially in the three volumes of *Law, Legislation and Liberty*. But the ideas in these later work are expressed also in his early writings, for instance, *Money, Capital & Fluctuations*, written in the 1920s and 1930s and published in 1984.

12. According to Peirce, the ideal of a moral standard, to which a logical norm is constructed as a correspondence, begins with a plan or a diagram, that is, "an iconic representation of ideal conduct . . ." (see 1958: 1.592 and following passages through 1.608, 609.

13. See Reilly on the element of expectation in Peirce, which includes the use of imaginary experience, especially with respect to the quest for theoretical and other esthetic signs of knowledge (1970:13,19,20). Peirce's concept of the experiential nature of cognition is discussed, especially on pp. 27 and 30, with reference to CP 5.540,542; 6.568; 8.144.

14. See Becker (1977:2–3; 32–39).

15. See Schmid (1978).

16. See Kevelson's discussion of *Has* and *Is* regarded as universals in language (1976).

17. On Peirce's idea of pure play see Chapter 9 of this volume.

18. See Wilkinson and Willoughby (1967) on Peirce's correct understanding of Schiller's *summum bonum* as *freedom*.

CHAPTER 15

Signs of the Naked and the Dressed

CONTRACT AND CAUSE IN LAW

The main focus of this chapter is the relation between the concepts or signs of contract and of cause in law. We have ascertained that the concepts and methods of discovery and interpretation in law from the perspective of legal realism parallel and extend Peirce's semiotic views on discovery and interpretation. In this chapter I will claim that not only is it in the history of the concepts of cause and contract that we find a cross-referential practice or definition and reinterpretation of these key ideas, but also in law, in philosophy, and in the physical sciences. In the particular case of the relation between Peirce's evolving concepts of cause and contract and the use of these concepts in law, especially since the advent of legal realism, it is expected that we will find that the respective redefinitions of these terms have consequences that ramify throughout the entire structure of social, institutional organization in the modern world.

In brief, with the general recognition that the universe is not a closed and completed system something of which one can say, in truth, "It is", and the acceptance of an open, infinite universe continually becoming—no less in process but differently in process than our ideas which signify the meaning of the reality of this judgment of a universal becoming—the traditional, still unresolved problems of causation assume new dimensions and are subsumed in new frames of thought. It is especially with reference to Peirce's logic of relations that the legal idea of contract, in connection with the idea of cause, is of particular interest in this semiotic approach to law.

Just as traditional discussions of causation were linked with discussions of change over time with respect to a conceptual structure or model of a static universe, the introduction of dynamic models of change in the universe required appropriate logics to account for the process of change, and, furthermore, sacred notions of the idea of time have had to be discarded and with them some of the most cherished beliefs of cause (von Wright 1967; Kevelson 1983c, 1987). It is not possible thoroughly to qualify these remarks here, but it still must be stressed that Peirce came to refute in his later years the Kantian notion of discrete temporal units, that is, individual moments. Instead, he asserted that at bottom the basic temporal unit was not a single moment but a relationship between such events which we call significant moments. Thus an event is a construction, that is, a sign representing a momentous, actual happening in the phenomenal world and the world of practical affairs.

Time is but one of several coordinating functions of this complex sign relation and is itself a complex relation rather than a single dimension or stage of a thing in motion, that is, in space. If one seeks for a prototypical representation of such an event, law furnishes us with this model and, as is assumed, furnished Peirce with such a model upon which he constructed his semiotic method as a representation of legal practice and discourse, not as it traditionally had been but as it might possibly become.

Peirce suggests that inquiry in general, or the investigation of an idea, or sign, is a community project wherein a community is more than a single person. In the sense that communication, even at its everyday levels, is purposeful, just as more specialized inquiry is goal-directed, meaningful discourse is always dialogic. If one intends to describe this process, that is, to construct a logic of inquiry, one must initially at a stage preliminary to the discourse itself establish what is meant by the terms to be used in the discourse. There must be an agreement.

This agreement admits of certain definitions and excludes other, nonpertinent definitions of the terms. The terms and the meanings of these terms, as agreed upon between participants in discourse, or meaning transaction, are the facts of the discourse. The facts of meaningful signs are nothing other than the materials of meaning distinguished from other possible grounds or contexts and are specified with respect to the inquiry in question. These facts, or terms, are then evolved to become the first objects of the inquiry itself. The factiveness of a term is inseparably connected with the agreement between participants to use a term in this and not that manner.

Subsequent to this agreement, the fact is generalized, that is, acquires a predominantly symbolic function in the discourse such that it is a representation, or sign proper of the terms of discourse. This preliminary fact-finding procedure, for Peirce, parallels the discovery procedure in law.

The inquiry cannot proceed until this stage of the process is worked through, for the establishment of the relation of fact constitutes the basis for the ensuing discourse. The fact, it might be said, sets the discourse in motion because without it nothing meaningful to the participants involved would be possible. The fact is a point of reference in Peirce's semiotics.

And what is a fact in law? The question of what constitutes a fact is no less problematic in law, throughout the history of law, than it has been throughout the history of science and throughout the history of philosophy. Following Peirce's semiotics, it will be assumed that a fact is a relation or composite of always more than one observable thing. According to Peirce, no matter how fine our instruments for observation may be, they are never absolutely perfect. Further, the method of corroborating whether an observable is in truth this and not that requires that one must infer some general principles from any number of individual or hypothetically individual observations. Thus for anything to be accepted as an observable it will have had to be judged as an observable. Even in this protological stage nothing is known without the mediation of signs, that is, without the mediation of reason and judgment. Therefore observation is fallible to begin with. But this fallible observation is all one has to work with, and one must allow for error.

The kind and degree of error may not be apparent for a long time. But, as Peirce argues, only a logic of inquiry which includes a method of revision and self-correction accurately describes the actual process of knowing more and more correctly the idea in the process of developing anything whatever. What is required, parallel to Peirce's contention of necessary falliblism, is the understanding in law that a fact is the result of testimony.

In early periods of the common law this testimony was a hearsay process of giving evidence, or of foreswearing as to the fact of the matter in question. A witness was a credible witness because one could rely on this person's ability to interpret in a manner understandable according to established conventions of meaning. One must be able and willing to report, to testify, in the appropriate language and not in a strange tongue or in a language not accepted as official by the court. With the disappearance of the hearsay testimony from the formal procedure of law, in its place the court appointed witnesses, or official legal actors whose responsibility it was to ascertain the facts of an exchange or contract.

Holmes reminds us that for many hundreds of years prior to the Norman invasion Anglo-Saxon law "required the election of a certain number of official witnesses, two or three of whom were to be called into every bargain of sale" (Holmes 1881/1963:201). Although the later function of witnesses was to furnish facts, or proof of debt, the earlier function was to verify whether the person charged with theft had come by the goods in question in an honest manner. Holmes shows that these witness functions remained after the Norman conquest but were modified and came to be known under William the Conqueror as "transaction witnesses" (Kevelson 1977). Eventually the presence of transaction witnesses was required only in cases involving the exchange of property.

But, as Holmes points out, the appropriate procedure for an investigation involving the question of failure to deliver promised property included and required the swearing of these transaction witnesses, or oath taking; this "accident of procedure" has very likely become one of the most important rules in substantive law.

> The rule that witnesses could only swear to facts within their knowledge, coupled with the accident that these witnesses were not used in transactions which might create a debt, except for a particular fact, namely, the delivery of property, together with the further accident that this delivery was *quid pro quo*, was equivalent to the rule that, when a debt was proved by witnesses these must be *quid pro quo*. (1881:200)

That is, there must have been an exchange, and presumably an equitable exchange or exchange of equivalent value, in the sense that one sign, represented by property of a definable kind, was equivalent in meaning or value with another kind, or value counter.

Holmes goes on to say:

> these debts proved by witnesses, instead of by deed are what we call simple contract debts, and thus beginning with debt, and subsequently extending itself to other contracts, is established our peculiar and most important doctrine that every simple contract must have a consideration. (1881/1963:203–204)

Cause and consideration are inextricably linked in law, and both are closely tied to the development of the idea of contract (see Chapter 11). But the problem of cause in law goes beyond the question of consideration and contract. In the following, some of the various notions of legal cause will be briefly discussed, with an attempt to relate some selected causal theories with Peirce's semiotics.

In the earliest sense one finds the Roman *causa* identified with consideration. The term *causa* continued to be used in this sense until rather late in the sixteenth century. Holmes reminds us that during the early Elizabethan the word *cause* is used "with reference to a covenant to stand seized to uses. . . ." He cites an anonymous case which indicated that *causa* referred to an "executed consideration furnished upon request, but without any promise of any kind, [which] would support a subsequent promise to pay for it."

Starting from this authority and the word *cause*, the conclusion was soon reached that there was a great difference between a contract and an assumpsit, and that, whereas in contracts

> everything which is requisite ought to concur and meet together, viz. the consideration of the one side, and the sale or the promise on the other side . . . to maintain an action upon an assumpsit the same is not requisite, for it is sufficient if there be a moving cause or consideration precedent for which cause or consideration the promise was made. (1881/1963:224)

The notion that a promise is implicit in a contract is a later development of the legal contract. And although the promise is common to all contracts since the Conquest, at least in common law, Holmes notes, the agreement to indebtedness predates promise implicit in the breach of contract, or assumpsit: ". . . a promise is not necessary to a liability in debt as formerly understood" (1881/1963:277).

Holmes says that the doctrine of cause fully developed in debt long before it occurred in equity. Cause in debt is the forebear of fact finding in our modern courts. The rule requiring consideration for simple contracts began with debt and extended to contract in general. Thus consideration or cause is the fact of obligation or indebtedness. But this fact, as is recalled, is not an object in the phenomenal world, nor is it a given as an axiom is given. It ultimately derived from the witnessing of data, that is, something given provisionally.

Berman points out, as I have said, that the notion of cause in law has been of major interest since long before Holmes found it in pre-Elizabethan common law. Berman traces it at least back to the time of Aristotle. But as a legal principle, he says, it began to emerge in the form of a systematic investigation of legal cause around the twelfth or thirteenth century, coincidental with the development of the first law schools in Milan and Bologna at the time of the rediscovery of the Justinian Codex.

The problem of legal cause follows closely upon the development of canonical law. At this time causation became closely linked with the concept of contract and to such subspecies of contract as agreement and promise. But, according to Berman, not all promises or agreements were regarded as binding. Only those agreements that were causally supported under canon law were regarded as valid in the eyes of the law. The cause, then, was said to cover the contract, that is, to "clothe it" (Berman 1983:246–47).

Roman law specified a number of ways in which contracts could be formed in law and provided various ways for contracting within each of the basic forms of contract. There were four major categories of contracts: the first required the exchange and articulation of formulaic expressions; the second had to be inscribed in a formal manner in ledgers created for this special purpose; the third was established by the actual delivery of the object specified in the contract; and the fourth was made by nonformal but verbally expressed agreement (ibid.:245). Later jurists added to these four other major classes of contract, of which the most important was the "unnamed" or innominate contract, which was of four distinct subtypes: the *do ut des*, or gift for gift; the *do ut facias*, or gift for act; the *facio ut des*, or act for gift; and the *facio ut facias*, or act for act (ibid.:245).

This typology of subcontract types presupposed that acts and things could be understood and agreed upon in terms of their equivalent value and, further, that the meaning of these acts and things could be assigned a monetary consideration such that the meaning of objects in question could be represented by the medium of money. Thus currency from the earliest times became through legal contract the token of the type, or sign of an object or "Representamen" in Peirce's terms, that is, an interpretant of an interpretant sign.

Later interpreters of the Justinian texts attempted to explain these classes of contract. Particularly, they needed to supply a basis for that whole category of unnamed or innonimate contracts. Indeed, without a basis or cause, the idea of consequent obligation or indebtedness was unthinkable. If there has been no consideration, and if the only consideration is the agreement that acts and gifts may have comparable value without naming the standard of reference which sets the currency value, how is one to place the transaction in a context with a definite frame of reference? In the words of the eleventh- and twelfth-century glossators, ". . . a naked agreement does not give rise to an action," and therefore the agreement must be presented in such a manner as to render it authoritative. The agreement in unnamed contracts, then, must be clothed. As Berman notes, "The word they picked out and turned into a general principle was 'naked'; to produce an action, an agreement must be 'clothed.' *Causa* was then defined as the presence of 'clothing,' (Berman 1983:246).

Eventually various kinds of clothing, or cause in law, came to be distinguished while the original purpose of providing justification for claims that certain contracts were binding under law was retained. It was not until two centuries later, Berman points out, after Aristotle's *Ethics* and *Metaphysics* were translated, that Aristotelian philosophical concepts of cause entered into legal discourse and provided opportunities for representing notions of final cause, efficient cause, proximate cause, formal and material cause, and so on as both procedural and substantive aspects of juridical practice and theory.

It is only after this assimilation of Aristotle into legal science that we find that promises are synonymous with contracts and that whether or not the contract is clothed it is caused. The evolved cause of the contract became the moral assumption that promises made must be promises kept. The shift was from a negotiable and provisional value equivalence to a moral edict. The consequence of providing moral substantiation to legal contracts was that emphasis shifted from equivalence to be decided and agreed upon in free exchange to equity which eventually required reference to moral authority, to an ultimate moral authority or sovereign.

The facts of the contract were superseded by the justness of the contract. It was the commingling of justness with truth and the truth statements of traditional logic that led Holmes in the twentieth century to assert his famous edict that the life of the law is not logic but experience and that law is concerned, primarily and properly, not with moral judgments but with facts.

As Berman points out, in the initial concern with establishing what is meant by a just contract the Romanists and canonists began with the marketplace as an index of fair and just price. But in time the opposition to profit making, usury, outcries against unfair competition and the need for some controls in the actual society in which moneylending was a political weapon of the Church brought about an ironic turn in the interpretation of *causa* in contracts. The Bible, which regarded usury as a sin, became authoritative against the papal custom of charging high interest in commercial contracts. The notion of *causa* became identified with moral obligation and conscience, and thus the naked contracts became clothed, or caused, as it were, in divine command (Berman 1983:248–251).

The displacement of the laws of contract by the idea of "due process" laws had its roots in canon law during the time of this metamorphosis of the idea of legal cause. But it recurred in the eighteenth century in the United States.

Benjamin Wright pointed out that due process represented natural law to the framers of the state and federal constitutions. Indeed, the social contract is presupposed in the idea of the laws of nature and thus contract, conscience, and the individual were all interrelated in the intentions of the framers of the Constitution in 1787 (Wright 1938:254–257).

During the nineteenth century when, as Wright notes, all persons could expect to become people of property and when the laws of contract no longer were needed as a "vehicle" for bringing in new ideas to the Constitution, the idea of contract became a kind of legal provision or tacit assumption but it "left to its successor, . . . [due process] the function of serving as the clause under which the courts attempt to reconcile the respective spheres of individual and social interests" (ibid.:258–59).

The actual decline, if not demise, of the contract clause occurred after 1890. The memorable eulogies written on the death of contract seem to mourn the passing away of an old and dear concept of individualism which presumed that persons entered into agreements on meanings and on values of all kinds.

What has not yet been written is the re-creation of what we may call a continuum in thought or cause. The idea of contract is reinterpreted in Peirce's semiotics. This idea of contract reentered American constitutional law through Holmes. The factive basis, or cause, of contract is reappraised by the legal realists, who show that when witnesses are not able accurately to represent the facts it is the judge who must then seek not one but two kinds of facts: those that are recoverable in the case at hand and those that evolve as part of the judicial process itself: ". . . while the witness is in this sense a judge, *the judge*, in a like sense, is a witness. He is a witness of what is occurring in his court-room" (Frank 1930/1963:114–115).

But in words that recall Peirce's semiotics, the judge is a "fallible witness," whose facts evolve into signs, or representations that in turn are interpretants toward the projected outcome of the inquiry, the judicial decision.

In closing this third part of the volume, I realize that at best such a brief introduction to the relation between contract and cause in law and Peirce's understanding of these matters does little more than unstick a warped door.

Yet, it is worth noting that Peirce in his later writings refutes the absolute notion of causation and insists that cause occurs by chance and is nourished by the intellect which consists of a "plasticity of habit." He notes that the concept of causation is at once the most resistant and the most significant object of modern inquiry. Everyone professes belief in the "great principle of causation," yet we have no general idea of what is variously meant by the term *cause* (CP 6.66 ff). He concludes that when he uses the term he means only, in commonsense speech, an explanation or justification of a judgment or decision.

Just as a Realist judge, in Frank's view, creates law and does not merely discover it, cause is simply an explanation, a sign construct based on the facts that the judiciary discovers as part of the process of inquiring into the case at hand.

Semiotics of law, following Peirce, and in agreement with Leon Green, would argue for indeterminacy as a principle of inquiry, especially with respect to the notion of proximate cause. But in all causal relations in law, Green says, the basic factor is fact. "Causal relation is the universal factor common to all legal liability. . . . the determination of causal relation in each case would be by the same process—an inquiry into the facts" and, further, ". . . in any given case the inquiry is not directed toward discovering *the* cause of the damage, but is whether the defendant's conduct was *a* cause . . ." (Green 1927:132, 134).

Finally, in the relation of cause and contract, one should inquire into the manner in which the "element of risk" enters the judicial decision, "a manner comparable to Peirce's Pure Chance" (Hart and Honore 1959:277–291).

PART IV

Interpretation and Value

The conservative believes that change is erroneous and undesirable; the radical insists that it is necessary and urgent. Mr. Justice Holmes simply urges that since change is inevitable, we must provide for its coming and see to it that the game is played in terms of the rules.

Harold J. Laski (1931:153)

CHAPTER 16

Origins and Development

HERMENEUTICS OF LAW AND POLITICS

> There is no direct communion between the minds of men; what-
> ever thoughts, emotions, conceptions, ideas of delight or suffer-
> ence we feel urged to impart to other individuals, we cannot
> obtain our object without resorting to the outward manifestation
> of that which moves us inwardly, that is, to signs. . . .
>
> (Lieber 1839/1963:2–3)

This contention by Lieber prefaces his now classic exposition on legal hermeneutics. It appeared in 1839, the year of Peirce's birth, and anticipates in significant ways, with special reference to law, the method of inquiry of semiotics.
It is appropriate here to introduce the topic of a semiotics of legal hermeneutics
by way of Lieber:

> The signs which man uses, the using of which implies intention, for the purpose of
> conveying ideas or notions to his fellow-creatures, are very various, for instance,
> gestures, signals, telegraphs, monuments, sculpture of all kinds, pictorial and hier-
> oglyphic signs, the stamp on coins, seals, beacons, buoys, insignia, ejaculations,
> articulate sounds, or their representations, that is, phonetic characters on stones, wood,
> leaves, paper, etc., entire periods, or single words, such as names in a particular
> place, and whatever other signs, even the flowers in the flower language of the East,
> might be enumerated. . . . These signs then are used to convey certain ideas, and
> interpretation, in its widest meaning, is the discovery and representation of the true
> meaning of any sign used to convey ideas. (Lieber 1839/1963:17,18)

To paraphrase the legendary Isaac: the thought is the thought of modern
semiotics, but the words are the words of Francis Lieber.

Our interest in Lieber, who wrote these thoughts on his theory of signs and the interpretation of signs and their relations some thirty years or so before Peirce spoke of signs in "Some Consequences. . . ." (1869), is restricted to semiosis in law and politics; but actually we find in reading Lieber that his major work on political ethics illuminates some of the most complicated relationships between logic, ethics, and esthetics, in Peirce's normative science division of his philosophy of signs.

For example, Lieber, as Peirce after him, concurs with Locke in denying the possibility of innate ideas. But, as Lieber points out, there is a problem: if, as Locke insists, opinion and conscience are developments of rational processes, whence comes the first mark on the blank surface of the moral human being? This problem of conscience, Lieber says, divides philosophy into two camps. It separates philosophers who uphold the notion of innate ideas from those who, like Locke (*Essay*, book 1, chap. iii), claim that all opinion is achieved through reason. Lieber's attempt to resolve what he calls Locke's confused explanation of the emergence of an ethical person leads him to the realization that we must not confound "the idea of artificiality, or unnaturalness, with that of development" (1839/1911:39).

If one can accept a "primordial" or primitive predisposition in human beings which, in a rudimentary but unmistakable way, is capable of discriminating right from wrong, then all else Locke says in his denial of innate ideas must be admissible. Thus a primitive predisposition must be seen as a material, factual function of the human being, enabling him to evolve this capability into what he calls conscience.

At first, there is a *consciousness* of right and wrong, Lieber says, and this consciousness is as basic as hunger, or sleepiness, for example; thus eating is to hunger, or sleeping is to sleepiness as a conscience is to being conscious of distinctions between good and bad, right and wrong. This consciousness is no more mysterious, according to Lieber, than any other aspect of the physical human being which distinguishes it from nonhuman beings. Consciousness, then, is such a thumb which functions in the construction of human communities.

Like Locke, Lieber maintains that concurrent with the development of conscience, people move out of a natural state (Locke's term) to a commonwealth; they do so, as Locke describes, through the process of natural law. Once there is mutual assent to natural law between people, the state of nature is left behind, and they have evolved into agents in community. Natural law is an interactive, dialogic process.

These concepts will not be discussed closely here but are mentioned in order to emphasize that to Lieber all acting is inseparable from exchange. He tells us correctly that we find widespread throughout the world that the word for action refers to a commercial house, a market, or a stock-exchange; the word *acting* is used synonymously with the carrying on of trade (1839/1911:28).

Further, Lieber says that if man is less restricted than nonhumans and more directive of his own purposeful actions than nonhumans, then one may rightly conclude that the notion of free action must imply the notion of free trade. One is unfree to the extent that one is bound by physical limitations, as animals are. One is free, however, in one's rationality. This notion of freedom accords with Locke's and is in line with the sense of Peirce's suggestion that our choice of action, of our process of choosing, before commitment, is an aesthetically marked freedom; it is the freedom characteristic of Schiller's notion of play, for example, as discussed above.

Lieber goes on to say that so long as a person is able to reflect and to make choices, and to act on these choices, he is self-determining. Rationality is freedom. In this sense all people who are rational are free to direct their manner of exchange with others. But precisely because of this freedom, because certain motives may lead one to make choices that are not ethically right, but ethically wrong, we see that the conclusion or consequence of an ethical action can be probably, but not absolutely, true.

One may significantly compare the quality of Lieber's consciousness of right and wrong with Peirce's category of firstness: one may say that the conscience, at each subsequent stage of interpretive development, is, in Peirce's sense, an interpretant sign.

For example, the testing of one's choice of action in the world of experience can be compared to the category of secondness through which the rewards and punishments of an act may be opposed and evaluated; finally, the choice of action becomes a law or is regarded as if it were a law. When certain ethical actions are referential in community—in the commonwealth of acting and of exchanging rational persons—the valued, customary act has a normative function and is a thirdness, according to Peirce's terminology. Whether or not the prevailing law-like ethical norm is legislated into practical law is another question, and this would lead into the investigation of practical law. Lieber carefully distinguishes theoretical law from practical law. Practical law includes that entire experiential domain he analyses in the *Political Ethics*.

Lieber argues against axiomatic, syllogistic thinking as a mode of deciding in both political ethics and theoretical or natural law. He says:

> Every science, even mathematics, has to start from some axioms, that is, from truths which must be either supposed to have been proved by other sciences, or are self-evident in their nature. . . . It appears to me that the only axiom necessary to establish the science of natural law is this: "I exist as a human being, *therefore* I have a right to exist as a human being." (1839/1911:67–68)

Although the principle of the precedent is essential in the development of all societies and should be sharply distinguished from dictation or command, every "progressive continuum" requires a precedent. But however we regard precedential decision to rest on law and reason, which is law itself, he says, no precedent is absolute. No precedent is unchangeable. "A precedent can be over-ruled," he insists, but only by the law, that is, only by the process of reason (1853:212).

How very close Lieber is here to Peirce's notion of the provisional aspect of judgment signs.

One further point must be made: Although Lieber took issue with Locke on many points and was indeed highly critical of Locke's actions, particularly with respect to Locke's contribution to the drafting of the Constitution of South Carolina (see Lieber 1853:211), they are of one mind in their evaluation of the importance of the individual, if not always on the meaning of *interpretation*.

For example, in order for man *qua* man to be an ethical being, Lieber finds it necessary to emphasize the supremacy of the individual person:

> Man's whole ethic character is materially founded upon or can be imagined only in conjunction with his individuality. Man's individuality and sociality form the two poles round which his whole life revolves. . . . The peculiarity in man is that he can fulfil his destiny in a state of society only, and that he has to bear weal and woe jointly with his fellow-creatures. . . . As to his individuality, it is necessary to observe that man is what he is, first and essentially, as an individual. His senses, perceptions, thoughts, pleasures, pains, emotions, his reasoning, appetites, and endeavors, are individually his own. Philosophically speaking, he cannot act through another; his acts are his own; for if he be forced to do anything against his will, he does not *act* in the philosophical sense of the term, but he *suffers*. . . . (1839/1911:56–58)

A point to be made here is that if one individual infers meaning from another individual, and they reach an accord together, in community, as inter-active agents in agreement about a sign they will hold together as a law, or general, then the entire process of inferring ethical values is an inductive process, or, as Mill said, we infer from individual to individual, from particular to particular. Such is Peirce's thesis, which cannot in his criticism of Mill be examined here. It must suffice to mention in passing, however, that just as logic, "the science of the general laws of signs" (CP 1.191), looks to ethics for leading principles, ethics, "the science of right and wrong, must appeal to Esthetics for aid in determining the *summum bonum*," as discussed earlier. But ethics must be more than the mere "conformity of action to an ideal," for that would be what Peirce calls "antethics." Ethics is a "sort of composite photograph of the conscience of the members of the community" (ms 283:39).

An ideal ethical sign, or pattern of interactive communal life, is a sign that is initially perceived in its iconic function, Peirce suggests, and is a kind of diagram. In a similar sense, Lieber says that "every idea has its caricature and the more unfailing so, the more actively and practically the idea is working in real life" (1853:213). Further discussion on ethics, the individual, and induc-tion in Peirce's semiotics considers closely his doctrine of chances. But in the following the "chance" *nonmeeting* of Lieber and Peirce is noted:

First, consider that Lieber had fled from Germany to England in the 1820s to escape persecution for his liberal views. In England he quickly became the respected and close associate of the then famous jurists Jeremy Bentham and John Austin. Recall that Peirce, also, was to reflect in a significant manner the influence—direct and indirect—of both Bentham and Austin. Although Peirce's differences with Bentham are numerous and important, Peirce acknowledges his indebtedness to Bentham's concepts of philosophical observation, namely, *coenoscopy* and *idioscopy* (19:81, [1905], CP 1.80–92, [1903]; 56–7). He also makes interesting use of the Benthamite notion of legal fiction. On a personal level, Bentham was known to Peirce through St. John Green, a co-member of the Metaphysical Club in Cambridge in the early 1870s, a disciple of Bentham, Peirce tells us, of whom he was most fond and describes

> as a skillful lawyer and a learned one . . . [whose] extraordinary power of disrobing warm and breathing truth of the draperies of long worn formulas was what attracted attention to him everywhere. In particular, he often urged the importance of applying Bain's definition of belief, as "that upon which a man is prepared to act." From this definition, pragmatism is scarce more than a corollary; so that I am disposed to think of him as the grandfather of pragmatism.

Let us recall, in passing, that if Bain is the grandfather of modern pragmatism, Berkeley, Peirce says, not Kant, is the "father of all modern philosophy . . . [and] the author . . . of modern 'pragmatism' . . ." (from a review of the works of George Berkeley by A. C. Fraser; (Ketner and Cook 1979:36; see also Fisch 1964.)

John Austin, a close, lifelong friend of Lieber, had been engaged in the now classic controversy with Holmes over Austin's assumption that law is the command of the sovereign. This controversy was at its peak around the time that the Metaphysical Club held its meetings.

An important link in the relationship between Lieber and Peirce and their respective theories of signs—even more important than their anti-Hegelian positions, than their mutual early and profound dedication to the poet Schiller's belief that freedom is the objective of aesthetics, even than their qualified but enduring indebtedness to Kant—is their direct line from Locke. As siblings, one might say, Peirce's and Lieber's descent from Locke had taken a curious route.

It is commonplace to show that Peirce adapts with little modification Locke's term *semiotic* from the *Essay concerning Human Understanding*. Locke is also credited with having taken "the first steps in profound analyses" of probable argument (CP 2.647–57, 2.658), a fact that is crucial for our understanding of why Peirce is to insist that although logic "depends upon mathematics," it depends "still more intimately upon ethics" (CP 1958:4.232–246). Peirce says that in the contemplation of ethical ideals we find an esthetic quality and that "Every man has certain ideals of the general description of conduct that befits a rational animal in his particular station in life, what most accords with his total nature and relations . . ." (CP 1.591). In discussing the subdivisions of the normative sciences, logic, ethics, and esthetics, Peirce points to the separation between the theoretical and the applied sciences, and although, as he observes, the practical sciences are rarely directly influenced by philosophy, it is primarily through ethics that the connection between the theoretical and the practical is effected. Peirce deplores the fact that "Ethics is courteously invited to make a suggestion now and then in law, jurisprudence, and sociology. Its sedulous exclusion from diplomacy and economics is immense folly . . ." (CP 1.251).

There is certainly little to be found in this or other of Peirce's often ironic comments on the mutual exclusion of the speculative and the practical sciences that warrants the widely shared opinion among Peirce scholars that Peirce was unconcerned with the world of practical affairs. For example, Bernstein's observation (1971:80) that "Peirce was almost totally indifferent to the concrete problems of social and political philosophy" is widely shared but wrong. It is true that there is little if anything in all of Peirce's writings to suggest he was even aware of the great Civil War in this country, or concerned that social, academic, economic, and political changes of revolutionary magnitude were taking place all around him with no less a public figure than Lieber at the center and in the thick of much of it. Yet, although we do not find explicit reference to Locke's *Letter Concerning Toleration* (1689) which is said to hold the key to his entire philosophy, or even much that would suggest that Peirce had closely studied Locke's *Two Treaties on Government*, we know these works were well known to him and known, perhaps, as well as the *Essay*, the influence of which is so much more apparent.

It is with enormous admiration that Peirce writes:

> Locke's grand word was substantially this: "Men must think for themselves, and genuine thought is an act of perception. Men must see out of their own eyes, and it will not do to smother individual thought—the only thought there is—beneath the weight of general propositions, laid down as innate and infallible, but really only traditional—oppressive and unwholesome heritages from a barbarous and stupid past."

Peirce goes on to say in his review of Fraser's study of Locke (*The Nation*, 1890):

> When we think of the manner in which the Cartesians, Spinoza, and the others had been squeezing out the quintessence of blindness from "First Principles," and consider to what that method was capable of bending itself, in religion and in politics, we cannot fail to acknowledge a superior element of truth in the practicality of Locke's thought. (Ketner and Cook 1975:95)

Lieber, at the time of the meetings of the Metaphysical Club, was nearing the end of his life. He had edited a thirteen-volume *Encyclopedia Americana*, had made major contributions to the study of criminology, and had edited important works on American prisons by his friends de Toqueville and de Beaumont.

He had enjoyed widespread acclaim for his three major works, the *Manual of Political Ethics* (1839/1911), the *Legal and Political Hermeneutics* (1839/1963), and for his most famous study, *On Civil Liberty and Self-Government* (1853). He had taught history and political economy for twenty years at South Carolina College, and in 1856 was offered a chair at Columbia College in history and political science. The years that followed this appointment caught Lieber up in the conflict between North and South and the Civil War. During this time he was a valued consultant for the War Department and became one of the nation's foremost authorities on both domestic and international law. He was responsible for drawing up a code of the rules of war, which was adopted by countries in Europe as well as in the United States States. But although the first chair in constitutional history and public law had been created for him at Columbia College's Law School, it was not through his teaching abilities that Lieber was able to realize his ambition, which was "to leave a work behind me, be it ever so small, which will live in spite of the changes of time. . . ." This he wrote to his friend Charles Sumner in the 1830s (Perry 1882/1926:82–83). Here he says that he will ". . . not rest until I *force* the political and legal world to quote me" (Brown 1851:16–18).

Among the great tributes to Lieber was Elihu Root's presidential address at the seventh annual meeting of the American Society of International Law, Washington, April 24, 1913, a year before Peirce's death. With a generosity almost extravagant Root cited the countless contributions Lieber had made to the cause of international law, to the enormous wealth of literature on law, ethics, and politics that Lieber had authored. Of his contributions to the science of signs, Root said nothing, nor has anything yet been said on this aspect of Lieber's work. Root said of Lieber:

> He was no dry student delving for knowledge he could not use; but a living soul instinct with human sympathy and love of liberty and justice, seizing eagerly the weapons of learning to strike blows in the struggle for nobler and happier life among men.

Of Lieber's life, Root said, "It was a wonderful career. . . . If our Society, at once national and international, were about to choose a patron saint, and the roll were to be called, my voice for one would answer, 'Francis Lieber.'"

Yet Peirce's debt to Lieber has not yet been acknowledged; too little is still known of Peirce.

Peirce's prolific writings, most of which are yet unpublished, which he continually rethought and revised throughout his long and thankless career, are rarely referred to by our seasoned jurisprudes and legal philosophers today, despite the fact that direct reference to legal practice and reasoning are significantly found in all stages of his work, and in relation to nearly all the major topics of semiotics which deeply concerned him.[1] All of logic, according to Peirce, should be regarded as semiotic.

As I stressed at the beginning of this volume, the impact of Peirce's thought, until only recently, has been greatest in the study of law upon some of the great revolutionaries in jurisprudence both in the United States and on the Continent, for instance, Holmes and Gény.[2]

It is in the context of an emergent social conscience that legal consciousness of correctable social inequity develops, for example, in Bentham's utilitarianism, in Mill's social and economic justice, and stimulates, directly and indirectly, the formulation of laws of juridical interpretation throughout the world, both in so-called civil law countries and in common law countries.[3]

Although the need for rules for legal interpretation has been felt since at least the first quarter of the nineteenth century, it was Peirce who contended that hermeneutics is not merely a theory and method of the exegesis of special texts— sacred on one end of the spectrum and profane on the other—but should be regarded as the method of methods of semiotics in order to ascertain not only how each field inquires into the objects of its special concern but also how the separate institutions of social value communicate with one another and therefore how such communication between systems results in the emergence of new values and new meaning in human intercourse, that is, in new signs and sign systems.[4]

Throughout his writings Peirce is careful to distinguish between the practical and the speculative sciences, linking the most speculative with the most abstract modes of developing an idea, that is, the mathematical sciences, and the most practical with the applied sciences such as law and economics. Semiotics is viewed as applying the principles of mathematical inquiry, for its purposes, to account for the structure and use of thought, in order to serve as referential model for those institutions that more directly interact with persons in society, such as the law. Thus semiotics mediates between speculative and practical acts. A legal system can be said to represent or to be a sign of that particular semiotic process most appropriate to it. By the same token, each mode, or style of a semiotic process or event—an occasion of inquiry—is a representation, or interpretative sign, of a more abstract process of discovery, which in turn takes its cues from the world of experience and observation and forms hypotheses as abstracted from the actual, practical world.[5] Therefore the actual practice of law, among other practices, is resourceful of the basic material upon which more theoretical investigations are developed.[6] In this sense, the higher the level of abstraction, the more authoritative the referent system so characterized, and the whole of semiotics is concerned with how one level may be translated into a different level, or method of inquiry. Peirce asks, "What does it mean to speak of the 'interpretation' of a sign? Interpretation is merely another word for translation . . ." (ms 282:100).

Understood in this manner, the legal system *interprets* its referent, which is to say that a particular structure of thought—a logical pattern—is a referent sign or authority, which as *type* becomes that upon which the legal acts of any given legal system are predicated, as *tokens* of that type.

Pragmatism, or pragmaticism, as Peirce redefines and distinguishes his concept of semiotics from other, then prevailing notions of pragmatism, refers to a *method* of inquiry. Semiotics is characterized by the pragmatic method precisely because the role of Peirce's logic is, as a whole, heuristic. The main agency in this logical role is to present a structure of procedure—a sign structure showing the process by which any idea, itself a sign, develops from one stage of interpretation to the next, according to rules for interpretation that are integral with the appropriately selected mode of reasoning. Thus Peirce's expanded logic, or semiotics, is not intended as a whole to reiterate *no more* in its conclusions than is given in its premises, but rather to invent, to discover, and to create new meaningful signs which, as provisional judgments, may act as subjects for continuing and even endless inquiry.

Elsewhere in this book the relation between authority and freedom is examined with respect to law. This relationship characterizes all of creative activity, the purpose of which is to make new meaning out of old and to realize that which is felt to be potentially valuable. In this context the concept of continuity is reexamined; the continuum of law is presumed here to be an aspect of the continuum of thought in general. According to Peirce, semiotics, as his expanded logic, serves in the creating of new values and value systems, as noted earlier. In this process, esthetics, considered as the science of values, is related to logic through the mediation of ethics. Peirce speaks further of the "ethics" of right thinking:

> "What is the use of thinking? . . . it is the argument alone that is the subject of logical goodness and badness . . ." and further, in this passage, ". . . an argument is sound if it necessarily must predict facts in the measure in which it promises to do so. . . . All this is entirely contrary to the doctrines of leading logicians of today. I make the soundness of an argument to consist in its conformity to the law of the facts." (ms 313.13, 15)

As early as the period between 1865 and 1867, Peirce writes in the logic notebooks that the phrase "the burden of proof" belongs in the courtroom "and has no place in speculative science where indefinite suspension of judgment is permissible. However, since several of the important questions of philosophy are matters of practical interest, it may be allowed to speak of a burden of proof in their practical reference" (MS 337).

A propos of the ethics of "right reason" in law, Justice Story's dilemma is recalled. The *tools* of reasoning with which he had to structure his liberal views on slavery cases were "formalistic" and thus incongruous with his judgment. According to Gilmore, Story was "driven" to present and justify his decisions in a "formalism" that was entirely foreign to the content of his convictions and liberal ideas and to the principles he had firmly stood for during his career (Gilmore 1917; Kevelson 1981) It is an uncommon instance of having the wrong reasoning for the right reasons.[7]

Story was as famous for his work on the codification of law as Lieber was for his work on legal hermeneutics and political ethics. They were close colleagues during the especially turbulent period in post-Civil War legal thought. Peirce selected both Story and Lieber to represent the "great men of the 19th century" in law (ms 1123:25).

Gilmore points out that formalism permitted Story an acceptable and political mode of deciding cases "according to the letter of a statute or of an established rule of law, without further inquiry," but, it must be noted, such resort severely compromised what Peirce would have called Story's ethics in reasoning.

In having to choose between a mode of interpretation that would accord either with that of legal interpretation or of doctrinal interpretation, Story chose the former and thus postponed for a later date, well into the twentieth century, the role of the activist judge in his role as legal hermeneuticist. Although Lieber (1839a:Chap. 3) was careful to distinguish legal hermeneutics from other kinds of interpretation, the first edition, as he later saw it, called for additional explanation. Thus, in the Hammond edition, issued in 1880, more than forty years after the first appearance of this major work, Lieber added more than a dozen appendices, each of which addresses special aspects of the concept of legal interpretation. It is particularly in Appendix C, "On the Province of Legal Hermeneutics," that Lieber distinguishes between legal hermeneutics as the interpretation of signs and other older notions of interpretation which tended to be understood in relation to "defective and imperfect laws. . . ." The entire appendix warrants close study, especially pages 245–250.

Story wrote during a period in the development of new juridical values when rules for interpretation had not yet become canonized and made an integral part of statutory law. Indeed, it was not until 1896 that the revised Cardinal Rules of Legal Interpretation are summarized, as in Beal (1896), Gény (1899/ 1963), Ross (1912), and others. Certainly Savigny must be acknowledged as one of the forerunners of the modern concept of legal hermeneutics, bringing forward a tradition of interpretation in law that dates back at least as far as early Roman law and indeed includes hermeneutic exegesis of sacred texts, such as the Talmud and the Koran.

Regarding, for a moment, the hermeneutics of sacred texts only—which until recently represented hermeneutics as a whole—much of the current literature on hermeneutics in the writings of Apel, Habermas, Gadamer, Ricouer, and others seems not to be concerned with the fact that the traditional purpose of hermeneutic, or interpretive, examination of sacred texts was primarily to clarify sacred law. Among contemporary hermeneuticists in this vein perhaps only Betti has maintained the link between sacred and profane interpretation. If one grants that the problems of theological interpretation are taken up by metaphysical inquiry, then one can readily understand Peirce's concern with explicating the relation between authority and liberty, and causation in continua, within the context of pragmatic method in semiotics. He comments on the subject: ". . . logic ought not to be founded on metaphysics; but on the contrary metaphysics ought to be founded on the science of logic. Logic ought to rest directly on those phenomena of life which nobody doubts" (1967:313.18).

But that which nobody doubts is precisely that which has become established in some system of belief as a sign of truth, an assumption of truth, a referent judgment or law-like representation of reality which members of any given community have come to accept and defer to as binding and which therefore becomes represented and codified in institutionalized, written law.

Peirce's contention is that the truth is not a property of a law any more than what we interpret as real is a property of the phenomenon in question— the object of our inquiry. Peirce does not deny that what exists is, indeed, real. But what we know to be true of existents we know because of the effects of their acts upon us. And further, we know what these acts mean to us by interpreting them, by inferring meaning in a cumulative manner with regard to the thing in question until we have settled doubts and achieve, through reason, some sense of certainty, which we hold and use as true. A judgment, whether it presumes to make or discover law, is, both in law as well as in ordinary life, a symbol of such truth. And a symbol, together with an index (such as a system of classification) and an icon (such as a pattern of thought or a procedure capable of being diagrammed) is the third of these coordinate co-functions of all signs. The dominance of one function over the other two depends primarily on context and purpose.

This concludes for the present a condensed discussion of Peirce's semiotic notion of interpretation as it affects or relates to legal hermeneutics, and that stands in opposition to the traditional juristic principle of hermeneutics which holds that *In claris non fit interpretatio* (When the text is clear there is no room for interpretation).

Regardless of whether one speaks of "usual" or "authentic interpretation," both of which Savigny tells us are implied by the term *legal interpretation* (1867:167–68), or of *doctrinal interpretation*, which calls upon, in the absence of rules for interpretation in the system of law which prevails, the ability of the judge to make decisions by employing a kind of free legislative and law-creative activity, semiotics insists that even the laws and rules for interpretation, in any given system of law, must themselves be regarded as provisional only and therefore subject to reinterpretation.

If ultimately, as Peirce argues, all observation is in error and all fact the result of a process of inference and itself a generalization of two or more observations—if ever a single observation could be isolated and defined—then all our premises in reasoning are, at bottom, hypothetical and not absolutely true. And if every interpretation of a law-like rule increases the meaning of that referent rule, or statute, the interpretation or sign that evolves is not a duplication of its referent but a new sign, the structure and internal relation and organization of which is the representation of a complex system of thought constituents that are not inherent in the referent but come into being—*become*—through the creative process of interpretation.

In Plucknett's words, "The more one examines the historical processes by which the judicature interprets the written and the unwritten laws, the laws that are enacted and the laws that are unenacted, the more clearly one sees that the office *ius dicere*, to interpret law, involves also the office *ius dare*, to make law" (1922:vii).

To illustrate this point further, consider Tedeschi's concern that Ascarelli's "anarchic" view of "free interpretation" in law will "lead to the elimination from the world of law of anything that is not a concrete, immediate relevant order" does not hold, especially when one introduces into this absolute freedom in interpretation the authority of those rules of the system that indicate procedure (Tedeschi 1967).

As Gény points out, the interpreter is constrained by rules for discovery and interpretation, "the best defined of which come from the formal sources of positive law" (1899/1963:565). Gény goes on to say that of the acknowledged constraints on the interpreter the main one is the written law. This exerts the primary authoritative source when it exists: "Statute as such is the expression of the authority of a man or a group of men, commensurate with their intelligence" (1899/1963:565). But we have already discussed legal hermeneutics substantially and mention it here only in passing.

In other words, because a statute carries forward the intention of its authors and the situation that was presumed to govern so that no statute "becomes an independent entity separate from the thought of its author," the process of legal hermeneutics must be regarded as a continuation of an idea. Thus a statute represents a general quality and a vague judgment. Every idea or statute so interpreted is like an answer to a question, a dialogue of the law with itself.

As I have noted, in Peirce dialogue is the basic structure of all sign interpretation and hence of semiotics as a whole. Peirce asks,

> What are signs for, anyhow? They are to communicate ideas, are they not? Even the imaginary signs called thoughts convey ideas from the mind of yesterday to the mind of tomorrow into which yesterday has grown. . . . But why should this idea-potentiality be so poured from one vessel into another unceasingly? Is it a mere exercise of the World-Spirit's Spiel-trieb—mere amusement?. . . It is a part, perhaps we may say the chief part, of a process of the Creation of the World. (ms 282.101)

Thus legal hermeneutics, like other interpretive processes, derives its impetus and takes its authority from what the poet Schiller spoke of as the transformation of values in the fusing of rule with liberty, in the free play of the imagination together with the inhibitory power of self-control in thinking. Boundaries link possibility with forms of thought which permit one to evolve vague notions into consequential judgments from which acts in the world proceed. Understood in this manner, one sees the domain of ethics governed by esthetics, and governing in turn what is called, variously, logic.

The choice of an appropriate or ethical mode of thinking in interpreting *vis-à-vis* law and legal systems depends, ultimately, on those values predicted to be realized *through* interpretation. In this sense all legal hermeneutics is teleological, the term *teleological* referring to the influence of future goals on the here and now, as a kind of precedential authority totally different from that notion of precedent so strongly criticized by the great legal realist Llewellyn. Thus modality, especially all degrees of the possible, becomes in legal hermeneutics the life of the law.

NOTES

1. See Fisch (1942:85–97). See also his paper on the reciprocation between Peirce and prominent lawyers of the nineteenth century (1964:3–32) and his introduction to vol. 3 of *Writings of Charles S. Peirce* (1986).

2. See Kevelson (1987). For discussion of the sovereignty of the people see Lieber (1839/1963, Hammond Edition: especially 206–227, 312–331.

3. Compare, for example, Britto (1927) and Betti (1948) with Plucknett (1922) on legal interpretation with respect to civil law countries, on the one hand, and England's common law tradition, on the other hand.

4. Peirce's method of methods is intended to interpret the method of inquiry that characterizes a specific science of discipline into the mode of communication of other disciplines inquiries; semiotics is seen to be the mediating process in intersystemic communication. See Kevelson (1987).

5. See Peirce's Manuscript 605 on the classification of the sciences. See also Manuscript 852 on semiotic philosophy as heuristic of categorical truths.

6. The actual practice of law corresponds with the notion of experience in Peirce, which he says is the basis for our investigations. Experience is predominantly contradictory and oppositional in its representational sign structure, according to Peirce, and thus corresponds with the typical factive sign. Note also Holmes's insistence that the law is primarily concerned with factive relations (1881/1963:   ). See also "The Path of the Law" (1897) and Summers's commentary on Holmes's fact–prediction relation in legal interpretation (1982:116–135).

7. See Gilmore's account of Story's applying the "wrong" logic to the "right" law ((1917/1977: especially pages 27, 38, 48, 50). In a similar sense Lieber criticizes Locke for his inappropriate use of axiomatic reasoning, for example, in the *Manual of Political Ethics* (1839/1911:67–68); and again, more specifically, in *On Civil Liberty and Self-Government* (1853: 211–212).

CHAPTER 17

American Realism

Earlier chapters investigated the hypothesis that there is a direct relationship between the theoretical concepts of philosophical systems of thought and rules that are an integral part of social systems such as institutions of law, economics, and government. A special area to be examined here is the impact of American pragmatism, as introduced by Peirce, on United States constitutional law through the direct influence of Holmes.

Holmes considered the Constitution to be an experiment upon which certain operations of thought could be performed so as to evolve, in a cumulative fashion, the meaning of constitutional law. This chapter compares Holmes's method of treating law as a science with the concept of "operations of thought," which derives from Peirce. The movement in law called legal realism originates with Holmes and hence indirectly with Peirce.

The major theories of Peirce's pragmatism are brought to bear on the kinds of legal practice, specifically, the process of decision making, which the proponents of legal realism describe in their various writings. This chapter suggests ways of confirming whether the historical changes in American law can be directly traced to the assumptions of the legal theorists and, through them, to pragmatism with its reaction against the Benthamite notion of complete legal codes.

The economic basis of modern law has also been examined at length. There it was appropriate to compare a bifurcation between civil and mercantile law in an earlier period of time with its apparent synthesis in modern society. It was noted that Hayek's contention is that the spontaneous activities characteristic of a free market and a maximally free society have been undermined by governmental intervention into the domains of law and economics. If not checked, this trend will lead away from new directions for law and philosophy into less freedom for society as a whole.

According to Hayek's thesis, the limits of human liberty are the boundaries of interpretation. In a previous chapter it was pointed out that by regarding the Constitution as an interpretable sign or experiment rather than as a fixed and complete system of law, freedom of interpretation by the judiciary would represent, or be a model of, social freedom in the larger sense.

Hayek regards the Constitution as an idea which grows, from which are derived or interpreted the laws that generate its own becoming, and which is in both theory and practice capable of being infinitely amended. In this sense, it is the idea of the constitutional amendment *as* an idea that may push the constraints on legal action to unprecedented frontiers of human liberty (Hayek 1960). This also is Holmes's view, as I have noted.

Hayek suggests that Peirce's pragmatic logic underlies and may account for the process of expanding human freedom through law. This chapter also examines Peirce's concepts to determine whether such pragmatic ideal can be or has been made effectual in the actual practice of American law.

Although there is an established body of literature that acknowledges the contributions of American pragmatism to the development of a movement in American law known as legal realism (Fuller 1934; Llewellyn 1962; Frank 1943b; Summers 1982; Cohen 1954; Hayek 1960; Pound 1931), most writings on this topic cite Peirce's followers, James and Dewey, as instrumental in introducing pragmatic theory into jurisprudence and legal procedure in the United States. Until recently, little has been written about Peirce's major contributions to American legal discourse and practice (Kevelson 1977, 1981, 1982b,d, 1985a,b,c, 1987). On the economic basis of American law, as noted, Hayek has been one of the few contemporary scholars to call attention to Peirce's influence on the social systems of law, economics, and politics (Hayek 1973; Machlup 1976).

If there has been little emphasis on philosophy's direct contribution to the social institutions of law, economics, and politics, in a general sense this omission may be due in part to the current policy of excluding the study of philosophical systems of thought from the curricula of law schools and departments of economics and political science. Usually the omission is claimed by philosophers who attempt to "apply" theory, however untested over time, to social issues without taking into account the bridge laws that are required to link theoretical systems with the systems of practical affairs. Attention is called in Chapter 18 to Rawls's (1971) uniqueness with respect to the first omission, especially in the area of law and ethics. In the special case of law school curricula, a survey course or seminar in jurisprudence may be required, but rarely do students examine larger philosophical issues outside the special area of jurisprudence. It has been suggested that the methodologies of law, economics, and government are considered to be at this time independent of philosophical foundations and that one need not subject the methodologies of the social sciences to close scrutiny against the background of philosophical theory. However, as hypothesized in this chapter, it may be the case that social issues that become recognized in legal, economic, and political practice as critical, that is, as warranting review and resolution, are the *result* of certain philosophical concepts which do become referential, especially in judicial decision making.

For example, with respect to problems in model building in the social sciences, it has been noted that "the methodological issues of interest . . . cannot be fully understood except against the backdrop of the larger philosophical problems that relate to each issue" (McClelland 1975:17).

The following discusses this significant omission in some detail in order to place Peirce's contributions to legal realism in appropriate context.

There is a widespread misconception that the speculative sciences, philosophy, for example, identifies the methodology of its inquiry with the subject under investigation. Thus an empirical method is appropriate for investigating physical objects, but nonmaterial objects of investigation require nonempirical method. But if explicitly questioned, no one will confine the inquiry into metaphysical problems to examinations of metaphysical phenomena. Rather, it has been implicitly accepted that the investigation of the most abstract principles must include investigation of the most concrete and physicalistic phenomena and those rules that are assumed to govern or account for their functions in existence. The classical hierarchical relational order of matter to spirit is completely overturned in modern science and especially so from the perspective of semiotics.

Thus the major problems of general philosophy are also among the major problems of science from a semiotics view.[1] Although these problems are, in actuality, never so conveniently separate as the proverbial "five philosophical problems" would suggest but are overlapping and interdependent, it has been traditionally convenient and useful to classify speculative investigation under the headings of these most general problems: mind–body, freedom and determination, cognition, justification of the belief in God, and ethics. It is apparent even to the man on the street that one cannot consider the relation between the mind and the body without also having to introduce the notion of predetermination which suggests a need, that is, a psychological need, to introduce causal factors. Thus, one also has to include in a close study of the mind–body problem the unsolved problem of the justification of the belief in God as well as all the other problems as they bear on causation. The analogy in law is implied by the terms: sovereignty, authority, precedent, rule of law, and so on. This problem of justification is not concerned only with affirming or denying whether people *believe* in God, but rather with logically demonstrating that this belief is true and the argument valid.

It is not valid within the constraints of traditional logics because the initial premises of such an argument are hypothetical only and never absolutely true.[2]

Similarly, the notion of causation is based on certain assumptions about first and/or final causes and on certain theories regarding the spatializing of time, and also on psychological rather than logical information which persuades that antecedents are related to causal factors, as in Mill and as far back as Aristotle. In selected mechanical processes the principle of causation still holds. In metaphysical theory it does not.

Again, the problem of determination versus freedom is tied to an initial prime mover, whether God, or mechanistic or natural forces, or genetic, that is, biological predispositions and encoding. The increasing popularity of the notion of behavior as biologically based tends to seal the coffin on freedom and to relegate this concept to the vast cemeteries of obsolescent ideas.

Analogously, the problem of ethics is problematic precisely because there is no absolute touchstone, or rule of law, that permits judgment to be passed on conduct as plus-or-minus ethical or moral. Rather, there are competing theories, none of which has satisfactory criteria for evaluating appropriate conduct. That is, moral conduct properly belongs to that sphere of social life which is generally understood as *legitimated* acts, whereas lawful conduct refers to a body of rules of law that act as precedents in judging the legality of public action.

The current tendency is to attempt to map legal acts onto the framework of legitimate behavior and to impose morals on law. This tendency is doubly problematic because the models of legitimacy have far less trustworthy foundations than institutionalized and codified legal order and legal system. That is, they are less certain than positive and codified law. But the *uncertainty* of foundations of legitimate conduct is valued honorifically, in Hayek's and in Peirce's views.

Legal realism, in its opposition to legal positivism—which acknowledges the rule of law to be absolute within a given system of law—is among those innovations in law in the twentieth century that would attempt to incorporate a social conscience, an ethical and moral watchdog, into the system of law as such. In so doing it has been severely criticized by positivists for removing whatever certainty the law may depend on in its judicial prouncements and in substituting instead the unsound, uncertain basis of morality.[3]

Criticisms against legal realism and its congeners, legal pragmatism, legal instrumentalism, and the like, are often given without a full understanding of the philosophical underpinnings of such legal practice. The problem is compounded because it is not always clear that the proponents and practitioners of legal realism and related approaches to legal theory and practice have themselves grasped the basic implications of their approach. It is the contention of this book that legal realism has often failed to realize its strength and pursue its purposes because it has not clearly grasped its theoretical bases, which are Peircean and therefore semiotic.

Not least of the five above-mentioned problems in relation to law is the problem of cognition: Here, a behavioristic, deterministic approach to the process of knowing is based on epistemological foundations which depend on Cartesian *a priori* assumptions. In the latter, freedom is permitted, but within circumscribed, determined, and foretold boundaries and therefore in a real sense is not freedom but rather relatively free movement and freeplay in a closed-system game in which the rules are given once and for all and are not open to change and improvisation. By contrast, a Peircean semiotic is concerned with the problem of cognition with its emphasis on real novelty, with the process of becomingness of the world, with the dynamic structure of the dialogic relation of knower and known; this concern permeates American realism, which has sought to transform the conditions, the process, and the knowledge as evidence in law.

The distinguishing logic of semiotics is not the logic of justification but the logic of discovery. The indisputable "fact" of the empiricists and the positivists in law becomes through semiotics a collective and consensual judgment, but provisional only. Evidential procedure is also the consequence of judicial evaluation, that is, of judgment, of selectivity among available pieces of data so that any evidence presented in a realist court is already a *qualified* set of facts and is a sign system in preparation for use as representation at trial and/or hearing.

As noted, the purpose of semiotics is not to *prescribe* how the courts may proceed. It is not deontic in this respect as is, for example, a Kantian categorical imperative. Rather, it is descriptive in an accountable manner, in a manner derived from, resembling in some respects, but never identical with, the method of science. It describes what the activist realist court actually does and how it does what it does in order to reach its conclusions. In other words, semiotics in law attempts to show the process of legal procedure as it develops in each case, and as the system of cases constitute the moving parts of that moving and developing whole which we may generally term in this case as the legal system. It is Peirce's thought process made large, visible, and mobile.[4]

When Peirce writes of his existential graphs and likens them to a motion picture process, he is attempting to emphasize that although each graph, because of physical limitation, must appear as a static representation, one must imagine each graph in relation with other graphs in a multidimensional structure, continuously in motion and change with respect to time–space coordinates.[5]

It is this same notion of continuous change that Hayek discusses throughout his philosophical writings on law and economics. Hayek's economic realism I am claiming is a counterpart to what is generally known in this country and abroad as legal realism. Little is known of Peirce's direct contribution to this movement. What is acknowledged is that these areas of law, economics, and politics, although usually and correctly referred to as the practical sciences, are

not merely technical fields of activity, or areas for application of theory, but that
the term *practical* should be understood as interactively relational with abstract
or speculative activity, as Peirce insisted.[6]

The most speculative or abstract of the sciences is mathematics, precisely
because it is the farthest removed from the world of our experience. Law,
economics, politics, and, to some extent, psychology are among the most significant of the practical sciences because they directly refer to and interact with
the world of experience. Yet we must remember that Peirce's pragmatism, the
term that stands for the *method* of semiotics, is derived from experience. Experience is the referent of semiotic pragmatics.

Peirce is quick to point out that the distinction between most abstract and
least abstract—or most and least practical—is not a value judgment with respect
to the comparative merit of each respective mode of inquiry. Rather, the hierarchy
that obtains between most and least is only in terms of their relative abstractness,
not in terms of their relative worth. Mathematics and physics, which is subordinate in terms of abstraction to mathematics, are dependent on the practical
sciences for their data, but the problems with which they are concerned are
themselves, abstracted from these data. Frequently, inquiry within these most
abstract of the sciences has little or no capability of returning to the data, which
are initially furnished by experience, in order to verify the conclusions of inquiry.
Rather, a previous solution to an abstract problem or set of data is used as a
starting point for subsequent analyses, such that investigation continuously builds
upon a series of quasi-nominalistic judgments, each in turn acting as a new topic
for investigation. But the practical sciences, so inextricably linked to the world
of experience, are checked and balanced by experience itself. Thus each general
conclusion, or judgment, is law-like only to the extent that and for as long as
subsequent experience sustains and does not negate or challenge this conclusion.[7]

In this chapter it may be useful to select a few of the distinguishing concepts
of Peirce's pragmatic semiotics which have directly and indirectly influenced
the shaping of legal realism. Not all of these concepts have received wide
audience even among long-time Peirce scholars. Some of these concepts, as they
relate to the development of legal realism, were discussed in the early decades
of the twentieth century with great interest but were not carried into the mainstream discussion of American jurisprudence. Although throughout this chapter
observations are directed mainly to American law, it has been noted that Peirce's
influence on the law is evident in France, Germany, and in Sweden, where
through Hagerstrom and Olivecrona we find an explicit movement called legal
realism which acknowledges its debt to Holmes.[8]

These ideas are:

1. Inclusion of traditional syllogistic reasoning within what Peirce calls
   his expanded logic, that is, a pragmatic logic.

2. Interpretation, which in Peirce as in legal hermeneutics is dependent on the rules for interpretation given by each particular system in question. Interpretation of signs is not an arbitrary activity nor is it the kind of creative approach described either by Eco (1976) or Roland Barthes (1968; 1977). In other words, the text is not authoritative and neither is the reader, but both together constitute a relationship which permits interpretation as transformation and growth of a shared sign or thought.

3. Discovery, which is possibly the most difficult of Peirce's contributions to modern thought and must be seen against his understanding that the universe is not finished and complete. Completeness would make discovery a mere finding of what already exists. Discovery in Peirce's sense partakes of invention and innovation, which is to say that real novelty and chance change that which continuously exists in the world.

A discovery procedure must be capable of seeing such new relations which are the result of new items in the world, that is, of discovering them as meaningful and unanticipated structures. At the same time discovery is linked to predictive theory in law, which is one of the hallmarks of legal realism. The decision of the courts must be predictable in a way not previously required because if the rule of law is no longer regarded as absolute, and if the decisions of activist, realist judges create new law, prediction must be the outcome of a systematic discovery procedure which minimizes the effects of uncertainty and instability on the legal system and on society as a whole.

4. Abductive reasoning, which is linked, on the one hand, with discovery and, on the other hand, with a displacement of spatializable structures such as arguments. For example, under the positivists, still dependent on the axiomatic governance of syllogistic reasoning, the arguments of law are amplifications and extensions or subdivisions of major premises. In the new realist law there is not a referent spatial system such as Euclidean geometry, of which legal discourse is an extension or token. Rather, legal principles may be "made visible," that is, become iconically present, according to principles of non-Euclidean geometry.

5. Reduction of the idea of causation to explanation. In this sense legal cause in all its various meanings becomes one of the leading assumptions of legal realism.

6. Contract, or the idea of agreement, motivated by reason, and indexically transactional in structure.

In law contract is derived from property. Both contract and property are ideas which are inseparable from the concept of the legal individual. The individual, as Peirce suggests, emerged in response to the nation–state, to the possibility of surplus goods and long-range capital investments, and, not least, to the restructuring of certain language systems, for example, the new syntactic structure of English as an analytic language and also as a language the structure of which emphasizes the dominant role of transitivity and object–subject relationship.

All six of the above-mentioned topics come to stand for aspects of possible freedom in a world of chance, of real novelty, of becoming, and of experience as the ground of the knowable.

Distinguishing features may be identified as follows: (a) emphasis on non-formal logic, which more accurately accounts for the actual growth of thought and ideas; (b) the system-specific role of interpretation in maintaining stability of order in the face of continuous change, and the understanding of discovery which is radically different from the previous notion of rearrangement of known and given parts within a defined universe; (c) self-corrective aspects of reasoning, which imply degrees of ethical behavior; that is, the freedom to release oneself from past judgments in the face of new evidence and new understanding is the freedom to break the constraints of an older order and to move intentionally into orders of one's choice; (d) inseparability of contract from freedom, both of which are submitted in the idea of the individual which itself is always an individual-in-community as a member of a society of like-minded individuals.

All of these ideas, which Peirce regarded as central to his semiotics, are assimilated and transformed to serve the practical sciences of law, economics, and politics.

This movement met, and still meets, with enormous opposition, and there is no simple accord among proponents with respect to particular concepts and specific practices in the practical world of human affairs.

Just as the so-called five problems in philosophy are not five distinct problems but are different aspects of continuing examination of central questions which remain unresolved, these topics and features that show Peirce's influence on American realism are not distinct but are different aspects of a new and unified approach to basic questions still unanswered by traditional approaches of both the practical and theoretical sciences.

To amplify further, semiotic methodology corresponds with the problem of knowing. The concept of provisional judgment in semiotics corresponds with the problem of justifying the belief in God. The concept of discovery corresponds with the freedom–determination question. The notion of contract in semiotics places the mind–body opposition in a new relationship which eliminates the need for an either/or, that is, a subordinate–superordinate approach. Finally, the problem of ethics becomes the question in semiotics of selecting the *appropriate* mode of reasoning for the task at hand where *appropriate* depends, ultimately, on the consensus of the given community.

What one gains through Peirce is a leap into new areas of freedom. What one loses through Peirce is certainty.

Of certainty Peirce says many things, among the most notable of which is that human beings create certainty because they suffer with uncertainty. They attempt to alleviate their suffering in four basic ways: (1) compliance with respect to the will of a coercive force,—a dictator, a totalitarian government, a legal system primarily punitive in intent; (2) Habit, that is to say, through having once achieved some satisfactory level of dependability with respect to a problem or set of problems and then deciding that too much has been invested in this pattern to change and to risk even when the pattern or habit becomes progressively less adaptable to similar problems and thus is a weakened source of satisfaction. But habit of thought symbolizes some hold on certainty; (3) achievement of certainty through testing one's own belief against the majority's belief; that is, common sense ensures a sense of security and certainty which many choose to place trust in, but the majority is not necessarily correct; and (4) reason, the least dependable way of sustaining certainty; it is the most free and in the long run is the mode based on the most solid ground.

Coercive authority gives us certainty but at the high cost of autonomy and freedom of inquiry. Habit is comforting, but clearly one sees that the habits of thought of others are different from one's own; therefore, unless one is altogether blind to experience, such certainty is achieved only at the cost of blindness to the world of others around us. Common sense which is the certainty of the general public is an untrustworthy certainty because it oversimplifies the problem. Thus the certainty which is most possible is that certainty which at every moment admits to the indeterminacy of the world and yet seeks for small reassurance some measure of stability or some criterion for the time being. This allows one to begin to resolve the more pressing and more immediate problem, that is, the case in point. The term, *pragmatism* has, unfortunately, been used interchangeably with experience, but this misses Peirce's message. It has been emphasized that few judges in the history of American law have permitted their philosophical ideas and ideals overtly to shape their decisions. Justices Cardozo and Holmes are among those singular judges who "thought it important to *have* a philosophy" (Cohen 1954:164–166).

In focusing on the relation between Peirce's philosophy and Holmes's effectualness in interpreting and changing constitutional law it may be useful to ask to what extent the *concept* of the legal system prevails at any one time in the history of a society and in what manner this prevailing idea of the legal system changes the actions of law. If, as noted by Lawrence Friedman (1975), what we call a legal system is actually a network of competing, conflicting legal subsystems, to what extent are the legal, economic, and political institutions of today reactions against the ideas of legal systems that predominated in an earlier period of social history?

It has been remarked that what is ordinarily referred to as our legal system at present is not a unified institution but a conflictual relation between attitudes with respect to the proper role of the judiciary.

On the one hand, there is the attitude expressed by Justice Marshall's famous dictum, "Judicial power, as contradistinguished from the power of laws, has no existence. Courts are mere instruments of law and can will nothing" (*Osborn* v. *Bank of United States*, 22 U.S., 9 Wheaton, 736,866, 1824).

The opposing view is Justice Holmes's "General propositions do not decide cases" (*Lochmer* v. *New York*, 198 U.S. 45,76, 1905).

As mentioned earlier, Holmes's attitude is the foundation for the development of legal realism. Holmes is referred to by Hayek as a spokesman for the progressive movement in law.

According to Pound's interpretation of this movement, legal actors, the highest of which is the judge, should not be "legal monks [who] pass their lives in an atmosphere of pure law," but they must also have an understanding of the way in which social and political factors enter into the legal process; further, legal thought is an extension of philosophical thought (Pound 1910:133–136). The philosophical thought to which Pound refers is, specifically, American pragmatism.

In presenting a historical evaluation of the legal realist movement in America, Fuller notes (1964) that although legal realism was the most powerful legal force of the twentieth century until the 1930s, the force of that movement has since become muted. Even during the years between the two World Wars legal realism was widely recognized as "the most significant development in American legal theory" (ibid.:4–15)). Fuller attributed the decline of the movement not only to the death of its outstanding proponents but especially to prevailing economic conditions which closed opportunity for investigation of the relations between pragmatic thought and the institutional practice of legal realism.

Fuller suggests that interest in a problem declines not only because a complex hypothesis comes to nothing, or even because the problem is resolved, but more often because practical considerations mandate cessation of research and development. Indeed, in 1928 an Institute of Law was established at the Johns Hopkins University for the purpose of inquiring into the relations between practice and theory in law, with special emphasis on the interaction between American pragmatism and legal realism. The institute lasted only five years, closing in 1933 for economic reasons.

Here, in summary, are the major questions raised by this chapter:

1. What is the impact of American pragmatism, following Peirce, upon the shaping of American law through Holmes and his followers in legal realism?
2. Given that Holmes regarded constitutional law as interpretable rather than fixed law, in what specific ways has his more than one-third contribution to constitutional law changed the patterns of American society?

3. In what sense and in what manner do Peirce's theories on discovery procedure, interpretation, causation, evidential procedures, and fact finding find analogous expression in legal procedures since Holmes?
4. Are there far-reaching verifiable consequences of American pragmatism outside the United States, such as are possibly manifested in the Scandinavian concept of legal realism?
5. Is the hypothesized relation between philosophy and law unilateral or is it reciprocal? If the latter, how does this reciprocity manifest itself? In the special instance of legal realism and American pragmatism, can one predict an impact on society as a whole, for example, in the form of a more open-ended social system?
6. Do judges create or discover law, as Frank asked (1942), and if the former, what becomes of the role of authority, or the "sovereign" in the future of American Law?

NOTES

1. See Patterson (1968:172–204). Patterson points out that "pragmatism began as a theory of method" (173). To Peirce, semiotics is the name of the theory that underlies the pragmatic method.

Patterson shows the development of pragmatism from Peirce through James to Holmes, and extending to Pound's theory of a sociological jurisprudence. Dewey, Patterson points out, directly brought a Peircean notion of inquiry and pragmatism to the close attention of the group of law teachers who studied under him at various seminaries throughout the 1920s. Dewey, as is well known, credits Peirce with providing the most important directions for a logic of inquiry which, Dewey finds, is the basis of juridical decision making. See particularly pages 172–179.

2. See Frank (1934:1063–1069). According to Frank, Holmes introduced non-Euclidean legal thinking into law. He says that this type of thinking permits the testing of "legal postulates by their results in human lives" (1066). As discussed in Chapter 7 of this volume, Peirce relates non-Euclidean geometric thinking to his existential graphs. See also Peirce's Manuscript 517.

3. See Holmes 1881/1963:104–129.

4. Peirce's existential graphs are discussed in relation to legal reasoning and the logic of questions and answers in Chapter 7 of this volume.

5. The idea of multidimensionality is connected with the Peircean idea of time as method, as discussed in Chapter 9 of Kevelson (1987). Multidimensionality also links the realists' vision of law as a dynamic rather than static system with the scientific community of the 1920s and the 1930s.

6. Peirce discussed the interdependence of the more abstract sciences, mathematics, physics, and philosophy, with the more practical sciences at various places throughout his voluminous writings. For detailed discussion on the classification of the theoretic sciences of research see Eisele (1976: vol 4, 15–35).

7. See Kevelson (1987: chap. 5 and 11).

8. See Fisch (1952:227–311). Here Fisch refers to Peirce's logic course at Johns Hopkins and remarks that "though logic had been defined as the art of thinking, or as the science of the normative laws of thought, he said these were not true definitions, for mere thinking accomplished nothing, even in mathematics. The true and worthy idea of the science was that it was the art of devising methods of research—the method of methods" (289).

CHAPTER 18

The Constitution as Interpretant Sign

Because of the wealth of his contributions to American law and to the shaping of the United States Constitution, and because of his principal role in interpreting Peirce's pragmatism and semiotic theory and method into what has developed as the most revolutionary movement in modern law, namely, legal realism and its congeners, the thought of Justice Oliver Wendell Holmes should be examined more closely than is possible within the scope of this book. The writings about Holmes, from the viewpoints of jurisprudence, social philosophy, and legal philosophy, are voluminous, raising questions far beyond those addressed in this introduction to legal semiotics; they warrant a separate study on Holmes, which is in preparation.

But in this chapter Holmes's ideas will be discussed primarily as they obviously bear on constitutional interpretation, where *interpretation* is to be understood as pivotal and basic to the process of semiosis according to the thought of Peirce.

This chapter explores a new area in constitutional law. But it does not advance claims with respect to specific issues in constitutional law as they center on Holmes and are related to Holmes's philosophy. The chapters on realism and on interpretation which this chapter supplements also further the idea introduced in the chapter on the economic basis of law. The present chapter introduces Holmes's notion that a system of law, the Constitution, for example, is an experiment or sign subject to change and correction through semiotic method.

Reference in this chapter will again be made to Lieber's contributions to legal and political semiotics. Lieber's influence on the United States Constitution was indirect, primarily through his close friends and colleagues Sumner and Story for whom Peirce, incidentally, expressed anything but admiration.

It has often been observed that political power and influence are direct outgrowths of political visibility. This is a general opinion but points up how semiotic processes actually occur in public life. Before judgment is reached and even before a competition can ensue, there is an image of a something or a someone that, as quality, is lifted out of the general background and "seen" in relief against that background in a significant manner. To put this process in semiotic terms, one may say that the visibility of potentially powerful forces and persons in political life is required as a predominantly iconic sign function. This iconicity develops semiotically into a predominant index, in relation to its given context.

The index is a sign function which expresses opposition, struggle, competition, and, in brief, the factiveness of experience. This index, to continue the analogy with the political forces of any given community, evolves to become predominantly symbolic. In the case of governmental and official positions in the political structure, the elected official, rather than the power behind the office, becomes the symbol of power and authority in the minds of the general public.

The traditional manner of conceding an election emphasizes the emergence of the predominantly symbolic sign out of the political campaign and out of the previous simple visibility of the candidates: The people have spoken. The elected official is a sign that a judgment—a provisional judgment in Peirce's sense—has been made. The judgment stands until overturned, until a new election takes place, until the opportunity for discovery of error. New elections imply that operations have been performed on thought and that detected error in earlier assumptions and judgments are to be revised.

The semiotic process takes place on many levels: in intrapersonal communication or inner dialogue; in interpersonal communication; in intersystemic communication, for instance, between physiological systems within a single person's body such as the vascular and endocrinal systems, or between different functions of a single social institution and also between distinctly different social institutions. This last level is what primarily concerns us here.

On the level of practical affairs we are never concerned simply with interaction between economic systems, political systems, and legal systems, as defined in their domains by constitutions and other documents describing the various parts and subsystems of social organization and governmental institutions. These defined system boundaries are themselves constituted of an infinite number of interlocking sign systems which influence and contribute to the development of each and hence to the development of overarching systemic relations.

It is helpful, perhaps, to compare the subsystems of an individual person with the subsystems of a social institution. Just as no individual person is isolate but is necessarily in relation with other, no social institution is isolate but interacts for its significance with other social institutions. The difficulty at this level in accounting for the growth and development of social institutions is apparent. But it is much more complicated by the fact that at every given moment one is dealing with this intersystemic relationship not only on a single level but always and simultaneously on many levels. Further, everything on all levels is moving and changing and admitting into its area novel elements by design and also by chance.

As Hayek remarked, we are as knowledge-seeking persons never able to know all of these levels which exist, much less all of those new elements emerging which are continually changing the complex situation of existence, *at all levels*.

Also, not the least of the problems which students of constitutional law share is how to account for the influence of legal studies which are not primarily from the perspective of the legal profession and jurisprudence. For example, it is well known that philosophy does enter into legal systems, even though many law schools at present offer, on the whole, little more than survey courses in jurisprudence and an occasional seminar on the philosophy of law. The first Round Table on Law and Semiotics (1987) suggests that a new creative union between legal professionals and legal philosophers may be emerging.

In recent years proponents of an ethical jurisprudence have looked outside the legal community for reinforcement of ethical principles which they themselves, as legal actors, hold as part of their personal moral creeds. These distinctions between morality and ethics have been noted. I have also remarked earlier that a Kantian or neo-Kantian concept of ethics dominates the newly established area of ethical jurisprudence. A neo-Kantianism in Rawls's *Theory of Justice* (1971) has received much attention. But this chapter will not argue against Rawls's basic premises, nor against his conclusions or against his questionable assumptions. Yet his book has, perhaps because of its "visibility," come to symbolize a "state of the art" of ethical jurisprudence. This is at best a provisional judgment, in the same sense that an elected official represents the provisional judgment or voice of the people.

Rawls's *Theory of Justice* must be discussed at least briefly here, primarily because it is antithetical to Holmes's view of the Constitution as experiment or sign of hypothesis. The legal profession has largely shown its appreciation for Rawls's virtuosity in balancing theories of justice with procedural prescriptions, especially with respect to his concept of "constitution making," but it is resistant to an imposition by a member of a system outside of the legal profession which exercises the kind of influence that Rawls expects his prescriptions to accomplish. As Ronald Moore says,

> Undeniably, Rawls is a master equilibrator. In *TJ*, he manages to traverse a lofty, treacherous, and remarkably complicated network of theoretic highwires while juggling a dazzling variety of conceptual devices; and throughout the performance he

> maintains the impression in his audience that he is moving on solid ground . . . [but]
> when we look more closely, the concentrated effort and the strain are evident. . . .
> First, by hanging some safety nets; the form of simplifying background assumptions,
> Rawls injects a false air of facility into the performance and invites an overbold use
> of the justice principle. . . . And, ultimately, the balance is lost when Rawls gives
> the justice principles an effective monopoly over competing forces of political values.[1]
> (1978)

The opposition of Moore to Rawls is twofold: Moore objects to the intrusion of constitution making by those who are not knowledgeable in the practical aims and procedures of the law. He objects even more strongly to the inconsistency of Rawls's argument. Here in this chapter we are primarily concerned with the fact that the argument is inconsistent because he is implicitly attempting to map a system of thought which is based on pragmatics and on experience upon a system of ethics which initially assumes that justice and liberty are *a priori* and thus given by the human condition. Justice is a concept in Rawls which is *prior* to the changing notions of justice principles in cases at hand.

Similarly, Rawls's notions of freedom or liberty, as these concepts are specified in the text of the Constitution, are self-evident to him and thus prior to experience. Although Rawls concedes that there may be many kinds of justice systems, he seems to assume that there is a general justice out of which the several justices are as tokens of a type. This general justice is eternal in Rawls, as in Kant, and of the nature of absolute truth. Also, his interpretations of liberty and freedom, although they are not the same concepts traditionally, are used interchangeably; he compares them as he compares ethical rights with civil rights. Rhetorically, Rawls defines one as the other and brings about a relation of equivalence. The problem of mapping morality onto law has been discussed in a preceding chapter. It is again stressed here that by strategically redefining each of these terms, liberty and freedom, we have equivalent terms; that is, Term I and Term II are as though equal in meaning. Rawls would be semiotically correct in doing this if a consensus affirmed it, which it does not.

Members of the legal system argue that Rawls's wish to bring liberty and freedom, as equivalent terms, together under the general rubric of justice is a manipulation of meaningful signs, each of which represents systems that are in large measure perhaps compatible but not identical. The objects or points of reference each interprets are different. Each stands for a totally different universe of discourse. Not that this difference, by subsequent rhetoric and arguments, could not be changed. The opposition to Rawls here is that through his changing the relation from dissociation to equivalence and his attempting to reshape the Constitution in the manner suggested in his book, the entire system of law and the purposes that law is intended to serve become subverted in the interests of something other than law, with nothing like law available to fill the role now served by the legal system.

Rawls's book has become part of the curriculum at many law schools.

Over and again the question that continues to be raised is why this study, which is primarily concerned with problems in social philosophy, should be given consideration in the curricula of law schools when rarely, if ever, are equally interesting books from equally related disciplines, sociology, economics, political science, given such special place.[2]

The main interest among lawyers and professors of law is that Rawls suggests that for their own good, and the good of the profession, the legal system should avail itself of and apply the ideas offered in his book. However, as Parker reminds us, it has been remarked that "Rawls' book reads as though the nineteenth century had not happened . . . that the United States is still governed by an eighteenth-century constitution."[3] But Parker stresses that Rawls's theses are already implicit in the Constitution as it now stands. A modification of the Constitution, as advocated by Rawlsian proponents, is in Parker's view simply another way of stating what is already stated in the Constitution. It is not really another interpretation, Parker suggests, but a paraphrase with emphasis on some aspects regarded today as more critical than they were yesterday. It is arguable whether a paraphrase is not, indeed, a reinterpretation.

The point that Parker makes clear is that having a constitution does not guarantee that everyone's constitutional rights are respected. "The United States Constitution sets standards that are often not met," Parker points out. The obvious but essential question is whether the Constitution merely sets standards on the letter of the law in all cases, or whether the discretion is juridical as to when and whether these ideal standards are to be supplied. Is not the Constitution altered by legislation that is not included in the legal system in question? In other words, is an additional legal system—a metalegal system—required in order to realize the intentions of the framers of the Constitution? If so, does the Constitution provide for a higher order of law than itself? The answer from most members of the legal profession is clearly no. The challenge from Rawls and his adherents is clearly yes. A higher order of justice and ethics would require a higher legal system to hold sway over and expedite the principles ideally included in the Constitution as it now stands.

Even granting that Rawls's thesis is correct, and there is strong argument to the contrary, does that assumed correctness itself provide authorization to resolve the problems of constitutional interpretation "by direct application of Rawls to principles of justice?"

According to Parker and others, one must bear in mind that "that would be to expect too much of theory and to give too little credit to the importance of the lawyers' craft."[4] Parker continues:

> Both Rawls' principles of justice and many of the most interesting provisions of the United States Constitution are too abstract to be mechanically applied. Their application requires practical wisdom, and skill in the arts of casuistry in which lawyers are trained.[5]

This observation brings us to the point of how Holmes as mediator did in fact link abstract theory to the practical wisdom of the trained lawyer and thus succeeded in bringing the systems of abstract thought of Peirce's pragmatism into the realm of practical affairs. Was Holmes a "metajurist"? This also brings us to a critical question, namely, are some theories less abstract and less adaptable than others? In point, does an abstract theory such as Peirce's pragmatic semiotics permit more appropriate adaptation, precisely because it is grounded on his revised and reinterpreted common-sensism, than does a Kantian or other system of thought which is based on eternal judgments and *a priori* knowledge?

The position taken here is that Peirce's semiotics is precisely that kind of link that permits, and indeed is designed to provide, a useful channel between the most abstract and the most practical of the social sciences.[6] There is in this case a "fit," which is not the case with respect to Rawlsian theory.

The assumption also held here is that a theory of economics rather than a theory of ethics is a more appropriate theoretical basis upon which to construct such linkages. Thus the proposal that the Constitution be interpreted from the perspective of economics is appropriate, that is, correct. This is the viewpoint of Hayek and his school. It is also the position taken by students of constitutionalism who are not explicitly Hayekian in their approach.[7]

The following section briefly examines some of the views that seek to base the Constitution on a monetary or economic foundation.

In the course of development of modern Western societies distinctions between public law and private law became confused. Up until the nineteenth century there were also clear divisions between civil law and mercantile law. As Hayek notes (1973), two distinct kinds of law have paralleled one another with the result that one *appears* to represent the other, whereas in actuality their purposes are unlike.

He says, for example, that *nomos*, the law of liberty, is not to be confused with *thesis*, the law of legislation. The law of liberty throughout the legal history of Western civilization has attempted to uphold the consensus that property should be protected and that boundaries separating properties should be clearly defined and protected. The law is not that which *assigns property*. But it is the rule of law which protects property rights, and related rights as they refer to or develop from a central and general concept of property. This, Hayek suggests, is the fundamental purpose of the law of liberty.

The conduct of persons toward one another with respect for the property of each constitutes, according to the law of liberty, the code of ethics that such a legal system implies. Thus the "rules of just conduct which govern the law of liberty are those same rules which are operative in a healthy and free economy" (1976:124). Hayek qualifies these views, however, but only moderately. He says he does not intend to suggest that the overall order of society which the rules of just conduct serve is exclusively a matter of economics. But so far only economics has developed a theoretical technique suitable for dealing with such spontaneous abstract orders, which is only now slowly and gradually being applied to orders other than the market.[8]

If Peirce's predictive theory of semiotics were developed into a predictive theory of law, it would uphold the predictability of the courts which is so necessary to a law of liberty in a spontaneous social order. The judge, in this system, is never blindly obedient to the status quo, Hayek reminds us, but is loyal to those principles underlying and substantiating the legal code upon which the rules of law rest.

A constitutional government, that is, a representative government such as that of the United States, is the development of ideas of freedom and rights and law which purport to uphold *as* rights the deepest values of the society they serve. The Constitution *represents* such values in all sign functions.

During this last century the value of freedom, until recently inextricably tied to private property, has been under attack by those who claim that private property serves only the special few. This is simplistic. A close analysis shows that the actuality of the situation is that the value of private property serves also those who at any given time have little or no claim to private property.

The justification of a free society as a whole rests on the concept of private property and on the rights of property owners to be protected by law.[9] A free society which is a "spontaneous order of actions" is served by that legal system Hayek calls Nomos, or the law of liberty. It is this law, which economics represents faithfully, that is evident in our Constitution. It is this same law of liberty and this same value of freedom which is absent from that other system of law referred to above, which Hayek calls Thesis, or the "law of legislation."

In brief, the purpose of the law of legislation is to regulate organizational roles of government. The purpose of the law of legislation, that is, the law of organization in government, is not of the same kind that enforces rules for conduct on interpersonal bases. It has nothing at all to do with ethics, nor should it have if it observes its own mandates and if it refrains from trespassing into other domains of law, on other properties. Properly speaking, a constitution is charged with the laws of legislation and is so charged because the law of liberty could not freely function unless these laws of legislation were operative. But they are not the same quality of law and are not intended to satisfy the same needs for law as the law of liberty does in a free society.

To extrapolate from Hayek's explanation of the reasons for the Constitution to function as a formal instrument of the law of legislation—a dignified and honored instrument, he says—one may compare the Constitution with syllogistic reasoning.

A propos of semiotic theory, Peirce recognizes the indispensability of syllogistic, formal logic, but he places it between abductive reasoning or discovery, on the one hand, and inductive reasoning, or verifiability in the actual world of common sense, on the other hand. It is for this reason, also, that formal logic with its tripartite divisions is dependent upon methodology or pure rhetoric in Peirce's expanded logic. It is rhetoric or methodology that makes freedom of thought and the acquisition of new knowledge possible. It is critic or formal logic that is charged with the organization of meaningful categories in the system of signs of language, that is, of thought acts spoken or not spoken, written or not written.

In some sense a Constitution is a "superstructure" of laws, a kind of overseer and protector of the basic law, that is, the law of liberty with which it is charged. But from another perspective it is the law of liberty that is the higher "metalaw" to which the Constitution is subordinate. However one positions these two systems of law or however one interprets "higher" it is without question the purpose of the Constitution to protect the values that motivate the law of liberty.

One of the problems in constitutional interpretation in modern times is monetary, that is, the economic basis of law. When the law of legislation claims revenue from the general public in order better to serve its charge, the law of liberty, it sets itself as a master and not as a servant and thereby creates a distancing between people freely engaging in spontaneous acts of exchange, and it obliges them to observe rules for conduct imposed upon them through financial and other considerations by those institutions that represent and are part of the system of the law of legislation.

Therefore, in place of an ethics based on relationship and on free exchange for the purpose of mutual well-being, the law of legislation has come to *determine* the nature of relationships. This law of legislation has extended its influence so that it not only regulates the organization of government but includes within its domain of governmental organization private citizens and private property. This, briefly, is the crisis Hayek and others describe. Hayek calls it the "transformation of private law into public law by 'social' legislation."[10]

In semiotics the term *public law* transforms its referent, *private law*, which is also a highly complex legal sign system, into a new meaning, or final interpretant.[11] This final interpretant is a judgment. The judgment is provisional and correctable, if tested against new hypotheses and further experience. But if such judgment is understood as reflecting prior and absolute truth, as the advocates of the social legislators seem to require, the judgment may *not* by reversed; the assumptions it represents and carries forward may, like many metaphysical claims, be unwarranted and unjustifiable according to the freedom of reason. Morality is thus imposed upon law through the use of inappropriate modes of reasoning.

So long as inappropriate methods of reasoning are used in analysis of the law and in interpretation of the Constitution one may continue to expect affirmation, on the one hand, of the aims of the social legislators and, on the other hand, plans for alternative constitutions. Such an alternative has been discussed at length in current literature.

As early as the 1960s Milton Friedman wrote that there is certainly the need for government to administer money, but just as certainly there is a need for a "dispersal of power."[12] Friedman examines the crisis and proposes a corrective "device" which he describes as an "independent central bank—to control monetary policy and to keep it from being the football of political manipulation. . . . The device is rationalized by assimilating it to a species of constitutionalism."[13]

In other words, a monetary constitution would be an interpretant of the existing constitution. It would mirror it, Friedman suggests, but would interpret it differently and for different purposes.

Kuhn, among others, has shown how new disciplines grow out of existing disciplines by precisely this method. Peirce's view is that each discipline or system of constitutionalism is an idea or sign. A sign grows through being interpreted by another sign and so transformed. A sign may be an entire science, an entire discipline, an entire constitution, an entire system of law—an entire system of anything which has been so bounded by definition as to be a property of some general idea or value.

Holmes referred to the Constitution of the United States as an experiment. It is an idea, or hypothesis in this context, that is, a sign capable of being interpreted by another sign. This is not the customary approach to constitutional interpretation, which restricts the act of interpretation to a dyadic structure in which an interpreter, usually human, explores and gives his best idea of meaning to the idea under inquiry.

Peirce's point is that signs are not restricted to written concepts, or to verbal concepts of any kind. Rather, anything we know or claim to know we know because it *is* a sign and interpretable. Persons, places, things, systems—are all signs. Peirce's argument is that signs interpret signs. It is only through the method of semiotics—the method of methods—that we are able to account for the process whereby one system of signs interprets another system of signs and thus evolves and grows, and give birth to new signs.

The notion of constitutional interpretation that yet must be discussed semiotically is the intent of the legislator. In the following chapter some important observations and arguments will be referred to, especially as they reflect the realists' attitude toward constitutional interpretation.

NOTES

1. See Moore (1979:238 268, especially 239, 240).
2. See also Parker (1979:269–295).
3. Ibid., 260.

4. Ibid., 272, 273.

5. Ibid.

6. Peirce (1967:302, 303, L75).

7. See McCloskey (1962:34–46); also Wright (1938).

8. See Siegan (1980). See also Posner (1977), especially pages 10–103, 212–396; also Weber (1925/1954: especially 68–71). See also Yeager (1962).

9. See Hayek (1973:115).

10. Ibid., 121.

11. Ibid., 141 ff.

12. See Friedman (1962:219–243).

13. Ibid., 219.

CHAPTER 19

Property I

Few concepts in law have undergone such profound changes during the past three quarters of a century as the concept of property. The dust has not yet settled and shows no signs of settling in the near future. The literature from the strictly legal perspective on property has been voluminous in recent years. Yet, prior to Locke's rather spare examination of property in law one finds little or no serious treatment of the topic. In philosophy, during the last two decades, we begin to find that property has become an appropriate area for philosophical investigation. In the main, the philosophical concern with property has been centered on the justification of private property and the relation between traditiional assumptions connected with private property and the issues of property rights as they relate to the problems of rights in general.

But, as Becker pointed out nearly ten years ago, the philosophical approach to the problems of property and property rights has yet to present arguments on any side of the problem that are not "seriously flawed." Mostly, according to Becker, the surface issues of the justification of property rights are disputed, but rarely do philosophers subject their own underlying philosophical assumptions to scrutiny (Becker 1977:2–3). To follow Becker, the concept of property as a relation of (a) moral philosophy, of (b) legal and practical frameworks, and of (c) logical aspects of the term *property* has been totally neglected.

Becker's project was to formulate a new theory of property intended to address the complex relations between (a) the concept of property rights in general and, in particular, what it means to justify a property right; (b) the strength of the traditional arguments for and against property rights; (c) the three-pronged approach to property rights, namely, from the largely incompatible arguments from utility, from liberty, and from labor theory. In other words, the traditional arguments justifying property rights have come from these three sources.

But these three frames of ideational reference are not mutually supportive and tend to cancel each other out.

Becker's project is admirable, and indeed he has clarified much of what he set out to do. However, as indicated above, like his predecessors whom he criticizes on this point, Becker also fails to establish (a) a clear picture of the relationship between the concept of property as a legal concept, (b) the concept of property rights as it has been taken up in recent years by moral philosophy, and (c) the underlying logics which, throughout the history of the concept of property, have been presupposed by jurists. We still lack a study showing the correspondence between one idea or interpretation of the general notion of property and its internal logic, and other ideas or interpretations of the general notion of property with respect to their particular internal logical structures.

A semiotics perspective on this problem would attempt to show that property in law is not one idea only. Rather, it is a multitude of ideas, or systems of thought, each of which is represented by this general term *property*. Further, semiotics assumes that a term or idea such as property refers to and represents its referent object which, one may assume, is the plan or structure—or map— which presents the bare bones of the idea before it is developed, resolved, and determined to some practical end. A logical structure, like a diagram, is such a plan or map or model. What is wanted is a reconstruction of the various ramifications of property in law to their respective plans or logical sources. In other words, each separate interpretation, or interpretant sign of property in Peirce's sense, has evolved from its own respective plan, or object sign. To use the language of the structuralists, there may be numerous signifying appearances of the term *property*, but we are not justified in assuming that each of these signifiers is tied to a single signified. On the contrary, it is precisely this unexamined assumption that has to date inhibited the clear and unambiguous account of property. One must begin to account for the fact of the various manifestations of this term before it can be justified on one philosophical ground or another.

There are at least two approaches to the problem of property in law from the perspective of legal semiotics. The first, discussed here, attempts to relate predominant interpretations of property to their underlying logical framework. The second should focus on the transactional aspects of property and on the exchange of equivalent values, where property in its largest sense is a commodity regulated by those norms in law which govern the rights of contract, consideration, and commerce. This second approach to property is developed in the following chapter. This chapter concentates on only the first of these yet distinct inquiries into the concept of property in law.

The purpose of thinking should determine the mode of reasoning appropriate to one's aim. As Peirce suggests, there are not only degrees of correctness in *manner* of reasoning about property, but degress of correctness in *mode* of reasoning about property. Thus, traditional reasoning in law about property and property rights in a deductive, syllogistic mode is, it is contended, inappropriate and therefore nonethical.

Further, in accord with Holmes's view that the life of the law is not logic but experience, and realizing that the logic Holmes refers to is traditional syllogistic reasoning, I propose that the concept of property in law is one of many, if not of all, major legal notions that may be ethically approached from the logical assumptions of semiotics and with the methodology semiotics employs for its purposes. Some of the main principles that would apply are discussed here.

In examining the notion of property semiotics may illuminate some aspects of problems attached to it which other approaches fail to disclose. Also, this inquiry may provide an example of how other legal issues and problems may be served by semiotics.

It is widely conceded that Locke's investigation of the concept of property is the first serious investigation that attempts to show the connection between primary philosophical assumptions and legal practices that derive from and presuppose such assumptions. Becker notes that there has been little or no discussion of what he calls the "warrant for the root idea" that property is justified by regarding it as an extension of labor, and that one's labor entitles one to the product or result of one's labor, that is, to property as an extension of one's self-possession. Becker finds, however, that there are two distinct arguments intertwined in the Lockean labor theory of acquisition and that these imply two distinct "conceptions of the root idea that labor entitles one to property" (Becker 1977:32,33). These two arguments are: (1) labor is an extension of one's possession of self, and (2) labor that is one's own is that which brings about the existence of a product, or property; thus the causative ingredient of labor entitles one to the product, necessarily.

The second argument suggests that there is such a product or property which is conceivable as a potentiality, separate and distinct from the laborer and his labor. In other words, there is an *idea* of a something which is not sufficient to bring into existence any particular laborer and particular labor. This argument assumes that such an idea has a kind of entity apart from the producer and that the joining together of producer with possible entity results in a realized product. This argument, largely Platonic and swathed in several levels of neoPlatonic metaphysics, is not our concern here, although the argument is widely enough believed and acted upon so that it should be taken up as a problem at another time.

It is the first argument that mainly concerns us here, although admittedly discussion of this first argument will unavoidably touch on certain aspects of the second. The first argument assumes that property, as a result of labor, should be understood as a "derivation from prior property rights" (Becker 1977:32). Thus the legal systems which have so interpreted Locke's theory are guided, either unconsciously or with careful consideration, by Locke's logic.

For example, the apple is the property of the apple tree; that is, the term "apple" is an extension of the term "apple tree," according to a mode of thought which holds that the fruit is immanent within the seed, or that the form in its general sense contains within it its possible and perfectible manifestation which, in this case, is its fruit as the realization of the function of the tree. This structure of reasoning is familiar to most readers. It is not only Platonic with emphasis on the immanence of the fruit, but Aristotelian also in the sense that the goal of the tree is to produce fruit; thus the action of the tree is teleological, tending toward the realization of that act which can be said to characterize the existence of the tree.

By drawing an analogy between trees and persons in society it may be then suggested that persons who are propertied, that is, who have property as a result of their labors, have achieved their purpose and have actualized their ideal beings in this particular way. By contrast, persons without property, manifest a significant absence (zero sign) with reference to a possibility of the whole person, as ideally conceived. Everyday language is so influenced by this mode of thinking that it is commonplace to say, if one loses an eye, a limb, or a tooth, that one *has* a missing tooth, limb, or eye, that is, one possesses in the absence. The system of this ideal person is conceived as complete, and where incomplete the lack is attributed to a variation or accident, that is, to a particular deviation or deformation from the ideal whole. The general class is an idea, or sign of the class, complete with all the conceived members of itself intact.

This general assumption rests on a prior idea which views the whole as a static and closed system, such that a part is always less than the whole and never a whole in itself equal to or greater than the original whole. Peirce objects to this logical framework, which is the framework for Euclidean geometry. He says that the greatest defect of Euclid's thinking—his fallacy of reasoning holding that a part is less than the whole—has done immeasurable harm in preventing us from understanding that terms of a first intention may become terms of a second intention, as in Boole's calculus; and that these evolved or developed terms of second intention are of a "special kind." Peirce says, "Genus, species, difference, property, and accident are the well-known terms of second inten-tion. . . . They relate particularly to the *comprehensions* of first intentions; that is, they refer to different sorts of prediction" (CP 3.43;4.180,186).

Although there is not sufficient time here to draw close parallels between Peirce's technical exposition of second-intention logic and its functions, it is important at least to mention the following in passing: Peirce understands by "concept of reference" three related ideas: (1) reference to a ground, (2) reference to an object, and (3) reference to an interpretant (CP 1.459). These three ideas of reference are co-functions of fundamental nature in "at least one universal science, that of logic. . . . Logic," according to Peirce, "is said to treat of second intentions as applied to first."

With respect to semiotics as a process of interpreting signs, by signs Peirce means ideas and the representation of ideas. In second-intention logic the object and the interpretant are the two primary references; the ground, or ultimate reference, is not accessible without the mediation of the sign, that is, the interpretant. Thus semiotics in its approach to property in law must take an approach very different from that assumed by Locke in his chapter on property in the second treatise on government.

Locke assumes that the ultimate object to which property refers is God, and this property, which is the whole earth god-given to man, is mankind's property, or real estate. As it is the given nature of mankind to labor, and as the material upon which mankind is given to perform his labors is the earth, then that which men produce of the earth and its several parts becomes by extension the property of those persons who bring about the produce of the earth and its several parts (Locke 1690/1955:21–29). Thus the reference of the property produced by human labor is divine. This divine reference, Peirce has suggested, is beyond our exhaustive comprehension. Therefore it is not the proper domain of logic. So Locke's concept of property evolves within a first-intention logic and does not permit the part alone to be regarded as a primary reference; the part as related to or extended from its ultimate object, or whole, is a derived primary reference.

Despite Peirce's great and frequently acknowledged indebtedness to Locke, especially Locke's examination of signs in the *Essay*, Peirce refutes Locke on major points, especially on Locke's "critic" in explaining the reference a word has to an idea in the mind of the speaker. Locke says that the word or the idea symbolizes its referent object; that is, it is a sign or representation of the idea referred to. Language, then, to Locke, is a mark of a mark, referring directly and faithfully to its source (Locke: *Essay*, Book 3, chap. ii, par. 4,5,6,7.)

One might say that this language, or those words produced by a speaker, are the property of that speaker and that they are produced by the mental labor or intellectual activity of his mind. Peirce says this is not the case. Rather, once words as signs are uttered and are recognized as signs of meaning value such that they are capable of being comprehended and interpreted as meaningful signs, they are no longer the property only of the speaker but are the common property of that community constituted of both speaker and listener. Further, they are the common property of that larger community referred to alike by both speaker and listener.

This commonality of meaning is a possible reference in the exchange and development of ideas and thought in the exchange of general ideas and their properties. The ultimate ground of reference is not of concern in the exchange

of meaning or of properties of a general idea because it is impossible, Peirce
claims, to disambiguate this ground, or ultimate reference (Harvard Lecture I,
1865; 1982:172–175).

The reference is twofold: one, to the referential object, which is the meaning
a symbol or sign has acquired in the context of a community or a universe of
discourse; two, to the interpretant, which is the mediated sign by which the
language represents the idea as presumably held in the mind of the speaker.
Thus, this reference to both a ground and to an interpretant sign is part of the
process of understanding. Second intentions are just those objects of understanding with which logic concerns itself.

Thus the Lockean idea of property as an extension of a person's labor may
be likened to a first intention. But the manner in which one interprets what is
meant by property involves semiotic representations of that first intention, "property," regarded as a symbol of a general idea. According to Peirce, the "rules
of logic hold good of any symbol," written and spoken symbols, symbols which
are thought, and, one might add, symbols which in a Lockean sense equate the
production of thought with one's thought as one's "inalienable possession" or
property in a general sense (CP 1.559).

Even the original thought, Peirce claims, is not, strictly speaking, the first
but is a copy or representation which in its primary stage was expressed as an
intended action, that is, a plan. A plan is a diagram or, to use Peirce's terminology, a predominantly iconic sign, as mentioned above.

Therefore, to have a sense of oneself, that is, to possess oneself freely,
means to Peirce to represent oneself to oneself as a plan of action. Similarly, to
connect oneself with one's acquisitions, made possible as a result of one's labor
in Locke's sense, is to represent oneself as a general idea together with one's
attributive parts, or properties: a new whole, or new general idea. It is Peirce's
point, however, which he successfully argues, that such properties are separable
from their primary source, and when made public they assume the value and
meaning which the object community and referent interpretant in context carry
forward and evolve. Both are the references in the order of "particular categories."

It has been frequently claimed that the Locke of the *Essay* and the Locke
of the *Treatises* seem to be two distinct Lockes, so contradictory do certain of
his ideas appear when comparing one work with the other. Yet those who see
little or no similarity in the Locke of both the *Essay* and the *Treatises* have failed
to examine the logic upon which the *Treatises* rest. The logic expounded in the
Essay and the logic presupposed in the *Treatises* are one and the same. As Peirce
shows, both are faulty, and, moreover, because they are faulty the reasoning of
both the *Essay* and of the *Treatises*, particularly on property as this topic concerns
us here, *is not ethical.*

The reasoning does not realize the goals of "ideal conduct," Peirce would
suggest. If, therefore, Locke's work on property has been criticized as lacking

sensitivity to the problems of inequities in the distribution of goods in society, the criticisms are correct, but the justification of these criticisms is inadequate. Locke's critics have reasoned no less badly than Locke, and from that point of view they offer neither logical nor ethical warrant for opposing viewpoints.

Recall that Peirce first published his "pragmatic maxim" in 1878 in *Popular Science Monthly*. He let it "fly forth," he tells us, to become part of the world, that is, a "property," so to speak, of the world, (CP 5.17). The pragmatism that Peirce produced as an idea of a logic of consequences, intended to be applied to the "doctrine of reality," strongly bears the influence of his Metaphysical Club days (1871, 1972), when he was exposed to many of the legal problems with which other juristic members of the club were concerned. This maxim, according to Peirce, rests on the assumption that belief is that which may be established in appropriate dress or form as a "guide to action." A belief, in this sense of Peirce's pragmatism, is like a rule or maxim of conduct (CP 5.25,26,27).

Pragmatism offers a rule for action, then, as a definition which expresses the belief that here is simply another means for achieving the same practical consequence as any other means. However, if someone says that there is a practical difference between this rule or definition and another, and that pragmatic rules or definitions are not merely alternative means to a common end, then pragmatism itself, Peirce says, is "completely volatilized" (CP 5.33). But, Peirce says, if it takes so little to undermine his proposed pragmatic logic, how does one arrive at a legitimate use of alternative rules of action?

In order to legitimize what Peirce claims for pragmatism, namely, a way of reaching the desired goal by any number of possible means, Peirce proceeds to show that our logic itself is nothing but an "application of the doctrine of what we deliberately choose to do which is Ethics." Thus logic in applying ethical norms represents truth, or correct arguments. *Ethics represents manifest efforts of will.* Esthetics is that highest division of the normative sciences which makes present, or brings up for perception, those general qualities or ideas that are to become determined through ethics and validated through logic (1958:5.36). By then first taking the highest, Peirce begins his justification of the legitimacy of pragmatism by phenomenologically examining the notion of universal categories.

The idea of category itself refers to the accepted understanding among philosophers that a category is the most general of general ideas. Further, there are two orders of categories: the particular and the universal. The order of particular categories "form a series," with one only of each series expressible at any one time. Thus this order embraces the consequential, the substitutable, the variable, the permutable, and the transformable. The universal categories, by contrast, are always and at once present in all phenomena.

In Aristotle, Peirce says, we do not find the two orders explicitly distinguished. He presumes that Aristotle's "predicables" correspond to the particular categories and that Aristotle's "predicaments" correspond to the universal categories. The predicables include the five subcategories of genus, species, difference, accident, and property.

According to the nineteenth-century logician and economist Jevons, who influenced Peirce's thought, "Property is a quality which belongs to the whole of a class, but does not enter into the definition of that class" (1879:698–700).

In other words, a class may have such and such a property, but the "possession" of such a property is not exclusive to that class but may also be an attribute of possession of any other or many other classes. There is, however, the notion of "peculiar property," which will not be discussed here. By analogy, a social class may be, for example, homeowners; that is, this class has the property of owning homes. But this property of owning homes is not the exclusive privilege of any given social class. Members of all social classes may own homes.

The point here is that the application of property from logic to practical spheres of interest has, historically, taken the route that, if privileged then propertied, and if propertied then rights must follow. Thus privilege and rights are made manifest through the particular category of property. Holmes also is explicit in the application of the distinction between property and possession in common law systems. Such distinction does not exist in legal systems derived from Roman law.

Larkins's classic study (1930/1969) shows the evolution and application of his association of privilege, right, and property in legal notions of property prior to and since Locke in England, France, and the United States. At certain times in history the order of categories was confused through legal interpretation, such that the predicables of genus and property lost their distinction. Thus the three major subcategories of the order of universal categories—presentness, factiveness, representation—were viewed as the basis for the justification of a subcategory of a distinct and separate order.

This "translation" of the structure of logic into the structure of law with regard to property may be somewhat strained, or perhaps too cursive to provide adequate explanation at this time. Yet it must suffice for now and will show, I hope, that a hierarchy of categorical orders was traditionally established in the interpretation of property in law in Locke's day. Although such a hierarchy, it can be claimed, may represent the common sense of a society and/or its legitimated customary values, *this order is not only illegitimate but invalid.*

In most cases, as Jevons reminds us, we are wise to consign the ancient terms for the parts of logic to antiquity. However, in the case of the five predicables he urges that these subcategories of logic, used by Aristotle and also by Porphyry in his introduction to Aristotle's *Organum*, are still useful in attempting to examine the processes of thought. These predicables, or more modern terms for them, may still help to discriminate between types of qualities. That quality of particular concern here is that of property. Further, it is second-intention logic, or what Peirce calls "Objective Logic" and finds to be not only the "larger part of formal logic" but the superior part and the "more beautiful and interesting" part. It is that special logic that examines the properties of ideas, in this case the properties of property (CP 3.80,81).

Peirce claims that his logic is particularly useful in examining those properties that are an "infinite series" and thus includes Locke's notion of property. Such a detailed examination would entail, to oversimplify Peirce's comments at this point, a *quantification* of the Lockean proposition that "labor in the beginning, gave a right of property . . . though afterwards . . . the several communities settled the bounds of their distinct territories, and, by laws within themselves, regulated the properties of the private men of their society, and so, by compact and agreement, settled the property which labour and industry began . . ." (Locke 1690/1955:35–36).

According to Peirce, a second-intention logic quantifies the quantified part of a proposition such that the laws of society regarding property in the Lockean sense perform the quantifying; they evaluate, in quantifiable terms, the references to signified property. That is, the term *property*, as interpretant sign of the idea of property, and the common contextual and general meaning of property in any given, particular society, are the dual references of the concept of property in law.

This is not to suggest or even to recommend that legislators study and apply second-intention logic to current issues and problems regarding property and property rights. What is suggested, if not advocated, is that attempts be made to understand, from a philosophical and semiotic perspective, what is meant by property in order to provide practical law with some instruments for examining judgments and laws and for inspecting the warrants that support such judgments and laws. A semiotics approach to property in law may provide such instruments for analysis which are not provided by other means of investigation.

It may be useful to point up some of the apparent contradictions associated with the meaning of the term *property* which are inherited by contemporary investigators from both the recent and the remote past. For instance, legal notions of property, derived from Locke, were applied in England, France, and the United States and at the same time carried forward much older notions of property which predate Locke's thesis by many centuries (Larkin 1930/1969).

Stocks points to the changing concept of property and shows that in so short a time as fifty years the predominant interpretation of the term underwent transformation. For example, in 1789, at the time of the French Revolutionary Convention, it was "solemnly declared [that] private property [was] . . . a sacred and inviolable right of man." But, as Stocks notes, in 1840 the voice of Proudhon and others announced in Paris that "property was theft." Again, while the revolutions of the eighteenth century considered private property to be the just and logical extension of each man's natural rights the socialism of the nineteenth century denied the rights of private property.

Locke's work provided a center for serious discourse on property and for laws regulating that to which the idea of property refers. The pendulum swings around Locke's view, which held that the primary end of government is to preserve and protect private property, where private property is to be regarded as an extension of the general idea of natural property. According to Larkin, England was the "first country to adopt on a grand scale a new philosophy of property" (Larkin 1930/1969:v–vii). Historically, Locke was looked upon as the "English apostle of economic individualism."

When Locke used the term *property* he included in it the ideas of "lives, liberties and estates." Private property, in Locke's sense, is a natural right "anterior to the State, and to protect which . . . the State came into existence." Larkin says in his interpretation of Locke that private property is the "outcome of human personality."

Larkin notes that in Locke there is no reference to "the moral obligations of ownership. . . . Emphasis [is] laid on individual rights rather than on social purpose." Locke then presents a formidable opposition both to the idea of property held by the Church and to the Aristotelian notion of property. Both the Church and Aristotle are alike in regarding the individual, including his possessed properties, as first of all obligated to act on behalf of the community which, as social institution, is in the interests of God and above the individual's will and self-interest. Locke, it must be admitted, gives God the nod, but only as initial property giver. The production of property through human labor and the results of such production are clearly separate from divine estates and clearly, in Locke, utilizable toward upgrading the human earthly condition. He suggests the pragmatic aspects of property which Peirce later develops.

Larkin points out that rarely do we find the opposition between Church and common law so marked as it is regarding property. As in ancient logic, the notion of tangible and private property in feudal England was of a conditional and contingent character, appropriate to that order of categories mentioned above, of which property in its logical sense is regarded by Peirce as a subcategory. At this time of significant transition in England, the twelfth and thirteenth centuries, property and contract under law were almost inseparable concepts. Furthermore, the commercial concepts of price and interest emerged in full force at that time because they were closely related to contract and property. The Church has alternately succeeded and failed, during periods of history since then, to impose moral restrictions on the production of property regarded as wealth, and by extension on the pursuit of gain and profit. But even as early as the sixteenth century, such moral restraints on economic self-interest, now widely identified with private property, had become nearly obsolete, and certainly outmoded. At the same time the idea of property "as a conditional or derivative right" was strained if not discarded altogether. Property, in a peculiarly Peircean sense, could be regarded as separable from the class or person that it characterized but that in former times it had tended to define.

The idea of property according to Larkin, was a "revolutionary force" in the seventeenth century. The England into which Locke was born was a context in which property had become its own referent term, or interpretant sign, and had become itself "widely distributed," in logic, in law, and in everyday life. Thus, to Locke, not even the "supreme power" can recall from any person a portion of his private property, "without his own consent" (*Civil Government* edition cited by Larkin, edited by Morely 1884, Book 2, chap. xi, par. 138).

Locke makes little distinction between the property of persons and the property of goods both movable and immovable, any more than the distinction at that time had been made in law between land and the produce of land or, further, between land, the products of the land, and the derivative manufactured products of the products. Thus a piece of furniture was an extension of a walnut tree which was also an extension of a piece of the person's real property; what it was equivalent to in goods was also, by extension, a property right of the person whose effort developed the land and was exchangeable according to the laws of contract and consideration. This notion is radically transformed in current interpretations of eminent domain in the "takings clause" of the United States Constitution.

There still existed in the England of the beginning of the eighteenth century a remnant of the freeholders or yeomen of Saxon times. The continued emphasis on the sanctity of private property was in part a continued protection of a rural middle class and not only a protection of the great property owner (Larkin 1930/ 1969:110).

The security of private property was regarded as the basis or opportunity for enormous commercial development which resulted in the production of further signs of property, that is, in more dependable and more unambiguously interpretable bills of exchange and promissory notes. This further extension of interpretant signs of property as idea was facilitated by supportive legislation and judicial decision. By the middle of the eighteenth century, Larkin notes, "not only was political organization based on property, but the policy of the age showed a special tenderness for the interests of property-owners" (1930/1969:114).

This policy extended to laws governing taxation. At this time the poor were exempted from taxes because, it was argued by Locke and others, taxes could not be borne by the poor for practical as well as sentimental reasons. But by the end of the eighteenth century oppressive tax laws on the general public, together with Rousseau's influence from France, brought about a strict reexamination of the Lockean notion of property. The anarchists, Paine and Godwin, for example, fought to exempt real property, that is, land, from the general concept of property and thus to relieve tenants of their absolute dependence on the will of landowners.

It was Godwin who pointed out that the idea of private property was rooted in the right of private judgment. But if this judgment should be represented by government, how then is it possible to separate the idea of private property under the protection of government from the judgment of private persons who produced the idea?

Neither Godwin nor the anarchists with whom he is associated have been able to reconcile the right to private judgment with the right to protection of such judgments by the institutions of government. Hence came Godwin's idea of private property, derived from the idea of the right of private judgment. But by the nineteenth century private judgment had become the inalienable right of all persons, whereas goods as property had become, in anarchist thought, part of the public domain. The anarchist approach to private property could not compete at that time with the Lockean notion of property in economics. In particular, law in the second half of the century was much more interested in the mixture of social fact and economics than in moral ideals and the distribution of goods. Larkin says that by the turn of the century "the theory that one can do what one likes with one's property, within the limits imposed by the state, became an integral part of the modern science of Economics" (Larkin 1930/1969:135). Thus Locke's view on property triumphed.

However, the economists who carried this view into the twentieth century were among those logicians whose ideas were examined and found faulty by Peirce. Economists such as Jevons, Ricardo, and Keynes are those who, according to Peirce, were mistaken in their logic and therefore mistaken in their economic theories and hence also mistaken in their interpretation of property.

Posner (1977:1) defined economics as the "science of human choice in a world in which resources are limited in relation to human wants." Further, Posner points out that economics in its broadest sense is concerned with ideas as potential property. He says that "ideas are discarded not because they are demonstrated to be false but because competing ideas give better answers to the questions asked. . . . Competition among ideas is the method by which truth is established. . . . An idea is false only if rejected in the marketplace . . ." (Posner 1977:308).

In Posner's sense, the realization of the truth of an idea is a "struggle," to use Peirce's characterization of the indexical sign, which, as the category of secondness, represents the structure of existence.

It is the symbolic *semiotic* representation of the idea, not merely the competition between ideas, that provides a point of reference and thus establishes its relative truth or rightness. A semiotic approach, then, begins with the notion of property as it appears, as a quality of an idea and as a symbol of that quality evolved to a series of judgments. Property, as a sign in semiotics, is a bundle of judgments. Property in law, correspondingly, is a bundle of rights.

According to Peirce, logical norms correspond with moral laws or those norms for ideal conduct that depend on some general quality or value, itself of a normative character. Reasoning is only a particular kind of moral conduct. One does not see the will at work in reasoning as clearly as one sees it in controlled or moral behavior. Yet these normative systems parallel one another just as they both are parallel with our value systems.

Thus a semiotic inquiry into property in law would seek correspondences between the predominant logic in legal reasoning, the predominant code of ethics in legal practice, and the referent esthetic norms, or values, that govern the ethics and the logic of property.

One might test, for example, as a way of initiating inquiry into property as a general idea or quality of modern social life, some hypotheses regarding property as general value. Then one would attempt to find this idea or referent interpretant sign interpreted by legal conduct, with respect to the concept of property in law.

Finally, one would want to ask whether the arguments supporting the rightness of legal ethics with respect to legal acts on property are valid or fallacious. One would designate the first interpretant or general idea on property in law as the immediate interpretant or sign; the ethical representation as a second or dynamic interpretant presenting the structure of competition, or opposition or factiveness; and the final interpretant or proof-like test would be whether the supporting argument was not only valid in the traditional sense but also appropriate to the topic in question.

Anywhere is a place to begin, according to Peirce's semiotics. Any first is free. Thus a general idea such as property in law is given as an object for inquiry because it is part of shared experience, part of the context of the cultures that produced it. The *idea* of property in law, therefore, is everyman's property. It is only the second stage, that of selecting the appropriate conduct of inquiry, that determines the status of the first, general idea.

It is hoped that this introduction to property in law provides a point of departure from which one can then proceed to examine the process of exchanging properties and those laws, peculiar to distinct legal systems, that regulate such use and exchange, or the withholding of use and exchange.

This investigation is the topic of the next chapter, Property II.

CHAPTER 20

Property II

The relationship between individual and property constitutes the basic relationship underlying every organized political order which is variously defined as the state.[1] In this chapter the problematic concept of the individual as counterpart to the concept of property falls outside the focus here and will be discussed only as it illuminates the object of inquiry, property. Similarly, the state as a concept will not be examined except to note that it is that which is constituted by the relationship between individual and property.[2]

The leading assumption here is that property is a value-laden sign in social organization which increases or decreases in value, both extensively and intensively, in direct proportion to the shared value of the idea of the individual. At present, such distinguished scholars as Hayek have argued that a free society is that value sign that *interprets* its referent object, that is, the interrelationship or immediate interpretant. Individual–property is a kind of binomial in the modern world of nation–states. Further, as Hayek and others suggest, if freedom is to continue to function as an interpretant sign, or basis for the emergence and development of new and noncoercive values in human societies, the relationship between property and individual must remain an assimilative and cumulative measure of the meaning of freedom.[3] The idea of freedom must incorporate, transform, and further this fundamental relationship if the ideal of free societies is to evolve as the continuing aim of free inquiry and as the final interpretant in legal discourse.

A free society rests on a consensus of shared, common values, each of which in relationship with all others becomes institutionalized into a network of social institutions or sign systems such as that which Lieber aptly called the "jural state."[4]

While the main focus here is on the legal system, it is evident that the legal system as such must be viewed as interdependent with all other systems such as economics, politics, and so on. But historically, from the somewhat different viewpoints of the speculative and practical sciences, it has been "the legal system," or the idea of the law, which has defined, on the one hand, properties in relation to logical subjects and, on the other hand, property and property rights in relation to existents and social individuals. Therefore an investigation of the meaning and function of the term *property* should begin by regarding it as a member or member sign within the general domain of law, while remembering at the same time that this domain has "fuzzy boundaries" and, indeed, simultaneously interpenetrates every other system at any given moment. Any changes occurring in systems other than the legal system effect movement and change in law.

An analogy may be made here between the coordinate function of social institutions, or sign systems, and the iconic, indexical, and symbolic functions of every sign in Peirce's semiotics. A particular function is predominant only with respect to context, and to an interpreter's point of view and purpose for investigation. But every function always implies its coordinates.

Authority, precedence, sovereignty: all of these near synonyms for cause, either first or final, have been shown by Hayek to be basic tenets of what he describes as the organized and unfree social order.[5] He opposes this coercive order—a deterministic order—with what he calls the spontaneous society, in which the dynamic interrelationship of individual and property plays a changing and crucial role.

Insofar as property is discussed in connection with moral philosophy or ethics in this chapter, it will be only to point up briefly again that the choice of how one reasons about property is an ethical matter and is governed by, in Peirce's sense, the highest of his normative sciences: esthetics or the science of values.

Thus it is first of all a matter of value whether one holds one's world to be open or closed. It is, therefore, a matter of value whether one opts for a free or a determined society. Once these choices are made, all that logic can do is appropriately describe the structure of one's selected value, that is, show the relation of the parts of meaning to the whole of the assumed value sign, or hypothesis.

The explicit value which informs this chapter, as well as the study as a whole, is that the world is becoming and that every operation on every significant thought increases the conceivable meaning of the value of one's world such that the world as real—as a complex system of real signs—actually grows and becomes that which our growing thought represents.

Philosophy has not regarded property in law as a respectable topic for investigation until very recently, in the 1960s. Even today it confines its questions to two or three selected and narrow aspects of the idea of property in law: justification of private property, relations between concepts of private property and property rights in both traditional and nontraditional frames of thought, and the relation between property rights and the problems of rights as a general topic. Questions regarding property rights have almost invariably been tied to old and still insoluble problems in moral philosophy. As discussed in the preceding chapter, Becker and others have noted that few philosophical arguments on property rights are not seriously flawed.[6]

A critical examination of these arguments exceeds the scope of this chapter and would involve confrontations with unfounded assumptions regarding the terms *cause* and *authority*[7] and, indeed, with prevailing beliefs that one can still maintain, despite evidence to the contrary, that our world is a closed system. Because of the vast literature on these topics only that which pertains to law and to related social systems is touched on here.

The problems of causation and authority in law have been discussed in some detail in separate chapters of this book and will only be referred to in passing here.

Simply put, one's investigation of property produces more property. That particular aspect of the concept of property in law which is examined here is the question, what in fact does constitute property? Of what does property consist? In what respect will our definitions of property alter the consistency and the uses to which it may be put and alter as well the consequences of property? To begin with, let us regard the nexus between property and individuals as a contract. In law, as discussed earlier, it is the contract that establishes the legitimacy of any claim that can be upheld by a legal system.

The initial relationship between property and individual is not a dyadic structure, but is triadic. Peirce understands the structure of all ideas representing real value in the world, that is to say, representing our world as knowable or as imaginable and as possible on many levels of possibility, as a triad. The problem of the potential in property, that is, in property that has not yet emerged as an empirical perceivable fact but is nevertheless a legal fact, will be discussed. The triadic structure of mediation from a realist's view will be mentioned.

Potential property includes the following examples: the crop of an orchard of apple seedlings; air space over a chemical-producing factory; mineral deposits crossing below the foundation footings of an apartment building; the vast, untapped, yet unexplored and moving emergent property in the depths of the sea; and the yet to be interpreted meanings of ideas or signs continuing from other and perhaps older contexts or universes of discourse. These are but a few of the problems of property with which legal systems are currently concerned. Here little will be said of the rights, that is, the specific property rights, of the unborn or of the deceased as they conflict and compete with other unborn and other deceased and, needless to say, with all the living. Neither will the potential force of ideal, yet-to-be signs, that is, mere qualities or only facts thus far, be examined in close detail.

The following section develops the relation between both kinds of property—legal and phenomenal—in American pragmatism.

Locke's discussion in the *Second Treatise* does not regard property as a problem but rather assumes that the relation between persons and their inalienable possessions, including the consequences of their labor, that is, goods produced through personal effort and ability, is a binding relationship. But the problematic notion of property develops as a critical issue from the early years of the nineteenth century into present times. Among the several reasons offered as to why property was not seriously investigated earlier was the fact that the old assumptions regarding the link between property and contract, both in civil law and common law systems, had not been doubted. The analogy between property in transitional logic and property as a tangible attribute of the person remained strong and still tied to Aristotlian logic. Aristotle observed that logic is a by-product of law.

When in the eighteenth century the United States interpreted the English tradition of common law, which was basically judge-made law, the tradition of deciding particular cases with reference to fixed and general principles—that is, the method and theory of precedent in law—was increasingly less adaptable to the emerging structure of its industrializing society.

Although on the surface the English tradition of common law remained the ostensible model for judicial decision making, actually the theory of precedent served to provide only an *apparently* stable foundation for law in the United States which contradicted the truth of the matter. Because the system of law that was evolving in the United States *resembled* the traditional system but actually *represented* it as an increase of new information, that is, as an interpretant in Peirce's sense, the new facts did not fit the old frame.

As discussed, systems of law that presume axiomatic and precedential codes of general principles for decision making are usually based on syllogistic reasoning. But such a method of reasoning, in other areas as well as in law, is not open-ended, does not conclude with more information than that given in the premises, and does not result in the growth of new knowledge. Therefore the limitations of the model, which was adhered to in principle but increasingly less so in fact, opened the way for a climate of revolution in legal thought that sloughed its skin in the name of legal realism.

As the renowned legal historian Grant Gilmore remarked in "Legal Realism: Its Cause and Cure" (1961:1041): ". . . no legal system provides answers in advance to questions that have not yet been asked." By asking new questions, that is, posing new problems, realism began to construct the frame of a new legal system.

As noted, it is one of the main premises of this book that the laws of contract and of property correspond with the major concepts of dialogic interaction and shared information in semiotics. The term *property* and *contract in law*, and in semiotic theory and method in general, do not statically retain fixed meanings but are, as ideas, signs that are continually undergoing change. Thus the realists attacked as a primary target old notions of property and contract. They raised serious doubts.

When an idea is selected by an investigator for closer inquiry because something new and surprising has occurred which leads one to question and reexamine previous assumptions and beliefs, one may say with Peirce that a semiotic analysis is in the process of being prepared for systematic inquiry. Doubt signals the advent of a problem, a threat to former stabilizing beliefs.

Thus laws of contract and of property in the United States since 1800 represent earlier laws but they transform them with respect to a new and changing phenomenal world, an industrializing society both here and abroad.

According to Gilmore,

> Our Courts in the early nineteenth century were writing on a largely clean slate. There is little in our law of contracts, for example, that has any recognizable ancestry before 1800. The explanation for this is not that we had discarded English law and were deliberately making a fresh start; there was in fact no English law for us to discard. . . . Our rules of contract came into existence in the course of the industrial revolution, . . . and as personal rather than real, property became the chief respository of wealth. (1961:1040)

But by the end of the nineteenth century, the method of case law precedent was incapable of adapting to the rapidly changing situation regarding contract and property. There was little illusion in the 1880s that revolution in law could be avoided.

Holmes at this time, influenced by what he then knew of Peirce's ideas from the 1860s Lowell Lectures and their association in the Metaphysical Club, expressed the idea that the courts would have to bring to decisions the value of their own experience. A model of legal reasoning must evolve, he contended, which is pragmatic, based in experience and not on eternal legal principles or law axioms.

But influenced by the work of Bentham on codification in law, together with the persuasive Justice Story, a friend and lifelong colleague of Lieber, the movement began which aimed to replace case law and precedential authority in the United States with legal codification. Ironically, the country's leading law school, Harvard under Christopher Langdell, adopted a strong emphasis on case law and opposed codification, and thus established the method of teaching law in universities. Until the present day case law has predominated in the theory of the schools, but codification began to characterize the practice of law. At this same time a system of codification was constructed which, although not so comprehensive as the French and German codes, became a firm replacement for the older rules of precedent.

Gilmore's important distinction between statute and code is of interest here: a statute, a term sometimes used incorrectly as synonymous with code, is a legislative enactment that is strictly limited in its application and does not carry the authority of a general precedential rule. But a code is a legislative enactment which "entirely pre-empts the field and which is assumed to carry within it the answers to all possible questions." Statutes become parts of statutory complexes, and the entire system or class of which such statute is a member must be consulted and referred to. A code not only wipes out all preexisting law but is always "its best evidence of what it means . . ." (Gilmore 1961:1043).

In this manner the codification of our legal system replaced fixed principles with respect to contract and property, for example, with different sets of fixed principles. Codification is general whereas statute is particular. Statute requires a referent class which it strengthens both quantitatively and qualitatively, as a unified network of ideas.

However, a statutory complex does not carry the self-evidential, persuasive, and rhetorical force of a code. Unfortunately, statute and code are still used interchangeably by many lawyers and law professors, such that when previous decisional law, as the case law rejected in Peirce's and Holmes's day, is enacted into statute it is commonly siad to be Codified. It is by observing these distinctions Gilmore makes that one can better understand a statute in modern law to correspond to a provisional judgment in Peirce's sense, which is not absolute but is a particular expression of a sign, the total force of which is assumed only when this statutory sign is brought into context with other class members in a "statutory complex."

The twentieth century has been the century of codifying the common law. As one may have predicted from the above, the codification of common law in this century became an increasingly controversial issue. Codification froze the law.

Law, like language and, indeed, like society as a whole, resists any rigid mold. Yet the American Law Institute succeeded in restating common law into codification, thus producing codes or restatements of almost all aspects of common law, including restatements of torts, and of property.

At the same time the once loosely drafted statutes became subject to precise rules for legal drafting, and this process of legal drafting, itself a part of legal semiotics, contributed to the standardization of rules of law and rules prescribing methods for reinterpreting and for deciding law. Needless to say, this process of standardization assimilated previous systematically vague and open-ended methods of discovery into technical procedures. The project of the realists was to react against this hardening of the life of the law.

This is the context into which legal realism emerges and states its purpose, which, in brief, opposes in many voices a system of law in the United States which has become not scientific in the sense envisaged by Holmes and advocated by Peirce but scientistic: a search for ideal form rather than a process of inquiry.

It was remarked above that the new legal realism had strong sympathies with anarchism. That Holmes was familiar with the writings of the European anarchists is known from his correspondence with his lifetime friend Harold Laski. He refers, for example, to Proudhon's famous essay, "Property Is Theft," with great admiration.

It is of interest that at this time state ownership of property was not equated with private ownership of property. Yet, later interpretations of oppressive property ownership are to include states as well as private property as instruments of authority in opposition to freedom (DeGeorge 1978:88–110). For example, Laski points out that administrative regimes can be approximated to industrial management and that the state in America is therefore totally different from anything called the state in Europe and elsewhere (1919/1969:114,116,355,356).

At the turn of the twentieth century government began to assume the role once played by private ownership, for instance, in railroads and the utilities. As the industrialist is today, government also came increasingly under the control of the legislation. The result was that the civil servant and the factory worker, that is, labor in general, moved toward common goals with respect to property. At the same time, management and administrative aspects of government seemed to become more alike. They aimed toward the realization of their common goals.

This new administrative syndicalism since the 1920s has met with strong opposition from jurists who wish to replace the divided loyalties within government with a new concept of sovereignty which would give additional and needed reinforcement of power to government and weld the division of labor schism *within administration.*

Laski says this is not a new power, nor a reinstatement of the notion of the state as absolute authority. Rather, it is recognition of what the state is, in its function as sign: The state is nothing but a "territorial society," he says, which is divided only in a formal sense into subjects and rulers. Administrative syndicalism is merely an index or warning sign that the government or state as a whole has not been competent in doing its work, that is, in providing proof that it has "satisfied the material and moral claims of those over whom it exercises control" (Laski 1919/1969:374). This kind of provision of satisfaction is the role of government. Such satisfaction, however, has come to be viewed as dissatisfaction on other levels through interpretation of the key terms "moral and material claims."

But if one looks more closely, it is clear that such dissatisfaction is more profound than it at first appears. Such dissatisfaction indicates and represents on all levels of sign function what Laski calls a "problem in organization. What it suggests is inherent error in the mechanism of the modern state. It suggests a redistribution of power" (1919/1969:375).

Paradoxically, in order for the purposes of government to be fulfilled it must be seen that some of the demands of government are unnecessary and oppressive. Anarchism is such a paradox, as will be discussed in a different context.

Anarchism represents, according to DeGeorge and others, an opposition to the "dangers of unlimited power, the need for rethinking the structure of government, and the necessity for developing new social models" (1978:107).

In this fundamental sense anaarchism is allied with semiotics, not so much because of its objection to the concentration of property in the hands of a few, but rather because of its objection to the concentration of power in the structures of institutions which have become self-referring closed circles and ossified instruments of authority without being capable of liberating themselves in order more freely to serve the aims of freedom in the name of which they were established.

Semiotics maintains that nominalism of any kind connected with any theory of freedom is no longer freedom but unthinking habit hardened into authoritative, axiomatic, predominantly symbolic signs of the truth.

The notion of the law, viewed as having crystallized to a system of absolute authority, is precisely what provoked the realists to experience such revolutionary notions of law that the counterrevolutionary critics of realism opposed in various ways:

For example, D'Amato (1978:468–513) recapitulates some of the major objections to legal realism, particular as expressed in Hart's *The Concept of Law* (1961 and other writings). Consistency, for example, is a requisite of any legal system. Part of that system's power is to appear stable. Inconsistency, on the other hand, weakens society's trust in the efficacy of its official legal actors and diminishes confidence in the law's ability to protect rights, including property rights of the people of the society.

According to critics, legal realism's emphasis on the need to reduce, if not altogether eliminate, the power of the authoritative precedent and the rule of law in general tends to weaken the cohesion of a society.

Yet, the consistent maintenance of public order is itself not sufficient to warrant the trust and confidence of the people, for it is obvious that a conquering nation may impose a consistent and effectual law through its agents, as may any totalitarian regime. Consistency goes arm in hand with power, D'Amato argues, but not necessarily with a system of law which operates in the best interests of the people, that is, in the interests of freedom.

Hart has called the realists' rejection of the absoluteness of the rule of law *rule skepticism*. He suggests that the law is a kind of game, the rules of which must be observed or else the very notion of scoring becomes meaningless.

Although D'Amato's criticism of Hart's law-game analogy is apt in defining a game as a set of strict rules, it is not correct, for it fails to account for the fact that the game may include the rules for rule breaking. Hart also fails to discuss this kind of improvisational game. Thus neither Hart's nor D'Amato's views fully show us that, indeed, the realists did perceive the law as a game, but one in which the game included rules for changing rules.

Lon Fuller, one of the most articulate of the contemporary Peircean realists, reminds us of what he calls the "rule-phobia of the left-wing legal realist 'nominalism'" (1934:444). This is an expression he attributes to Morris Cohen. Fuller notes that although the realists have liberated American law from nominalism by "inculcating in it a healthy fear of such very real demons as Reified Abstraction, Omnibus Concepts, and Metaphors—Masquerading as Facts . . . we are now in danger of carrying the crusade against conceptualism too far" (1934:443)

In opposition to Berkeley and other nominalists who identify the concept in the mind with a thing, and aspects of that thing with properties of that thing, we may carry this analogy into law such that an idea of a person with properties may include not only the person's material things, but by extension also the ideas that are associated with that person as his properties or possessions for example, his good name. Fuller insists that a concept may be represented by a thing but that this representation involves a process of transformation such that the initial idea, or sign, is transformed or "thingified" by a mode of thinking that converts a "mental activity into logical terms" (1934:447)

But a concept is not a container, that is, a thing. Yet it may be represented as a thing with some distortion, through logical operation upon one's thought. In this sense Fuller is very close to Peirce's method of developing interpretants as a process of thinking. But, Fuller suggests, if we are now regarding property as a term in law according to neither the rules of logic nor the rules of law, which are not applicable but which extend a Berkeleyan mode of thinking as applied to law, then we need to understand how law may more appropriately conceive of property. How may it "thingify" some iconic representations of the concept of property into tangible things?

Fuller suggests that a property–thing is a transformation of an idea of relationship between persons in community, as imaged or represented by a concrete object.

In his article "Mediation: Its Forms and Functions" (1971:305–339), Fuller insists that not only property but contract as a whole is that which results from a legal process, that is, an idea *represented* by a thing, in this case a legal system. Particularly when one refers to the contract "implied in fact" one has to refer to the "modes by which contractual obligations arise tacitly out of human interaction . . . [and] present structure and process in an uncomfortably intimate embrace . . . the thing that emerges from the process—the 'contract'—is, as it were, simply an aspect of the process itself" (p. 306).

Fuller also draws an analogy between the law as a process and an event of collective bargaining which involves a mediator. The mediator is the concrete representation of the idea of a sign interpreting other signs, with respect to the legal process. Fuller maintains that only this mediating function is capable of resisting a tendency to submerge every kind of ordering under the rule of power or authority.

Prior to realism, Fuller says, a conflict over properties and property rights would have fallen to a judge who would have attempted to persuade both parties to look at the norms or rules regarding the problem and "accommodate" themselves to these norms, that is, to the structure established by such norms. But there is a significant difference between the procedure of the traditional judge and the procedure of the judge as mediator. The former "orders the parties to conform themselves to the rules, while the mediator persuades them to do so. . . . Mediation is commonly directed, not toward achieving conformity to norms, but toward the creation of the relevant norms themselves. . . . there is no preexisting structure that can guide mediation. It is the mediational process that produces the structure" (1971:308). Similarly, the property in question is not an object, distinct from the process; it is a value function and thus a *part* of the process.

Thus the rule of property and property laws under realism would be to create structures of equivalence, that is, value functions that become part of the structure which would then create further mediational processes.

The age-old purpose of resolving property disputes was to establish a satisfaction to both parties through the creation of property equivalences if the same, that is, the exact, property in question could not be *simply* exchanged.

But a realist's approach, based on semiotic notions of creating satisfaction or certainty by producing values that are equivalent to rightful claims, turns and transforms a logical idea of equivalence into *equivalent things*. "Things" facilitate and leave open the freedom for negotiation of freedom as value. Things are also the source of qualities, that is, the starting point of a new process of exchange.

Dewey, who has written astutely on qualities, also correctly brought together Peirce's notion of property with Locke's and has unified the relation between property in law and property in the logic of semiotics (1974:205–220). In this paper Dewey takes issue with several misconceptions and misreadings of Locke's notion of knowledge. It is not Locke's primary but his secondary qualities that are "frankly relational in the modern sense of relational" (1974:208).

Briefly stated, a property is that which produces an effect and is always relational. One's knowledge of properties is knowledge of relations of cause–effect kinds of perceived change which derives from a sense of property as a relation between something and something else. Property, whether it refers to an idea with force or to an object that represents an ideational force, is a power between existents; that is, it is that which produces change.

According to Dewey, a correct reading of Locke would reveal the errors in his thinking as well as the obstinacy with which he clung to old and treasured beliefs in the inviolable inner constitution of a thing. In this context Dewey cites Berkeley's recognition of the main problem in Locke: "The connection of ideas does not imply the relation of cause and effect, but only of a mark or sign with the things signified" (1974:220). Dewey adds this qualification:

> Primary qualities cease to be the counterparts of traditional essential attributes and the efficacious causes of secondary. They are those qualities of things which serve as the most accurate, dependable, and comprehensive signs; the qualities most important and most available for reasoning in the implication relation. (1974:220)

This interpretation of Locke's understanding of relations in knowledge also furthers his notion of property, as in the *Second Treatise*. Locke's property underlies the liberalism of the nineteenth century, which became transformed and even distorted by some of the realists but was again retrieved by the liberal economists of the twentieth century, Hayek and Friedman, for example.

Free contract as the basis of legitimate property rights under a freedom-seeking, freedom-protecting, and freedom-creating system of law is the basic tenet of Peirce's theory of signs.

What must be closely considered is the concept of an economically based legal system, in relation to Peirce's view of economic systems as models for semiotic processes. It is the price system which, according to Hayek, is the primary index or sign of freedom in society. This is discussed in a subsequent chapter. The relation between property as tangible goods and property as a function of knowledge in Peirce's semiotics is also discussed later.

The connections between law, economics, politics, and semiotics are manifold. But among the most important of these connections is the similar, although distinctly different, way in which the idea of contract has been understood, as discussed earlier. To recapitulate its function in semiotic theory briefly, contract stands for an agreement between a speaker and a listener to regard the communicative signs they share, that is, to exchange and interpret in the process of transacting meaning, as carrying certain general value, that is, mutually intelligible representations of a mutually shared universe of discourse.

The underlying structure of all semiosis, as mentioned, is dialogic. Although the participants in this process in the most abstract sense are signs or sign systems (interpretants), on the level of human society persons may be regarded as logical tokens of the interpretant sign as type. A dialogue between persons may take place between one person and a wholly other, or, as in the case of Peirce's concept of "inner dialogue," between oneself of the present moment and other aspects of oneself in earlier, future, or simply different representations of oneself to oneself.

"Self" is one's symbolically predominant sign, one's enduring identity *as* sign. But regardless of how analysis represents the participants of a semiotic process, that is, a dialogic transaction of meaningful signs, there must be an agreement or contract which affirms that the counters of exchange will carry the same or equivalent value to both participants. Analogously, property is that term the referent of which is a thing capable of ownership. It carries with it certain claims or rights for the owner and sometimes for the user who is not also the owner in deed, for instance, a tenant, a lessee, an heir to some extent, an inventor or other patent-holder of ideas, and so forth.

Property is a product and function of contractual agreement between the individual who claims the property in question and the rest of society which acknowledges that claim. Property, when it refers to things that have negotiable value, such as all marketable goods, including even inalienable possessions (for example, the parts of one's body and one's personality and talents), carries with it an equivalent cash value. This cash value, however it may fluctuate, should hold for any given time according to the rules of the marketplace. Thus in organized society everything has a price, or equivalent value which permits members of that society to measure goods, although some properties are virtually priceless because their esteemed value exceeds anyone's ability to pay, or because the property through the will of the owner is not available for any price. This "exclusive" right is rarely binding any longer. Nevertheless, all property has traditionally been regarded as equivalent to some measure of currency, that is, bills of exchange, or acts of exchange, or, in some manner, measurable sums of reciprocity.

Property is based on contract. A common motive or consideration is equivalent to reasons supporting it. In an earlier age property was viewed as an instrument *for something*. In more recent times property is viewed as an instrument for *someone*; that is, the character of expectancy which was associated with the notion of property is no longer expectancy for the exclusive benefit of the owner. Rather, the owner of property has by the fact of ownership a contract with all non-owners. There is, therefore, an expectancy on the part of the non-owners which the owner agrees either explicitly or tacitly to satisfy. Thus property is a mode of production, as has been variously argued by anarchists, liberals, conservatives, socialists, and others.

How it is a mode of production and why it is a mode of production are two basic questions that separate the whole body of interlocutors on property into their respective camps. These distinctions will not be discussed here, although the fact that there are such distinctions brings home the earlier observation, based on Peirce's semiotics, holding that it is value on which ethics depends and which in turn calls forth an appropriate method of reasoning. The mode of reasoning which has traditionally characterized conservatives, anarchists or socialists is an implicit value belief in a utopian or idealized end of human society and human interaction. It is argued in all these otherwise differing value systems that the marketplace must serve utopian ideals and is subordinate to them. But the method of the libertarian serves not as a means to utopia but as a model for a free society. This point on the distinction between free and perfect societies and their respective "models" of reasoning is discussed later.

There is little disagreement that property is not only in its derived sense a bundle of rights, but in a more elemental sense also a bundle of expectations (Atiyah 1979). According to Atiyah, property signifies the responsibility of the property owner, that is, of the person in whom the property is legally vested, to the society as a whole. Property value is sustained if and only if the property is in some manner placed at the service of the community. In this basic sense property implies a contract between owner and non-owner. Something ceases to be property with an exchange value or equivalent currency measure when it no longer is significant within a society. In a real sense, when property ceases to be a commodity it not only loses negotiable value also it loses real significance. It ceases to become an active sign. It produces nothing. It is dormant or dead.

Contract has been indissolubly bound with property since the inception of the idea of property. On the one hand, the value of property derives from the legitimate and legal measure of its value, as agreed upon. On the other hand, in this dialogic or semiotic interaction and interpretation of one idea with another, for example, contract and property as interpretants, so engaged, a kind of meaning exchange takes place between these two ideas or signs such that the meaning accumulated through this interaction continues to grow and develop in a process described as "semantic reversal."

One may conceive this process as a game in which meaning is the object transferred back and forth among participants. Gadamer, for example, refers to the process of interpretation of meaning as such a game but mistakenly observes that it is the game that plays the players; that is, it is the consistent and eternal value and meaning of the idea in exchange which catalyzes the players, while at the same time it remains platonically constant (1976).

In a closed system this is the most that can be anticipated. But in an open system nothing remains static. Everything is in flux: the players, the game, the value in exchange. Atiyah, who describes this interaction between property and contract, suggests that property, as associated with possession and control, that is, with one's free will, should be regarded and often has been regarded as the earlier of the two concepts. He says that the "concept of freedom of property was a precursor, and a necessary precursor, to the age of freedom of contract" (1979:85). Yet the impetus of the idea of absolute ownership, "of the absolute right of the owner to exploit and develop land (i.e., real property) as he thinks best," has in the twentieth century entirely disappeared from English law, from American law, and from the legal systems of nearly all free countries. In the process of this change both the practice and the idea of contract were altered. Indeed, contract has suffered through overregulation by swollen government bureaus and through zealous antiliberal actions—where the term *liberal* is used in the traditional sense, closely associated with state protection of private property rights. Libertarian may be, today, a more apt term.

These "ethical" movements, which in the interests of determining what a just society should look like and how it must act, have squeezed the freedom out of contract and consequently have created, as Atiyah points out, a "new kind of property, which is also unfree. . . . The creation of these unfree forms of property, which have not otherwise existed since the feudal era, has a tendency to freeze the existing situation, and to discourage economically desirable chance" (1979:728).

Thus interference with freedom of contract affects the future relation of property with contract such that the relational idea that bound them cannot, in any dynamic semiotic process, retrospectively recover itself. But it acquires this new meaning. The idea increases, but the process loses in value.

In recent years not only has there been a perceptible reduction in the "importance attached to consent, promise or intention in the law," but also in the world of experience which the legal system and the judicial process represent more directly than does speculative activity there has occurred a "whittling down of freedom of property" (Atiyah 1979:729). Atiyah suggests that unless there is a movement to construct a new theoretical notion of contract which will place it firmly within an ethics of obligation the ideal of a free society will not survive. Atiyah's three-point structure for contract, based on obligation (that is, on deontic assumption), will not be discussed here. For reasons explained elsewhere, a deontic structure of contract eliminates the relational structure between freedom of property and freedom of contract which presupposes the question of expectations, referred to above. The presupposition of question requires an open-ended interrogative structure, a modal logic capable of accounting for possibility at many levels, such as envisioned by Peirce and applied to the fields of law, economics, and philosophy by Hayek and others in more recent years.

Hayek's famous essay "Competition as a Discovery Procedure" (1968, Nishiyama and Leube 1984:255, 256) suggests that what he calls competition is a structure of opposition closely resembling Peirce's index: the representation of the structure of experience and the guideline for the discovery of new value. Hayek regards competition in the free market as a "procedure for the discovery of such facts as, without resort to it, would not be known to anyone, or at least, would not be utilized."

Neither to Hayek nor to Peirce, nor to Duhem and others, is a fact identical with an observable. Rather, a fact is a complex shared judgment regarding a thing in question. Thus what is meant by a fact is a measure of meaning that holds its value through a contractual act by the several judgments to regard it as such and such, that is, as fact. The factive structure is oppositional and represents the structure of experience which is manifested through the interactivity of competition.

According to Hayek, an "economic equilibrium never really exists" (1984:259). Neither does a legisign represent to Peirce the final interpretant of an idea achieved once and for all. This abstracted economic equilibrium is nothing other than a judgment of an ideal kind in semiotics, or a law that holds but provisionally until new evidence *as problematic* invites a reexamination of the problem and thus invites a new investigation leading to an overturning of a previous judgment and hence to reformulated economic equilibrium in the marketplace.

The remaining pages of this chapter will attempt to show how Hayek's index of a free society corresponds with Peirce's semiotic index of free inquiry. Both begin with a visualizable, iconic representation of how things primarily appear in their spatial relations as a map, a graph, a quality abstracted from its usual ground; they proceed with the facts of the matter, which are the data defined and thereby judged comparatively—a this and not that, index. Indices function to prepare for their caption or title or symbol, that is, for transferable meaning as sign.

According to Hayek, in a free society in which free contract and free property are in a healthy interdependence, property as a relation of individuals becomes the touchstone of spontaneous and free interactivity:

> In our society, in which the knowledge of the relevant facts is dispersed among many people, the price system is the only mechanism that communicates information. The price system is a system of signals that puts us in the situation of adopting to circumstances and experiences of which we know nothing. Our whole modern order and well-being rest on the possibility of adapting to processes that we do not know (Nishiyuma and Leube 1984)

Ultimately we do not know this phenomenal world of which we are a part. But we do know or are capable of knowing that which we construct as a means of knowing better and more fully the unknowable, everchanging circumstances of existence. How we construct such models of representation will permit us with greater or lesser freedom to act in fellowship and with justice toward others. Of that much maligned *nouveau arrivé(e)* who proverbially knows the price of everything and the value of nothing, one might note that in some respects Wall Street "smarts," as Peirce called them, and Main Street common sense have, with semiotics, come into their own.

The upwardly mobile person has almost lost the stigma with which a closed society stained him in the past, and the values of past ages with their determinist structures and rules for coercive interrelationships are no longer springboards for our ethical judgments. It will be interesting to trace the evolution of the idea of property in modern times to see whether society loses or gains in the transaction.

The death of contract was certified as long ago as the 1930s. With its demise began the undermining of the vitality of free property rights. We are at a crossroads. Property is not entirely dead. It is on a kind of life-support system awaiting some new injection or infusion, or touch of creative expectation. The recapitulation of the demise of contract in law will be mercifully brief: this

chapter concludes with the question posed throughout this century in jurisprudential circles: What is property?

NOTES

1. Lieber writes that a political state is nothing other in its basic sense than a society comprised
of individuals in relation with one another for the purpose of achieving shared values. This fundamental relationship binds people into a state, or society. A free state, or "jural state," is characterized by representatives of its members, he writes (1839/1911:147 ff.). In the same study Lieber
distinguishes between representative government in a free society and mob rule which is passed off
as the will of the people (181 ff.).

2. See M. Cohen (1933) in which he stresses that the meanings of such terms as *rights*,
duties, and *fault* have both a legal as well as a moral significance, and these distinct frames of
reference ought not be confused such that the state appears to stand behind a standardized moral
code which attempts to construct a legal system to correspond with and reflect it. There are no fixed
legal rules governing conduct, Cohen says, and that is precisely why there is law: "Laws are made
precisely because no uniformity exists." He goes on to say that Holmes performed a great service
by pointing out that a morally "bad" man, at the same time, may be a law-abiding person. This is
not a contradiction but only appears so if one confuses one system of thought with another, when,
one might add, one wants to know how and what the relations and lines of communication are
between two such different systems and, further, how they interpenetrate in subtle ways. See
especially pages 204 ff. On page 208 Cohen, with reference to Peirce, says that law ought not be
seen as in any way identical with custom. The establishing of such identity, or equivalence, removes
from the individual that margin of choice and divergence from customary norms that is otherwise
open to him.

3. Hayek discusses the relation between degrees of explanation available with degrees of
freedom and risk which individuals are capable of acting upon (1967:3–21).

4. Lieber (1853) says that "self-government may be said to be liberty in action, . . . self-
government implies self-institution. . . . It does not create nor tolerate a vast hierarchy of officers,
forming a class of mandarins for themselves, and acting as though they formed and were the
state. . . ."

5. See Becker (1980). Becker suggests (187–191) that the kinds of property have become
confused with the kinds of property rights. "Property rights" is a category that justifies uses of things;
"property" identifies and defines classes of what may be used. This distinction has yet to be worked
through in both legal and philosophical literature.

6. See Bingham on distinction between scientific cause and legal cause (1914:162–170). In
law a sequence of phenomena must be constructed selectively, and the whole construction constitutes
that which will be used as the "laboratory of the lawyer and jurist," such that procedure itself is the
means of presenting a functional, legal cause (162, 163).

7. According to Peirce, any dynamic system must be able to account for potentialities. In
such a system the traditional laws of contradiction are not applicable. See especially manuscript
137.

Inquiry as Method of Freedom

The law of fashion is a law of life. . . . I think it one of the glories of man that he does not sow seed, and weave cloth, and produce all the other economic means simply to sustain and multiply other sowers and weavers that they in their turn may multiply, and so *ad infinitum*, but that on the contrary he devotes a certain part of his economic means to uneconomic ends—ends, too, which he finds in himself and not elsewhere. . . . It is still only the minority who recognize how the change of emphasis which I have called the law of fashion has prevailed even in the realm of morals.

Oliver Wendell Holmes in,
"Law in Science–Science in Law" (1899/1921)

CHAPTER 21

Inquiry and Discovery Procedures

Little attempt will be made in this chapter to discuss in detail Peirce's methodology except to clarify it with respect to interpretation and discovery procedures in law. To recapitulate briefly: Peirce's semiotic methodology, or speculative rhetoric, is the highest division of his expanded pragmatic logic: It seeks to account for the development of meaning in verbal signs in all acts of inquiry, such that a sign is shown to interpret its previous sign, or referent in discourse, and to bring a cumulation of meaning forward in a dynamic and open-ended process. The result of any given inquiry is a judgment which corresponds to the conclusion of a logical argument.

From the perspective of pragmatics, as defined by Peirce, a judgment is a value sign that acts to furnish an end which ultimately has effectual bearing on practical affairs in society. According to Peirce's scheme, ethics, or conduct in practical affairs, is governed by value signs and value systems which are networks of interrelating signs. All of logic, or possible modes of reasoning, is in turn dependent on ethical systems. Thus, while speculative rhetoric, or methodology as the highest level of reasoning, underlies the process of developing values and value systems, the whole of possible choices of modes of reasoning is subordinate to value judgments which are themselves the consequents of previous processes of inquiry.

A system of value judgments in general may be said to correspond with a code of law in that it functions as a point of reference. However, in Peirce's view no code is ever complete, and thus all judgments may be regarded as provisional only, capable of reinterpretation and reformation. Peirce's insistence on the incompleteness of codes, or law-like judgments, is directly opposed to the Benthamite conviction holding that a code in law must be in all respects complete. Bentham presupposes a closed system of inquiry, whereas Peirce's concepts of indeterminacy, infinity or open-endness, and interpretation in inquiry stress the dynamic development of all systems of thought. In this regard, the legal system and its encoding-decoding process is of concern. From the Peircean perspective, a logic of justification in the traditional sense is inadequate to the task of describing a continually changing, evolving process. Rather, it is a logic of discovery and inquiry which is not only more appropriate, but, because more appropriate, more ethically suited to the task of accounting for the actual procedures in practical life which, prototypically, we find in the legal procedures of discovery and interpretation in open or relatively open social systems such as the United States.

As I have written elsewhere (Kevelson 1980, 1981, 1983a), there is strong evidence for assuming that not only was Peirce critically influenced by issues and problems in the law during the last half of the nineteenth century, but he was influential in a radically new approach to discovery and interpretation in the practice of law. He may be said to stand behind the whole movement in American law known generally as legal realism. Such is claimed here.

I have pointed out that legal realism is not a term that stands for a homogeneous approach to the law, and neither does it represent a unified and systematically cohesive theory of jurisprudence. Rather, the term may be regarded as indicating certain characteristics in the transformation of American law in the period roughly between the 1870s and the 1930s.

By demarcating the sixty years, more or less, of this period in which some of the most important spokesmen for legal realism practiced and preached, one should not assume that this movement sprang into being whole like Athena from Zeus's head nor ended abruptly at a time coincident with the Great Depression. On the contrary, as I have mentioned the first major expression of a semiotic approach to legal discovery and interpretation is to be found in Lieber's *Legal and Political Hermeneutics* (1839/1963), which was itself a major reaction against Savigny's theory of legal interpretation. In significant ways it anticipated Peirce's philosophy of signs and sign interpretation, or semiotics, and forecast Holmes's effectual transformation of American constitutional law and his impact on the development of legal realism both in this country and abroad.

In this chapter focus is on Peirce's contribution to legal realism through which processes of discovery and interpretation in American law were raised as problems and issues in the law and have subsequently become modified, sometimes radically transformed, and consequently have come to be seen in current practice as significant areas in the law in need of critical investigation.

It should be noted in passing, without close discussion at this time, that a semiotics perspective on law, which this chapter assumes and carries forward, is not to be confused with some recent structuralist approaches to law, which sometimes are confused with what is called here legal semiotics. Although, from a historical point of view, the emergence of structuralism and semiotics in this country coincided in the early 1960s totally different philosophical assumptions underlie each of these approaches despite certain surface similarities. Furthermore, although there are important correlations between a semiotic approach to legal interpretation and the popular Continental movement in hermeneutics, the relationship between the latter and a Peirce-grounded semiotics and its method of interpretation and inquiry is not so much superficial as reflective of a divergence between the objectives of these two distinct modes of sign interpretation.

It is the task of the investigator of a Peircean semiotics to recognize and distinguish Peirce's influence in semiotic studies of law and other areas which are not so explicitly labeled. It is the further task to persuade that although Peirce's enormous contributions are rarely directly discussed, they do actually constitute the basis of realism in law and its related movements, for example, legal pragmatism and legal instrumentalism.

Although James and Dewey are most often cited as the philosophical forebears of these movements in American law, and Peirce's work is largely neglected in the literature, this oversight may be attributed to the fact that the great bulk of Peirce's writings was not available to the early writers on realism and indeed has become accessible only in very recent years. Thus a legal semiotics as proposed here intends not only to correct this oversight but also to show how Peirce's thought *in toto* may provide new directions and even some solutions to current problems in interpretation and discovery and in those closely related institutions of economics and politics.

More than forty years ago (1942) Fisch showed clearly the relation between Peirce's pragmatism and the prediction theory in law which is generally associated with Holmes. Less than a year before Fisch's paper, Edwin Garlan opposed the then and still current practice of our official legal actors "still struggling against a frame of reference predicted upon premises, principles, and methods characteristic of eighteenth-century rationalism and nineteenth-century evolutionism and utilitarianism, attitudes which have already been seriously questioned and modified in other social disciplines" (1941:3). Garlan correctly understood that the law must also move in a new direction toward a "pragmatic philosophy of law" (1941:3).

Legal realism is such a movement and its purpose, according to Garlan, is dual: it intends law as an "experimental and fact-controlled method" and also—inseparably also—as a process of "functional interpretation" of its assumptions, rules, statutes in which law is always to be regarded as coordinate with other social institutions and therefore capable of being "tested by its contributions to the larger whole" (1941:4).

We have made much of Holmes's assertion that the Constitution of the United States is nothing but an experiment. An experiment in semiotic terms is an operation or series of operations upon an hypothesis, or possible idea. An idea, which is, to Peirce, simply another word for a possibility, is a *sign*. An idea, then, is a representation of some realizable aim or goal. It is a complex structure that is not fixed and permanent but rather malleable and cultivatable. An idea, regarded as an area of thought, may be so defined and circumscribed by boundaries which, for the purposes of experimentation and investigation, distinguish it from its customary ground or context. It is growable and thus capable of quantitative as well as qualitative change, increasing in its extensive and its intensive dimensions. Inquiry as a process is such a method for increasing the yield of an area of thought, or idea, or sign and, in our case, of law itself as an experiment.

If the main purpose of correct reasoning in general is to reduce uncertainty in selected instances, the main purpose of law in particular is to reduce uncertainty with respect to social interactions which fall within the province of institutional jurisdiction.

Within the institution of law itself the legal practitioner or lawyer is primarily concerned with prediction, not only as it bears on the theoretical problems of judicial interpretations and opinions, but also because prediction, as a theory of law, permits some limited certainty with respect to the future action of the courts (Garlan 1941:6). Thus legal realism attempts a thoroughgoing pragmatic transformation of the idea of law such that no contradiction should separate legal theory from legal praxis but that the lawyer, no less than the legal philosopher, would be engaged in the same acts of law—where *act* is both on the level of ideas and their development in thought and in the courts with respect to practical legal procedure.

What is needed, Peirce stressed, is not a doctrine but a method such that the consequences of discovery and inquiry in thought may be understood as representations of actual phenomenal processes in the world of experience. Thus Peirce's semiotics was intended to represent, as a whole, actual processes of inquiry in experience.

The prototypical experience has long been regarded as the relation between persons in society and the law, just as the legal argument is assumed to be the prototype of ordinary argument (Toulmin 1958). As claimed elsewhere and briefly repeated here, Peirce's expanded logic, or semiotics, is a representation of this legal relation. His method of methods may be understood as a model for interpreting models of inquiry of which signs and systems of signs constitute the material for the understanding.

Garlan writes, "What realism has attacked is . . . not logic but the tendency to use logic along with insufficient concern for any but the formal character of the premises. Its own aim is an adequate, though thus far unobtainable, logical structure" (Garlan 1941:9,10).

Garlan was not singular in his failure to recognize that in Peirce's expanded logic, or semiotics, the legal realists had precisely what they claimed was needed. It remains for present-day investigators to bring to the attention of the legal community Peirce's thought as it bears directly on some of the most difficult issues in law, which include the economic basis of legal interpretation as well as the interpretation in the courts of economic issues.

It is of special importance to show that some of the major conflicts between legal realists themselves, and between legal realists and their opponents, derive from an inadequate grasp of the pragmatic assumptions that underlie realism and give it its impetus as a movement in American law. For example, neither James's nor Dewey's version of pragmatism carried forward certain of Peirce's ideas which still need to be examined in this context. Also, because Peirce did not conceive of a direct application of his pragmatics, or "pragmaticism" as he later termed it, to practical affairs, there has been a general tendency to disregard his actual and significant contributions to law and to legal-economic theory and practice. Fortunately there have been outstanding exceptions to the general disregard of Peircean thought in the practical sciences of law, politics, and economics. Hayek's views on the economic bases of law in a free society oppose Keynesian thought in a manner that recalls Peirce's own rejection and refutation of Keynesian economics and Benthamite utilitarianism.

This chapter raises the question whether proposed reforms in civil discovery law, especially in the United States, will bring about reductions in obstructions to justice in the courts by significantly minimizing the predominant adversarial system of adjudication that prevails today. The adversarial system as currently practiced is harshly criticized from many quarters as an unwanted vestige of the "sporting theory of justice." These criticisms spring from those who also advocate stronger federal codification of rules and regulations governing commerce. It may be suggested that the strongest objections to more inclusive and comprehensive discovery charge discovery with promoting "overdiscovery," and that such "use of discovery is so excessive as to cause unnecessary expense and delay and to permit the better-financed litigant to coerce his opponent into an unfair settlement" (Levine 1982:115).

What is lacking in the current controversy is a well-defined model of a logic of discovery that is appropriate not to closed systems of thought or closed societies but to such open, pluralistic societies as characterize modern democracies. These systems are representations of multidimensional, open, "motion-picture" systems of thought such as Peirce attempted to account for in those aspects of his existential graphs that were primarily concerned with the modalities of possibilities, that is, with hypothetical and experimental investigations.

As I have mentioned, legal realism was one of the major concerns of the Institute of Law established at the Johns Hopkins University in the late 1920s. Not through lack of interest or because of any failure to develop significant relations between pragmatic philosophy and legal problems, but rather because of lack of funding brought about by the Great Depression, this important research came to a virtual standstill. Inquiry into this and related topics became dormant.

The Johns Hopkins Institute was seen as a victim of economics in its demise, but its mission has reemerged in the 1960s with modern semiotics.

Rumble's opinion (1968) that legal realism is founded on pragmatism is widely shared. The literature on this aspect of the relationship between American philosophy and American law is enormous. Rumble points out that for more than three-quarters of a century the link between pragmatism and the new law has been acknowledged. But what has been lacking until recently is a thorough-going inquiry into the influence of pragmatism on law.

Although it seemed unmistakably clear to the legal realists to identify the influence of Dewey, Pound, and Holmes, one finds little or no mention of Peirce.

Thus not only has this first step not been completed, but it cannot be properly even initiated until Peirce's semiotics is firmly put in place as the ground from which and against which this movement was brought forward.

Pragmatism, Rumble notes, "was the dominant current of philosophical thought in the 1920s and 1930s. The realists were not, in general, philosophers who applied ready-made systems to the law. They were lawyers first and foremost," who concurred with Dewey's assertion that the "logic of rigid demonstration" is inadequate and what is needed is a "logic of search and discovery . . . an experimental logic . . . a logic of inquiry" (Dewey 1931: 126–134). In these remarks, prefatory to his major work in the logic of inquiry in which he recovers much but not all of Peirce's semiotic method of inquiry, Dewey unmistakably shows the constructivist aspect of all systems of thought as models of action in the world. Thought itself is viewed as significant actions that are oriented to goals and consequences and are not merely reflective of, or extensions of, antecedents and referents.

Such a view presents serious problems, not only for semiotics or logic but also on a workaday level, for law. If the referential function of a legal code is no longer to be regarded as a complete and fixed authority, and yet if the rules for open-ended inquiry and discovery in law are to be specified with respect to any given system of law, how is discovery to proceed when the guidelines or rules determining discovery are provisional only and modifiable in response to the outcome of discovery procedures? Are discovery and interpretation not only to be antithetical to the "sporting theory of justice" but to go beyond the old adversarial "sporting" system by infusing the processes at every stage with an element that resembles, at the surface, caprice? How can chance be integrated with the logic of inquiry proposed by the pragmatists yet not at the same time force judicial interpretation and discovery into institutional instability?

Furthermore, if the rules for interpretation and discovery are said to be a part of any given system of law that they govern, then it must be conceded that the system of law as a whole is unstable and that this instability is desirable. What should be apparent here is that legal reasoning, from the realists' point of view, if it is faithful to its pragmatic ground, must violate the traditional laws of contradiction; that is, a legal system in the process of becoming rather than one that is, at least ideally, existent and in place is their goal.

The traditional laws of thought are inadequate to describe actual processes of evolving ideas, and logics must be constructed that sustain paradox and account for contradiction and do not attempt to impose reductive solutions (Rumble 1968:8; Kevelson 1984).

Given the scope of this chapter, a historical recapitulation of the development of theories of legal interpretation is not possible. It might be pointed out, however, that the concern with systematic interpretation, back as far as the earliest professional law schools in Western civilization, was primarily with the notion of a legal system as a closed system in response to a relatively closed society within a fundamentally completed, circumscribed, and finite universe.

When Savigny undertook in the eighteenth century to describe procedures for the interpretation of law, his fidelity to the Roman codes as such was in an important sense atavistic (Savigny (1867:166–268). Subsequent approaches to legal interpretation in reacting against Savigny emphasized the responsibility of interpretation to a changing society and changing social values. Lieber stressed the consensual nature of interpretation required in the defining of terms or signs (1839/1963).

Edward Beal (1896) presumed that such a consensus exists and that agreement obtains on the meaning of special, technical legal terms.

But definition remained as a paramount task, preliminary to interpretation in the courts. Up until this time the juristic principle, "When the text is clear there is no room for interpretation" (*In claris non fit interpretatio*) was generally assumed, so that usual or authentic interpretation referred to the interpretation of law for which rules governing interpretive processes were provided by the legal system in question and were an integral part of that system. Doctrinal interpretation, on the other hand, referred to interpretation in the absence of rules for interpretation. This doctrinal interpretation, regarded as anomalous in traditional approaches to interpretation, becomes central from the perspective of legal realism.

Holmes says that the capacity to call into question one's first principles marks the "civilized man."

Frank (1930) affirms the need for legal rules. Rules like codes, when absolutely binding, are a form of legal fundamentalism and as such have no place in modern society or its institutions. Frank speaks of the construction or hypothesizing of doubts with regard to so-called established truths. Doubts, for Frank as for Peirce, become the means to systematic and scientific interpretation and thus to greater freedom from dogmatic authority. Frank says, "Increasing constructive doubt is the sign of advancing civilization. We must put question marks alongside many of our inherited legal dogmas, since they are dangerously out of line with social facts" (1930:159). With this book, *Law and the Modern Mind*, Frank explored new territory in legal theory and practice. He was no less a pioneer than was Peirce.

What Frank opposed was not so much the rules of law, but the myth of certainty in the rules of law. With respect to the rules of interpretation, Frank was explicit in his refutation of some of the earliest formulation of interpretation rules which appeared, as mentioned before, at the close of the nineteenth century. In particular he opposed such doctrines of interpretation as Bele's *Cardinal Rules of Legal Interpretation* (1896) and its congeners. He opposed also the notion of legal absolutism, advanced by Harvard law professor Joseph Beale. Joseph, not Edward, was the target of Frank's epithet "Bealism," which came to stand to the realists for all of legal absolutism which they opposed (Paul 1959:35–38).

The kind of "word magic" that Frank accused Beale of practicing was, in a legal context, none other than the denunciatory "nominalism" that Peirce levelled at his opponents. Frank follows the path of the law that Holmes had cut through. Frank says:

> Rules, whether stated by judges or others, whether in statutes, opinions or text-books by learned authors, are not the Law, but are only some among many of the sources to which judges go in making the law of the cases tried before them. . . . (1930:127)

Frank goes on to say, "The law, therefore, consists of *decisions*, not of rules. If so, then *whenever a judge decides a case he is making law. . . .*" He is careful to qualify what he means by *decisions*; they are signs that point to future decisions or, in Peirce's terms, *indexical signs* (1930:127,128). The legal decision is discussed earlier in this volume.

Frank speaks of the "if-y" and the "chancy." Although there is little or no direct reference to Peirce's semiotics in Frank's voluminous writings, it is fair to assume that what he means by these terms is what Peirce describes, with respect to the former as hypothetical reasoning, and to the latter as the element of chance that must be taken into account in a universe that becomes, rather than is, in an infinite universe without end which we create as makers of reality with its laws as our sign constructions.

It is Peirce's influence that finds one of its ripest and most receptive carriers in Frank, for example, Frank's exposition of non-Euclidean geometry which he adapts to legal reasoning. Frank did not "discover" Peirce until 1942. Frank had by this time begun to think beyond three-dimensionality to multidimensionality, which presupposes a logic "which studies the conceptual frame of a dynamic world, a world of change and flux. . ."—a world in which contradiction plays a major role and not one in which paradox is to be resolved and eliminated (von Wright 1969:14–32).

For many of the legal realists the problem of interpretation was tantamount to a rejection of legal positivism. This position is exemplified by Kelsen who contrasts positive law with sociological jurisprudence. In some ways Kelsen is compatible with Peirce although he is clearly opposed to the position of sociological jurisprudence which he identifies with the "American legal realists." Kelsen contrasts his position by stating that a normative theory of the law attempts to prescribe how rules govern men in their practical affairs through the mediation of legal and other deontic systems. The object of sociological jurisprudence, he points out, intends only to describe how persons actually do behave and how a legal system of rules merely extends actual behavior in an authorized and responsive manner. Actual behavior is the starting point for observing general principles which can then be written into legal rules. Society, then, is the model for a legal system only if *model* is not confused with *ideal*. But Kelsen also opposes the positivists who hold that the law is the model for right social conduct (1941:53).

As noted, Peirce's position is that semiotics is descriptive rather than prescriptive. His methodology attempts to account for the process of evolving thought and does not attempt to impose commands of an ethical or moral nature on the phenomenon of thinking.

In this respect, as in others, Dewey is at variance with Peirce. Dewey does wish to use a logic of inquiry as an instrument for bringing about correct thinking, especially with respect to indeterminate situations and apparent paradoxes. This is an essential distinction, and it should be marked as perhaps the most significant difference between the positivists and the realists.

Kelsen's notion that a rule of law is, "like the law of nature, a hypothetical judgment that attaches a specific consequence to a specific condition" is Peircean in this respect and not unlike the realism of Pound, for example, or even Llewellyn (Kelsen 1941: 51).

On the one hand, according to Kelsen, rules for interpretation are hypotheses, but these hypothetical or provisional rules exert a deontic force: they are to be regarded at least on the surface as binding and *as if* they were commands that ought to be followed, that is, referred to precedentially. Thus the need for legalisms and legal fictions which honor the imputed permanence of provisional rules perpetuates the myth, as Frank also claimed.

Kelsen denies the coercive force of a rule in law. He denies that law exerts an enforced obedience and insists that the moral and psychic sanction that members of society experience in the violation of fundamental rules of conduct is merely transferred to the legal system which carries out society's moral condemnation in a specifiable and concrete manner.

Kelsen argues that "the law is not, as Austin formulates it, rule 'enforced' by a specified authority, but rather a norm which provides a specific measure of coercion as sanction" (1941:57, 58). In effect, Kelsen's theory—the "pure theory of law"—conflates values with ethics and shows the normative character of the law as a mechanism for fulfilling ideal social goals and for repairing the ideal fabric of society which is rent by its delicts. From this view, an ideal whole is presupposed. But from Peirce's view, and from the view of the realists, the idea of wholeness in society in general or in law as a particular social institution is at best a working idea, a model subject to change and correction, or, in a word, an experiment.

If a positive jurisprudence intends to reinforce belief in a stable and nonchanging code, a system of law that is predominantly under the influence of the positivists may actually regard rules for interpretation, as well as interpretation in each case, as provisional but will superimpose over the provisionality of rules a semblance of absoluteness, such that the interpretive acts of the judiciary appear to be discovery rather than the invention in law which they actually are.

On the other hand, the realists' position at its most extreme is found in the writings of Fuller, who states that "all forms of legal positivism have the common characteristic of being *formal* in their method; they deal not with the content of the law but with its form and sanction" (1940: 133–34). Fuller is generally regarded as following in the tradition of legal realism and is customarily included as a spokesman for its special concepts of law (see, for instance, Summers 1982).

Fuller argues for greater judicial autonomy over and against the traditional sovereignty of the legislator. Interpretation, in Fuller's proposed system, becomes the responsibility of the judge to deliberately evolve a rule so that the former becomes subsumed in the latter—that is, its meaning becomes part of the accumulated meaning of the new decision which does not merely extend the old rule but, in effect, transforms it into a new sign, or new law. This new law is, in semiotics, an interpretant.

In any given process of inquiry the object or rule in question is the immediate interpretant. Its factiveness, or agree-upon definition with respect to the case at hand in the inquiring experience, is the dynamic interpretant. The adaptation to the case at hand by means of qualification, revision, redefinition, or any of the available means by which meaning is increased in a term results in a judgment arrived at through interpretation. This judgment is the final interpretant. This final interpretant conveys a kind of certainty in the law until, or unless, in the future some "surprising fact" or novel aspect of another case impels fresh doubt and hence fresh inquiry into the relation between the law, now as a provisional given, in the situation at hand. Thus every case brings with it at least the possibility of doubt, and therefore the possibility of a new inquiry emerges which results in a new judgment, or law, or final interpretant.

Fuller mentions, in a footnote to his argument in favor of judge-made law, the school of legal realism in Sweden which derives from the writings of Hagerström and is best known to English readers through *Law as Fact* by Olivecrona

(1938). There is little evidence to support the thesis that Hagerström and his disciples, including Olivecrona, were familiar with Peirce's work. But indirectly, through Dewey, and more recently, Enrico Pattero (1986), one expects to find a Peircean semiotics there in full play.

Fuller's claim, which is supported by the Swedish realists, is that the judge plays an active role through interpretation in shaping common morality. He does so in dialogue with society, in response to the changing values of a changing community.

Realists such as Fuller are intent upon reasserting the malleable, revisable character of a common law. They want to show that the rule of the judiciary today in shaping extralegal or moral attitudes is in large measure comparable to the prestatutory period of the common law when the dialogue between the highest judge in English common law, the king, was clearly of a dialogic and responsive nature. This dialogic structure, as discussed, is describable by a logic of questions and answers—an erotetic logic to which a deontic logic is subordinate and derived (Kevelson 1977).

Fuller, it should be noted, does not go as far as others known as realists, however. For example, Roland Gray, as early as 1909, set about to refute Austin's theory of the sovereign and to show that the judge is the actual force in the making of law and the keeping of legal unity. Gray failed to regard a judicial act such as an interpretive decision, as an act but viewed such acts as commentary only. Holmes, on the other hand, and more than a dozen years earlier, had shown that a judicial decision is effectively more than mere commentary or words and is in fact consequential action (Gray 1909/1921; Holmes 1920:167). In this context one notes that Peirce and the pragmatists who followed him also believed that all thought was action but of a form that differed from observable physical acts. As noted, Peirce regarded ideas as phenomena and maintained that one could observe the development of an idea by mapping it or by representing it diagrammatically. In terms of movement toward the realization of a goal, Peirce's predictive semiotic method assumed that visible physical motion and process were no more and no less action than the growth of a thought, which is phenomenal because its consequences or extensions may be readily ascertained as a fact by any community of thinking persons.

The concluding few pages of this chapter discuss the idea of the *fact* from the shared perspective of the realists and the pragmatists. What facts are admissible in discovery? What is needed for something to function as a fact in discovery? How does a logic of discovery for law account for the selection of facts? These concluding pages are intended more to open questions than to resolve them. In particular, they are intended to indicate how Peirce's semiotics, rejecting both positivism and nominalism, places the process of inquiry within an open-ended frame for creating relations out of novel material as well as creating new structures of relationship between the given and the new. Although Peirce's published writings were scant at the time that the realist movement was being shaped by Holmes and others, his thought was widely known through lectures and discussion among the legal theorists of his day. He was profoundly influenced by his juristic colleagues in the development of his pragmaticism and his general theory of sign, and it is not imprudent to suggest strongly that legal realism was reciprocally indebted to him (see Fisch 1986:xxix–xxxv).

This chapter has discussed inquiry as a method of discovery which is describable by a logic of questions and answers. Interrogatory procedures have traditionally been a part of legal discovery in law and have developed as one among other methods of discovery. When William Petheram wrote his treatise *The Law and Practice Relating to Discovery by Interrogatories Under the Common Law Procedure Act, 1854* (1864), it was evident that not all interrogatories might be conducted as means through "which discovery may be sought," but rather only those interrogatories for which rules of procedure and interpretation had been established. It is the courts that establish those rules that determine what kinds of interrogatories may be administered and how they are to be administered.

The problem of interrogatory formerly included the selection of appropriate affidavits and testimony which are preliminary to the administering of interrogatories. Not all interrogatory implies oral questioning of litigants in court. An important feature of this early examination of discovery is that the shaping of discovery was largely in the context of equity proceedings.

In 1912 Robert Ross published what appears to be the first comprehensive treatise on the laws of discovery. This treatise set forth the rules relating to discovery in general in law and the related rules, both general and particular, governing interrogatories. Here, too, it is the court, or judge, who decides (1) whether interrogatories will be permitted, (2) if permitted, which will be permitted, and (3) which interrogatories, if any, are even to be considered. The criteria for the allowing of documents related to proposed interrogatories have to do both with the question of fairness with respect to the case and also with the economic costs involved. Thus the problem of cost and discovery was as crucial seventy years ago as it is in the present especially in defining legal and economic relations.

If interrogatories are allowed, they must be confined only to those questions that enable the interrogating party to obtain information directly related to the material facts at issue. In discovery all of the procedure permitted or disallowed is entirely at the discretion of the judge.

Disclosure of evidentiary documents and inspection of such documents are clearly distinguished. In a similar fashion, Peirce would hold that the selection of a "quality" is equivalent to the disclosing of a potential fact. But the examination of the so-called fact is a different stage of the discovery process, both in legal procedure and in Peirce's phenomenological inquiry, preliminary to semiotic analysis. A fact, to Peirce, is not yet a sign. Analogously, the admissibility of evidence or facts in court is a prior stage to the interpretation of the fact with respect to the settling of a claim.

As noted earlier, Peirce's phenomenology, a preliminary stage to the semiotic inquiry as such, corresponds methodologically to discovery in law. What is needed is a point-by-point discussion of the correspondence between Peirce's discovery procedures and his justification of such procedures within a logic of discovery and discovery in law as preliminary to the court's judgment on the case. This is a task for the immediate future of legal semiotics.

It should be pointed out that Peirce had not worked out a logic of discovery but had discussed it in much detail. G. Gore, at the end of the nineteenth century, was among the first to point to the need for a logic of discovery as a means of accounting for the transition from felt values to ethical conduct in scientific inquiry to a testing of such values in a logical manner according to the method of a logic of discovery.

Carmichael (1930) equates a logic of discovery with a logic of creativity. If this is the case, then he believes it highly unlikely that "a science of inference from the known to the unknown can be developed." But this is not the major problem that Carmichael sees. He says that the major stumbling block is that "discovery is relative to the point of view" and that therefore one would need not *a* logic of discovery (1930:42–44). This is precisely Peirce's point when he stresses that the aim of semiotics is to make clear and accessible a method of methods, that is, a method of inquiry that permits inquiry into not one but a countless number of points of view, or systems of thought. Further, Peirce held that we need such a method of methods to see how these various thought systems are related, or become related, or give birth to new relations. The method of semiotics would provide a means of deriving the most general principles upon which the judiciary decides. Rather than focus on the arbitrariness of individual judicial decisions, semiotics would seek the *principles* of inquiry that relate even opposing judges, as each represents a *system of thought*. Peirce's methodology—an inquiry into inquiry—seeks to bridge systems of thought, that is, create new relations between them.

It has long been accepted, albeit as a controversial issue, that what we call a "material fact" is not a single, observable phenomenon. Rather, a fact is a complex organization of prior judgments. Peirce, anticipating the inquiry of science—in law as in physics—into the unity of the fact itself, the empirical and presumably verifiable "thing," explains how even the first glimpse of an observable is never actually a first glimpse, but is an inference from previous judgments of former glimpses which only appear single but at every stage are *relations of judgments of the observable fact in question*. Thus at every stage, beginning with the admission of a quality of an observable in one's attention, facts are always relationships. No factual relationship can ever truly be established on infallible ground. No matter how fine our instruments, Peirce insists, no individual can discover a fact. A fact requires the testimony of two or more persons who agree to agree on the fact as such.

So long as we no longer regard individuals as atomistic particles of society, or regard law as a discrete institution in a social context, discovery procedures in law, with reference to system-specific rules for discovery, must represent the possibilities for stretching the definitive boundaries of rules so that conceivable freedom becomes realized in the law as a system of signs.

CHAPTER 22

Conflict of Laws

A COMPLEX INDEXICAL SIGN

The problem of conflict of laws centers on the making of judicial decision in those cases wherein two or more legal frameworks are juxtaposed as competitors for dominant authorial legal reference. The situation is viewed as a relationship between incompatible systems. Structurally, the unit of opposition may be compared with an "indeterminate situation," in Dewey's sense; it presents all the characteristics of paradox. The issues of paradox in resolving problems by means of the method of practical logic, or semiotics in Peirce's sense, will be discussed more fully below.

The claim made here is that the special problems of conflict of laws in legal semiotics require an approach that is pragmatic but does not resolve the paradoxical structure. Rather, despite the fact that decision must be based ultimately on one or the other of the competing legal systems involved, the indeterminate or paradoxical situation is not resolved. Decisions in conflict of laws cases do tend to be provisional and *ad hoc*, as Peirce claims that judgments in semiotic reasoning ought to be.

There are various rules in the history of conflict of laws that have been established for the purpose of determining which system, in each case, is to take precedence over the other. But this does not resolve the paradox. It recognizes that the paradoxical situation holds, that an action must be taken, and that this action must be taken in only one direction at the given time. This is precisely Peirce's point (Kevelson 1982a).

Although Holmes stressed that "the whole outline of the law is the resultant of a conflict at every point between logic and good sense" (cited in Dewey 1924:17,18), this chapter is concerned with how the special kinds of conflict of laws are prototypical of legal conflict in general and of semiotic oppositional relations as well.

Thus the approach here will be to (1) define conflict of laws from a jurisprudential perspective; (2) give a brief account of the development of the problem over time; (3) cite examples of the problem in the twentieth century; and (4) attempt to bring, on the one hand, Peirce's thought to bear on the problem in law and, on the other hand, to show how this problem in law may be used as a paradigm of semiotic problems of a conflictual and paradoxical nature.

In brief, the problem of conflict of laws will act as an interpretant, in Peirce's sense, for understanding further developments of the idea of paradoxically structured semiotic sign systems in other areas of inquiry.

It may be useful in concluding this introductory section to name a few examples of cases that fall under the heading of conflict of laws:

1. When partners in a contract of any kind are citizens of different countries, and there is a breach of contract or other failure to complete the terms of the contract to mutual satisfaction and expectation, to which country's courts is appeal made? And which courts have the decision-making privilege?
2. When agreements made in treaties are in opposition to domestic national laws, which takes precedence? In the United States constitutional law prevails.
3. With regard to settlement of wills, trusts, and estates, the laws of different states may come in conflict with respect to the domicile of the deceased, the location of properties in question, the residences of heirs, and so on. The conflict of laws between states will be mentioned here only in passing, except to note briefly that in the United States the laws of states are subordinate to constitutional law where the Constitution is explicit and/or interpretable with respect to the given case.

Currie, among others, offers clear analysis of several of the above-mentioned examples (for example, 1963). The term *conflict of laws* is sometimes referred to as "choice of laws." The term *law of the forum* refers to the court responsible for the making of decision in international cases; for instance, the Nurenberg trials involved conflict of laws, and the military court established was a forum court, or mediating legal instrument. The notion of mediation, especially from the perspective of semiotics, is an important feature of conflict of laws problems.

The problems inherent in the topic challenge but continue to resist attempts in law to reconcile and resolve special types of differences, especially in the areas of interstate and private international law. Conflict of laws, sometimes referred to as "collision in law," emerged at a time that coincided with the emergence of the global recognition of sovereignty of nation–states. During these past centuries problems of conflict in laws have been largely neglected by philosophers of law and by sociopolitical philosophers. To date, they have not been examined within the special framework of legal semiotics or from the broader perspective of general semiotics.

However, theorists and practitioners in practical law need no introduction to this topic. The predominant official position is that conflict of laws falls within the broad domain of private international law. This classification is controversial, as will be discussed further.

The juristic debates over questions of conflict of laws is sometimes referred to in the literature as "mixed questions" (Harrison 1919). Savigny, whose writings on legal interpretation, or legal hermeneutics, are classic especially with respect to Roman law, refers to the problem of conflict of laws as a "limitation upon arising from place" (cited in Harrison 1919).

Lieber, commissioned to draft the first code of war following the Civil War in the United States, was responsible for laying the foundation for what is now generally the basis of modern private international law and especially of modern public international law, that is, the *ius gentium* of classical jurisprudence. Lieber infused his approach to international law with ethical premises derived largely from Kant and to some extent from Savigny; these premises are inherited by the twentieth century.

In our modern, complex international exchanges between industrial and nonindustrial states, as the distinction is often made, there are special problems regarding how one nation may encroach on the sovereignty of other nations without recourse to any established court. More will be said below on the role of international corporations and codes of business which are used as if they were codes of law. Law is the interpretant of the commercial code, and this leads to unprecedented problems in conflict of laws.

As mentioned above, conflicts arise when it is not clear which nation's laws are to take precedence, for example, in international crises—for instance, in the "skyjacking" of a craft belonging to one nation, carrying passengers who are citizens of other nations, landing on a third nation's soil, held captive by members of still another nation, or, as is often the case, by members of groups that lack national sovereignty and national courts that are recognized by the world community *as* courts. Here the problem of conflict of laws is especially critical. In what country should the skyjackers be tried? Under which laws? Are they, under all the laws in question, even criminals? Is there a case? Traditionally, the question, Where is the jurisdiction? was primary in the problem of conflict of laws. But even this primary question is no longer adequate. Clearly, no decision can be expected without the underlying problems of definition addressed and resolved. The matter of definition is central to all semiotic method. Any approach to this aspect of conflict of laws in the area of legal semiotics must take into account the pitfalls of nominalism, which Peirce discusses throughout his work.

Another kind of problem of conflict of laws arises in countries that tolerate two and sometimes three coeval legal systems. One such system might be essentially customary law, inseparable from the religious laws central to the society in question. A competing system often is an imported legal system which has been implanted by acts of war and conquest. Still a third coexisting legal system might be a system of interpretants for international business. Such codes obtain across nations through the interests of multinational corporations and multinational business networks. These are the obvious and open partners in many modern conflicts of laws cases. But this says little about the fact that anything that we term a legal system is, actually, a *network of competing legal subsystems*, each vying for power with the others (L. Friedman 1975; Kevelson 1984). Thus each of the systems referred to above is a complex multisystem.

These are but a few of the several kinds of dispute that fall under the rubric of conflict of laws. These problems are not unlike certain logical paradoxes wherein two frames of reference are actually operative but not explicit on "the surface." Thus, according to Harrison (1919), these apparent paradoxes, which in Peirce's definition are genuine paradoxes, are resolved by structuring the paradox as a conflict (see Kevelson 1984). Conflicts, that is, logical conflicts, are logically settled by subsuming one claim within the other, by subordinating one of the apparently contradictory terms to the other, as token to type, rather than type versus type, or class against class. Again, special recourse to definition is wanted, and it is here that semiotics has a significant role to play in the resolution of the problem of conflict disputes.

But the problem of conflict of laws may be a misnomer. If we are showing opposition between sovereign states, then each is justified in claiming that *its* law is the law. Traditional logic is inadequate to this task; an informal or pragmatic logic is required. A logic that assumes that a process of resolution involves the transformation of the constituent terms is precisely the expanded logic of Peirce's method. It is this sense of logic that he says is synonymous with all of what he means by semiotic.

It will not be possible to examine attempts to apply a semiotic or Peircean logic to the problem. We note in passing that several attempts have been made and largely from the ranks of the legal realists, as mentioned above.

Perelman, as early as the 1950s, attempted to defend the validity of certain paradoxical arguments. In fact, the topic of pragmatic paradoxes was given a great deal of attention throughout the 1950s. But to date the problem has not crossed over from philosophical to juridical domains. Perhaps it remains for semiotics to perform the role of link between systems, just as its role is to account for intersystemic communication of all kinds, including that particular kind involved in conflict of laws cases.

At the present time the problem of paradox in philosophy has not been satisfactorily resolved according to the laws of thought underlying traditional and formal logics. On the practical side, in the law, the tendency has been to juxtapose two competing frames of reference. Resolution of conflict through juxtaposition results in a compromise of both positions in many but not in all cases. If the place of jurisdiction has been determined and agreed upon, the conflict may then be resolved with reference to the laws that govern the presiding court. But when the fact of place—of court, of action in question, or of residence of litigants—is not a satisfactory answer, then juxtaposition in conflict will tend to modify and transform the frames of reference that are in conflict. Thus either the decision must agree with an agreed-upon system of law, or the laws themselves must be changed to accord with the decision. The practice of modifying the law of the land is not uncommon in those cases wherein multinational commerce codes effect changes in the laws of the nations they deal with (Kline 1985).

Kline, in his study of international business codes, points out that over the last thirty years multinational corporations "have revolutionized business patterns and generated a global debate over their proper political control" (1985:3–6). International codes of the conduct of multinational corporations have emerged, he says, as useful "instruments of international relations." These codes are the result, in large part, of efforts of labor organizations. These codes have generally been seen as "toothless" because they are not enforceable by law. Yet they remain as central movements in most anticipated, effective legal control over the multinational corporations. Governments, especially in emerging nations, negotiate such codes because they are useful as diplomatic instruments; that is, they function to "bridge international differences while still preserving the sovereign rights of national governments to intervene on a case-by-case basis" (Kline 1985:4).

There are several implications for investigations by legal semiotics here:

1. The law-like codes in use for multinational corporations represent actual codes; they are, in other words, dynamic interpretants of the immediate interpretant of the idea of legal code.
2. The use of these codes for diplomatic purposes is a rhetorical use of particular kinds of procedure; this rhetorical function should be viewed as a methodological function from the point of view of a Peircean legal semiotics.
3. When participation in the encoding of these law-like business rules involves official and nonofficial members of the host society, there is

another kind of semiotic representation at play here. This concept of representation in government, as a standing for a body of constituents, refers to a semiotic function well described by Hanna Pitkin (1967).

One further implication is this: When host governments feel they are losing control and have insufficient say in the decision making of multinational corporations, the view is often advanced that any international system of business law that could control the corporations could also gain control over other involved nations. But when the local officials work harmoniously with corporation officials the interpretation becomes quite different: The corporations are viewed as a source of "potential global benefits . . . as well as a framework" (Kline 1985) which acts as a force within, or as a form within which to bring together public interests with those of corporations, to the mutual enhancement of both. This view transforms the customary practices of the host society and tends to transform the native legal system. The influence of customary law on the codes attempts to infuse the code with considerations of local concepts of justice. However, justice is a concept variously defined with respect to different cultures.

Thus the situation appears to be one in which any presumption of a universal law, presumed to underlie the multinational corporations' dealings with emergent nations, must be seriously doubted. Rather, what will eventually emerge, one may predict, is not universal law, but increasingly a more pluralistic global legal system, that is a more complex and provisional system of dealing with international problems in both private and public law.

One can only remark in passing that such a pluralistic system of law characterizes the legal theory advanced by more than a few proponents of legal realism in the United States. Before giving a brief historical account of the development of the concept of conflict of laws, it may be useful to review some of the basic principles currently used in the settling of cases (quoted phrases are from Currie 1963:188):

1. Courts should generally "look to the law of the forum as the source of the rule of decision."
2. Whenever the law of a foreign state rather than the law of the forum should "furnish the rule of decision, the court should investigate social, economic, or administrative policy" to determine whether these policies are expressed by the law of the forum, and whenever so, the law of the forum can then be said to provide the "source of the rule of decision."
3. Sometimes the policies and laws of the foreign state have a "legitimate interest" in applying their law to the case at hand.
4. If the forum state has no such law and policies which pertain but the foreign state does, then preference is given to the foreign state.

5. With respect to applying laws and policies of states, the forum state takes precedence over the foreign state.

The point was made above that conflict of laws falls into the broad category of private international law (and not) public international law, or *ius gentium*. The problem of conflict of laws does not arise during the period of classical Roman civil law. The concept of the *ius gentium* does not apply to conflicts among sovereign states. According to Harrison, for example, the Romans would have found the idea of a society of friendly nations resolving disputes an inconceivable possibility. The concept of resolving conflicts through dialogic interaction between equals does not emerge until much later. Bartolus, in the first quarter of the fourteenth century, noted the distinction between laws of nations derived from territorial laws and feudal custom, and the laws of various tribes and settlements of "crowds of conquering races."

Territorial law became the basis for international public law and the source of civil law. This was totally different in concept from the kind of personal law that was "applied to the various mingled races amongst the subjects of each particular sovereign." When the problem of conflict of laws became recognized as such, it was assigned to the class of private international law; decisions regarding conflicting claims were made with respect to the place where the contract occurred. The law of the place was then, and still remains, one of the main principles governing decision in conflict of laws (Harrison 1919:112 ff.).

Whereas Continental law traditionally distinguished between persons and things, the prominent analytic jurists, that is, those who characterized common law, (Austin and Bentham, for instance) made little or no distinction between laws of persons and laws of things. Locke's concept of property provides fair reason why this distinction was not made in Anglo-American law to the extent that it was and is made in Continental law. There is a marked difference between property and possession in common law history which, as Holmes points out (1881/1963), does not occur in Continental civil law. The analytic jurists of England saw no need to distinguish between real statutes and personal statutes. They argued against the distinction on the grounds that what was needed was a general concept so that one could analyze law according to scientific method (Harrison 1919:113). But, as we recall, a code of law in Bentham's view must be complete and complete in all its parts. This view is at total variance with that of Peirce, for example, who understands a code to be always incomplete and subject to revision and change. The crux of the difference lies in the manner in which the authoritative reference is regarded: in Peirce it is never absolute.

Thus a legisign, in Peirce's lexicon, is law-like but provisional. It is a judgment subject to correction. One of the major contributions modern semiotics has to make in this area is with respect to the notion of the given: a given is a predominantly symbolic sign but is of the nature of a mental construction only. There are no real data, says Peirce.

When Harrison proposes that conflict of laws be regarded as part of an intermunicipal law and thus separated from traditional notions of international law, both public and private, he is advocating a law of "compound jurisdiction" (Harrison 1919:131). This idea may be fruitfully examined from the viewpoint of general semiotic theory which regards the exchange of messages between addresser and addressee as involving a continuous shifting of authorities.

The following will briefly present aspects of conflict of laws with respect to American law. Ehrenzweig, for one, suggests that there is a "hidden order of law just as there is such an undisclosed or hidden 'order' of art" (Ehrenzweig 1967:60). He further suggests that part of the "crisis of American conflicts law" derives from various choices of law rules which are "based on the 'legitimacy' of 'reasonableness of interest. . . .'" He calls this a mistake, because such terms as legitimacy and reasonableness, like jurisdiction and significance, are "deduced from a nonexisting superlaw" (Ehrenzweig 1967:63).

Although there is a need, Ehrenzweig stresses, to establish a structure for conflicts rules, the idea of a rational structure presupposes modes of reasoning that will have to account for paradox and simultaneous authority, that is, coexisting and equally "true" givens, without having to dissolve one of the factors within the other.

Finally, the conflicts of laws problem may be approached through a method that permits a correlation of equals. A shift from authorial to dialogic communication would characterize the development of the process. It is a semiotic process. Such a process and development are described by Bakhtin, Volosinov, Mukarovsky, and others and can be applied to the legal problem as well as to other problems of intersubjective communication (see Kevelson 1981).

It has been argued that law serves as a model for arguments in general (Toulmin 1958) and that a legal system is prototypical of all other semiotic systems (Kevelson 1987). This problem of conflicts of law may be seen as the type of problem of paradoxical structures as a whole and thus may provide insight into the process whereby codes of conflicting reference become transformed and new values emerge as a result of mediating, transforming semiosis.

CHAPTER 23

The Means–End Process of Freedom in Law

The predominant emphasis in this book on the affinities between Peircean semiotics and common law traditions in a modern Anglo-American legal system may convey to the reader the idea that a legal semiotics is applicable only to systems of law that share a general background with common law countries, on the basis of cultural customs, consensus, contract, property, and the like. This is not the case; the theories are widely applicable to all legal systems. But an introduction to legal semiotics is more readily given with respect to common law because fundamental concepts are shared by both, in different ways, but in ways that permit intersystemic communication between philosophy and law to be more apparent to the newcomer to this point of view.

Although the implication has been that some legal orders are more compatible than other orders which subsume an ethics based on absolutes of right and on a *summum bonum* which is only peripherally concerned with the basic value of freedom, this implication must be qualified.

First of all, a semiotic method should not only provide a systematic means of bringing together legal systems of given societies with other systems, both on its own level of practical science as in economics and politics, and on different levels of abstraction such as in philosophy or mathematics. A semiotics of law should also be able to show how the constituents in any given system ideally called the law are really a network of competing legal systems which, as Friedman has shown (1975), are social subsystems in semiotic interaction.[1]

Furthermore, a semiotics of law should also be capable of accounting for such intersystemic communication between systems the origins of which are culturally, historically, and ideologically different from the various branches and outgrowths of common law—for example, civil law systems as a whole, systems and orders of law in the Middle East, such as Islamic and Mosaic laws—as *types* of systems. The legal systems of the Far East, for instance, those of Japan and China, and those of all indigenous legal orders of third-world countries are part of what an overall legal semiotics includes among its charges.

Still further, what is now referred to as international law subsumes, requires, and implies semiotic accounts of individual systems involved and their relation in the larger international unity. The traditionally separate law of the sea (maritime law) is a no less vast and encompassing category than is international law, common law, civil law, or the once distinct mercantile law.

Is it the case that the object sought is one world, one law? Is it the case that overriding systems of rights shall be assumed to supersede and coerce culture-specific legal systems into compliance? Is it the case that the presumption of a world government is a general aim, and, if so, is it possible to achieve this unity without coercion and the force necessary to bring it about and to fortify its effectualness in the world? There are many persons in academic disciplines as well as some in political life who eagerly assent to means-justifying-ends positions. There are, however, great oppositional forces among equally careful and concerned thinkers who reject the denial of freedom and free choice in the name of some eventual global utilitarianism. The respective values held by each group influence and determine the mode of inquiry in each case.

In earlier chapters mention was made of the growing interest among legal semioticians in legal drafting and artificial intelligence, in computer science as a tool to assist in the process of legal drafting, the purpose of which is to disambiguate, insofar as natural language may be disambiguated, the language of rules and statutes, that is, the law language. Such approaches are mentioned only in passing here. The usual understanding of legal interpretation, similarly, is concerned with disambiguating the language in which a law has been written, often at a much earlier time when different uses of a common language, at different periods of its development, were predominant, that is, customary. Thus the problem of interpretation in law is not merely the problem of agreeing on basic concepts, but that of agreeing that when they are articulated by different persons there is some general common meaning that permits law to be something more stable than an idiosyncratic exposition on certain principles that may lie outside the frame of the law itself.

The problem of paraphrase is central to legal drafting.[2] But paraphrase is a higher level of generalization than the finding of synonymous terms of technical and pivotal terms of a rule of law.[3]

It is of interest, then, that we find civil law countries producing treatises on systematic legal interpretation before such documents appear with respect to interpretations of common law. Yet John Cowell's *The Interpreter*, published in 1607 is a landmark in common law interpretation. The voluminous writings that, as a whole, constitute the canonical texts of other legal systems, for instance, Mosiac law and Islamic law, have become referential for ideology and morality, rather than the reverse, as is presumed to be the case in common law wherein morality is said to be underscored and articulated by the document of law. The United States Constitution, it is believed, articulates the underlying legal order based on custom. The interpretation of constitutional law is thus presumed to hold faith with an underlying legal customary order.[4]

But civil law countries are less closely bound to underlying legal orders. Rather, the initial project of civil law was to liberate a legal system from underlying ties to moral orders felt to be no longer tenable. Certainly the attempt in civil law to dissociate the notion of the sovereign from the rule of law was a manifest attempt to free law from theocracy. With the emergence of modern science in the sixteenth century, this new system provided a more useful referent system for law than the closed system of older theocratic law.

The break between systemic alliances is never abrupt and rarely observable. Yet it is a phenomenon that we know by its consequences, by its acts as "facts" of the world.[5]

Thus the phenomenal facts of unions and disunions between social systems become for legal semiotics one of its most pressing challenges. To what extent do archaic and obsolete theocratic vestiges cling to modern legal systems? To what extent do indigenous legal orders based on unwritten customary law fuse and confuse with mercantile law such that two or more legitimated legal systems coexist, each charged in this division of labor with responsibility for less than well defined aspects of practical life?

It is pointed out in passing that the mercantile system is never simply a single system but is also a composite or network of competing systems, comparable to the conflict between the law of liberty and the law of legislation. For example, the legal order in an emergent nation–state is seen to be layer upon layer of law until, it is assumed, the core of the union will appear as something solid resembling the primeval legal system of that given society. To attempt to find such a core at center is an exercise in futility. Dual legal systems have existed for millenia.

One must be aware of the sustained coexistence of multiple legal systems over a long period of time, for example, in England following the Norman conquest when two legal systems coexisted and influenced each other until for the sake of clarity and unification the law language of the time, the official formulaic language of the thirteenth and fourteenth centuries, became a marquetry of both systems. "To have and to hold" is one such expression among many in law which fuse not only the linguistic origins representing different legal systems but also the underlying moral order and ideology of each.

"To have and to hold" became a single expression, but it consists of terms that are not synonymous and not in any sense originally representative of a single idea or meaningful sign. Thus a simple phrase like this one becomes symbolic of the semiotic relation between two systems. It is a judgmental phrase, legislating that not one or the other system is dominant but only both together are legal and binding.

This introduction to the law as a system of signs merely scratches the surface of a new universe of discourse. Clearly, with respect to this universe of discourse we are at such a primitive stage as our forebears were when they discovered existence. In approaching our task one attempts not to find the smallest indivisible element or subatomic particle of this phenomenon called a legal system, but rather to conceive first of all of the greatest and most general relationship.

This approach resembles that of the functional linguists, for example, as contrasted with the linguistic method of transformational or generative grammar.[6] This approach is also in marked contrast to that of the positivists, who begin with the single most general concept and then proceed to break it down into its constituent parts.

Semiotics is both analytic and synthetic in the sense that it begins not with a single most general idea but with a relation between general ideas. It must discover or hypothesize its "general" and may not simply accept it as given, that is, as truth.

One might object that a higher generality that includes the relationship between ideas is not fundamentally different from a positivist approach. But it is fundamentally different, because, as stated, the general idea of unification or relation between two or more general ideas is not given as a postulate, or axiomatic truth, but is a working idea that abductive reasoning constructs or invents, which at its best is explicitly provisional. It is, Peirce says, a supposition and, even, a guess.[7]

The structure of such a guess is always in the form of hypothesis: "If, if . . . then if and then, then." This structure resembles the "If, if . . ." proposition of the Stoics' logic. As has been mentioned earlier, the Stoics were among the effectual influences on Peirce's semiotics despite what he called their materialism. They lacked the element of play, of permitting nonexistents to act as agentive forces and to supply causative, that is, explanatory force as a leading assumption. They lacked a high and serious level of play, as a mode of guessing and inventing Peirce suggests.

At every level of the semiotic investigation of law, investigation may be accounted for and described according to a logic of inquiry. A deontic logic, such as has often been held to characterize legal reasoning, does not involve the investigator's role in the analysis, although it is also dialogic in underlying structure.

A new context emerges, cutting across nation–state borders, across defining theological canons, ideological constraints, cultural customs, and sublegal systemic assumptions: this new territory, which a legal semiotics must also explore, is the uncharted domain of technology.

The late Ithiel de Sola Pool speaks of technology as an entirely new context and one in which such notions as rights, as guaranteed in our Bill of Rights, require interpretation[8] (de Sola Pool 1983:1–5).

De Sola Pool is primarily concerned with the transformation of the value of freedom in this modern technological context. For example, what was formerly the function and occupation of translators across national language boundaries is now the work of electronics. This process, generally referred to as "convergence of modes," establishes general meaningful signs which appear to bring together the diverse channels of the written word, the telegraph, the press, radio, and television, into a common language. By a single instrument all of the various language types are simultaneously translated into common denominator form and dispersed in translation to as many codes as one may conceive. There is not a single channel for this operation, but the process itself is capable of distinguishing the most appropriate channel for the message in question: wire, cable, airway, voice, print, or whatever. The picture is further complicated by the fact that economic interests converge in the form of cross-ownership.

Further, there is no agreement, tacit or explicit, on the meaning of terms. The multielectronic communications take place across all traditional borders in codes loosely assumed to be understandable.

Still further, there is not only an ideal and abstract listener, but also a composite sender such as has no historical precedent.[9] The laws that were enacted in the 1920s to regulate and enforce broadcasting rights, according to the then current understanding of the First Amendment, are long obsolete. The basic terms in which such legislation is stated are now irrelevant in large measure. The problem is still further complicated by national constraints against free expression in broadcasting and other more recent modes of electronic communication. The need for cryptography, similar to the transmittal of messages in time of war, is apparent. However, the cryptographic element in an already complex mode of simultaneously translating messages into many codes removes a measure of responsibility from the sender and at the same time imposes on listeners unwanted and often harmful information in the form of delegated responsibility. This is based on an implicit notion of contract between any sender and any receiver; metamessages of a nonverbal nature are part of communications in general.

The ideal of a free press, for example, which has access to channels is to an unknown extent now governed by political regulation. But the rights to transmit are not the same as the rights guaranteed by the First Amendment. Rather, the one has to do with traditional property rights and the other with how far one may extend the "property" of one's speech. At the same time, the traditional laws governing the enforcement of private property have become attenuated. Thus issues which would have appropriately belonged within the domain of property and contract pass over into the domain of free expression.[10]

In line with a tendency to carry over into a new system ideas and practices that are applicable to older systems, the advent of cable brought with it carryovers from broadcasting. For instance, it is wrongly assumed that the "spectrum" of cable was as limited a resource as were the older broadcast channels. Yet, according to de Sola Pool, utilization of a resource withdraws it from alternative uses. Information is an exceptional resource for which this is not true. Giving information to one person does not reduce the meaning of it available for another person. Here de Sola Pool's argument resembles that of Machlup, noted earlier. Thus: "Spectrum shortage is . . . no longer a technical problem but only a man-made one. . . . What is lacking is a legal and economic structure to create incentives to use extant technologies in ways that would provide broadcasting in abundance" (1983: p. 151).

It is clear that the argument from "shortage" is based on a mode of thinking that assumes a finite structure of the world and, like most utility-based concepts, presumes a finite maximum resource of any given society at any given time.

But logic which is grounded in an infinite world with infinitely developing resources would not reason from the position of shortage. It is not only a new legal and economic institutional structure that is wanted, according to de Sola Pool, but a structure of thinking, a mode of reasoning to which our social systems may refer and which they may correctly represent.

The great and growing number of symposia since the 1920s continue to treat the problem as a violation of First Amendment rights. It is not so much the problem of censorship, however, with which one ought to be most concerned, although that is surely a problem of great magnitude with respect to freedom, but with a different problem in a different frame of reference. The issue here is that the concept of censorship, or restrictions against free speech, has been used as a way of opposing and challenging the regulators of the available "spectra" for communicating information of all kinds.

The two remaining subsystems of legal semiotics to be mentioned in this chapter are maritime law and international law. The latter was set in motion, as it were, by Lieber nearly a half-century after publication of his *Legal and Political Hermeneutics* (1839). The recent history of international law and the problems of human rights are competently examined by Paul Sieghart (1983).

Also of particular interest in this context is the Sebenius study, *Negotiating the Law of the Sea* (1984). For example, Sebenius reconstructs the Third United Nations Conference on the Law of the Sea of 1974. His main purpose is to show how different nations, through their representatives, are engaged in contract making on the meaning of the terms involved. These studies point up the need for legal semioticians to begin with the largest rather than the smallest element.

Sebenius shows a new dimension of contract in law: Maritime law, subsuming private and public law of participating nations as well as major precepts of international law as vaguely and inadequately assimilated within nation-specific legal systems, is spread out as part of a total international contract, as a phenomenological picture of the contractual events leading up to a contract in law. Phenomenological aspects of legal semiotics are a topic that greatly exceeds the scope of this book, but the preparatory function of phenomenology requires critical attention.

Also essential is the comparatist approach to legal semiotics. Wigmore's classic approach (1928) to comparative legal history as analysis of legal signs in commerce and transaction merely opens the door.

What is still needed also is a method of methods or "quest of quests," in Peirce's sense, which will permit semiotics to investigate the relations among all systems presently included under the rubric of law. This kind of inquiry into the ways in which different systems structure their respective goal seeking (for instance, how they justify and explain their goals to others, how they create in the process of inquiry new goals and fuse these with other systems)—all of this is included in what Peirce intended by his method of methods with respect to all methods of inquiry in general.

A comprehensive legal semiotics would include examination of the central position of the normative sciences of logic, ethics, and esthetics and would investigate each body separately and also in relation with the others. A full picture would also show that a phenomenological account, or protosemiotic analysis of law, follows value, and therefore it would also show the relationship between the normative sciences with respect to law and a metaphysics of law in Peirce's view. Not least, through the relation between the metaphysical and the phenomenological stages of the total process it would be able to explain in greater measure than is now possible equivalent values of appearance and reality as principles of law in motion and in change.

The creation of new law is all of this dynamic process that semiotics attempts to understand and interpret.

NOTES

1. See Kevelson (1977).
2. See Dickerson (1981).
3. See Betti on legal interpretation (1948); also Ross on interrogatives, interpretation and discovery in law (1912); Tsune-Chi Yu, a student of Lieber and correspondent with Holmes, on interpretation of international treaties (1927);
4. See Dewey (1924:17–27), especially page 21, where Dewey refers to Holmes's use of a logic of search and discovery, as opposed to a logic of rigid demonstration.

5. See de Sola Pool (1983:1–5).

6. Ibid., 22–54.

7. Ibid., 149 ff.

8. Ibid., 151 ff.

9. Kevelson (in preparation).

10. Kevelson, "Freedom of Speech: Two Kinds of Utterance"; *Proceedings of IVR* 1987 (will appear in 1988).

References

Aarnio, Aulis. 1978. *On Legal Reasoning*. Turku: Turun Yliopisto.

Ackerman, Bruce A. 1978. *Private Property and the Constitution*. New York: Yale University Press.

———. 1984. *Reconstructing American Law*. Cambridge MA: Harvard University Press.

Adjukiewicz, Kazimierz. 1974. *Pragmatic Logic*. Trans. O. Wojtasiewicz. Dordrecht: D. Reidel.

Adams, E. M. 1969. "The Philosophical Grounds of the Present Crisis of Authority." In *Authority: A Philosophical Analysis*, ed. R. Baine Harris, 3–24. Birmingham: University of Alabama Press, 1976.

Adler, Mortimer. 1963. "Legal Certainty." In *Essays in Jurisprudence*, ed. *Columbia Law Review*, 363–380. Westport, CT: Greenwood Press, 1977.

Alleman, Gellet Spencer. 1942. *Matrimonal Law and the Materials of Restoration Comedy*. Wasslingford, PA: University of Pennsylvania Press.

Allerton, D. J., and E. Carney, eds. 1979. *Function and Context in Linguistic Analysis*. Cambridge: Cambridge University Press.

Anderson, Alan Ross. 1967. "The Formal Analysis of Normative Systems." In *The Logic of Decision and Action*, ed. N. Rescher, 147–205. Pittsburgh: University of Pittsburgh Press.

Apel, Karl-Otto. 1967. *Charles S. Peirce: From Pragmatism to Pragmaticism*. Trans. J. M. Krois. Amherst: University of Massachusetts Press, 1981.

Arnold, Thurmond W. 1962. "Law as Symbolism." In *Sociology of Law*, ed. V. Aubert, 46–51. Harmondsworth, Middlesex: Penguin Books, 1969.

Ashworth, E. J. 1974. *Language and Logic in the Post-Medieval Period*. Dordrecht: Reidel.

Association of American Law Schools. 1950. *The Legal Philosophies of Lask, Radbruch, and Dabin*. Editorial committee. Trans. Kurt Wilk Intro. E. W. Patterson. Cambridge, MA: Harvard University Press.

Atiyah, P. S. 1979. *The Rise and Fall of Freedom of Contract*. Oxford, England: Clarendon Press.

Austin, John. 1879. *Lectures on Jurisprudence: Or the Philosophy of Positive Law*. London: John Murray. Especially lectures 14–20 in Vol. 1.

Austin, J. L. 1968. *Philosophical Papers*. Eds. J. O. Urmson and G. S. Warnock. London: Oxford University Press.

———. 1975. *How to Do Things with Words*. Eds. Marina Sbisa and J. O. Urmson. Cambridge, MA: Harvard University Press.

Bacon, Francis. 1960. *The Advancement of Learning and the New Atlantis*. London: Oxford University Press. (Originally 1605 and 1627).

Baker, Edwin C. 1980. Starting Points in the Economic Analysis of Law. *Hofstra Law Review* 8:939–972.

Bakhtin, Mikhail. 1973. *Problems of Dostoevsky's Poetics*. Trans. R. W. Rotsel. Ardis.

Baran, Henryk, ed. 1976. *Semiotics and Structuralism: Readings from the Soviet Union*. White Plains, NY: International Arts and Science Press.

Barker, Sir Ernest, ed. 1947. *Social Contract: Essays by Locke, Hume, and Rousseau*. London: Oxford University Press, 1977.

Barry, Brian. 1973. *The Liberal Theory of Justice*. Oxford, England: Clarendon Press.

Barthes, Roland, 1977. *Elements of Semiology*. Trans. A. Lavers and C. Smith. New York: Hill and Wang.

Basham, A. L. *The Wonder That Was India*. 1954. New York: Grove Press.

Battray, R. S. 1911. *Ashanti Law and Constitution*. New York: Negro University Press, 1969.

Baumgarten, Alexander. 1964. *Baumgarten's Meditationes Philosophicae de Non Nullis ad poema pertiventibus*. Trans. and eds. Karl Aschenbrenner and William B. Holten. Berkeley: University of California Press. (Originally published 1735)

Beal, Edward. 1896. *Cardinal Rules of Legal Interpretation*. London: Steven & Sons, Ltd.

Beale, Joseph Henry, Jr. 1900. *A Selection of Cases on the Conflict of Laws*. Cambridge, MA: Harvard Law Review.

Becker, Lawrence. 1977. *Property Rights: Philosophic Foundations*. Boston: Routledge and Kegan Paul.

———. 1980. The Moral Basis of Property rights. Eds. J. Pennock and J. Chapman. *Nomos* 22: 187–200 (Series on law and economics). New York: New York University Press.

Belnap, Nuel D. Jr. 1966. Questions, Answers, and Presuppositions. Symposium on Questions. *Journal of Philosophy* 63.20: 609–611.

Benditt, Theodore. 1978. *Law as Rule and Principle*. Stanford: Stanford University Press.

Bentham, Jeremy. 1948. *The Principles of Morals and Legislation*. New York: Hafner Press. (Originally published 1780)

Berle, Adolphe A. 1959. *Power Without Property*. New York: Harcourt, Brace, and World.

Bentham, Jeremy. 1960. (1) "On Interpretation" (pp. 158–163). (2) "Signs of a Law" (pp. 152–155). Ed. H. L. A. Hart. *Of Laws in General*. London: Athlone Press.

Berman, Harold J. 1983. *Law and Revolution*, Cambridge: Harvard University Press.

———. 1977. The Origins of Western Legal Science. *Harvard Law Review* 90.5, 894–944.

Bernstein, Richard J. 1978. *The Restructuring of Social and Political Theory*. Phila.: University of Pennsylvania Press.

Bernstein, Richard J., ed. 1965. *Perspectives on Peirce: Critical Essays on Charles Sanders Peirce*. New Haven: Yale University Press.

———. 1965. Action, Conduct, and Self-Control. Ed. R. J. Bernstein, ed. *Perspectives on Peirce* (pp. 75–87). New Haven: Yale University Press.

———. 1971. *Praxis and Action*, Philadelphia: University of Pennsylvania Press.

Berolzheimer, Fritz. 1912. *The World's Legal Philosophies*. Trans. R. S. Jastrow. Boston: The Boston Book Company.

Bett, Henry. 1925. *Johannes Scotus Erigena: A Study in Medieval Philosophy*. Cambridge, England: Cambridge University Press.

Betti, Emilio. 1948. *Le Categorie Civilistiche Dell' Interpretazione*. Milano: Dott. A. Giuffre.

Brown, Thomas. 1977. *Inquiring Into the Relation of Cause and Effect*. Delmar, N.Y.: Scholars' Facsimiles and Reprints. (Originally published 1835)

Bingham, Alfred M., and Redman, eds. 1934. *Challenge to The New Deal*. New York: Falcon Press.

Bingham, J. W. 1914. Legal Philosophy and the Law. *Illinois Law Review* 9:99–119.

Bird, Otto. 1976. *Cultures in Conflict.* Notre Dame: University of Notre Dame Press.

Black, Donald and Maureen Mileski, eds. 1973. *The Social Organization of Law.* New York and London: Seminal Press.

Blair, Roger D. and D. C. Kaserman. 1983. *Law and Economics of Vertical Integration and Control.* N.Y.: Academic Press.

Bodenheimer, Edgar. 1976. *Jurisprudence: The Philosophy and Method of the Law.* Cambridge: Harvard University Press.

Bodenheimer, Edgar. 1977. "Hart, Dworkin, and the Problem of Judicial Lawmaking Discretion." *Georgia Law Review* 11.5: 1143–1172.

Brady, James B. 1972. Law, Language and Logic: The Legal Philosophy of Wesley Newcomb Hohfeld. *Transactions of the Charles S. Peirce Society,* 8(2): 246–263.

Braudel, Fernand. 1982. *The Wheels of Commerce.* Trans. S. Reynolds. New York: Harper & Row.

Britto, Antonio, R. C. 1927. *Systema de Hermeneutica Juridica.* Rio de Janeiro: Livraria Francisco Alves.

Brkic, Jovan. 1970. *Norm and Order: An Investigation into Logic, Semantics, and the Theory of Law and Morals.* York: Humanities Press.

Brokerick, Albert, ed. 1967. *Law and the Liberal Arts.* Washington, D.C.: The Catholic University of America Press.

Bromberger, Sylvain. 1966. Questions. *Journal of Philosophy* 63.20: 597–606.

Buchler, Justus. 1979. *Toward a General Theory of Human Judgment.* New York: Dover Publications. (Originally published 1951)

Bunge, Mario. 1963. *The Myth of Simplicity.* Englewood Cliffs, NJ: Prentice-Hall.

Burrell, David B. 1965. "C. S. Peirce: Pragmatism as a Theory of Judgment." *International Philosophical Quarterly* 5: 521–40.

Cahn, Edmund, 1981. *The Moral Decision: Right and Wrong in the Light of American Law.* Bloomington: Indiana University Press. (Originally published 1955)

Cairns, Huntington. 1949. *Legal Philosophy from Plato to Hegel.* Baltimore: Johns Hopkins Press.

———. 1977. "The Valuation of Legal Science" In *The Theory of Legal Science.* Westport, CT: Greenwood Press, 1977. (Essay originally appeared 1941)

Calabresi, Guido. 1961. "Some Thoughts on Risk Distribution and the Law of Torts." *Yale Law Journal* 70: 499.

———. 1982. *A Common Law for the Age of Statutes.* Cambridge: Harvard University Press.

Campbell, John. 1980. "Locke on Qualities." *Canadian Journal of Philosophy,* 10(4):567–86.

Carmichael, R. D. 1930. *The Logic of Discovery.* Chicago and London: Open Court.

Carzo, Domenico, and Bernard Jackson, eds. 1985. *Semiotics, Law and Social Science.* Gangemi Editore and Liverpool Law Review.

Casner, A. James, ed. 1952. *American Law of Property.* Vols. 1–7 and supplement. Boston: Little, Brown, 1977.

Caws, Peter, 1959. "The Functions of Definition in Science." *Philosophy of Science* 26: 201–228.

Channels, Noreen L. 1985. *Social Science Methods in the Legal Process.* Totewa, NJ: Rowman & Allanheld.

Cherry, Colin. 1966. *On Human Communication.* Cambridge, MA: M.I.T. Press.

Clark, Malcolm. 1987. *The Enterprise of Law.* St. Paul and New York: West Publications.

Clark, Herbert H. 1976. *Semantics and Comprehension.* The Hague and Paris: Mouton.

Coase, Ronald H. 1960. "The Problem of Social Cost." *Journal of Law and Economics* 3:1.

Cohen, Felix S. 1933. *Ethical Systems and Legal Ideals.* NJ: Falcon Press.

Cohen, Julius. 1963. "The Value of Value Symbols." *Columbia Law Review: Essays in Jurisprudence.* Westport, CN: Greenwood Press, 1977.

Cohen, Morris. R. *Reason and Nature.* 1931. Glencoe: Free Press, 1953.

————. 1933. *Law and the Social Order.* New York: Harcourt, Brace.

————. 1950. *Reason and Law.* Glencoe, IL: Free Press.

————. 1954. "Legal Thought." In *American Thought: A Critical Sketch,* Chap. 6, Glencoe, IL: Free Press.

Cole, Peter, and Jerry L. Morgan, eds. 1975. *Syntax and Semantics: Speech Acts.* Vol. 3. New York: Academic Press.

Collingwood, R. G. 1933. *An Essay on Philosophic Method.* Oxford: Clarendon Press.

Corbin, Arthur L. 1960. "Legal Analysis and Terminology." In *Landmarks of Law,* ed. R. D. Henson. Reprinted from *Yale Law Review,* 1919.

Cover, Robert M. and Fiss, Owen M. 1979. *The Structure of Procedure.* Mineola, N.Y.: Foundation Press.

Cribbet, John E. 1975. *Principles of the Law of Property.* Mineola, NY: Foundation Press.

Cunningham, W. 1878. "Political Economy as a Moral Science." *Mind* 3: 369–383.

Currie, Brainerd. 1963. *Selected Essays on the Conflict of Laws.* Durham, NC: Duke University Press.

D'Amato, Anthony. 1978. "The Limits of Legal Realism." *Yale Law Journal* 87:468–513.

Daube, D. 1979. "Roman Law of Property.' In *Theories of Property,* A. Parel and T. Flanagan, eds., 35–50. Waterloo: Wilfred Laurier University Press.

Davis, William. 1972. *Peirce's Epistemology.* The Hague: Martinus Nijhoff.

De George, Richland T. 1978. Anarchism and Authority. Eds. J. R. Pennock and J. W. Chapman. *Nomos* 19: 91–110 (Issue titled *Anarchism*).

D'Entreves, A. P. 1963. "Legality and Legitimacy." *Review of Metaphysics* 16: 687–702.

De Sola Pool, Ithiel. 1983. *Technologies of Freedom.* Cambridge: Harvard University Press.

Dewey, John. 1916. "The Pragmatism of Charles S. Peirce." *Journal of Philosophy* 13:709–714.

————. 1920. *Reconstruction in Philosophy.* Boston: Beacon Press, 1948. Enlarged ed.

————. 1922. *Human Nature and Conduct.* New York: Henry Holt.

————. 1924. "Logical Method and Law." *Cornell Law Quarterly* 10:17.

————. 1929. *The Quest for Certainty.* New York: Putnam, 1960.

————. 1931. Justice Holmes and the Liberal Mind. In *Mr.Justice Holmes,* ed. F. Frankfurter, 33–45. New York: Coward-McCann.

————. 1934. *Art as Experience.* New York: Paragon, 1979.

————. 1935. "Peirce's Theory of Quality." *Journal of Philosophy* 32:701–708.

————. 1938. *Logic: The Theory of Inquiry.* New York: Holt. Especially pp. 46 ff.

Dickerson, Reed. 1981. *Legal Drafting.* St. Paul: West Publishing. Eds. D. Black and M. Mileski, New York: Seminal Press.

Dietze, G. 1964. The Limited Rationality of Law. Ed. Carl Friedrich. *Rational Decision.* New York: Atherton Press.

Dolle, Hans. 1956. The Economic Order and the Law. Eds. R. Merton and A. Peterson. *Science and the Economic Order* (57–84). Frankfurt am Main: INH Breidenstein.

Durkheim, Emile. 1964. "Types of Law in Relation to Types of Social Solidarity." In *The Division of Labor in Society,* ed. V. Aubert, 68–132. Glencoe, IL: Free Press.

Ebenstein, William. 1945. *The Pure Theory of Law.* Madison: University of Wisconsin Press.

Ebersole, Frank B. 1953. "Definition of Pragmatic Paradox." *Mind* 62 (Jan.) 80–85.

Eco, Umberto. 1976. *A Theory of Semiotics.* Bloomington: Indiana University Press.

Edie, James M. 1976. *Speaking and Meaning: The Phenomenology of Language.* Bloomington: Indiana University Press.

Ehrenzweig, Abbot A. 1967. *Private International Law: A Comparative Treatise on American International Conflicts Law.* Leyden: A. W. Sijhoff, and New York: Oceana Publishing.

Ehrmann, Henry W. 1976. *Comparative Legal Cultures.* Englewood Cliffs, NJ: Prentice-Hall.

Eisele, Carolyn. 1976. *The New Elements of Mathematics of Charles S. Peirce*. Four vols. of five. The Hague: Mouton.

———. 1979. *Studies in the Scientific and Mathematical Philosophy of Charles S. Peirce*. Ed. R. M. Martin. New York: Mouton.

Eliade, Mircea. 1959. *The Scared and the Profane*. Trans. W. R. Trask. New York: Harper and Row.

Engel, Salo, and Rudolf A. Metall, eds. 1964. *Law, State, and International Legal Order: Essays in Honor of Hans Kelsen*. Knoxville, TN: University of Tennessee Press.

Fann, K. T. 1970. *Peirce's Theory of Abduction*. The Hague: Martinus Nijhoff.

Feibleman, James K. 1941. *An Introduction to the Philosophy of Charles S. Peirce*. Cambridge, MA: M.I.T. Press.

———. 1962. *Foundations of Empiricism*. The Hague: Martinus Nijhoff.

Feinberg, Joel. 1980. *Rights, Justice and the Bounds of Liberty*. Princeton: Princeton University Press.

Fillmore, C. J. 1972. "Subjects, Speakers, and Roles." *Semantics of Natural Language*, eds. D. Davidson and G. Harmon, 1–24. Dordrecht: D. Reidel.

———. 1975. "An Alternative to Checklist Theories of Meaning." *Berkeley: Proceedings of the First Annual Meeting of the Linguistic Society*, ed. G. Harmon, 1–24. Dordrecht: D. Reidel.

———. 1977. "Topics in Lexical Semantics." *Current Issues in Linguistic Theory*, ed. R. W. Cole, 76–138. Bloomington: Indiana University Press.

Fisch, Max. 1942. "Justice Holmes, the Prediction Theory of Law and Pragmatism." *Journal of Philosophy* 39(12):85–97.

———. ed. 1951. *Classic American Philosophers*. New York: Appleton-Century-Crofts.

———. 1952. "Peirce at the Johns Hopkins University," in Studies in the Philosophy of Charles Sanders Peirce. Ed. P. P. Weiner and F. H. Young. Cambridge: Howard University Press.

———. 1954. Alexander Bain and the Geneology of Pragmatism. *Journal of the History of Ideas* 15:413–444.

———. 1964. "Was There a Metaphysical Club in Cambridge?" Eds. E. C. Moore and R. S. Robins, *Studies in the Philosophy of Charles S. Peirce*, 3–32. Amherst: University of Massachusetts Press.

———. 1978. "Peirce's General Theory of Signs." Ed. T. Sebeok. *Sight, Sound, and Sense* (64–66). Bloomington: Indiana University Press.

———. 1980, 1982. "The Range of Peirce's Relevance." Parts 1, 2. *The Monist*.

Fisch, M., K. Ketner, and C. N. Kloesel. 1979. "The New Tools of Peirce Scholarship, With Particular Reference to Semiotic." *Studies in Peirce's Semiotic*. Institute for Studies in Pragmaticism, Lubbuck: Texas Tech University.

Fitzgerald, John J. 1976. "Ambiguity in Peirce's Theory of Signs." *Transactions of the Charles S. Peirce Society*: 127–134.

———. 1968. "Peirce's Theory of Inquiry." *Transactions of the Charles S. Peirce Society* 4:130–143.

Flanagan, T. E. 1979. "F. E. Hayek on Property and Justice." *Theories of Property*, A. Parel and T. Flanagan, eds., 335–360. Calgary: Wilfred Laurier University Press.

Folsom, Gwendolyn B. 1972. *Legislative History: Research for the Interpretation of Laws*. Charlottesville: University Press of Virginia.

Frank, Jerome. 1930. *Law and the Modern Mind*. New York: Doubleday and Company, 1963.

———. 1933. "Mr. Justice Holmes and Non-Euclidean Legal Thinking." *Cornell Law Quarterly* 17:568, 572–579.

———. 1934a. "A Conflict with Oblivion: Some Observations on the Founders of Legal Pramatism." *Rutgers Law Review* 9:425–463.

———. 1934b. *Realism in Jurisprudence*. American Law School Journal 7:1057–1076.

————. 1950. "Modern and Ancient Legal Pragmatism; John Dewey & Co. v. Aristotle." *Notre Dame Lawyer* 25:207–257, 460–504.

Frankena, William K. 1964. "Decisionism and Separatism in Social Philosophy." *Rational Decision*, Ed. Carl J. Friedrich, 18–25. New York: Atherton Press.

Frankfurter, Felix, ed. 1931. *Mr. Justice Holmes*. New York: Coward-McCann.

————. 1938. "Justice Holmes Defines the Constitution." *Atlantic* 162:484–495.

————. 1938. *Mr. Justice Holmes and the Supreme Court*. Cambridge: Harvard University Press.

Fried, Charles. 1982. *Contract as Promise*. Cambridge: Harvard University Press.

Friedman, Lawrence M. 1973. *A History of American Law*. New York: Simon and Schuster.

————. 1975. *The Legal System*. New York: Russel Sage Foundation.

Friedman, Milton. 1962. "Should There Be an Independent Monetary Authority." Ed. Leland B. Yeager, *In Search of a Monetary Constitution*. Cambridge, MA: Harvard University Press.

Friedman, Wolfgang. 1959. *Law in a Changing Society*. Berkeley: University of California Press.

Friedrich, Carl. 1964. *Rational Decision*. Ed. Carl Friedrich. New York: Atherton Press.

————. 1973. *The Philosophy of Law in Historical Perspective*. Chicago: University of Chicago Press. (Originally published 1958)

Fuller, Lon L. 1934. "American Legal Realism." *University of Pennsylvania Law Review*, 429–461.

————. 1940. *The Law in Quest of Itself*. Chicago: Foundation Press.

————. 1964. *The Morality of Law*. New Haven: Yale University Press.

————. 1966. "Reason and Fiat." In *The Nature of Law*, ed. M. Golding, 161–172. First published in *Harvard Law Review*, 59 (1946): 377–389.

————. 1971. "Mediation: Its Forms and Functions." *Southern California Law Review*, 44: 305.

Furer-Haimendorf, C. 1967. *A Study of Values and Social Controls in South Asian Societies*. Chicago: University of Chicago Press.

Gadamer, Hans-Georg. 1976. *Truth and Method*. New York: Seabury Press.

————. 1983. *Beyond Objectivism and Relativism: Science, Hermeneutics, and Praxis*. Philadelphia: Pennsylvania University Press.

Gandhi, Ramchandra. 1974. *Presuppositions of Human Communication*. Bombay and Delhi: Oxford University Press.

Garlin, Edwin N. 1941. *Legal Realism and Justice*. New York: Columbia University Press.

Geldart, William. 1975. *Elements of English Law*. 8th ed. Ed. D. C. M. Yardley. London: Oxford University Press.

Genons, Carey K., and Richard W. Pearce. 1965. *Law and Science*. Homewood, IL: Richard D. Irwin.

Gény, François. 1963. *Méthode d' interprétation et sources en droit privé positif*. Paris: Trans. J. Mayda. St. Paul, MI (Originally published 1899)

Gilmore, Grant. 1961. "Legal Realism: Its Cause and Cure." *Yale Law Journal* 70:000–000.

————. 1974a. *The Ages of American Law*. New Haven: Yale University Press. (Originally published 1917)

————. 1974b. *The Death of Contract*. Columbus, Ohio: Ohio State University Press.

Gilmore, Myron P. 1941. *Argument from Roman Law in Political Thought, 1200–1600*. Cambridge: Harvard University Press.

Goffman, Erving. 1976. "Replies and Responses." *Language in Society* 5(3):257–313.

Golding, M., ed. 1966. *The Nature of Law*. New York: Random House.

Goldman, Alvin I. 1970. *A Theory of Human Action*. Princeton, NJ: Princeton University Press.

Gore, G. 1878. *The Art of Scientific Discovery*. London: Longmans, Green.

Goudge, Thomas A. 1969. *The Thought of C. S. Peirce*. New York: Dover Publications.

Gould, James, 1832. *A Treatise on the Principles of Pleading*. Boston: Lilly and Wait.

Gould, Josiah B. 1970. *The Philosophy of Chrysippus*. Leiden: E. J. Brill.

Gray, J. C. 1892. "Some Definitions and Questions in Jurisprudence." *Harvard Law Review* 6:264.

———. 1909. *The Nature and Sources of Law*. Cambridge, MA: Harvard University Press.

Green, Leon. 1927. *Rationale of Proximate Cause*. Kansas City, MO: Vernon Law Book Co,

Greenawalt, Kent. 1977. "Policy, Rights, and Judicial Decisions." *Georgia Law Review* 11(5):991–1054.

Greimas, A. J. 1976. "Analyse semiotique d'un discours juridique." Collaboration avec Eric Landowski. *Semiotique et sciences sociales*, 79–128. Paris: Editions du Seuil.

Greimas, A. J. and E. Landowski, 1983. *Pragmatique et Semiotique. Actes Semiotique.*

Grey, Thomas C. 1975. "Do We Have an Unwritten Constitution?" *Stamford Law Review* 27:703–718.

———. 1980. "The Disintegration of Property." *Property, Nomos XXII*, ed. J. R. Pennock and J. W. Chapman, 69–86.

Grice, H. Paul. 1968. "Logic and Conversation." Unpublished manuscript.

Grimes, Joseph E. 1975. *The Thread of Discourse*. The Hague: Mouton.

Grimke, Frederick. 1948. *The Nature and Tendency of Free Institutions*. Ed. J. Ward. Cambridge, MA: Belknap Press. Harvard University Press.

Gutteridge, H. C. 1946. *Comparative Law*. Cambridge: Cambridge University Press.

Haack, Susan. 1978. Philosophy of Logics. Cambridge: Cambridge University Press.

Haas, William Paul. 1964. *The Conception of Law and the Unity of Peirce's Philosophy*. Fribourg, Switzerland: University of Fribourg Press.

Hahm, David E. 1977. *The Origins of Stoic Cosmology*. Columbus: Ohio State University Press.

Haines, Charles G. 1959. *The American Doctrine of Judicial Supremacy*. New York: Russell & Russell.

Halliday, M. A. K., and Ruquiya Hasan. 1973. *Cohesion in English*. London: Longman's English Language Series.

Hamblin, C. L. 1958. "Questions." *The Australasian Journal of Philosophy* 36(3):159–169.

Hamburger, Max. 1942. *The Awakening of Western Legal Thought*. Trans. B. Miall. New York: W. W. Norton.

Hamburgh, Max. 1971. *Theories of Differentiation*. New York: American Elsevier.

Hamilton, William G. 1808. *Parliamentary Logick*. London: Pall Mall, Thomas Payne.

Hand, Learned. 1954. *The Spirit of Liberty*. Ed. I. Dillard. London: Hamish Hamilton.

Hanson, Norwood Russell. 1958. *Patterns of Discovery*. Cambridge: Cambridge University Press.

Hare, R. M. 1971. *Practical Inferences*. London: MacMillan Press.

Harrah, David. 1961. "A Logic of Questions and Answers." *Philosophy of Science* 28:40–46.

Harris, J. W. 1979. *Law and Legal Science*. Oxford: Clarendon Press.

Harrison, Frederic. 1919. *On Jurisprudence and Conflict Laws*. Oxford: Clarendon Press.

Harrison, Jane. 1959. *Prolegomena to the Study of Greek Religion*. New York: Meridian Books. (Originally published 1903)

Hart, H. L. A. 1953. *Definition and Theory in Jurisprudence*. Oxford: The Clarendon Press.

———. 1961. *The Concept of Law*. New York and London: Oxford University Press.

———. 1963. "The Ascription of Responsibility and Rights." In *Essays in Logic and Language*, ed. A. Flew, 145–166.

Hart, H. L. A., and Honoré, A. M. 1959. *Causation in the Law*. Oxford: London Press.

Hartzler, H. Richard. 1976. *Justice, Legal Systems and Social Structure*. New York: Kennikat Press.

Hayek, Friedrich A. 1967. *Studies in Philosophy, Politics, and Economics*. Chicago: University of Chicago Press.

———. 1973, 1976, 1981. *Law, Legislation and Liberty*. 3 vols. Chicago: University of Chicago Press.

———. 1978. *The Constitution of Liberty*. Chicago: University of Chicago Press. (Originally published 1960)

——. 1984. *Money, Capital and Fluctuations*. Ed. R. McCloughby. Chicago: University of Chicago Press.

Hegel, G. W. F. 1975. *Natural Law*. Trans. T. M. Knox. Philadelphia: University of Pennsylvania Press. (Originally published 1802–1803)

Herbert, Wray. 1981. "Semiotics: Fad or Revolution." *Humanities Report* (Jan):4.

Herrick, Frederick M. 1890. *The Attic Law of Status, Family Relations and Succession in the Fourth Century, B.C.*, Dissertation, Columbia College. New York: Middlesex.

Hill, Walker H. 1940. "Peirce's 'Pragmatic Method'." *Philosophy of Science* 7:168–171.

Hintikka, Jaakko. 1976. *The Intentions of Intentionality and Other New Models for Modalities*. Dordrecht and Boston: D. Reidel.

——. 1976. *The Semantics of Questions and the Questions of Semantics*. Amsterdam: North-Holland Publishers.

Hiz, Henry, ed. 1978. *Questions*. Dordrecht: Reidel.

Hobbes, Thomas. 1971. *The Art of Rhetoric with a Discourse of the Laws of England*. Ed. J. Cropsey. Chicago: University of Chicago Press. (Originally published 1681)

Hocutt, Max O. 1962. "The Logical Foundations of Peirce's Aesthetics." *Journal of Art and Aesthetic Criticism*: 157–166.

Hohfeld, Wesley N. 1964. *Fundamental Legal Conceptions as Applied in Judicial Reasoning and Other Legal Essays*. New Haven: Yale University Press.

Holderness, Clifford. 1985. "A Legal Foundation for Exchange." *Journal of Legal Studies* 14(2):321–344.

Holmes, Oliver Wendell. 1881. *The Common Law*. Ed. M. D. Howe. Boston: Little, Brown, 1963.

——. 1921. *Collected Legal Papers*. New York: New York University Press, 1952.

——. 1931. *Representative Opinions of Mr. Justice Holmes*. Ed. A. Lief. Forward by H. J. Laski, New York: Vanguard.

——. 1943. Letters to William James. In *The Mind and Faith of Oliver Wendell Holmes*, M. Lerner, ed. Boston: Little, Brown.

Hook, Sidney, ed. 1966. *Art and Philosophy*. New York: New York University Press.

——. 1974. *Pragmatism and the Tragic Sense of Life*. New York: Basic Books.

Horovitz, Joseph. 1972. *Law and Logic: A Critical Account of Legal Argument*. New York and Berlin: Springer-Verlag.

Howe, Mark De Wolfe. 1957. *Justice Holmes: The Shaping Years, 1841–1870*. London: Oxford University Press.

Howell, W. S. 1961. *Logic and Rhetoric in England, 1500–1700*. New York: Russell & Russell.

Huizinga, J. 1955. *Homo Ludens*. Boston: Beacon.

Humphreys, Willard C. 1968. *Anomalies and Scientific Theories*. San Francisco: Freeman, Cooper & Co.

Hutcheson, Jr., J. C. 1929. "The Judgment Institute: The Function of the 'Hunch' on Judicial Decision." *Cornell Law Quarterly* 14:274.

Hutchinson, T. W. 1984. *The Politics and Philosophy of Economics*. New York: University Press.

Ihering, Rudolf von. 1924. *Law as a Means to an End*. New York: MacMillan.

Ilbert, Sir Courtenay. 1901. *Legislative Methods and Forms*. Oxford: Clarendon Press.

Ivanov, V. V. 1973. "The Significance of M. M. Bakhtin's Ideas on Sign, Utterance, and Dialogue for Modern Semiotics." In *Semiotics and Structuralism*, ed. H. Baran, 310–367. Trans. W. Mandel, H. Baran, and A. J. Hollander. Moscow: Moscow University, 1976.

——. 1974. "The Theoretical Framework of Modern Poetics." *Current Trends in Linguistics*. Vol. 12, part 3. *Linguistics and Adjacent Arts and Sciences*, ed. T. A. Sebeok, 835–861.

Jacobson, Harold K. 1984. *Networks of Interdependence*. New York: Alfred A. Knopf.

Jackson, Bernard S. 1985. *Semiotics and Legal Theory*. Routledge and Kegan Paul.

Jakobson, Roman. 1960. "Linguistics and Poetics." *Style in Language*, ed. T. A. Sebeok, 350–377. Cambridge, MA: M.I.T. Press, 1968.

Jensen, O. C. 1957. *The Nature of Legal Argument*. Oxford: Basil Blackwell.

Jardine, Lisa. 1974. *Francis Bacon: Discovery and the Art of Discourse*. Cambridge: University Press.

Jenks, Edward. 1912. *A Short History of English Law*. 2nd ed. Boston: Little, Brown.

Jevons, W. Stanley. 1879. *The Theory of Political Economy*. 2nd ed. London: MacMillan.

———. 1883. *Money and the Mechanism of Exchange*. Part 1. Humboldt Library 50. New York: J. Fitzgerald. 49–153.

———. 1973. *The Principles of Science*. London: MacMillan. (Originally published 1879)

Jolowicz, H. F. 1963. *Lectures on Jurisprudence*. London: Atherone Press.

Jones, H. W. 1966. "Legal Realism and Natural Law." In *The Nature of Law*, ed. M. Golding, 261–274. New York: Random House. Reprinted from Columbia Law Review 61 (1961): 799–809.

Kagan, K. 1955. *Three Great Systems of Jurisprudence*. London: Stevens.

Kahneman, D., Paul Lovic, and Amos Twersky, eds. 1982. *Judgment Under Uncertainty: Heuristics and Biases*. Cambridge and London: Cambridge University Press.

Kalinowski, Georges. 1959. "Y a-til une logique juridique?" *Logique et Analyse* 5:48–53.

———. 1965. *Introduction à la logique juridique: Eléments de semiotique juridique, logique des normes et logique juridique*. Paris: R. Pichon et R. Durand-Auzias.

Kallen, Horace M. 1942. *Art and Freedom*. Vol. 2. New York: Duell, Sloan and Pearce.

Kanowitz, Leo. 1973. *Sex Roles in Law and Society*. Albuquerque: University of New Mexico Press.

Kant, Immanuel. 1956. *Critique of Pure Reason*. Trans. M. Muller. New York: Doubleday Anchor. (Originally published 1781)

———. 1958. *Critique of Practical Reason*. Trans. L. B. Beck. Indianapolis: Bobbs-Merrill. (Originally published 1788)

———. 1965. *The Metaphysical Elements of Justice*. Part 1 of *The Metaphysics of Morals*. Trans. John Ladd. Indianapolis: Bobbs-Merrill. (Originally published 1797)

Kantorowicz, Hermann. 1958. *The Definition of Law*. Ed. A. H. Campbell. Cambridge: Cambridge University Press.

Karcevskij, Serge. 1967. Dualisme Asymetrique du Signe Linguistique. Ed. J. Vachek. *A Prague School Reader in Linguistics*. Bloomington: Indiana University Press. (Originally published 1929).

Kapferer, Bruce, ed. 1976. *Transaction and Meaning*. Philadelphia: Institute for the Study of Human Issues.

Kaufman, Irving R. 1981. "Charting a Judicial Pedigree." *The New York Times*. 24 Feb., 23.

Kelsen, Hans. 1941. *General Theory of Law and State*. Trans. A. Wedberg. Cambridge: Harvard University Press.

———. 1941. "The Pure Theory of Law and Analytic Jurisprudence." *Harvard Law Review*, 55: 44–70.

———. 1957. *What Is Justice?: Justice, Law and Politics in the Mirror of Science*. Berkeley: University of California Press.

Kennedy, W. B. 1924. "Pragmatism as a Philosophy of Law." *Marquett Law Review* 9:63–77.

Kent, Beverly. 1976. "Peirce's Esthetics: A New Look." *Charles S. Peirce Transactions* 12(3):264–281.

Ketner, K. L., and J. E. Cook, eds. 1975, 1978, 1979. *Charles Sanders Peirce: Contributions to The Nation*. Parts 1, 2, and 3. Lubbock: Institute for Studies in Pragmaticism.

Kevelson, Roberta. 1976. *Style, Symbolic Language Structure, and Syntactic Change*. Lisse: Peter de Ridder.
———. 1977. *Inlaws/Outlaws*. With Peter de Ridder. Bloomington: Research Center for Semiotic and Structural Studies.
———. 1978a. "Reversals and Recognitions." *Semiotica* 19(1/2):29–58.
———. 1978b. "Wittgenstein's Language Games as Systematic Metaphors." *Semiotica* 19(3/4):281–320.
———. 1980. "Relations of Something to Nothing." *ARS Semiotica* 2(3):295–326.
———. 1981. "Semiotics and the Art of Conversation." *Semiotica* 32(1/2): 53–80.
———. 1982a. "Peirce's Dialogism and the Continuous Predicate." *Transactions of the Charles S. Peirce Society* 18(2):110–126.
———. 1982b. "Legal Speech Acts: Decisions." *Linguistics and the Professions*, ed. R. DiPietro, 121–132. Norwood, NJ: Ablex.
———. 1982c. "Semiotics and Structures of Law." *Semiotica* 35(1/2): 182–192.
———. 1982d. "Peirce as Catalyst in Modern Legal Science: Consequences." *Semiotics 80*, ed. M. Lenhart and M. Herzfeld. New York: Plenum Press.
———. 1983a. "Peirce's Phenomenology and Solipsism." In *Sign, Structure, Function*, ed. T. Winner *et al*. The Hague: Mouton.
———. 1983b. "Francis Lieber and Legal Hermeneutics." In *Semiotics 81*, ed. M. Lenhart and J. Deely. New York: Plenum Press.
———. 1983c. "Time as Method in Charles S. Pierce." *American Journal of Semiotics* 2(1/2):267–276.
———. 1983d. "Bridge Laws." Evaluative review of T. Sebeok's *The Sign and Its Masters* (1978). *American Journal of Semiotics* 2(1/2): 84–108.
———. 1984. "Peirce's Speculative Rhetoric." *Philosophy and Rhetoric* 17:1.
———. 1985a. "Toward a Global Perspective on Legal Semiotics." In *Semiotics, Law and Social Science*, ed. D. Carzo and B. S. Jackson, 81–93. Gangemi editore and the *Liverpool Law Review*.
———. 1985b. "Semiotics in the United States." In *The Semiotic Sphere*, ed. T. Sebeok and J. Umiker-Sebeok. New York: Plenum Press.
———. 1985c. "Semiotics and Law." In *Encyclopedic Dictionary of Semiotics*, ed. T. Sebeok and J. Umiker-Sebeok. DeGruyter.
———. 1985d. "Semiotics and Methods of Legal Inquiry: Interpretation and Discovery in Law from the Perspective of Peirce's Speculative Rhetoric." *Indiana Law Journal*, 61(3): 355–371.
———. 1987. *Charles S. Peirce's Method of Methods*. John Benjamins Publishers.
———. In preparation. *Representation and Law. Récherches Semiotiques/Semiotic Inquiry*.
Kirzner, Israel M. 1960. *The Economic Point of View*. Princeton, NJ: Van Nostrand.
Kline, John M. 1985. *International Codes and Multinational Business*. Westport, CT; Quorum.
Koestler, Arthur. 1964. *The Act of Creation*. London: Pan Press.
Korner, Stefan. 1955. *Kant*. Harmondsworth, Middlesex: Penguin Books.
Kretzman, Norman. 1982. *Infinity and Continuity in Ancient and Medieval Thought*. Ithaca: Cornell University Press.
Kuhn, Thomas. 1977. *The Essential Tension*. Chicago: University of Chicago Press.
Kuno, Susumu. 1972. "Multiple WH Questions." *Linguistic Inquiry* 3(4):463–488.
Labov, William, and David Fanshel. 1977. *Therapeutic Discourse: Psychotherapy as Conversation*. New York: Academic Press.
Lancaster, Robert S. 1958. "A Note on Peirce, Pragmatism, and Jurisprudence." *Journal of Public Law* 7:13–19.
Lanigan, Richard L. 1977. *Speech Act Phenomenology*. The Hague: Martinus Nijhoff.

Larkin, Paschal. 1930. *Property in the Eighteenth Century with Special Reference to England and Locke.* New York: Kennikat Press, 1969.

Laski, Harold. 1931. "Mr. Justice Holmes." Ed. Felix Frankfurter, *Mr. Justice Holmes.* New York: Coward-McCann.

———. 1968. *Authority in the Modern State.* Cambridge, MA: Archon Books. (Originally published 1913)

Lasswell, Harold D., Nathan Leites, and Associates, eds. 1949. *Language of Politics: Studies in Quantitative Semantics,* 11–23, 173–230. Cambridge, MA: M.I.T. Press. 1965.

Lawson, F. H. 1958. *Introduction to the Law of Property.* Oxford: Clarendon Press.

Lenzen, Victor F. 1969. An Unpublished Scientific Monograph by C. S. Peirce. *Transactions of the Charles S. Peirce Society* 5:5–24.

———. 1967. *Principles of Reasoning.* New York: Dover.

Lerner, Max, ed. *The Mind and Faith of Oliver Wendell Holmes.* Boston: Little, Brown.

Lea, Henry Charles. 1886. *The Duel and the Oath.* Ed. E. Peters. Philadelphia: University of Pennsylvania Press, 1974.

Leonard, Henry S. (1959). "Interrogative, Imperatives, Truth, Falsity and Lies." *Philosophy of Science* 26:172–185.

Letwin, William. 1965. *Law and Economic Policy in America.* 1954. New York: Random House.

Levine, Julius B. 1982. *Discovery: A Comparison between English and American Civil Discovery Law with Reform Proposals.* Oxford: Clarendon Press.

Lewis, C. I. 1946. *An Analysis of Knowledge and Valuation.* La Salle, IL: Open Court.

Lieber, Francis. 1839. *Legal and Political Hermeneutics.* St. Louis: G. I. Jones, 1963.

———. 1839. *Manual of Political Ethics.* Vols. 1 and 2. 2nd ed. Ed. T. D. Woolsey. Philadelphia and London: J. B. Lippincott, 1911.

———. 1853. *On Civil Liberty and Self-Government.* Philadelphia: J. B. Lippincott.

———. Special collections of Lieber manuscripts. Huntington Library, San Marino, California, and Library of Congress, Washington, D.C.

Lindahl, Lars. 1977. *Position and Change: A Study in Law and Logic.* Dordrecht: D. Reidel.

Llewellyn, John E. 1964. "What Is a Question?" *Australasian Journal of Philosophy* 42:69–85.

Llewellyn, Karl. 1962. *Jurisprudence: Realism in Theory and Practice.* Chicago: University of Chicago Press. (Originally published 1931)

Locke, John. 1690/1955. *Two Treatises on Civil Government.* Gateway Editions, 1955.

Long, Douglas, G. 1977. *Bentham on Liberty.* Toronto: University of Toronto Press.

Loevinger, L. 1958. "Facts, Evidence and Legal Proof." *Western Reserve Law Review* 9:154–175.

Lorenzen, Ernest G. 1947. *Selected Articles on the Conflict of Laws.* New Haven: Yale University Press.

Lovejoy, Arthur O. 1908. "The Thirteen Pragmatisms." *Journal of Philosophy, Psychology and Scientific Methods* 5:5–12, 29–39.

Luria, Alexander. 1932. *The Nature of Human Conflict.* Trans. W. H. Gantt. New York: Liveright Press, 1976.

Lyons, John. 1977. *Semantics.* Vol. 2. Cambridge: Cambridge University Press.

Lukasiewicz, J. 1958. *Aristotle's Syllogistic.* Oxford: Clarendon Press.

Lotman, J. M., and B. A. Uspenskij. 1976. "Myth—Name—Culture." *Semiotics and Structuralism,* ed. H. Baran. White Plains, NY: International Arts and Sciences Press.

Longacre, R. E. 1976. *An Anatomy of Speech Notions.* Lisse: Peter de Ridder Press.

MacDonald, A. J. 1933. *Authority and Reason in the Early Middle Ages.* London: Humphrey Milford, Oxford University Press.

MacKay, D. M. 1969. *Information, Mechanism, and Meaning.* Boston: M.I.T. Press.

———. 1975. "Formal Analysis of Communicative Processes." *Non-Verbal Communication,* ed. R. A. Hinde, 3–26. Cambridge: Cambridge University Press.

──────. 1975. "Formal Analysis of Communicative Processes." *Non-Verbal Communication,* ed. R. A. Hinde, 3–26. Cambridge: Cambridge University Press.

Machlup, Fritz, ed. 1976. *Hayek.* Hillsdale College Press.

──────. 1980. *Knowledge: Its Creation, Distribution and Economic Significance.* Vol. 1: *Knowledge and Knowledge Production.* Princeton: Princeton University Press.

MacRae, Duncan, Jr. 1980. "Scientific Policy Making and Compensation for the Taking of Property." J. R. Pennock and J. W. Chapman, eds., *Property, Nomos* XXII, 327–340.

Madden, E. 1952. "The Enthymeme: Crossroads of Logic, Rhetoric, and Metaphysics." *Philosophical Review* 61:368–376.

Maine, Henry S. 1886. *Dissertations on Early Law and Customs.* New York: Holt.

──────. 1963. *Ancient Law.* 10th ed. Boston: Beacon Press. (Originally published 1861)

Maitland, F. W. 1909. *The Forms of Action at Common Law.* Ed. A. H. Chaytor and W. J. Whittaker. Cambridge: Cambridge University Press, 1971.

Makkreel, Rudolph A. 1975. *Dilthey: Philosopher of the Human Studies.* Princeton, NJ: Princeton University Press.

Mann, W. Howard. 1963. "The Marshall Court: Naturalization of Private Rights and Personal Liberty from the Authority of the Commerce Clause." *Indiana Law Journal* 38:117–238.

Marshall, James. 1966. *Law and Psychology in Conflict.* New York: Bobbs-Merrill.

Maruyana, M. 1974. Paradignatology and its Application to Cross-disciplinary, Cross-professional, and Cross-cultural Communication. *Dialectica,* 28:135–196.

Mates, Benson. 1953. *Stoic Logic.* Berkeley: University of California Press.

Matejka, Ladislav, and I. R. Titunik, eds., 1976. *Semiotics of Art: Prague School Contributions.* Cambridge, MA: M.I.T. Press.

Maxwell, P. B. 1953. *Interpretation of Statutes.* 10th ed. London: Sweet & Maxwell. (Originally published 1875)

Mayda, Jaro. 1978. *François Gény and Modern Jurisprudence.* Baton Rouge: Louisiana State University Press.

Mazzeo, J. A. 1978. *Varieties of Interpretation.* Notre Dame, IN: University of Notre Dame Press.

McCarty, L. Thorne. 1977. "Reflections on TAXMAN: An Experiment in Artificial Intelligence and Legal Reasoning." *Harvard Law Review* 90(5):837–893.

McClelland, Peter D. 1975. *Casual Explanation and Model Building in History, Economics and the New Economic History.* Ithaca: Cornell University Press.

McCloskey, R. G. 1962. Economic Due Process and the Supreme Court. *Supreme Court Review* 13:34–61.

McDermott, John S. 1976. *The Culture of Experience.* New York: New York University Press.

Mead, George H. 1938. *The Philosophy of the Act.* Chicago: University of Chicago Press.

Merritt, Marilyn. 1976. "On Questions Following Questions in Service Encounters." *Language in Society* 53:315–358.

Merryman, John Henry. 1969. *The Civil Law Tradition.* Stanford, CA: Stanford University Press.

Meron, Theodor. ed. 1984. *Human Rights in International Law.* Oxford: Clarendon Press.

Michelman, Frank I. 1982. "Ethics, Economics and the Law of Property." J. R. Pennock and J. W. Chapman, eds. *Nomos* XXIV, 3–40. New York: New York University Press.

Minogue, Kenneth R. 1980. "The Concept of Property and Its Con-Temporary Significance." *Property,* Eds. J. R. Pennock and J. W. Chapman. *Nomos* XXII, 5–27.

Moerman, Michael. 1973. "The Use of Precedent in Natural Conversation: A Study in Practical Legal Reasoning." *Semiotica* 7:193–217.

Morawski, Stefan. 1974. *Inquiries into the Fundamentals of Aesthetic.* Cambridge, MA: M.I.T. Press.

Moles, Abraham. 1966. *Information Theory and Esthetic Perception.* Ed. J. E. Cohen. Urbana: University of Illinois Press.

Moore, Edward C., and Richard S. Robin, eds. 1964. *Studies in the Philosophy of Charles Sanders Peirce*. Amherst: University of Mass Press.

Moore, Ronald, 1979. *Legal Norms and Legal Science: A Critical Study of Kelsen's Pure Theory of Law*. Honolulu: University of Hawaii Press.

Morris, Charles. 1932. *Six Theories of Mind*. Chicago: University of Chicago Press.

———. 1938. *Foundations of the Theory of Signs*. International Encylcopedia of Unified Science. Chicago: University of Chicago Press.

———. 1939. "Esthetics and The Theory of Signs." *Journal of Unified Science* 8:131–150.

———. 1946. *Signs, Language and Behavior*. New York: George Braziller.

———. 1970. *Signification and Significance*. Cambridge: M.I.T. Press.

Murphy, Walter F. 1964. *Elements of Judicial Strategy*. Chicago: University of Chicago Press.

Mukarovsky, Jan. 1964. Standard and Poetic Language. Ed. Paul Gavin. *A Prague School Reader in Poetics* (pp. 17–30). Washington, DC: Georgetown University Press.

———. 1970. *Aesthetic Function, Norm and Value as Social Facts*. Trans. M. Suino. Ann Arbor: University of Michigan Press.

———. 1976. *Structure, Sign and Function*. Trans. P. Steiner and J. Burbank. New Haven: Yale University Press.

Nagel, E. 1979. *The Structure of Science*. Indianapolis, IA: Hackett.

Nagel, E. and Newman, J. R. 1964. *Godel's Proof*. New York: New York University Press.

Nauta, Doede, Jr. 1973. "Information—Measurement and Meaning." In *Linguistics*, 95–104. The Hague: Mouton.

Nelson, William E. 1975. *Americanization of the Common Law: The Impact of Legal Change on Massachusetts Society 1760–1830*. Cambridge: MA: Harvard University Press.

Nisbet, Robert. 1975. *Twilight of Authority*. New York: Oxford University Press.

Nishiyama, Chiaki, and Kurt R. Leube, eds. 1984. *The Essays of Hayek*. Stamford: Hoover Press.

Ockham, William. 1974. *Ockham's Theory of Terms*. Part 1 of the *Summa Logicae*. Trans. M. J. Loux. Notre Dame, IN: University of Notre Dame Press.

O'Connor, D. J. 1948. Pragmatic Paradoxes. *Mind* 57:358–59.

Ogden, C. K. 1959. *Bentham's Theory of Fictions*. Paterson, NJ: Littlefield, Adams.

Olivecrona, Karl. 1938. *Law as Fact*. Copenhagen: Einer Monksgaard, and London: Humphrey M. Ford.

Ong, Walter J. 1958. *Ramus: Method and Decay of Dialogue*. Cambridge, MA: Howard University Press.

Parel, A. and T. Flanagan, eds. 1979. *Theories of Property*. Waterloo: Wilfrid Laurier University Press.

Parker, R. B. 1979. "The Jurisprudential Uses of John Rawls." In *Constitutionalism*, ed. J. R. Pennock and J. W. Chapman. *Nomos* XX, 169–295.

Pattee, Howard H., ed. 1973. *Hierarchy Theory: Challenge of Complex Systems*. New York: George Braziller.

Pattero, Enrico. 1986. *"Uses and Functions: Legal language and Semiotics."* Proceedings in preparation. First U.K. Conference on Law and Semiotics.

Patterson, Edmund G. 1930/1968. "Can Law Be Scientific." *Illinois Law Review* 25, 118–124.

Patterson, Edwin W. 1953. "The Restatement of the Law of Contracts." *Columbia Law Review* 33:397–427.

———. 1963. "Theories of Law." *Columbia Law Review: Essays in Jurisprudence*. Westport, CN: Greenwood Press.

Peirce, Charles Sanders. 1931–1935. *Collected Papers*. 8 vols. Eds. P. Weiss, C. Hartshorne, and A. Burks. Cambridge: Harvard University Press, 1958.

———. 1967. Microfilm collection: 30 reels of manuscript, with R. Robins's Annotated Catalogue. Amherst: University of Massachusetts Press.

———. 1979. *Charles Sanders Peirce: Contributions to the Nation,* 1869–1908. Three vols. Eds. K. L. Ketner *et al.* Lubbock: Center for Studies in Pragmaticism.

———. 1982, 1984, 1986. *Writings of Charles S. Peirce.* New ed. Vols. 1, 2, 3. Eds. M. Fisch, K. Kloesel, and E. Moore.

Pekelis, Alexander. 1950. *Law and Social Action: Selected Essays.* Ed. M. R. Konvitz. Ithaca and New York: Cornell University Press. Especially pp. 42–74.

Pennock, J. R., and J. W. Chapman, eds. 1978–1982. *Nomos* series on Law and Economics. New York: New York University Press.

Perelman, Chaim. 1963. *The Idea of Justice and the Problem of Argument.* London: Routledge and Kegan Paul.

———. 1964. "La theorie pure du droit et l'argumentation." In *Law, State and International Legal Order,* ed. Engel, Salo and R. Mitall. Knoxville: University of Tennessee Press.

Perelman, Chaim, with L. Olbrechts-Tyteca. 1969. *The New Rhetoric.* Trans. J. Wilkinson and P. Weaver. Notre Dame, IN: University of Notre Dame Press.

Percival, W. Keith. 1975. "Grammatical Tradition and the Rise of the Vernaculars." *Current Trends in Linguistics,* ed. T. A. Sebeok, Vol. 13: *Historiography of Linguistics,* 231–274. The Hague: Mouton.

Perry, F. B. 1954. *Realms of Value.* Cambridge: Harvard University Press.

Perry, Ralph B. 1926. *General Theory of Value.* New York and London: Green.

Petheram, William C. 1864. *The Law and Practice Relating to Discovery by Interrogatives Under the Common Law Procedure Act of 1864.* London: Wm. Maxwell.

Petofi, J. S. 1971. "Analysis of Different Types of 'Works of Art'." *Semiotica* 3(4):365–380.

Pettit, Philip. 1980. *Judging Justice: An Introduction to Contemporary Political Philosophy.* London: Routledge and Kegan Paul.

Pinborg, Jan. 1975. "Classical Antiquity: Greece." In *Current Trends in Linguistics,* ed. T. A. Sebeok, vol. 13, 69–126.

Philbrick, F. 1938. "Changing Conceptions of Property in Law." *University of Pennsylvania Law Review,* 86:691–732.

Plamenatz, J. P. 1968. *Consent, Freedom and Political Obligation.* 2nd ed. London: Oxford University Press.

Pitkin, Hanna F. *The Concept of Representation.* Berkeley and Los Angeles: University of California Press.

Plucknett, Theodore F. T. 1922. *Statutes and Their Interpretation in the First Half of the Fourteenth Century.* Preface by H. D. Hazeltine. Cambridge: Cambridge University Press.

Posner, Richard A. 1977. *Economic Analysis of Law* (2nd ed./1st ed., 1973). Boston: Little, Brown.

Pound, Roscoe. 1931. "The Call for a Realist Jurisprudence." *Harvard Law Review* 44:697.

———. 1934. "Law and the Science of Law in Recent Theories." *Yale Law Journal* 43:525.

———. 1943. *Outlines of Lectures on Jurisprudence.* Cambridge, MA: Harvard University Press. (Originally published 1920)

———. 1956. *An Introduction to the Philosophy of Law.* New Haven: Yale University Press. (Originally published 1922)

Powell, Thomas Reed. 1918. "The Logic and Rhetoric of Constitutional Law." *Journal of Philosophy* 15(24):546–658.

Prall, D. W. 1936. *Aesthetic Analysis.* New York: Thomas Y. Crowell.

Pratt, Mary Louise. 1977. *Toward a Speech Act Theory of Literary Discourse.* Bloomington: Indiana University Press.

Presser, Stephen B., and J. S. Zainaldin. 1980. *Law and American History: Cases and Materials.* St. Paul: West Publishing.

Prior, A. N. 1976. *Papers in Logic and Ethics.* Eds. P. T. Geach and A. J. Kenny. Amherst: University of Massachusetts Press.

Prior, Mary, and Prior, Arthur. 1955. "Erotetic Logics." *Philosophical Review* 64(1):43–59.

Probert, Walter. 1928. *Landmarks of Law.* Ed. R. D. Henson, 158–179. Boston: Beacon Press, 1960.

Radin, Max. 1940. *Law as Logic and Experience.* New Haven: Yale University Press.

Ranulf, Svend. 1964. *Moral Indignation and Middle Class Psychology.* Introduction by Harold D. Lasswell. New York: Schocken Books. (Originally published 1938)

Rapaport, Anatol. 1974. *Fights, Games, and Debates.* Ann Arbor: University of Michigan Press.

Rawls, John. 1971. *A Theory of Justice.* Cambridge, MA: Howard University Press.

Rayfield, David. 1972. *Action: An Analysis of the Concept.* The Hague: Martinus Nijhoff.

Reddie, James. 1840. *Inquiries Elementary and Historical in the Science of Law.* London: Longman, Orme, Brown, Greene, and Longmans.

Reeves, N. 1973. In *The Social Organization of Law.* Eds. D. Black and M. Mileski. New York: Seminal Press.

Reichenbach, Hans. 1947. *Elements of Symbolic Logic.* Toronto and New York: MacMillan. Expecially pp. 336–444.

———. 1956a. *The Philosophy of Space and Time.* Trans. M. Reichenbach and J. Freund. New York: Dover. (Originally published 1927)

———. 1956b. *The Direction of Time.* Berkeley: University of California Press.

———. 1976. *Law, Modalities, and Counterfactuals.* Berkeley and Los Angeles: University of California Press.

Reid, John Robert. 1943. "Analytic Statements in Semiosis." *Mind* 52(Oct.):314–30.

Reilly, Francis E. 1970. *Charles Peirce's Theory of Scientific Method.* New York: Fordham University Press.

Rescher, Nicholas. 1964. *The Logic of Commands.* London: Routledge & Kegan Paul, Ltd. and New York: Dover Publications.

———. 1967. The Logic of Decision and Action. Pittsburgh, PA: University of Pittsburgh Press.

———. 1969. *Introduction to Value Theory.* Notre Dame, IN: University of Notre Dame Press.

Reuschlein, Harold G. 1951. *Jurisprudence— Its American Prophets.* Indianapolis: Bobbs-Merrill.

Rizzo, Mario J. 1979. *Time, Uncertainty, and Disequilibrium.* Lexington, WA: D.C. Health.

Roberts, Don. 1973. *The Existential Graphs of Charles S. Peirce.* The Hague: Mouton.

Romeo, Luigi. 1976. "Heraclitus and the Foundations of Semiotics." *Versus* 15(5): 73–90.

Rommen, Heinrich A. 1947. *The Natural Law: A Study in Legal and Social History and Philosophy.* London: B. Herder.

Rommetveit, Ragnar. 1968. *Words, Meanings, and Messages.* New York: Academic Press.

Ross, Alf. 1946. *Toward a Realistic Jurisprudence.* Copenhagen: Einar Munksgaard.

Ross, Robert E. 1912. *The Laws of Discovery.* London: Butterworth and Toronto: A. C. Forster Boulton.

Rotenstreich, Nathan. 1977. *Theory and Practice.* The Hague: Martinus Nijhoff.

Royce, Josiah, and Fergus Kernan. 1916. "Psychology and Symbolic Methods." *Journal of Philosophy* 13:701–709.

Rumble, Wilfrid E., Jr. 1968. *American Legal Realism.* Ithaca, NY: Cornell University Press.

Sacks, Harvey, E. Schegloff, and G. Jefferson. 1974. "A Simplest Systematics for the Organization of Turn-taking in Conversation." *Language* 50(4):696–735.

Sadock, Jerrold M. 1974. *Toward a Linguistic Theory of Speech Acts.* New York: Academic Press.

Sambursky, S. 1959. *Physics of the Stoics.* London: Routledge and Kegan Paul.

Sandbach, F. H. 1975. *The Stoics.* New York: W. W. Norton.

Sanders, Gerald A. 1969. "On the Natural Domain of Grammar." Bloomington: Indiana Linguistic Reprints.

Sarles, Harvey B. 1970. "An Examination of the Question–Response System in Language." *Semiotica* 2:79–101.

Sartorius, Rolf E. 1975. *Individual Conduct and Social Norms.* Encino and Belmont, CA: Dickenson.

Savan, David, 1976. *An Introduction to Peirce's Semiotic, Part I*. Publication of Toronto Semiotic Circle, Toronto, Canada.

Savigny, Friedrich Carl von. 1979. *System of the Modern Roman Law*. Vol. 1. Tran. William Holloway. Westport, CN: Hyperion Press. (Originally published 1867)

Sayre, Paul, ed. 1947. *Interpretations of Modern Legal Philosophies*. New York: Oxford University Press.

Scheiber, Harry N. 1978. "Property Law, Expropriation and Resource Allocation by Government, 1789–1910." In *American Law and the Constitutional Order*, ed. L. Freidman and H. N. Scheiber. Cambridge: Cambridge University Press.

Schiller, F. C. S. 1939. *Our Human Truths*. New York: Columbia University Press.

Schiller, Griedrich. 1967. *Letters on the Aesthetic Education of Man*. Ed., trans., intro. by E. M. Wilkinson and L. A. Willoughby. Oxford: Clarendon Press. (Originally written 1793–95)

Schmid, A. A. 1978. *Property, Power and Public Choice*. New York: Praeger Press.

Schur, Edwin M. 1968. *Law and Society*. New York: Random House.

Schwartz, Bernard. 1965. *A Commentary on the Constitution of the United States*. New York: MacMillan.

Schwarz, David S. 1977. "On Pragmatic Presupposition." *Linguistics and Philosophy* 1:247–257.

Scott, Charles T. 1965. *Persian and Arabic Riddles: A Language-centered Approach to Genre Definition*. Bloomington, Indiana and the Hague: Mouton.

Searle, Johur R., ed. 1971. *The Philosophy of Language*. London: Oxford University Press.

Searle, John. 1976. "A Classification of Illocutionary Acts." *Language and Society* 5:1–23.

———. 1969. *Speech Acts: An Essay in the Philosophy of Language*. Cambridge: Cambridge University Press.

Sebeok, Thomas A., ed. 1970–1976. *Current Trends in Linguistics*. Vols. 1–14. Bloomington: Indiana University Press.

———. 1976. *Contributions to the Doctrine of Signs. Studies in Semiotics 5*. Bloomington: Indiana University Research Center for Language and Semiotic Studies, with the Peter de Ridder Press at Lisse.

———. 1978. *The Sign and Its Masters*. Austin and London: University of Texas Press.

Sebenius, James K. 1984. *Negotiating the Law of the Sea*. Cambridge: Harvard University Press.

Shannon, Claude E., and Warren Weaver. 1949. *The Mathematical Theory of Communication*. Urbana, Chicago, and London: University of Illinois Press, 1975.

Shapiro, Michael, and Marianne Shapiro. 1976. *Asymmetry: An Inquiry into the Linguistic Structure of Poetry*. Amsterdam, New York: North-Holland.

Shklar, Judith N. 1964. *Legalism*. Cambridge, MA: Harvard University Press.

Shriver, Harry C. 1940. *The Judicial Opinions of Oliver Wendell Holmes*. Buffalo, NY: Dennis.

———. 1978. *What Justice Holmes Wrote and What Has Been Written About Him*. Fox Hills Press.

Sieghart, Paul. 1983. *The International Law of Human Rights*. Oxford: England; Clarendon Press.

Siegan, Bernard H. 1980. *Economic Liberties and the Constitution*. Chicago: University of Chicago Press.

Simmel, Georg. 1978. *The Philosophy of Money*. Trans. T. Bottomore and D. Frisby. London: Routledge and Kegan Paul. (Originally published 1907)

Smith, John. 1978. *Purpose and Thought: The Meaning of Pragmatism*. New Haven: Yale University Press.

Smith, John F. 1965. "Community and Reality." In *Perspectives on Peirce*, ed. R. J. Bernstein. New Haven: Yale University Press.

Spencer, Herbert, 1980. *Essays: Moral, Political, and Aesthetic*. New York: Appleton.

Srzednicki, Jan. 1976. *Elements of Social and Political Philosophy*. The Hague: Martinus Nijhoff.

Stammler, Rudolf. 1925. *The Theory of Justice*. Trans. I. Husik. New York: MacMillan.

Steiner, George. 1976. *Language and Silence*. New York: Atheneum Press.

Story, Joseph. 1844. *Commentaries on the Law of Agency as a Branch of Commercial and Maritime Jurisprudence*. 2nd ed. Boston: Charles C. Little and James Brown.
Summers, Robert S. 1982. *Instrumentalism and American Legal Theory*. Ithaca: Cornell University Press.
Taylor A. 1948. *The Literary Riddle Before 1600*. Berkeley: University of California Press.
Tedeschi, G. 1967. "Insufficiency of the Legal Norm and Loyalty of the Interpreter." *Proceedings of the Israel Academy of Sciences and Humanities* 1(3):1–19.
Tomas, Vincent, ed. 1964. *Creativity in the Arts*. New Jersey: Prentice-Hall.
Toulmin, Stephen. 1958. *The Uses of Argument*. Cambridge: Cambridge University Press.
Tsune-Chi Yu. 1927. *The Interpretation of Treaties*. New York: Columbia University Press.
Tully, James. 1982. *A Discourse on Property: John Locke and His Adversaries*. Cambridge: Cambridge University Press.
Twining, William. 1973. *Karl Llewellyn and the Realist Movement*. London: Weidenfeld.
Uchenko, Andrew P. 1929. "The Logic of Events: An Introduction to a Philosophy of Time." *University of California Publications in Philosophy* 12(1):1–180.
Uhr, Leonard. 1973. *Pattern Recognition, Learning, and Thought*. Englewood Cliffs, NJ: Prentice-Hall.
Unger, Roberto M. 1976. *Law in Modern Society*. New York: Free Press.
———. 1976. Knowledge and Politics. New York: Free Press.
Vaihinger, Hans. 1924. *The Philosophy of 'As If'*. Trans. C. K. Ogden. New York: Harcourt, Brace.
Volosinov, V.N. 1976. *Freudianism: A Marxist Critique*. Trans. I. R. Titunik. ed. with N. H. Bruss. New York: Academic Press.
———. 1973. *Marxism and the Philosophy of Language*. Eds. L. Matejka and I. R. Titunik. New York: Seminar Press.
von Mises, Ludwig. 1966. *Human Action: A Treatise on Economics*. 3rd ed. Chicago: Contemporary Books. (Originally published 1949)
von Wright, G. H. 1967. "The Logic of Action—A Sketch." *The Logic of Decision and Action*, ed. N. Rescher, 121–136. Pittsburgh: University of Pittsburgh Press.
———. 1969. *Time, Change and Contradiction*. Cambridge: Cambridge University Press.
———. 1980. "Freedom and Determinism." *Acta Philosophica Fennica* 31:1.
Wasserstrom, R. 1961. *The Judicial Decision: Toward a Theory of Legal Justification*. Stanford, CA: Stanford University Press.
Weber, Max. 1925. *Law in Economy and Society*. ed. M. Rheinstein. 2nd ed. Cambridge, MA: Harvard University Press, 1954.
Weeks, John. 1981. *Capital and Exploitation*. Princeton: Princeton University Press.
Wennerberg, Hjalmar. 1962. *The Pragmatism of C. S. Peirce*. Lund: C. W. K. Gleerup and Copenhagen: Ejnar Munksgaard.
Whewell, William. 1858. *History of Scientific Ideas*. London: John W. Parker.
———. 1845. *The Elements of Morality Including Polity*. 2 vols. New York: Harper.
White, Morton, ed. 1955. *The Age of Analysis*. New York: Mentor Books.
Wickelgren, Wayne A. 1938. *How to Solve Problems*. San Francisco: W. H. Freeman, 1974.
Wiener, Philip P. 1958/1966. *Charles S. Peirce: Selected Writings (Values in a Universe of chance)*. New York: Dover, 1966.
Wigmore, John H. 1928. *A Panorama of the World's Legal Systems*. 3 vols. St. Paul: West Publishing.
Wilkinson, Elizabeth M., and L. A. Willoughby, eds. 1967. *Friedrich Schiller on the Aesthetic Education of Man*. Oxford: Clarendon Press.
Winetrout, Kenneth. 1967. *F. C. S. Schiller and the Dimensions of Pragmatism*. Ohio: Ohio State University Press.
Winner, Irene Portis, and Jean Umiker-Sebeok, eds. 1979. *Semiotics of Culture*. The Hague: Mouton.

Winner, Thomas G. 1976. "Jan Mukarovsky: The Beginnings of Structural Semiotic Aesthetics." *Sound, Sign, and Meaning*, Ed. L. Matejka, 433–455. Ann Arbor: Michigan Slavic Contributions.

Winston, Patrick H. 1977. *Artificial Intelligence*. Reading, MA: Addison-Wesley.

Wittgenstein, Ludwig. 1945–1949. *Philosophical Investigations*. Trans. G. E. M. Anscombe. New York: MacMillan.

———. 1965. *The Blue and Brown Books*. New York: Harper Torchbooks.

Wortley, B. A. 1933. "Francois Gény." *Modern Theories of Law*. Ed. W. I. Jennings. London: Oxford University Press.

Wright, Benjamin F., Jr. 1938. *The Contract Clause of the Constitution*. Cambridge: Harvard University Press.

Wright, Richard W. 1985. "Actual Causation vs. Probabilistic Linkage: The Base of Economic Analysis." *Journal of Legal Studies* 14(2):435–446.

Yeager, Leland B., ed. 1962. *In Search of a Monetary Constitution*. Cambridge: Harvard University Press.

Zabeeh, Farhang, E. D. Klemke, and A. Jacobson, eds. 1974. *Readings in Semantics*. Chicago, IL: University of Chicago Press.

Zeman, J. 1974. "Modality and the Peircean Concept of Belief." *Semiotica* 3:205–220.

Index